CHINA'S ENVIRONMENT AND THE CHALLENGE OF SUSTAINABLE DEVELOPMENT

CHINA'S ENVIRONMENT AND THE CHALLENGE OF SUSTAINABLE DEVELOPMENT

Foreword by N.T. Wang

Kristen A. Day, Editor

An East Gate Book

M.E.Sharpe
Armonk, New York
London, England

An East Gate Book

Copyright © 2005 by Columbia University

Library of Congress Cataloging-in-Publication Data

China's environment and the challenge of sustainable development / edited by Kristen A. Day.
    p. cm.
    "An east gate book."
    Includes bibliographical references and index.
    ISBN 0-7656-1470-7 (hardcover: alk. paper)—ISBN 0-7656-1471-5 (pbk: alk. paper)
    1. Economic development—Environmental aspects—China. 2. Environmental policy—
China. 3. Environmental protection—China. 4. Sustainable development—China. I. Day,
Kristen.

HC430.E5C43 2005
338.951′07—dc22

2004017118

Printed in the United States of America

BM (c) 10 9 8 7 6 5 4 3 2 1
BM (p) 10 9 8 7 6 5 4 3 2 1

In memory of Nian-Tzu (N.T.) Wang

1917–2004

Contents

List of Illustrative Materials

Tables

Figures

Maps

Boxes

Foreword

The present volume draws from a series of papers presented to the University Seminar on China: International Business at Columbia University during the 2002–3 academic year. The main purpose of the ongoing seminar, as with many other University Seminars, is to bring together academicians as well as practitioners from Columbia and elsewhere for discussions on topics of mutual interest. The seminar is also an integral part of the China-International Business Project, of which I am the director under the auspices of the university's Graduate School of Business and the School of International and Public Affairs.

The project was initiated in 1979 in anticipation of the need for greater mutual understanding about business relations between China and the rest of the world when China's new policy of reform and opening up became evident at the end of the 1970s. The project's seminar became one of the University Seminars in 1982. Between its inception in 1980 and mid-2002, the seminar had more than 120 meetings on topics relevant to the theme in question.

The seminar greatly benefited other components of the project. In particular, it provided invaluable information and insights for participants in the Columbia graduate course China: International Business Relations, as well as for those attending similar courses on China; it supplemented major international conferences on the subject that involved a large number of distinguished speakers and audiences and yielded conference publications; it facilitated executive training and outreach; and it aided numerous research projects and publications—those authored and edited by the present writer alone amounted to six books and over 100 articles.

At the beginning of the 2002–3 academic year, when the director of the University Seminars, Robert Belknap, approached me about the possibility of publishing a volume of selected papers from the seminar, my reaction was enthusiastic. It was agreed that the planned publication should focus sharply on a single topic—China's environment—and that speakers at the seminar would be invited to prepare papers with a view to publication.

There are many reasons why the environmental issue is most timely for business with China. From a broad perspective, the state of the earth has reached a point at which the capacity to sustain human development on the land, the sea, and in the air has been greatly strained. The rapid disappearance of many species, as in the case of dinosaurs millions of years ago, may be irreversible and raises the question of the ultimate survival of humans. The decline in biodiversity not only upsets ecological balance but also threatens human well-being in our time. For example, while nutritionists are extolling the value of fish, many fish stocks are now only one-tenth of those of half a century ago. The increasing desertification of many poor lands has deprived those already on the verge of the poverty line of their livelihood. The drying up of lakes or the impending rise of the sea level, resulting from the careless discharge of greenhouse gases, threatens many inhabitants in low-lying areas and islands. At the same time, the scarcity of water and clean air has already become a major problem in a growing number of countries.

Because of China's size and the greater-than-ever connectedness across the globe, the world needs China to deal with environmental issues, and China needs the rest of the world for its experience and know-how on managing environmental problems. For example, China's dust storms are already affecting the health of residents in many neighboring countries. In past decades, it was assumed by China and many developing countries that priority must be given to development and that the environmental problem could be put on hold in the poorer countries; moreover, it was felt that the developed countries, as the main culprits, not only should but also could afford to deal with the problems of their own creation. Only in recent years have both the common person and the government of China re-evaluated the relationship between development and the environment.

To be sure, development remains a national priority for the eradication of ongoing poverty, despite decades of a sustained rise in the gross national output and draconian measures of population control. Yet the conventional national accounts ignore the fact of environmental damage as negative output. For example, careless up-stream logging has caused floods, thus not only reducing future production but also leading to health problems and deaths. The promotion of the export of wool has caused overgrazing and desertification. While a detailed accounting of the negative output of environmental damage may be both difficult and debatable, it is evident that it constitutes a substantial portion of the total growth of China's aggregate output in recent years. Moreover, some of the damage, such as the disappearance of certain species, may not be translatable in monetary terms. Many instances of the impact of environmental damage, such as the thousands of deaths caused by the Great Smog of 1952 in London, will remain unknown until future research reveals the facts. In some cases, such as the rise of the sea level, the negative effects will be borne by future generations.

From the point of view of international business, it no longer can be assumed that China is an "underpolluted" area that will trade environmental damage for development. Certainly, there is already a new environmental consciousness and a set of laws and institutions to deal with offenders. Even if enforcement of the statutes continues to lag, the risks for offenders are bound to increase with time, partly because it will be more difficult to hide the facts from international activists and others, and partly because transnational corporations are ever more aware of global governance issues.

The new awareness of environmental issues is, therefore, not at odds with the development objectives of the host country or good corporate governance of international business. To be sure, the aim can hardly be zero pollution, and any reduction is likely to entail costs. Thus, the replacement of coal by hydro, nuclear, wind, or solar sources may have its own problems and entail high costs, at least until new technologies are invented. The calculus of a delicate balance between the twin goals of development and environment requires input from many disciplines as well as political wisdom—locally, nationally, and internationally. Fortunately, such an effort is consistent with age-old Chinese values. The *Book of Changes*, one of the earliest Chinese classics embraced by Confucians, emphasized harmony between human beings and nature. Traditional family values pay great attention to future generations rather than to the pursuit of selfish instant happiness at the expense of offspring.

To be sure, any major issue, environment not exempted, can become politicized and controversial. The best minds may passionately disagree and violent confrontations may be used to promote hidden agendas. As the product of an educational institution, the present volume seeks to propagate existing knowledge about the current state of affairs regarding China's environment, that is, what has been done about it and relevant experiences elsewhere. Even though the editor, as well as members of the editorial board and invited readers, may have expressed certain views for the consideration of the contributors, the final responsibility for the views expressed rests with each author.

The material presented in this volume is neither complete nor totally based on state-of-the-art research. Many areas, especially micro-case studies, could be added. In the area of policy suggestions, numerous possibilities also present themselves. For example, would more emphasis on conservation be desirable or effective? This evidently runs counter to the mentality and habits of an affluent society, where waste is part of the exercise of free expression of affordability as well as personal choice. Few reflect on the habits of throwing away a significant portion of food on the plate, discarding clothing considered less fashionable, or keeping lights or air conditioning on when no longer needed. These same habits are being cultivated in developing countries by the nouveaux riches. If habits are difficult to change, should fiscal policy make it costly to engage in some antisocial habits?

Many stories of successes and failures could also be added to guide future policies and engage readers' interest. Yet, in spite of the limitations, it is hoped that this volume will call attention to the role of the environment in human welfare both in China as well as globally. Moreover, it is not limited to the interests of people in business and economics but is also relevant to all disciplines and walks of life.

I congratulate Kristen A. Day, the editor of this volume, for her indefatigable energy in putting together a sufficient number of relevant papers and for her skills in persuading the contributors to make the necessary revisions. As chair of the editorial board, I also wish to thank other members, notably Ming-Jer Chen and John Z. Yang, for their contributions, in spite of their busy schedules. Gratitude to other readers is also expressed in individual papers. Lastly, without the guidance and intellectual stimulus of the director of the University Seminars and heads and colleagues of the Weatherhead East Asian Institute, the Graduate School of Business, and the School of International and Public Affairs, in which the China-International Business Project is located, and the generosity of the donors to the project, this volume would not have been possible.

N.T. Wang
Director, China-International Business Project
Graduate School of Business and
School of International and Public Affairs
Columbia University

Acknowledgments

Many people gave me their time and provided valuable assistance with this project. I particularly would like to express my appreciation for the many contributions of the late N.T. Wang, who chaired the Editorial Board for this project. N.T., who provided me with this opportunity to explore China's environmental challenges, passed away shortly before this book went to press. Were it not for his invitation and the guidance that he provided throughout the process, this book would not have been produced. He was a remarkable person of great wisdom and will be deeply missed. I also thank the other members of the editorial board, especially Ming-Jer Chen, who was responsive to my every query and provided both encouragement and practical assistance.

Jennifer L. Turner of the Woodrow Wilson International Center for Scholars in Washington, D.C. gave me tremendous support from start to finish. She took time out of a busy schedule to share her encyclopedic knowledge of green developments in China and to direct me to other experts in the field. I also greatly appreciate the kind assistance of Jingjing Qian, who never said no when I came to her with a request.

I acknowledge with gratitude the support and involvement of my advisers at Calico Group: Teji Bindra, Piya Chatterjee, Russell Langworthy, Alan Schindler, Frank Wang, and N.T. Wang. They are my brain trust and have been advisers for this project in the truest sense of the word. I particularly thank Frank Wang and Alan Schindler for their insight, encouragement, and substantial contributions.

This project would not have been possible without the encouragement of Robert Belknap at Columbia University. I express my appreciation to the University Seminars at Columbia University for their help in publication. The ideas presented have benefited from discussions in the University Seminar on China: International Business.

Alicia Hetzner, my copy editor, provided essential feedback and refined many rough edges. I also thank the following people for reviewing manuscripts from July 2003 through January 2004. The perspectives and expertise they shared with the authors in this volume were invaluable:

Pamela Baldinger	Alan Schindler
Peter Carroll	Judith Shapiro
Ledford Day	Jennifer L. Turner
Richard J. Ferris Jr.	Min Wang
Yuhong Jiang	James Wen
Russell Langworthy	Fuqiang Yang
Song Li	Youlin Yang
Benjamin Liebman	Emily T. Yeh
Chris Nielsen	Hongjun Zhang
Jingjing Qian	

My family, especially my husband, Nick Liu, and parents, Barbara and Ledford Day, not only encouraged my efforts, but also provided all manner of practical support. Helen Hongneng Liu helped a great deal on the home front, enabling me to concentrate on this project. Last, but not least, very special thanks to Katrina Yang-Wen Day for the light she has brought to my life and to Serena Yang-Lin Day, a bundle of joy.

Introduction

Through globalization, our world has become increasingly interconnected, and local fortunes have become linked more than ever to forces that often lie well beyond national borders. This higher level of international integration is a double-edged sword—with enormous benefits in information exchange, communications, economic growth, and international trade accompanied by concomitant negative environmental and social impacts, the effects of which span international boundaries. Nowhere are the costs and benefits more apparent than in the People's Republic of China (PRC). By joining the World Trade Organization (WTO) in 2001, the PRC tethered its national development ambitions to the global economy. The WTO reports that from 2000–2002, China's trade rose by 30 percent, while world trade stagnated.[1] The environmental consequences of such rapid expansion and China's growing role as a major supplier for many economies are worthy of consideration, as they are, and will be, felt far beyond China.

Examples of these emerging impacts are grabbing media attention. "Foul Water and Air Part of Cost of the Boom in China's Exports," states one recent headline.[2] How will China's breakneck economic growth be powered? asks "China's Dark Days and Darker Nights: Industrial Growth Exceeds Supply of Electrical Power."[3] The article describes the rolling blackouts that have recently been instituted in major Chinese cities. Is China's surging demand for natural resources such as wood depleting forests in neighboring countries? queries the article "Felling Asia's Forests: China's Insatiable Appetite for Timber. . . ."[4] Or consider the bigger question raised by this situation: to what extent can trade based on comparative advantage, such as that espoused by the WTO, result in negative environmental externalities?

Other recent articles consider whether China's rapid economic growth may bring about the depletion of basic resources. Examples include "Water Crisis Looming for China, Officials Warn"[5] and "Dry, with a Chance of Grain Shortage."[6] Indeed, are current and future generations of Chinese destined to live in an unhealthy, seriously degraded natural environment plagued by shortages of basic necessities? These important questions must be considered, along with the considerable benefits of economic growth for China's 1.3 billion citizens.

This volume explores the sustainable development challenges that China faces as it pursues a rapid pace of economic development, while coming to terms with the environmental and natural-resource-related costs.[7] This is an enormous topic that impacts virtually every aspect of China's national development. It involves disciplines, institutions, and issues that extend well beyond those conventionally linked to the environment. We begin with an overview of the scope and scale of these challenges, contained in chapter 1, followed by a unique cross-section of views that analyze the inherent tensions between economic development and environmental protection.

Subsequent chapters analyze specific social, political, economic, and environmental forces that contribute to China's environmental challenges. These examinations by experts from various disciplines—including Chinese and Western academics, lawyers, environmental consultants, scientists, and environmentalists—enable the reader to develop a greater appreciation of China's current environmental situation. Furthermore, the chapters illuminate the social, political, and economic dynamics that will determine the future direction of the world's most populous nation and explore whether sustainable development is an attainable goal.

Chapter 1, by Cynthia W. and Michael C. Cann and Gao Shangquan, outlines China's environmental sustainability challenges at the macro level. It describes the nation's pressing environmental issues and introduces many of the themes elaborated by the following chapters. Chapter 1 also considers some of the policies and actions that China has taken toward achieving sustainable development and recommends steps that can be taken to remain on this path.

The second chapter, by Yok-shiu F. Lee, looks at environmental attitudes and consciousness within Chinese society. Do Chinese citizens have a realistic view of their country's environmental problems? Is economic growth more important to them than the quality of their environment? Lee examines evidence accumulated on many aspects of the public's environmental perceptions, attitudes, and values—evidence replete with conflicting data. Nonetheless, the data suggest that environmental concerns rank relatively low among the Chinese in comparison with other concerns.

Beyond the environmental questions that are its direct focus, chapter 2 also touches on two other important issues. One is the reliability of statistics and qualitative information in and about China. As the author describes in detail, statistical information and data from China vary and may even conflict. The second is the role that external factors play when interpreting data in any study.[8]

Chapters 3 through 6 analyze the effects of China's evolving legal and bureaucratic systems on its efforts at environmental protection. Historically, party politics, political directives, and China's powerful bureaucratic infrastructure have had an enormously detrimental impact on the country's environment. One well-known example is the "three great cuttings" (*san da fa*), representing the three major periods of deforestation in modern Chinese history. The first was the Great Leap Forward (1958), when forests were cut to fuel a campaign to produce steel throughout the country. Next was the Cultural Revolution (1966–76), when forests were cut to produce grain based on the ideological "learn from Dazhai" campaign.[9] The final cutting occurred following early economic market reforms in the 1980s, when villagers rushed to cut down their trees after being given semiprivate ownership rights, fearing that those rights would be short-lived. A more recent example (2001) is a government policy in Xinjiang that resulted in the misuse of pesticides to destroy pests' natural enemies, enabling aphids and red spiders to devastate the cotton crop.[10]

In recent years, however, the central government generally has assumed a less direct role in environmental management, devolving some authority to provincial or local jurisdictions, while permitting new domestic and international forces to emerge. These new actors are a major impetus behind many of the more promising efforts to improve China's environment and are described in detail in chapters 4, 5, and 6.

Chapter 3, written by Richard J. Ferris Jr. and Hongjun Zhang, reflects the more than twenty years of combined experience of two practicing attorneys working within China's multilayered bureaucracy and complex regulatory system. Ferris and Zhang offer unique insights based on their personal experiences, particularly Zhang's role in drafting some of China's national environmental laws and his involvement in their implementation and enforcement during his tenures at China's Legislative Office of the Environmental Protection and Natural Resources Conservation Committee and the National Environmental Protection Agency (now the State Environmental Protection Administration). Chapter 3 introduces China's environmental regulatory system and tracks the country's progress in strengthening its environmental protection regime. It also considers the practical compliance challenges faced by investors and shares insights on how to meet those challenges.

In chapter 4, Elizabeth Economy considers the difficulties of enforcing China's extensive network of environmental regulations. She argues that human and financial resource constraints and susceptibility to political pressure undermine the ability of China's environmental regulators to effectively enforce the law. The chapter also describes a very interesting development, given China's history of tight government control: efforts by China's recent leadership to compensate for governmental limitations by opening the door to outside forces from civil society for help with enforcement.

Chapter 5, by Jennifer L. Turner and Eric Zusman, explores the extra-bureaucratic opportunities for policy innovation created by the presence of these civil-society groups. It tracks the growth in international interest in China's environment and the increasing role of international nongovernmental organizations (NGOs) and multilateral organizations in influencing China's environmental policy. Based on their experience observing and working with a number of these organizations, the authors describe how different types of international organizations have enhanced communication among China's bureaucracies, opening the door to innovative policies, improved interagency coordination, and more effective environmental management.

How do international models for environmental protection in China actually work on the ground? What challenges do joint government-NGO projects face? To what extent are Western market-oriented approaches transferable to China's market socialist system? Chapter 6, written by Richard D. Morgenstern and others, recounts an Asian Development Bank–funded collaborative effort between the Chinese municipal government in Taiyuan, Shanxi Province, the Washington-based NGO Resources for the Future, the Chinese Research Academy of Environmental Sciences (CRAES), and the Norwegian Institute for Air Research. It describes the challenges and opportunities created by efforts to implement a market-based emissions trading program to improve air quality in the city of Taiyuan.

Chapters 7 to 9 focus on topics emblematic of the challenges of balancing economic growth with environmental protection. No sector has a greater environmental impact or a closer link to China's economic growth than energy. Energy demand in China has doubled since the 1980s and is projected to double again within the next two decades.[11] Coal has fueled China's remarkable economic expansion, accounting for 64 percent of its energy consumption, but coal is also the single greatest cause of China's environmental degradation.[12] Compiled by Frank Wang and Hongfei Li, chapter 7 quantifies the impact of China's energy consumption on its environment and assesses the prospects for adoption of cleaner energy sources in the future.

The natural by-product of China's burgeoning consumer economy and booming export market is waste.[13] In chapter 8, Dan Millison examines the ground-level realities of China's hazardous waste management within the context of developments elsewhere in East Asia. Millison also considers prospects for mitigating hazardous waste and other industrial pollution problems through better management of inputs and production processes, also known as clean production (CP). Chapter 8 describes how both hazardous waste management and CP programs in China have lagged behind regional development patterns due primarily to a misperception that technology rather than improved management will solve the country's environmental problems.

Chapter 9 considers in detail one important subset of China's environmental degradation: desertification in north China. It provides perspective on the impact of human beings' economic activities on an area that has received global attention in recent years. In 2002, for example, the presence of 5-to-10-day-old arsenic, copper, and zinc in emissions from smelting operations in China was detected by monitoring stations in Hawaii.[14] Similarly, dust from China's sandstorms has affected air quality in China and neighboring countries. This discussion by desertification scientists Wang Tao and Wu Wei assesses the costs of desertification and the commitments that will be required to effectively combat it. The authors' call to action, which includes promoting public participation, developing incentives to discourage exploitation of fragile ecosystems, and strengthening China's legal framework, is also applicable to addressing China's other environmental issues.

This volume concludes with a bibliographic examination by James D. Seymour of the Western-language literature that addresses China's environment. Seymour provides an overview of many of the topics that are at the core of discussions on this important issue—history, energy, agriculture, water, quality of life, politics, and law—and surveys useful literature and Web-based references for anyone interested in further exploring this subject.

For China to achieve sustainable development, the complex, multifaceted, and multidisciplinary issues discussed in this book need to be debated and resolved. The authors in this volume raise many important questions: How important is public awareness in changing behavior toward the environment? What rule of law and enforcement challenges exist in a nation that still lacks an independent legal system and powerful enforcement mechanisms? What tensions exist among economic development, geopolitical realities (such as energy and natural resource endowments), and environmental protection? What is the emerging role in China of civil institutions such as nongovernmental organizations and the media? How can technology and innovative approaches to pollution prevention and control be implemented effectively?

The authors here provide no simple answers. Sustainable development has not yet been attained in China. Nevertheless, there are reasons to hope that the country will find a balance between economic and environmental demands. While these are often judged to be two opposing goals, increasingly, many policymakers and experts are realizing that a healthy economy requires a healthy environment, and vice versa.[15]

The wealthier Chinese cities have been making rapid progress in integrating these goals through the implementation of more environmentally responsible policies. An example worth noting is the upcoming Beijing 2008 "Green Olympics." As a part of its comprehensive planning for this event, Beijing has earmarked US$3.6 billion for environmental projects, including replacing coal with natural gas, curbing auto emissions, planting trees, and treating medical waste and sewage.[16] While some of the measures being taken may have the effect of simply relocating pollution sources beyond city limits, others, such as resource conservation efforts, clean energy sourcing, and environmentally responsible building design, will create useful examples for other Chinese cities to follow. In addition, and perhaps more importantly, the "Green Olympics" may promote environmental awareness among Chinese citizens that will serve as a catalyst for environmental improvement and promote sustainable development in the long term.

Many Western countries had the luxury of following a "pollute now, clean up later" approach to development. For China in the twenty-first century, this is not a viable option. Increasingly, China and the rest of the world are affected by other nations' economic and environmental decisions. Fortunately, the Chinese government has moved environmental quality up on its list of priorities and is actively investigating and implementing novel solutions. In a positive indication that it recognizes the severity of the problem, the Chinese government has welcomed input on environmental solutions from other countries, and a number of projects and collaborations have begun to be successfully applied in China.[17] I am hopeful that, as China matures as a full partner in the world's market economy, it will team up with other nations and other institutions within Chinese society to develop new solutions to the yet-unresolved tensions between economic development and environmental protection.

Kristen A. Day, Editor
Co-Chair, University Seminar on China: International Business
Columbia University

Notes

1. World Trade Organization, *The World Trade Report 2002,* www.wto.org/english/res_e/statis_e/its2003_e/chp_0_e.pdf.

2. Joseph Kahn, "Foul Water and Air Part of Cost of the Boom in China's Exports," *New York Times,* Nov. 4, 2003, A1.

3. "China's Dark Days and Darker Nights: Industrial Growth Exceeds Supply of Electrical Power," *Washington Post,* Jan. 5, 2004, A1.

4. David Lague, "Felling Asia's Forests," *Far Eastern Economic Review* (Dec. 25, 2003), www.feer.com/articles/2003/0312_25/p026china.html.

5. Jehangir Pocha, "Water Crisis Looming for China, Officials Warn," *Boston Globe,* Jan. 2, 2004.

6. Lester R. Brown, "Dry, with a Chance of a Grain Shortage," *Washington Post,* Dec. 14, 2003, Outlook Sec., B5.

7. China's GDP growth rate exceeded 7 percent per annum for most of the 1990s through 2002.

8. Because of this variability and the influence of external factors (e.g., the impact of party politics, conflicts of interest), the editor has not attempted to reconcile the results of all the studies cited in this volume. Differing public and private organizations compile statistics based on varying assumptions and biases. It is incumbent on the reader to regard statistics and survey findings with a degree of skepticism based on the source of the information.

9. Dazhai, a poor mountainous area in Shanxi Province, was glorified during the Cultural Revolution for its rural production brigades and collectives. Subsequently, it was determined that local leaders had falsified acreage reports and grain production figures.

10. See James Seymour, this volume, p. 252. Source: New China News Agency, U.S. Foreign Broadcast Information Service, Sept. 14, 2001 (via Internet).

11. See Frank Wang and Hongfei Li, this volume, p. 181. Source: United States Energy Information Administration, *International Energy Outlook 2003* (Washington, DC: Government Printing Office, 2003), 181.

12. Ibid., p. 181.

13. For a detailed account of anticipated impacts of trade expansion on China's water, air, and solid waste, see Hu Tao and Wanhua Yang, *Environmental and Trade Implications of China's WTO Accession: A Preliminary Analysis,* prepared for the Working Group on Trade and Environment, China Council for International Cooperation and Development, Sept. 2000, 4–5, www.iisd.org/pdf/china_wto_accession.pdf.

14. See Richard J. Ferris Jr. and Hongjun Zhang, this volume, p. 68. See also Andrew Bridges, "Dirty Air Has Gone Global," *Toronto Star,* June 1, 2002, J5.

15. Economic losses attributed to environmental degradation and pollution in China range from 3 percent to 5 percent of annual GDP to as high as 13 percent of GDP per year, effectively wiping out the country's annual economic growth. See Dan Millison, this volume, p. 224. One source of information is Vaclav Smil and Yushi Mao, *The Economic Costs of China's Environmental Degradation: Project on Environmental Scarcities, State Capacity, and Civil Violence* (Toronto: Committee on International Security Studies of the American Academy of Arts and Sciences, 1998).

16. "China Going Green Over Olympics," *Sydney Morning Herald*, Dec. 24, 2003, www.smh.com.au/articles/2003/12/24/1072239713847.html.

17. See Jennifer Turner and Eric Zusman, this volume, pp. 133 and 139. See also Jennifer Turner, ed., "Inventory of Environmental and Energy Projects in China," *China Environment Series* 6 (2003): 199, which contains a more comprehensive inventory of environmental and energy projects in China.

CHINA'S ENVIRONMENT AND THE CHALLENGE OF SUSTAINABLE DEVELOPMENT

—— Chapter 1 ——

China's Road to Sustainable Development

An Overview

Cynthia W. Cann, Michael C. Cann, and
Gao Shangquan

Sustainable development is "Development that meets the needs
of the present generation without compromising the ability of
future generations to meet their own needs."[1]

Sustainable development is essential to China's future, and the future of the world. As this giant sleeping dragon awakens from her economic slumber, the whole world is watching. The People's Republic of China (PRC) has been experiencing extraordinary economic growth over the last ten to twenty years.[2] The GDP of China has quadrupled since 1978 and, in 2002, the estimated official GDP growth rate was 8 percent.[3] China has become a formidable presence in the global economy. Perhaps the most visible single event in China's development occurred on October 15, 2003, when China joined a very elite group of nations by becoming only the third country on earth to launch an astronaut into space.

China and the world stand at a critical crossroads. Will the dramatic increase in consumption of resources and the concomitant production of waste that goes along with China's rapid economic development become a model of sustainability for many of the developing, as well as developed, countries of the world? If the most populous country in the world does not achieve an environmentally sustainable pattern of growth, the carrying capacity of the earth will rapidly be exceeded.

China's conversion from a centrally planned economy to a socialist market economy has the potential to pose many problems for the rest of the world, as well as for the PRC.[4] China's entry into the WTO in 2001 and the requisite conformity with the WTO's rules and obligations have complicated the country's growth and development.[5] As the world globalizes, the effect that the development of one nation has on the rest of the world is exacerbated. With China's population of 1.3 billion people,[6] its sheer size alone mandates its integration into the world economy and world ecology, and requires careful consideration of the country's development. For example, China's increased demand for many raw materials needed to support its rapidly increasing economy has created worldwide shortages and dramatically increased prices around the world.[7] In fact, to supply its growth and development, China's imports rose 40.5 percent—to US$398.56 billion—in the first nine months of 2003 compared to the first nine months of 2002.[8] Table 1.1 illustrates the growth in volume for certain specific commodities.

Even before China embarked on the road toward a new market economy, the country was faced with many economic, social, and ecological problems. These problems emanate, in large part, from a burgeoning population, a lack of clean and potable water, insufficient arable land, and an inefficient industrial base.[9] Population problems include more than just issues of birth control. Adding to the complexity of population growth are increasing unemployment, rural-to-urban migration of farmers, growth of the urban poor, an aging population, and a rising gender imbalance.[10] To address these issues, the government formulated China's Agenda 21, a white paper on growth and sustainable development in China in the twenty-first century.[11] This plan will be discussed in more detail below.

An emerging nation of such size and importance cannot follow in the footsteps of many other nations by continuing the practice of "pollute now and treat later."[12] To achieve long-term economic growth, the country must find a road to sustainable development (SD). China's espoused plan is to replace the old model of growth with the new model of SD.[13] In the new model, problems are addressed by bringing together public, private, and government sources. The objective for China is to produce successful growth such that the economy, society, and the environment are in harmony with one another.[14] This objective reflects the "Triple Bottom Line" approach to SD, which regards the economy, society, and the environment as a synergistic system. "Triple Bottom Line" was coined by the nongovernmental organization (NGO) SustainAbility as a way to present a formula for the business case for SD. The term is used to explain how to achieve growth while minimizing any harm to the environment or society resulting from growth activities.[15] Following this logic, China has attempted to approach sustainable growth in a comprehensive way. The immediate targets include control of population growth and the negative effects of urbanization, agricultural and

Table 1.1

Commodity Imports to China (January–September 2003)

	Volume (tons)	Growth in volume (%)
Cotton	642,524	596.3
Copper	1.99 mn	36.9
Iron ore	110.67 bn	33.1
Diamonds	9.11 mn	8.7
Timber	19,436	5.5

Source: Wonacott, "China Saps Commodity Supplies," *Wall Street Journal*, Oct. 24, 2003, C1.

industrial restructuring, efficient use of resources, development of substitute and reproducible resources, realization of zero discharge of pollutants, and environmental protection.[16] According to the Communist Party of China Central Committee, China's SD plan must satisfy the people's increasing material needs, improve the people's standard of living, establish a fair and just social income distribution system, and, at the same time, provide for a content society, a clean environment, and conservation of resources.[17]

In this chapter, we look at some of the challenges that China faces in achieving SD and some of the policies and actions China has taken toward achieving this goal. Finally, we provide suggestions on what China should do in the future as it treads the road toward SD.

Challenges to Achieving Sustainable Development in China

Environmental degradation in China is severe, and this degradation, along with her massive population and unprecedented economic development, presents significant barriers to SD. Economic development has led to an insatiable appetite among China's burgeoning middle class for consumer goods (especially automobiles) and meat and dairy products, as well as a concomitant rapidly rising demand for energy. This economic development threatens not only to further degrade China's environment but also leads to major questions as to how China will feed herself. The following sections touch on some of the challenges that China faces in her drive to achieve SD.

Water

China is confronted with serious water problems, including pollution, distribution, and flooding. According to the World Resources Institute (WRI), most of China's domestic and industrial wastewater is released untreated into its waterways. In 1996 only 5 percent of household waste and 17 percent of industrial waste received any treatment, and little has improved since. Approximately one-half of the drinking water in China is contaminated with human and animal feces. Furthermore, because China ranks number one in the world in the consumption of synthetic nitrogen fertilizers, its nutrient runoff from agricultural lands is tremendous.[18]

China's seven largest rivers—Huai, Hai, Liao, Songhua, Chang (Yangtze), Zhu (Pearl), and Huang (Yellow)—all are severely polluted. The quality of the water in more than half of the monitored sections of such rivers is designated as class 5 (the lowest Chinese category of graded waters; see Table 1.2) or below. The majority of the 50,000 kilometers (km) of China's major rivers are so polluted that 80 percent no longer support fish. Chromium, cadmium, and other serious toxins have so polluted the Yellow River that most of it is unfit for either human consumption or irrigation.[19]

Discharge of waste from coastal cities and oil from offshore operations are contaminating the shoreline. Of the four seas that border China, the pollution in the East Sea is the worst, with the quality of more than half of the water in this sea rated as grade 4 or worse.[20] From 1999 to 2001, the number of red tides in these seas increased by a factor of 5 (seventy-seven red tides in 2001). Estimates indicate the total direct loss caused by marine disasters, including red tides, reached 10 billion renminbi (RMB).[21] Although the causes of red tides are not well known, some scientists believe that coastal pollution from pesticides and nutrients are underlying factors.

Although China ranks second globally in overall water resources, it provides only 33 percent of the world average in water on a per capita basis. China faces critical water deficiencies, particularly in the north, which has 66 percent of the agriculture, while 80 percent of the water supply is in the south, primarily in the Yangtze River Basin.[22]

China relies heavily on water to produce grain, with about 80 percent of its grain coming from irrigated land, compared to 20 percent in the United States and 60 percent in India.[23] With irrigation as a major contributing factor, from 1982 through 2000 the Yellow River ran dry for as much as two-thirds of each year.[24] In part because China's surface waters are so polluted, there is an overreliance on groundwater. Aquifers in northern China have been depleted faster than they can be replenished. Levels have dropped by 50 to 90 meters in the Hai Basin, and in cities such as Tianjin and Jinan serious subsidence has occurred.[25]

Poor efficiency of water use contributes to China's water-availability issues. Some estimates indicate that up to 60 percent of the water used for irrigation is lost due to such factors as evaporation from canals and from

Table 1.2

Classes of Water Use in China

Class	Description of use
I	Water that flows through national nature reserves
II	Sources of municipal drinking water (first grade conservation area), conservation areas for rare aquatic species, and areas for fish spawning
III	Source of municipal drinking water supplies with treatment required (second grade conservation area), conservation areas for common aquatic species, and areas for swimming
IV	Source of industrial water supply and recreational use other than swimming (boating, fishing)
V	Source of industrial cooling water, irrigation water, and ordinary landscape

Source: National Standards of the People's Republic of China, "Environmental Quality Standards for Surface Water," http://svr1-pek.unep.net/soechina/water/standard.htm.

fields, and poor maintenance of an outdated supply infrastructure.[26] Continued rapid economic development and industrialization will put increasing demands on China's water resources. For example, urban water demand in northern China is expected to increase by 85 percent between 2000 and 2050.[27] China also is plagued by chronic flooding. In July 2003, flooding affected 100 million people in southern, eastern, and central China. The death toll amounted to 298, with economic losses estimated at US$800 million.[28] During the summer of 1999, the worst flooding in fifty years claimed 4,000 lives.[29] Significant deforestation in the Yangtze and Yellow River watersheds has exacerbated flooding. Estimates indicate that over fifteen years, starting in the early 1980s, these watersheds have lost over 30 percent of their forest cover due to indiscriminant logging.

Air

China's air pollution is recognized as some of the worst in the world. According to the World Health Organization (WHO), seven of ten of the earth's most polluted cities are in China.[30]

As a result of air pollution, China's population suffers from a high incidence of respiratory diseases (lung cancer, pulmonary heart disease, bronchitis). Women in certain industrialized areas of China are reported to have the highest rates of lung cancer ever recorded in the world.[31] Emissions of sulfur dioxide, resulting in large part from the combustion of coal, produces acid rain, which affects about 30 percent of China's total land area. Central and southwestern China are the most seriously affected, with pH levels as low as 3.7.[32] Particulates, which also are largely a result of the burning of coal, are especially high in northern China. The growing number of cars, trucks, and buses that clog China's highways faster than new roads can be constructed increasingly contributes to this problem.

Soil

Estimates indicate that due to soil erosion and economic development, China has lost one-fifth of its agricultural land since 1949.[33] Although China and the United States have comparable grazing-land area, from 1961 to the present China's livestock population has grown by a factor of three. China now has a livestock population of 400 million, compared to 97 million in the United States. Overgrazing and overplowing in northwestern China have expedited desertification. In late winter and early spring, dust storms inundate Chinese cities such as Beijing and Tianjin. Countries to the east of China such as Japan and Korea are also affected.[34]

Energy

The rapid economic development of China since the 1980s has been accompanied by a doubling of energy demand. With the current annual 3.5 percent per annum increase in energy use, China's energy needs will double again in approximately twenty years.[35]

Coal accounts for 65 percent to 70 percent of China's total energy needs, and this proportion is unlikely to change significantly in the coming decades.[36] With 12 percent of the world's proven reserves, China has ample coal, with estimates indicating that, at current consumption rates, China's coal reserves will last for 100 to 200 years.[37] Fortunately, most of this coal has less than 1 percent sulfur. However, most coal-fired power plants lack sufficient pollution controls. In addition, significant quantities of coal are burned in homes and factories in which all the flue gas products are vented directly into the atmosphere. Thus, atmospheric concentrations of sulfur dioxide (SO_2) are high, and China is plagued with acid rain, as mentioned. Furthermore, the major coal reserves lie mostly in the northern areas of the country, and transporting coal to more populated and industrialized areas presents a challenge, not to mention the damage to the earth and wastes produced by mining and processing it.

Coal also produces approximately twice the amount of carbon dioxide per unit of energy as methane, and one-third more than fuel oil, and thus is a major contributor to global warming. Although on a per capita basis China emits less than one ton of carbon dioxide per year (the comparable figure in the United States is more than five tons), China emits 12 percent of the world's total carbon dioxide, which is second only to the United States' 25 percent.[38] As global warming results in rising sea levels, coastal Chinese cities will be dramatically affected. For example, a one-meter increase in sea level would inundate one-third of Shanghai.

With China's rapidly growing appetite for electricity and automobiles, the country's increase in greenhouse gas emissions over the next thirty years likely will equal that of the rest of the developed world.[39] Although developing countries, including China, are exempt from restrictions on greenhouse gas emissions by such treaties as the Kyoto Protocol, any additional international discussions of limiting these gases undoubtedly must include China.

Recent numbers from the National Bureau of Statistics indicate that encouraging reports of declining coal use in China are unfounded and that coal consumption actually increased by 7.6 percent in 2002.[40] China's consumption of coal may dip in the latter half of this decade as hydroelectric projects such as the Three Gorges Dam come on line, but it is expected that this dip will only be temporary.[41]

China has gone from being one of the largest exporters of oil outside of the Organization of the Petroleum Exporting Countries (OPEC) in the 1980s to importing more than 30 percent of its oil needs in the 1990s.[42] Although using a greater percentage of oil for electricity production would diminish greenhouse gas emissions, China's leaders are reluctant to further increase China's dependence on foreign oil.

Transportation

The high energy demand and the accompanying pollution resulting from the rapid increase in motor vehicle use will add to the challenge of SD.[43] From 1984 to 1994, the number of motor vehicles in China tripled, to reach 9.4 million. Predictions indicate that in the first two decades of the twenty-first century the number of motor vehicles in China will increase by a factor of 13 to 22. In Beijing, as of August 2003, the number of motor vehicles doubled to two million, with 2,000 new license plates being issued each day.[44] In the first nine months of 2003 alone, vehicle sales increased 30 percent.[45] This rapidly emerging car culture will not only exacerbate China's appetite for energy but also create copious amounts of air pollution and urban sprawl. Production of cars in China has risen from 1.8 million cars to 3.8 million in the last three years, ranking China fourth behind only the United States, Japan, and Germany. In four years, China will likely surpass Germany and become a net exporter of cars.[46] Demand for new cars in China is growing at 20 percent to 30 percent per year.[47] In the next decades, the addition of millions of cars to China's highways will not only add to the existing severe air pollution problems, but the highways and parking lots that will be necessary to accommodate them will take up many hectares (ha) of cropland, exacerbating China's food supply issues. In response to China's declaration in 1996 that automobiles would be a growth industry, a host of prominent Chinese scientists penned a white paper that strongly recommended against this policy, expressing concerns about its implications on future food production. They concluded that a mass transit system consisting of urban light rail, buses, and bicycles should be the model for China's growing transportation needs.[48] However, officials in Shanghai appear to be moving in the opposite direction and recently announced a ban on the use of bicycles on major streets to make way for automobiles.[49]

Population

From 1950 to 1985 China's population virtually doubled to over one billion people, a milestone reached by no other country. To stem the tide of this mushrooming population, in 1979 China initiated a one-child-per-couple policy. According to the China Population Information and Research Center, since 1979 the population of China has increased by 315 million to 1.29 billion in 2003.[50] The population of China is projected to increase to 1.5 to 1.6 billion by around 2040 and then begin a gradual decline.[51] This additional population increase, along with rising living standards, will continue to significantly strain housing, food, and transportation and almost certainly will increase pollution.

In addition, China is a rapidly aging society. Traditionally, family members have cared for the elderly, but this custom faces substantial challenges as Chinese society evolves and the burden falls on the single child of the one-child family.

Food

China faces a significant test of how to feed its growing population. Although China is about the same size as the United States, much of its land is mountainous or desert and only one-tenth is suitable for cropland.[52] As indicated previously, China has lost over one-fifth of its cropland since 1949. This trend continues as a result of overgrazing, overplanting, industrialization, and increases in roads, parking lots, and housing. As the economic status of the Chinese population rises, demand for meat, poultry, eggs, milk, butter, and ice cream has dramatically increased. In the United States, grain use amounts to about 800 kilograms (kg) per person, while in China it is approximately 300 kg.[53] This large discrepancy is attributed primarily to the significant reliance on animals and animal products in U.S. diets, in contrast to the primary reliance on grains in the Chinese diet. The increased demand for animal products in China will significantly increase the amount of grain necessary to feed each person and will put additional stress on China's food resources and its already overburdened water resources. While human needs for drinking water are rather minimal at four liters (L) per day, the need for water to provide food varies from 2,000 to 4,000 liters per day for people who rely heavily on animal products for food.[54] U.S. Department of Agriculture (DOA) figures indicate that from 1999 to 2003, China's total annual harvest of coarse grain, corn, barley, sorghum, oats, and rice fell from 411 million tons to 378 million tons.[55]

As China's demand for grain grows, the world watches in apprehension that the country will have to rely heavily on imports to satisfy her growing hunger. This reliance already may be evident. In the first nine months of 2003, China imported the largest amount of soybeans ever from the United States. "The USDA expects China to import a record 808 million bushels of soybeans over the next year, up 55 million bushels from its Oct. estimate and more than double the amount China imported from all sources during the 2002 marketing year."[56] This surge in the import of soybeans by China is dramatically affecting world soybean supplies and costs. According to the Chicago Board of Trade, soybean prices jumped from just over US$5.00 a bushel in the beginning of 2003 to almost US$8.00 per bushel at the end of October 2003.[57]

Increased global temperatures from anthropogenic greenhouse gases may also add to China's impending food/water shortage. China's major rivers originate in the Himalayas, from which rains and melting spring snows provide water for communities downstream. Any increase in rainfall and concomitant decrease in snowfall due to higher temperatures will result in increased flooding during the rainy season and less mountain snow mass, which provides water during the dry season. China's wheat and rice production would likely be severely affected.[58]

China's Progress in Sustainable Development

As China continues to grow, the juggernaut of economic development may be moving in a more environmentally positive direction than once believed. There are some encouraging indications that SD may be possible. In preparation for developing and implementing the new market economy in a sustainable manner, China has established a cadre of ambitious plans, policies, and projects, some of which are described below.

Two Major Plans Affecting Sustainable Development

Agenda 21 is a broad plan of action that addresses the issues of environment and development around the world. Agenda 21 was established in 1992 at the United Nations Conference on Environment and Development (UNCED) held in Rio de Janeiro. Each member nation of the United Nations was given the task of employing Agenda 21 at the national and local levels.[59]

In light of Agenda 21, China laid out strategic plans, policies, goals, objectives, and action plans that include changes and development in numerous areas of the economy, society, and the environment. The real challenge for China is implementing this agenda. The Program for Formulating and Implementing China's Agenda 21 began in May 1993.[60]

In addition to Agenda 21, the Communist Party of China (CPC) Central Committee formulated China's *Tenth Five-Year Plan 2001–2005 (FYP) for National Economic and Social Development,* which also addresses SD.[61] The CPC encourages each province/locality to develop a tenth Five-Year Plan (FYP) with SD as an underlying theme. In fact, sustainable development is a major theme of the FYPs at all levels, specifically, national water conservation, clean energy, sustainable agriculture, waste and pollution reduction, innovation and development of technology, and improved environment and production in the western region.[62]

Assessing China's Progress

China has made progress in many areas related to SD. To help address the burden of implementation, China has welcomed some input from the international community. In 1992 the State Council of China established the China Council for International Cooperation on Environment and Development (CCICED) "to further strengthen cooperation and exchange between China and the international community in the field of environment and development."[63] The council reviews China's progress and provides advice on issues related to the impact of development on the environment.

The 2002 report, "Summary on Implementation of CCICED Recommendations," synopsizes the feedback and reports from sixteen ministries and departments in response to the recommendations made by CCICED. The report covers seven areas: environmental economics, sustainable agriculture, forest grassland, biodiversity, cleaner production and pollution control, transportation, and trade environment.

The 2002 CCICED report, with other sources, has provided a foundation for reviewing China's progress on SD. Examples of specific projects, funding, studies, policies, and regulations implemented at the national and provincial levels are presented in the following sections.

Funding for Sustainable Development

According to China's Vice-Minister of Science and Technology, Li Xueyong, the government is the major source of funding for SD.[64] For example, in August 2002 as part of the tenth FYP, China allocated ten billion yuan (US$1.2 billion) to enhance science and technology research on SD. Another example is the government's investment of US$5.1 million in Alxa League, Inner Mongolia, to restrain desertification. Rapidly advancing desertification is causing recurring sandstorms, which are devastating the local economy. To protect natural forests and grasslands, the government invested RMB 25.8 million in Alxa in 2001 and plans to add another RMB 490 million over the next three years.[65] Minister Li also advocates that China should reach out to the international community to procure funding to help the country pursue SD.

One of the chief sources of external funding for SD in China has been the Asian Development Bank (ABD). ADB has provided major funding to improve economic efficiency, promote growth to reduce poverty in inland provinces, and improve environmental and natural resource management (Box 1.1). The World Bank is another heavy contributor of funding to China for SD.[66] Examples of the World Bank's SD support appear later in this chapter.

Funding for limiting the production of greenhouse gases has come from the Clean Development Mechanism (CDM) under the Kyoto Protocol. Funds will be used to develop a 4.5 megawatt (MW) wind farm that will have the potential to eliminate 675,000 tons of carbon dioxide emissions over its first ten years of operation.[67]

Water

As indicated previously, there is major concern across China about water pollution, water distribution, and flooding. China is facing major water shortages in 500 of its 700 major cities, aquifers are running dry,[68] and cropland is turning to desert.[69] The State Economic and Trade Commission (which in March 2003 merged with the National Development and Reform Commission), in conjunction with the State Tax Administration, has completed "The Report on Industrial Water Price, Water Resource Fees and Water Discharge Fees."[70] China is beginning to place a monetary value on this scarce resource and to put a price on water to discourage use.

China depends very heavily on irrigation, with four-fifths of its grain harvest coming from irrigated land.[71] Currently, the PRC is expanding drip irrigation technology, the most efficient way to water crops.[72] Following this course has the potential to irrigate land at a much lower cost yet increase the yield of crops per volume of water used. The combination of increased rice

Box 1.1

Asian Development Bank Support for Sustainable Development in China

The Asian Development Bank (ADB) provides funding and technical assistance to its members. Since China became a member in 1986, it has received in excess of US$10 billion in loans from the ADB. For 2001 the ADB allocated funding to China based on three objectives:

1. Improving economic efficiency
2. Promoting growth to reduce poverty in inland provinces
3. Improving environmental and natural-resource management.

A summary of these ADB loans and technical assistance grants and their intended uses follows:

Loans: $997 million in 2001	*Technical assistance grants:* $12.4 million in 2001
Two road projects–western region	Two grants focus on poverty reduction
One railway project; carefully designed and monitored to ensure sustainable expansion	Three grants focus on environmental protection
Acid rain control and environmental improvement project	Two grants help the government develop human resources and improve capital use in the western region
Power transmission project	Thirteen grants support policy-oriented studies and promote capacity building
Project to improve flood management along the Yellow River	A $970,000 grant supports a planning study for preparation of the Yellow River Law, which will reduce poverty related to environmental causes and establish sustainable methods of watershed and land degradation management, with the long-term goal of reducing sedimentation and flooding of the Yellow River

Source: Asian Development Bank, *Annual Report 2001,* People's Republic of China, www.adb.org.

yields per acre plus more efficient irrigation practices enabled farmers in the Yangtze River Basin to quadruple water productivity from an average of 0.65 kg (1966–78) of rice per ton of water to an average of 2.4 kg (1989–98).[73]

Another approach to water conservation is to produce foods that need less water to grow. In parts of China, the government is encouraging farmers to switch from less efficient, water-intensive crops, such as rice, to more efficient crops, such as wheat. To raise water productivity per acre, farmers around Beijing have been ordered to replace 23,300 ha of rice with less water-intensive crops by 2007.[74]

China is also giving consideration to other wasteful water practices, such as the use of "flush and forget" toilets. A typical Chinese family of five uses 150,000 liters of water per year to flush away human waste using a conventional water toilet. A better alternative is composting toilets, which were pioneered by the Swedish. Composting toilets are being used in some Chinese villages.[75]

As indicated earlier, water pollution is another significant concern in China. It is now mandatory for anyone wanting to dump waste in the ocean to register for approval and to obtain a license from the State Ocean Administration.[76] The State Environmental Protection Administration (SEPA) is pushing for faster construction of sewage treatment plants and waste treatment plants in the Three Gorges Reservoir, better management of pollution from ships, and control of industrial pollution. As of June 1, 2003, thirteen sewage treatment plants were in operation in the reservoir area. Ten more were slated to go online by the end of 2003, and a total of RMB 39.3 million (approximately US$4.75 billion) has been reserved to further prevent pollution and protect the environment in the region.[77] SEPA has also put in place *The Plan for Prevention and Control of Water Pollution in Yangtze River Basin, Yellow River and Songhuajiang River*.[78] Box 1.2 provides an overview of the progress on managing the Yellow River project. Ningxia Province began construction on the Yellow River–Shapotou water conservancy project in 2000. This project will increase irrigation capacity to over 66.6 thousand ha of land, supply water to 10,000 ha of land, and generate 600 million kilowatt (kW) hours of power.[79]

Sustainable Agriculture and Food Production

One of China's main concerns is the production of enough food to feed her ever-growing population. Agricultural yields have declined in part due to loss of arable land, insufficient water for irrigation, and the Turn Farmland to Forest and Grassland Project.[80] In addition, heavy use of chemical fertilizers and pesticides has damaged the soil and ecosystems.

Box 1.2

Progress in Managing the Yellow River

- Water use in the Yellow River Basin is 70 percent, far exceeding the recommended 40 percent for any river.
- Manipulation of water resources.
  - Five dams in operation in the Upper Yellow River, three under construction, five with some preparatory site work underway, and another twelve in the design phase.
  - When the entire series of reservoirs is completed in 2020, the generating capability will be approximately 16.3 gigawatts.
- To deter unrestrained water use, the Yellow River Conservancy Commission (YRCC) and Ministry of Water Resources raised the price for raw, untreated water delivered to urban and industrial wholesale water systems by over 1,000 percent.
- In 2002, for the first time in many years, the river did not run dry before reaching the ocean.

Source: "Managing the Upper Reaches of the Yellow River," United States Embassy in China, An April 2003 Report from Embassy Beijing, www.usembassy-china.org.cn/sandt/Upper-River.htm.

Some progress is evident in the area of sustainable agriculture. Special funding has been allocated through the state ministries for a variety of agricultural projects, including the establishment of base farms as demonstration projects for ecofarming, support of the revision of laws pertaining to agriculture, and support of the development of the agriculture infrastructure.[81] In addition, funding has been allocated to conserve grasslands, promote agricultural technologies, train farmers, and establish quality assurance of agriculture and related services systems, as well as to support research and surveys that relate to ecofarming. In 2002 the Ministry of Land Resources organized a workshop that focused on the transfer of information on agricultural geological research and how it relates to socioeconomic development and sustainable agriculture.[82] Many provinces have established ecofarming demonstration projects to promote agricultural technologies, water conservation, irrigation techniques, and organic farming. Liaoning Province has implemented a program to develop "green" food.[83] Shanghai is educating farmers about environmental issues,[84] while Hebei Province is providing environmental education to citizens.[85] To ensure sustainable agricultural development in the coastal regions, the State Ocean Administration continues to monitor red tides and provide warnings of approaching disasters.[86]

One Chinese industry in jeopardy is the fishing industry, due to overfishing. To relieve this problem and soften the economic blow to fishermen, China has embarked upon a five-year fishing-vessel-scrapping program funded at US$33 million per year. This project aims to shrink the number of vessels by 30,000 over five years, resulting in a 7 percent reduction in China's 440,000-ship fishing fleet.[87]

China also is trying to divert the five million people currently working in the wild capture sector of the fisheries industry to aquaculture, but funding is scarce. The Bureau of Fisheries is working to discourage poor farmers from becoming fishermen. To further relieve some of the pressure of overfishing, the bureau has instituted fishing moratoria, which are activated regularly.[88]

China has made impressive gains in land productivity by multiple cropping. In southern China, triple crops of rice have been produced, while in northern China, double-cropping of corn and winter wheat has doubled land productivity.[89]

As the world population increases and, at the same time, moves up the food chain, meat consumption has increased by a factor of 5, to 240 million tons, from 1950 to 2002. Meat consumption per person has more than doubled during this period. As mentioned, China's population is moving from a starch/grain-centered diet to consuming more protein (fish, poultry, and meat). This trend is putting additional stress on China's grain production, since a weight gain of one pound for an animal requires several kilograms of grain. For example, feedlot beef requires seven kilograms of grain per day, while herbivorous fish require fewer than two. To exploit this difference, China is leading the way in aquaculture, with two-thirds of the world's production. In addition, to fertilize the fishponds and increase the fish yield, farmers are using waste from pigs, ducks, and other animals. It is interesting to note that the aquaculture industry in China is employing an alternative energy source—geothermal—to heat ponds.[90]

Forest and Grassland

China is facing the challenge of increasing food production while dealing with the issues of desertification, conservation of ecological systems, and reforestation. To help address these intertwined problems, the Ministry of Finance, together with the State Forestry Administration, did a cost-benefit analysis of the forestry industry and set aside money to monitor and evaluate environmentally friendly food agricultural resources, the forest industry, wetlands, rare and endangered plant species, and desertification.[91]

To reduce environmental disasters such as flooding, loss of topsoil, and desertification, China has a program that pays farmers in vulnerable areas to replace the crops that they normally would plant with trees. The plan is to cover more than ten million hectare of grain-land—which equals at least one-tenth of China's current grain-land area—with trees by 2010.[92] The Chinese have planted more than thirty-five billion trees since 1981.[93] According to the National Greening Commission, more than 16 percent of the land in China is now forested, a 4-percent increase over the last twenty years. It should be noted, however, that some questions remain as to the long-term survival of these trees and the accuracy of these statistics. In addition, in 1998 the government announced a curb on tree cutting in natural forest areas to alleviate flooding.[94]

In April 2002 a US$93.9 million loan was approved by the World Bank to support the China Sustainable Forestry Development Project. This loan is in addition to a US$26 million grant from the Global Environment Facility (GEF) and a US$15 million grant from the European Commission. Such generous funding has been granted because the forestry industry is important to China's economy and growth.[95]

The funds will be used to protect watersheds, natural forests, and their biodiversity, and to alleviate flooding. They will also provide support for loggers affected by bans on logging.[96] Individual provinces are doing their parts to reclaim forests from farmland by regulating and, in some instances, banning logging.[97]

Biodiversity

Progress is also being made in the area of biodiversity. The Ministry of Land Resources (MLR) has established forty-four national geological sections and geological heritage reserves. The Ministry of Agriculture (MOA) has put in place national germplasm banks and thirty-two perennial and asexual propagation crop germplasm nurseries to protect wild plants.[98] A legal framework has been established for wildlife conservation and administration. As a result, RMB 200 million has been allocated to a network of ecosystem research in China.[99] In addition, marine nature reserves have been established in the country's coastal regions.

At the provincial and municipal levels, similar advancements in the area of biodiversity have taken place. For example, Tianjin Municipality is working to restore and protect ecosystems and is enforcing regulations to keep out an invasion of alien pests. Liaoning Province has implemented the *Development Plan for Nature Reserves in Liaoning* and *Notice on Strengthening Wildlife Conservation,* which calls for the establishment of sixty nature reserves that encompass 9.7 percent of the land in the province.[100] Guizhou Province has established seventy-nine nature reserves and fifty-three scenic areas.[101] Hainan Province has a number of pilot cities and counties that have implemented sound ecological practices such as pollution control, encouragement of ecoindustry, and environmental conservation.[102]

Cleaner Production and Pollution Control

Many environmental laws in China and the rest of the world are aimed at preventing the dispersion of toxic chemicals into the environment. These "command and control" laws are also known as "end-of-the-pipe solutions," and they restrict emissions of pollutants and impose fines for emissions above set limits. While such legislation helps to prevent hazardous substances from entering the environment, pollution controls of this type inevitably fall short. China has begun to pass laws, such as the *Cleaner Production Promotion Law* (June 29, 2002), that "move up the pipe" to discourage the use or production of hazardous substances.[103] Cleaner production regulations encourage companies to find alternative nontoxic substances to replace the toxic materials that they currently use. In addition, laws of this type encourage increased efficiency of resource use, the use of renewable resources, and a reduction in energy consumption. They not only protect the environment but also promote better human health, conservation of natural resources, and SD. China is the first nation to pass a law with cleaner production as a national policy.

The field of green, or sustainable, chemistry is blossoming in China. Green chemistry is defined as the reduction or elimination of the use or production of hazardous substances.[104] Green chemistry also seeks to minimize energy use and waste generation, and to promote the efficient use of resources (renewable resources if possible) during the synthesis of chemicals and chemical products. Examples of green chemistry include reduced-risk pesticides, production of biodegradable polymers from renewable resources, and greener syntheses of pharmaceuticals.[105] Each year, beginning in 1998, China has hosted an international green chemistry conference, and is one of a growing number of countries to boast a chapter of the Green Chemistry Institute. The establishment of green chemistry in China comes at an opportune time because the Chinese chemical industry has been growing at an annual rate of 15 percent.[106] One example of green chemistry in China is a new focus on greener pesticides.

To encourage recycling and cleaner production, the State Economic and Trade Commission (SETC) (now part of the National Development and Reform Commission) and the Ministry of Finance have issued a *Notice on Policy*

Issues Concerning the Value-added Tax for the Comprehensive Utilization of Certain Resources and Other Products. This regulation provides for a tax refund when certain products are made from recycled materials or comprehensive utilization of resources has been employed to make the products. Half of the value-added tax is also refunded for cases in which power generation is the result of "gangue, peat, shale, oil and wind."[107]

Many of the provinces have built demonstration projects to reduce industrial pollutant emissions. Jiangxi Province is involved with the restructuring and upgrading of industry and auditing for cleaner production and has begun ISO 14000 environmental certification and management. To control pollutant emissions, the Tibet Autonomous Region has shut down fifteen polluting organizations from various industries and has barred construction of five new operations with similar polluting tendencies.[108] Qinghai Province reduced pollution by assisting industry to invest in new, less polluting technologies and to implement new processes. The province encourages reduced waste, recycling, and more "environmentally friendly end-of-pipe discharging."[109]

Energy

The State Economic and Trade Commission (which, as mentioned earlier, was subsequently merged with the National Development and Reform Commission) is implementing plans to conserve energy based on a legal framework that promotes energy conservation and the development of a new energy industry. The SETC also advocates certification of energy-efficient products, an energy efficiency standard, and labeling. The commission is responsible for more than 100 energy conservation projects in metallurgy, nonferrous metals, building materials, chemical engineering, power, and paper-making industries.[110]

The Ministry of Water Resources has developed the *Plan on Ecological Conservation by Replacing Fuels with Small Hydro Power Plants* to help with clean energy production.[111] In 2001 the Ministry of Water Resources established 400 small hydropower projects in rural counties in China to further the plan for alternative power generation laid out in the tenth FYP. As of 2002, 3,500 MW of hydropower had been generated in these small plants, with more capacity to be installed over the tenth FYP period.[112] Currently, China has a total installed hydroelectric capacity of 79,000 MW.

As of the beginning of 2003, ten projects on the main stream were completed, with a total installed capacity of 8.92 million kW.[113] The Three Gorges Dam Project is expected to be completed by 2009. At that time, the installed hydroelectric capacity from the project is expected to be 18,200 MW, or approximately 24 percent of the current total hydroelectric capacity in all of China.[114] In addition to the Three Gorges Project, twenty-five hydroelectric power projects are being developed on the Yellow River. The combined installed hydroelectric capacity for this latter project is expected to be 15,800 MW.

It is important to mention that, although hydroelectric power may be considered a renewable resource, it is not without considerable environmental and social costs. Environmental problems that result from dams include wildlife habitat destruction and division, silting of waterways, increased emission of methane (a greenhouse gas), and the leaching of toxic heavy metals from the soil. Some of the social costs are displacement of people from their homes and workplaces (more than one million people were displaced as a result of the Three Gorges Project), division of people from their neighbors, loss of natural and archeological treasures, and loss of crop and grazing land.

According to the Clean China Council, efforts to produce more energy-efficient appliances and buildings are beginning to bear fruit. This is of particular importance, since China is the world's largest market for electrical appliances, and the unprecedented high-rise building boom is transforming the skylines of China's cities.[115]

China has ample wind resources. However, wind power in China is approximately twice the cost of electricity from coal. To alleviate the cost, the Chinese government has reduced by half the value-added tax on wind-generated electricity. As of 2002, China had installed 460 MW of wind power, which is about one-quarter of India's wind power capacity, one-tenth that of the United States, and about one-thirtieth that of Germany, which is the world leader in wind power resources. However, in its tenth FYP, China indicates implementation of a threefold increase in wind power.[116]

The MOA has started small energy projects in China's rural regions. In 2001 the MOA committed to invest RMB 100 million per year on these projects. So far, 30,000 biogas pits, 177 small biogas projects, 112 stalk gasification projects, 4,727 small wind power systems, 70,000 solar stoves, and 100 solar energy houses have resulted from the investments.[117] In 2002 the Asian Development Bank approved a loan of US$33.1 million for China to develop clean energy from agricultural biomass wastes.[118] Furthermore, farmers are being trained in clean energy, and regulations are being developed that require using cleaner energy sources to replace fuels such as coal. In 1994 and 1996, China cut coal subsidies by US$750 million and another US$250 million, respectively, in order to raise the price of coal to more realistic levels. In addition, a high tax was placed on sulfur emissions.[119] Replacement of coal burning boilers, for example, will reduce pollutants such as sulfur dioxide in the atmosphere.

Cleaner Air and Transportation

By 2001, China's State Power Corporation, which has been divided into five companies, had achieved sulfur dioxide emissions reductions of 700,000 tons. Reduction of an additional 25 percent is expected by 2005.[120]

The Ministry of Transportation is committed to building environmentally sound public transportation systems and encouraging use of clean fuel for vehicles. Most provinces are following suit by developing new and improved public transportation systems, including rail systems, with priority given to the use of clean fuel. The ministry is promoting environmental management of these systems. Banishment of certain types of vehicles from the urban areas has already begun, and prevention and control of pollution from vehicle exhausts is underway. Leaded gasoline was banned in 2002.[121]

Over RMB 52 billion is slated for investment to reduce pollution in Beijing. The municipal government ordered city vehicles to convert to liquefied petroleum gas and natural gas. In addition, the city installed pollution control devices on 190,000 vehicles and 36,000 taxis. By 2002, Beijing had the world's largest fleet of natural gas buses—a total of 1,630 vehicles. Air pollution reduction efforts also include expanding subway and light rail systems and increasing the number of buses from 15,400 to 18,000 by 2007.[122]

Barriers to the Implementation of Sustainable Development

Although it appears that China is making progress toward implementation of SD on numerous fronts, not all of the efforts are going smoothly. Many plans have been created to infuse SD into China's national development, but only a limited number of these plans have been implemented and fully executed. A case in point is the experience in Heilongjiang Province. Heilongjiang has taken the lead in wetland preservation since 1999, when it became the first province to ban development of wetlands. However, when an ambitious program was proposed to encourage sustainable growth of the province by establishing a legal framework, implementation became problematic.[123]

Heilongjiang comprises 400,000 square km in northeast China and borders Russia. The province has been under pressure by the central government to grow and develop the Ussuri watershed region. However, there are concerns that this area should not be developed at the expense of the ecosystem. The provincial government undertook a scientific study with cooperation of individuals from other countries on two continents. The Cooperative Group, as they are called, wrote a plan to develop the Ussuri watershed area in a sustainable manner.[124] An interesting aspect of this plan is that it involved the development of an additional area using a similar approach in

Russia, across the border from Heilongjiang Province. Heilongjiang was attempting to establish "use zoning" through the establishment of a legal framework that sets aside land for planned, coordinated development but constrains the usage.[125] Although a plan was in place, the legal framework was never implemented.

The group encountered a number of hurdles in trying to achieve the political goals associated with the project while trying to preserve the environment. Some of the barriers included transborder bureaucratic obstacles; incompatibility of new policies with existing policies in China and Russia; the stress associated with SD; competing interests among bureaucrats, environmental planners, and foreign consultants; and insufficient support at the local level.[126] As with most endeavors, support of the local constituency is critical to achieving any goal.

At this time, the project to protect wetlands in Heilongjiang continues. Regulation is once again underway. In addition, the ADB has provided funding for a Canadian environmental development company to restore marshlands along the Songhua River to their original condition.[127] Although this project has not developed as originally planned, progress is nonetheless being made.

The Heilongjiang experience suggests that trade-offs between economic development and ecological protection are necessary to implement economic growth without degrading the ecosystem. Another important lesson learned is that local support or buy-in is absolutely imperative to achieving movement toward the goal of SD.

The problems that Heilongjiang Province experienced in implementation are not unique.

> The central government in Beijing has had repeated difficulties in forcing provincial governments to pursue recent efficiency programs. China no longer has the central planning mandates to order improvements, but has not yet developed market-based incentives, like higher prices, to encourage people to curb their consumption of fossil fuels.[128]

A fundamental challenge to the implementation of SD is the ongoing debate over the appropriate balance between economic growth and environmental conservation.[129] Where does that leave the implementation of SD in China in the future?

The Future

Are we exceeding the carrying capacity of the earth? Are we depleting the earth's resources and generating waste faster than the earth can absorb it and convert it back into resources? Rees, Testemale, and Wackernagel have developed the concept of an *ecological footprint* as a way to measure the sustainability of our actions. Our ecological footprint takes into account the resources that humans consume and the waste that we produce and, based on them, calculates the amount of biologically productive space necessary to provide these resources and convert the waste back into resources.[130]

Studies indicate that, as of 1997, the ecological footprint in China is 1.2 ha per person, compared to 10.3, 6.1, 5.2, 4.3, 3.4, and 0.8 ha for the United States, Hong Kong, United Kingdom, Japan, Republic of Korea, and India respectively.[131] Estimates show that there is 1.7 ha per capita of biologically productive space on earth, and it is clear that all of the above ecological footprints exceed this level, with the exception of those of China and India.[132] However, because China has such a large population and only 0.8 ha of biologically productive space per capita within its borders, this suggests that the aggregate ecological footprint of China's people oversteps her boundaries. Since the ecological footprint generally is a direct function of economic development, China—and the world—must watch China's ecological footprint as China continues its rapid pace of development. To stay within her boundaries and grow in a sustainable manner:

1. China must continue to rigorously control her population.
2. Businesses in China must ardently practice the triple bottom line, with social and environmental benefits being on an equal or greater footing with economic benefits.
3. China must implement and enforce strict pollution standards. More importantly, China must promote pollution prevention and resource and energy conservation at the source. Clean production practices must be implemented across the country. Use of renewable energy resources should be a national priority.
4. China must promote the use of mass transit rather than automobiles. In cases in which cars and trucks are a necessity, they should be held to strict gas mileage standards and pollution standards.
5. SEPA must have greater monetary support and political clout. The local environmental protection boards (EPBs), which are largely responsible for implementing and enforcing environmental regulations, must be given greater authority to impose and collect fines. Fines also must be increased to make it economically prohibitive to pollute.
6. Nongovernmental organizations (NGOs) that are advocates for the environment, such as Friends of Nature, must be allowed and even encouraged to grow in number and strength.
7. The Chinese should lead the way in promoting the United Nations

Decade on Education for Sustainable Development (2005–15). Conservation must be instilled in the minds of all the people, and the three R's—reduce, reuse, and recycle—must become a way of life. The government must provide incentives for this. Additionally, China must invest in the education and development of human capital. In 1998–99 China spent only 2.2 percent of its GDP on education—less than any other developing country.[133] As the gap widens between the haves and the have-nots, China risks social unrest. Providing an education to all will reduce that risk and broaden the probability of growth and SD through innovation.

8. China must focus on conservation of cropland, increasing land and water yields of crops, and reforestation.

9. China must do full cost accounting, which strives to incorporate both environmental and social costs into traditional accounting systems. In addition, the country should eliminate subsidies of pollution-creating and resource-consuming activities and provide disincentives through taxation. At the same time, financial incentives should be provided for activities that focus on resource and energy conservation and prevent pollution at the source.

Conclusion

The model of economic development based upon ever-increasing consumption, which is common in many developed countries, should not be the paradigm that is followed by China. Will China's development be one that simply imitates that of many Western nations, or will China's growth provide the prototype of SD for the entire world to emulate?

Whether China develops in a sustainable manner depends on the policies and practices set forth and implemented today and tomorrow. China's future lies in the hands of its leaders and citizens. The concept and practice of SD must become part of the psyche and actions of all the Chinese people, who must be taught that whether the future of their country holds great promise or despair depends on the path that is taken today. Current choices will determine whether the future lifestyle of the Chinese people is comfortable and pleasant, or debased by environmental degradation and shortages of basic necessities. The world is watching China, for as goes the world's most populous country, so goes the world.

Notes

The authors acknowledge the contributions of Wang Wanfei to an earlier version of this chapter.

1. UN Brundtland Commission, *Brundtland Report (Our Common Future)* (New York: 1987), www.unesco.org/education/esd/english/international/unced.shtml.

2. Many of the statistics referenced in this paper are from Chinese government sources. Their limitations and those of nongovernmental statistical data on China must be acknowledged. These limitations are true particularly for more sensitive information in which there may be an incentive to over- or under-report. Nonetheless, we believe the information used in this paper is useful for general assessment purposes.

3. "China," in U.S. Central Intelligence Agency, *The World Factbook 2003—China*, www.cia.gov/cia/publications/factbook/geos/ch.html#Econ.

4. State Environmental Protection Administration of China (SEPA), "China's Agenda 21-White Paper on China's Population, Environment, and Development in the 21st Century," chap. 4, www.zhb.gov.cn/english/SD/21cn/write_paper/writepaper-c4.htm.

5. World Trade Organization, WTO News: 2001 Press Release, "WTO Successfully Concludes Negotiations on China's Entry," Sept. 17, 2001, www.wto.org/english/news_e/pres01_e/pr243_e.htm.

6. China Population Information and Research Center, "China Population," www.cpirc.org.cn/eindex.htm.

7. Peter Wonacott, "China Saps Commodity Supplies," *Wall Street Journal*, Oct. 24, 2003, C1.

8. Ibid.

9. Michael Pickles, "Implementing Ecologically Sustainable Development in China: The Example of Heilongjiang Province," *Georgetown International Environmental Law Review* 14 (3) (Spring 2002): 577–93.

10. China Population Information and Research Center, "China Population."

11. SEPA, "China's Agenda 21," Chapters and Programme Areas of the White Paper, www.zhb.gov.cn/english/SD/21cn/index.htm.

12. Ibid., chap. 1.1, www.zhb.gov.cn/english/SD/21cn/write_paper/writepaper-c1.htm.

13. Ibid., chap. 4.2, www.zhb.gov.cn/english/SD/21cn/write_paper/writepaper-c4.htm.

14. *People's Daily Online*, "Hu Stresses Harmony Among People, Resources, Environment," Mar. 10, 2003, english.peopledaily.com.cn/200303/10/eng-20030310_113015.shtml.

15. SustainAbility, "SD Issues, The Triple Bottom Line," www.sustainability.com/philosophy/triple-bottom/tbl-intro.asp.

16. *People's Daily Online*, "CPC Central Committee Proposal for Formulating Tenth Five-Year Plan (Summary)," Oct. 18, 2000, english.peopledaily.com.cn/200010/18/eng20001018_52942.html.

17. International Labor Office, Government of the People's Republic of China, Tenth Five-Year Plan for National Economic and Social Development—People's Republic of China, "Making Improvement in the People's Living Standards as the Basic Starting Point," www.logos-net.net/ilo/150_base/en/init/chn_1.htm#kuva.

18. World Resources Institute (WRI), Health and Environment, Air Pollution and Health, "The Environment and China: Water and Air Pollution," www.wri.org/wri/china/water.htm.

19. Edward O. Wilson, "The Bottleneck," Scientific American.com, Feb. 24, 2002, www.sciam.com/print_version.cfm?articleID=000E5878–3E45–1CC6–B4A-8809EC588EEDF.

20. UN University, Environment and Sustainable Development Programme, "Coastal Hydrosphere Project, China," http://landbase.hq.unu.edu/Sampling%20Plan%202002/China.htm /China.htm.

21. One RMB (renminbi) or Chinese yuan (CNY) equals approximately US$0.12; conversely, RMB 8.28 equals US$1.

22. Wilson, "The Bottleneck."

23. Lester R. Brown, *Plan B: Rescuing a Planet under Stress and a Civilization in Trouble* (New York: W.W. Norton for Earth Policy Institute, 2003), 117, www.earth-policy.org/Books/PlanB_contents.htm.

24. Eric Zusman, "The River Runs Dry: Examining Water Shortages in the Yellow River Basin," *Economic, Social and Legal Issues in China's Transition to a Market Economy* (Los Angeles: UCLA Asia Institute, 2000), 1, http://repositories.cdlib.org/asia/eslictme/chntrans12/.

25. World Bank et al., "China: Agenda for Water Sector Strategy for North China, Vol. 1: Summary Report," Washington, DC, 2001, 6, http://lnweb18.worldbank.org/eap/eap.nsf/Attachments/WaterSectorReport/$File/Vo11v13A4a1.pdf.

26. Carmen Ravenga, "Will There Be Enough Water?" WRI, Earth Trends: The Environmental Information Portal, Oct. 2000, http://earthtrends.wri.org/text/FRE/features/FRE_fea_scarcity.htm.

27. World Bank et al., "China: Agenda for Water Sector Strategy," 44.

28. International Federation of Red Cross and Red Crescent Societies, "Red Cross Assists as Floods Affect Close to 100 Million in China," July 10, 2003, www.ifrc.org/docs/news/pr03/5503.asp.

29. BBC News, "China's Floods: Is Deforestation to Blame?" Aug. 6, 1999, http://news.bbc.co.uk/1/hi/world/asia-pacific/413717.stm.

30. WRI, "The Environment and China."

31. Ibid.

32. China Internet Information Center, "Acid Rain in China," http://us.tom.com/english/1902.htm.

33. "China/Environment/Current Issues," in U.S. Central Intelligence Agency (CIA), *The World Factbook,* see www.cia.gov/cia/publications/factbook/geos/ch.html.

34. Lester R. Brown, "China Losing War with Advancing Deserts," Earth Policy Institute, Aug. 5, 2003, www.earth-policy.org/Updates/Update26.htm.

35. P. Andrews-Speed, Liao Xuanli, and R. Dannreuther, "Searching for Energy Security: The Political Ramifications of China's International Energy Policy," *China Environment Series* 5 (Washington, DC: Woodrow Wilson Center, 2002), 13–14.

36. Ibid., 14.

37. U.S. Energy Information Administration, "International Energy Outlook 2003: Coal," Report released Aug. 1, 2003, www.eia.doe.gov/oiaf/ieo/coal.html.

38. Bernie Fischlowitz-Roberts, "Carbon Emissions Climbing," Earth Policy Institute, 2002, www.earth-policy.org/Indicators/indicator5.htm.

39. Keith Bradsher, "China's Boom Adds to Global Warming," *New York Times,* Oct. 22, 2003, late edition-final, sec. A1, 3.

40. Brown, *Plan B,* 215.

41. Bradsher, "China's Boom."

42. P. Andrews-Speed et al., "Searching for Energy Security," 3.

43. WRI, Health and Environment, Air Pollution and Health Effects, "Poor Ambient Air Quality Prevails," 1998–99, www.wri.org/wr-98–99/prc2air.htm.

44. Julie Chao, "Pacific Currents: China Trying to Cope with Burgeoning Car

Culture," *Seattle Post-Intelligencer,* Sept. 8, 2003, http://seattlepi.nwsource.com/national/138451_pac08.html.

45. Wonacott, "China Saps Commodity Supplies."

46. Keith Bradsher, "China's Factories Aim to Fill Garages Around the World," *New York Times,* Nov. 2, 2003, late ed.-final, sec. A8, 3.

47. Dan Ackman, "China's Hot Wheels," *Forbes,* Dec. 16, 2002, www.forbes.com/2002/12/16/cx_da_1216topnews.html.

48. Brown, *Plan B,* 146.

49. News Interactive, "Shanghai to Increase Bike Ban," *Herald Sun,* Dec. 9, 2003, http://heraldsun.news.com.au/common/story_page/0,5478,8113685%255E1702,00.html.

50. China Population Information and Research Center, "China Population."

51. International Institute for Applied Systems Analysis, Data—Population, "The Impact of Fertility Assumptions on Total Population Projections in China" (1999), www.iiasa.ac.at/Research/LUC/ChinaFood/data/pop/pop_22.htm.

52. Lester R. Brown, *Who Will Feed China? Wake-up Call for a Small Planet* (New York: W.W. Norton, 1995), 54.

53. Ibid., 45.

54. Brown, *Plan B,* 25.

55. FAS Online, "Grain: World Markets and Trade," Foreign Agricultural Service Circular Series, Nov. 2003, www.fas.usda.gov/grain/circular/2003/11–03/graintoc.htm.

56. Scott Kilman, "U.S. Crop Prices Soar as China Fuels Demand," *Wall Street Journal,* Nov. 13, 2003, A2, 3.

57. Ibid.

58. Brown, *Plan B,* 68.

59. UN Department of Economic and Social Affairs, Division for Sustainability, "Agenda 21," Mar. 24, 2003, www.un.org/esa/sustdev/documents/agenda21/index.htm.

60. PRC, "China's Agenda 21, Summary, Formulating and Implementing China's Agenda 21," www.undp.org/seed/cap21/china.html.

61. China Development Gateway, "Look into the Next Five Years: Premier Zhu Rongji's Explanation of 10th Five-Year Drafting," 2001, www.chinagate.com.cn/english/e-plan/index.htm.

62. Ibid.

63. China Council for International Cooperation on Environment and Development (CCICED), Phase III (2002–2007), "2002 Report on Summary on Implementation of CCICED Recommendations," www.harbour.sfu.ca/dlam/history.html.

64. *People's Daily Online*, "China Issues Sci-tech Program on Sustainable Development," Aug. 15, 2002, http://english.peopledaily.com.cn/200208/15/eng20020815_101497.shtml.

65. West Development, China Development Gateway, "China Invests US$5.1 Million to Curb Desertification in Inner Mongolia," http://211.147.20.14/chinagate/focus/west/news/i001/20020422invest.html.

66. Leah Nathans Spiro, "Why a Wealthy China Gets World Bank Backing," *Business Week,* Sept. 29, 1997, www.businessweek.com/1997/39/b3546008.htm. Also see chapter by Zusman and Turner, this volume, p. 129.

67. IT Power News, "First Kyoto Protocol Project to Go Ahead in China: Chinese Win Carbon Funding for Windfarm," Nov. 12, 2003, www.itpower.co.uk/NEWS30.HTM.

68. Brown, *Plan B,* 115.

69. Ibid., 48.

70. CCICED, "2002 Report," 21.

71. Brown, *Plan B,* 28.

72. Sandra Postel, Paul Polak, Fernando Gonzales, and Jack Keller, "Drip Irrigation for Small Farmers: A New Initiative to Alleviate Hunger and Poverty," *Water International* 26 (1) (2001): 3–13.

73. Brown, *Plan B,* 121.

74. Ibid.

75. Ibid.

76. CCICED, "2002 Report," 17.

77. *People's Daily Online,* "More Sewage Treatment Plants Operational in Three Gorges Reservoir Area," June 6, 2003, http://english.peopledaily.com.cn/200306/06/eng20030606_117791.shtml.

78. CCICED, "2002 Report,"16–17.

79. Hong Kong Trade Development Council, Business Alert—China, "Local Adaptations of Tenth Five-Year Plan," 12 (4) (Dec. 15, 2000), www.tdctrade.com/alert/cba-e0012.htm.

80. Chinadaily.com, "No Strain for China's Grain," *China Daily,* Nov. 21, 2003, www.chinadaily.com.cn/en/doc/2003–11/21/content_283673.htm.

81. CCICED, "2002 Report," 5.

82. Ibid., 6.

83. Ibid., 7.

84. Ibid., 8.

85. Ibid., 3.

86. Ibid., 7.

87. U.S. Embassy in China, "China Combats Overfishing and Illegal Fishing," A Feb. 2003 report from Embassy Beijing, 1, www.usembassy-china.org.cn/sandt/Illegal-Fishing.htm.

88. Ibid., 2.

89. Brown, *Plan B,* 21.

90. Ibid., 38, 140.

91. CCICED, "2002 Report," 9.

92. Brown, *Plan B,* 149.

93. Forests.org, "Battling China's Deforestation," Mar. 28, 2001, http://forests.org/archive/asia/battchin.htm.

94. Peichang Zhang, Guofan Shao, Guang Zhao, Dennis C. Le Master, George R. Parker, John B. Dunning Jr., and Qinglin LI, "China's Forest Policy for the 21st Century," *Science* 288 (June 23, 2000): 2135–36.

95. DevNews Media Center, "World Bank Supports Sustainable Forestry in China," Apr. 18, 2002, http://web.worldbank.org/WBSITE/EXTERNAL/NEWS/0,,contentMDK:20041156~menuPK:34460~pagePK:34370~piPK:34424~theSitePK:4607,00.html.

96. Ibid.

97. CCICED, "2002 Report," 10, 11, 12.

98. Ibid., 12.

99. Ibid., 13.

100. Ibid., 14.

101. Ibid., 15.

102. Ibid., 14.

103. Cleaner Production in China, "Cleaner Production Promotion Law," Approved

by the Standing Committee of the National People's Congress (NPC) of the People's Republic of China in the 28th Session on June 29, 2002, www.chinacp.com/eng/cppolicystrategy/cp_law2002.html.

104. Paul T. Anastas and John Warner, *Green Chemistry: Theory and Practice* (Oxford: Oxford University Press, 2000).

105. Michael C. Cann and Marc E. Connelly, *Real-World Cases in Green Chemistry* (Washington, DC: American Chemical Society, 2000).

106. Patricia Short, "China Stars at SCI in Barcelona," *Chemical and Engineering News* (Oct. 30, 2003): 14.

107. CCICED, "2002 Report," 16.

108. Ibid., 20.

109. Ibid.

110. Ibid., 21.

111. Ibid., 9.

112. Ibid., 21.

113. Yellow River Conservancy Commission (YRCC), "The Outline of Hydraulic Multipurpose Project," Dec. 22, 2002, www.yrcc.gov.cn/eng/gc/index1.phtml.

114. ChinaOnline, "Three Gorges Dam Project," www.chinaonline.com/refer/ministry_profiles/threegorgesdam.asp.

115. Bradsher, "China's Boom."

116. Brown, *Plan B*, 215.

. 117. Roger Raufer and Wang Shujuan, "Navigating the Policy Path for Support of Wind Power in China," *China Environment Series* 6 (Washington, DC: Woodrow Wilson Center, 2003), 37, http://wwics.si.edu/topics/pubs/4-feature_3.pdf.

118. CCICED, "2002 Report," 22.

119. ADB.org, News Release No. 1 193/02 23, "Biomass Use to Reduce Pollution in People's Republic of China," Oct. 2002, www.adb.org/documents/news/2002/nr2002193.asp.

120. CCICED, "2002 Report," 18.

121. Ibid., 25.

122. *People's Daily Online,* "Beijing Boasts World's Largest Fleet of Gas-Burning Buses," Apr. 10, 2002, http://english.peopledaily.com.cn/200204/13/eng20020413_93968.shtml.

123. Pickles, "Implementing Ecologically SD," 2.

124. Ibid., 2.

125. Ibid., 3.

126. Ibid., 2.

127. Ibid., 8.

128. Bradsher, "China's Boom," 3.

129. Ibid.

130. Redefining Progress, Sustainability Indicators Program, Ecological Footprint Analysis, www.redefiningprogress.org/programs/sustainabilityindicators/ef/.

131. The Earth Council, Ecological Footprints of Nations, "Ranking the Ecological Impact of Nations," www.ecouncil.ac.cr/rio/focus/report/english/footprint/ranking.htm.

132. The Earth Council, Ecological Footprints of Nations, "Ecological Benchmark: How Much Nature Is There per Global Citizen?" www.ecouncil.ac.cr/rio/focus/report/english/footprint/benchmark.htm.

133. David Wessel, "The People's Republic May Neglect People by Starving Schools," *Wall Street Journal,* Oct. 23, 2003, A2.

Bibliography

Ackman, Dan. "China's Hot Wheels." *Forbes,* Dec. 16, 2002, www.forbes.com/2002/12/16/cx_da_1216topnews.html.

ADB.org (Asian Development Bank). News Release No. 1 193/02 23, "Biomass Use to Reduce Pollution in People's Republic of China." Oct. 2002. www.adb.org/documents/news/2002/nr2002193.asp.

Anastas, Paul T., and John Warner. *Green Chemistry: Theory and Practice.* Oxford: Oxford University Press, 2000.

Andrews-Speed, P., Liao Xuanli, and R. Dannreuther. "Searching for Energy Security: The Political Ramifications of China's International Energy Policy." *China Environment Series* 5. Washington, DC: Woodrow Wilson Center, 2002.

Asian Development Bank. *Annual Report 2001, People's Republic of China.* www.adb.org.

BBC News. "China's Floods: Is Deforestation to Blame?" Aug. 6, 1999. http://news.bbc.co.uk/1/hi/world/asia-pacific/413717.stm.

Bradsher, Keith. "China's Boom Adds to Global Warming." *New York Times,* late edition-final, Oct. 22, 2003.

————. "China's Factories Aim to Fill Garages Around the World." *New York Times,* late edition-final, Nov. 2, 2003.

Brown, Lester R. *Plan B: Rescuing a Planet under Stress and a Civilization in Trouble.* New York: W.W. Norton for Earth Policy Institute, 2003. www.earth-policy.org/Books/PlanB_contents.htm.

————. "China Losing War with Advancing Deserts." Earth Policy Institute, Aug. 5, 2003. www.earth-policy.org/Updates/Update26.htm.

————. *Who Will Feed China? Wake-up Call for a Small Planet.* New York: W.W. Norton, 1995.

Cann, Michael C., and Marc E. Connelly. *Real-World Cases in Green Chemistry.* Washington, DC: American Chemical Society, 2000.

Chao, Julie. "Pacific Currents: China Trying to Cope with Burgeoning Car Culture." *Seattle Post-Intelligencer,* Sept. 8, 2003. http://seattlepi.nwsource.com/national/138451_pac08.html.

China Council for International Cooperation on Environment and Development (CCICED). Phase III (2002–2007). "2002 Report on Summary on Implementation of CCICED Recommendations." www.harbour.sfu.ca/dlam/history.html.

CHINAdaily.com. "No Strain for China's Grain." *China Daily,* Nov. 21, 2003. www.chinadaily.com.cn/en/doc/2003–11/21/content_283673.htm.

China Development Gateway. "Look into the Next Five Years: Premier Zhu Rongji's Explanation of 10th Five-Year Drafting," 2001. www.chinagate.com.cn/english/e-plan/index.htm.

China Internet Information Center. "Acid Rain in China." http://us.tom.com/english/1902.htm.

ChinaOnline. "Three Gorges Dam Project." www.yrcc.gov.cn/eng/gc/index1.phtml.

China Population Information and Research Center. China Population. www.cpirc.org.cn/eindex.htm [in Chinese].

Cleaner Production in China. "Cleaner Production Promotion Law." Approved by the Standing Committee of the National People's Congress (NPC) of the People's Republic of China in the 28th Session on June 29, 2002. www.chinacp.com/eng/cppolicystrategy/cp_law2002.html.

DevNews Media Center. "World Bank Supports Sustainable Forestry in China." Apr. 18, 2002. http://web.worldbank.org/WBSITE/EXTERNAL/NEWS/0,,content-MDK:20041156~menuPK:34460~pagePK:34370~piPK:34424~theSitePK:4607,00.html.

The Earth Council. Ecological Footprints of Nations. "Ecological Benchmark: How Much Nature Is There per Global Citizen?" www.ecouncil.ac.cr/rio/focus/report/english/footprint/benchmark.htm.

————. Ecological Footprints of Nations. "Ranking the Ecological Impact of Nations." www.ecouncil.ac.cr/rio/focus/report/english/footprint/ranking.htm.

FAS Online. "Grain: World Markets and Trade." Foreign Agricultural Service Circular Series (Nov. 2003). www.fas.usda.gov/grain/circular/2003/11–03/graintoc.htm.

Fischlowitz-Roberts, Bernie. "Carbon Emissions Climbing." Earth Policy Institute (2002). www.earth-policy.org/Indicators/indicator5.htm.

Forests.org. "Battling China's Deforestation." Mar. 28, 2001. http://forests.org/archive/asia/battchin.htm.

Gonzales, Fernando, and Jack Keller. "Drip Irrigation for Small Farmers: A New Initiative to Alleviate Hunger and Poverty." *Water International* 26 (1) (2001): 3–13.

Hong Kong Trade Development Council. "Local Adaptations of Tenth Five-year Plan." Business Alert-China 12 (4) (Dec. 15, 2000). www.tdctrade.com/alert/cba-e0012.htm.

International Federation of Red Cross and Red Crescent Societies. "Red Cross Assists as Floods Affect Close to 100 Million in China." July 10, 2003. www.ifrc.org/docs/news/pr03/5503.asp.

International Institute for Applied Systems Analysis. Data—Population. "The Impact of Fertility Assumptions on Total Population Projections in China" (1999). www.iiasa.ac.at/Research/LUC/ChinaFood/data/pop/pop_22.htm.

International Labor Office. Government of the People's Republic of China. Tenth Five-year Plan for National Economic and Social Development—People's Republic of China. "Making Improvement in the People's Living Standards as the Basic Starting Point." www.logos-net.net/ilo/150_base/en/init/chn_1.htm#kuva.

IT Power News. "First Kyoto Protocol Project to Go Ahead in China—Chinese Win Carbon Funding for Windfarm," Nov. 12, 2003. www.itpower.co.uk/news/new_offices.htm.

Kilman, Scott. "U.S. Crop Prices Soar as China Fuels Demand." *Wall Street Journal,* Nov. 13, 2003, A2, 3.

News Interactive. "Shanghai to Increase Bike Ban." *Herald Sun,* Dec. 9, 2003. http://heraldsun.news.com.au/common/story_page/0,5478,8113685%255E1702,00.html.

People's Daily Online. "Beijing Boasts World's Largest Fleet of Gas-Burning Buses." Apr. 10, 2002. http://english.peopledaily.com.cn/200204/13/eng20020413_93968.shtml.

————. "China Issues Sci-tech Program on Sustainable Development." Aug. 15, 2002. http://english.peopledaily.com.cn/200208/15/eng20020815_101497.shtml.

————. "CPC Central Committee Proposal for Formulating 10th Five-Year Plan (Summary)." Oct. 18, 2000. http://english.peopledaily.com.cn/200010/18/eng20001018_52942.html.

————. "Hu Stresses Harmony Among People, Resources, Environment." Mar. 10, 2003. http://english.peopledaily.com.cn/200303/10/eng20030310_113015.shtml.

————. "More Sewage Treatment Plants Operational in Three Gorges Reservoir Area." June 6, 2003. http://english.peopledaily.com.cn/200306/06/eng20030606_117791 shtml.

People's Republic of China. "China's Agenda 21, Summary, Formulating and Implementing China's Agenda 21." www.undp.org/seed/cap21/china.html.

Pickles, Michael. "Implementing Ecologically Sustainable Development in China: The Example of Heilongjiang Province." *Georgetown International Environmental Law Review* 14 (3) (Spring 2002): 577–93.

Postel, Sandra, Paul Polak, Fernando Gonzales, and Jack Keller. "Drip Irrigation for Small Farmers A New Initiative to Alleviate Hunger and Poverty." *Water International* 26 (1) (2001): 3–13.

Raufer, Roger, and Wang Shujuan. "Navigating the Policy Path for Support of Wind Power in China." *China Environment Series* 6. Washington, DC: Woodrow Wilson Center, 2003. http://wwics.si.edu/topics/pubs/4-feature_3.pdf.

Ravenga, Carmen. "Will There Be Enough Water?" World Resources Institute, Earth Trends: The Environmental Information Portal. Oct. 2000. http://earthtrends.wri.org/text/FRE/features/FRE_fea_scarcity.htm.

Redefining Progress. Sustainability Indicators Program. Ecological Footprint Analysis. www.redefiningprogress.org/programs/sustainabilityindicators/ef/.

Short, Patricia. "China Stars at SCI in Barcelona." *Chemical & Engineering News* (Oct. 30, 2003): 14.

Spiro, Leah Nathans. "Why a Wealthy China Gets World Bank Backing." *Business Week* (Sept. 29, 1997). www.businessweek.com/1997/39/b3546008.htm.

State Environmental Protection Administration of China (SEPA). China's Agenda 21-White Paper on China's Population, Environment, and Development in the 21st Century. Chap. 1.1-Preamble. www.zhb.gov.cn/english/SD/21cn/write_paper/writepaper-c1.htm.

———. China's Agenda 21-White Paper on China's Population, Environment, and Development in the 21st Century. Chap. 4-Economic Policies for Sustainable Development. www.zhb.gov.cn/english/SD/21cn/write_paper/writepaper-c4.htm.

———. China's Agenda 21-White Paper on China's Population, Environment, and Development in the 21st Century. Chap. 4.2-Economic Policies for Sustainable Development. www.zhb.gov.cn/english/SD/21cn/write_paper/writepaper-c4.htm.

———.China's Agenda 21-White Paper on China's Population, Environment, and Development in the 21st Century. Chapters and Program Areas of the White Paper. www.zhb.gov.cn/english/SD/21cn/index.htm.

SustainAbility. The Triple Bottom Line. SD Issues. www.sustainability.com/philosophy/triple-bottom/tbl-intro.asp.

UN Brundtland Commission. *Brundtland Report (Our Common Future)*. New York: 1987. www.doc.mmu.ac.uk/aric/eae/Sustainability/Older/Brundtland_Report.html.

UN Department of Economic and Social Affairs. Division for Sustainability. "Agenda 21." Mar. 24, 2003. www.un.org/esa/sustdev/documents/agenda21/index.htm.

UN University. Environment and Sustainable Development Programme. "Coastal Hydrosphere Project, China." http://landbase.hq.unu.edu/Sampling%20Plan%202002/China.htm .

U.S. Central Intelligence Agency (CIA). *The World Factbook 2003*. www.cia.gov/cia/publications/factbook/.

———. "China Combats Overfishing and Illegal Fishing." A Feb. 2003 report from Embassy Beijing. www.usembassy-china.org.cn/sandt/Illegal-Fishing.htm.

U.S. Embassy in China. "Managing the Upper Reaches of the Yellow River." An April 2003 report from Embassy Beijing. www.usembassy-china.org.cn/sandt/Upper-River.htm.

U.S. Energy Information Administration. "International Energy Outlook 2003: Coal." Report released Aug. 1, 2003. www.eia.doe.gov/oiaf/ieo/coal.html.

Wessel, David. "The People's Republic May Neglect People by Starving Schools." *Wall Street Journal,* Oct. 23, 2003, A2.

West Development. China Development Gateway. "China Invests US$5.1 Million to Curb Desertification in Inner Mongolia." http://211.147.20.14/chinagate/focus/west/news/i001/20020422inest.html.

Wilson, Edward O. "The Bottleneck." Scientific American.com, Feb. 24, 2002. www.sciam.com/print_version.cfm?articleID=000E5878–3E45–1CC6-B4A-8809EC588EEDF.

Wonacott, Peter. "China Saps Commodity Supplies." *Wall Street Journal,* Oct. 24, 2003, C1.

World Bank, Sinclair Knight Merz and Egis Consulting Australia, General Institute of Water Resources and Hydropower Planning and Design (MWR), Institute of Water and Hydropower Research (Beijing), Institute of Hydrology and Water Resources (Nanjing), and Chinese Research Academy for Environmental Sciences (Beijing). "China: Agenda for Water Sector Strategy for North China, Vol. 1: Summary Report." 2001. http://lnweb18.worldbank.org/eap/eap.nsf/Attachments/WaterSectorReport/$File/Vo11v13A4a1.pdf.

World Resources Institute. Health and Environment, Air Pollution and Health Effects. "Poor Ambient Air Quality Prevails." 1998–99. www.wri.org/wr-98–99/prc2air.htm.

———. Health and Environment, Air Pollution and Health. "The Environment and China: Water and Air Pollution." www.wri.org/wri/china/water.htm.

World Trade Organization. WTO News: 2001 Press Release. "WTO Successfully Concludes Negotiations on China's Entry," Sept. 17, 2001. www.wto.org/english/news_e/pres01_e/pr243_e.htm.

Yellow River Conservancy Commission (YRCC). The Outline of Hydraulic Multipurpose Project, Dec. 22, 2002. www.yrcc.gov.cn/eng/gc/index1.phtml.

Zhang, Peichang, Guofan Shao, Guang Zhao, Dennis C. Le Master, George R. Parker, John B. Dunning Jr., and Qinglin Li. "China's Forest Policy for the 21st Century." *Science* 288 (June 23, 2000): 2135–36.

Zusman, Eric. "The River Runs Dry: Examining Water Shortages in the Yellow River Basin." *Economic, Social and Legal Issues in China's Transition to a Market Economy.* Los Angeles: UCLA Asia Institute, 2000. http://repositories.cdlib.org/asia/eslictme/chntrans12/.

—— Chapter 2——

Public Environmental Consciousness in China

Early Empirical Evidence

Yok-shiu F. Lee

In the West, the volume and quality of research on public environmental consciousness have been enhanced by approximately four decades of social scientists' research. In comparison, the research base for China's environmentalism is still in its infancy (Feng and Wang 2002). Only recently have researchers in the People's Republic of China (PRC) begun to unveil the complex contours of China's collective environmental consciousness (Hong 1997, 1998; Xi and Xu 1999; Yang 2002a, b).

This conspicuous time lag between China and the developed world in generating and implementing a research agenda on environmental problems raises the question of why such a noticeable gap occurred in the first place. This time lag is regrettable, given that, since the early 1960s, China's socialist-inspired industrialization program has done enormous and widespread damage to the country's natural resources (Edmonds 1994; McElroy 1998; Smil 1984, 1993; Shapiro 2001). Furthermore, rapid economic growth following reform measures introduced in the early 1980s has exacerbated the degradation of environmental conditions in and near human settlements, both urban and rural (Ash and Edmonds 2000; Cannon 2000; Murray and Cook 2002; Stockholm Environment Institute 2002; World Bank 2001).

Some leading Chinese officials who oversee environmental protection policy matters argue that the beginning of the modern era of environmental protection in contemporary China can be traced back to 1973, when the First National Conference on the Environment was held (Wang 1999; Wu 1999; Xu 1999). Early efforts in promoting the concept of environmental protection—initiated in the late 1970s and early 1980s—were concentrated on organizing nationwide public campaigns that propagated general environmental themes, with the general public being the primary audience (Wang 1999). Only a small number of environmental laws were enacted at that time, and they were rarely observed by polluters and seldom properly enforced by the authorities. This apparent long absence of a sense of the importance of protecting the living and the natural environment was attributed to a lack of knowledge, on the part of both the rulers and the ruled at that time, of the nature of environmental degradation, its adverse impacts on human and ecosystem health, and effective measures to deal with the problem (Wang 1999).

Beginning in the late 1980s and early 1990s, driven by both heightened public environmental consciousness inside China since the mid-1980s[1] and the increasing concern for global environmental problems expressed by the world community (especially since the 1992 Rio Earth Summit), central government officials have shown a marked increase in expressed concern for environmental protection matters (Chan 1999; Peng 2002; Wang 1999).[2] "Environmental protection" as a national policy issue gradually was moved forward from the back burner—where it had stayed from the late 1950s to the early 1980s—and placed near the top of the central authorities' agenda in the late 1980s.

Two questions immediately spring to mind. First, to what extent, and how, has such long-term, large-scale destruction of the country's natural resource base and a general, continuing decline in environmental quality of life in cities and countryside influenced the public's perceptions and awareness of major environmental issues? Second, to what extent, and how, have the public's environmental values and attitudes influenced their behavior toward the environment?

Several nationwide survey studies have been sponsored by major organizations of both domestic and foreign origin. In addition, an increasing number of local, city-based, and single-institution–oriented studies organized by city governments—mostly by local environmental protection bureaus[3]—and university students have been conducted on the issue of public environmental consciousness since the early 1990s. Major particulars of these studies are summarized in Table 2.1. Although different conceptual frameworks have been adopted, and varied methodological approaches have been employed by researchers conducting these studies, the empirical evidence generated has provided clues to help us to begin to partially address the above two questions. Extensive and systematic data have not yet been collected to allow a cogent picture of the changing dynamics of public environmentalism to be drawn up. However, the amount of data generated thus far by these studies is sufficient to enable researchers to sketch the basic outline of the Chinese people's awareness, knowledge, attitudes, and, to a limited extent, degree of commitment to the universally accepted norm of environmental protection.

How Important Is the Environment to the Chinese People?

Before we examine in detail major findings of recent survey studies on this topic, several caveats are in order as to the reliability of environmental data reported by Chinese authorities, as well as the comparability of survey results on public environmentalism gathered through various methodological approaches. As has been the experience of many China scholars, the problem of the lack of certain essential information on this topic has been compounded by the fact that complex, and sometimes inexplicable, factors have led to the production and reporting of inconsistent and conflicting data. These data were purportedly prepared by government offices, although operating at different levels of jurisdiction, on the same phenomena. Glaring examples of inconsistencies and contradictions will be referred to in the ensuing discussion of the empirical data gathered on China's public environmental attitudes.

Moreover, given that Chinese researchers studying public environmental attitudes are working in relatively uncharted territory, it is not surprising to find that a diversity of methodological approaches has been adopted at different times and in disparate localities to gauge the public's environmental attitudes. Not unexpectedly, these diverse approaches have produced results that are not fully compatible across space and time. Thus, it is necessary to point out at the outset that data presented here should be considered within broader historical and spatial contexts. They also should be interpreted in a way to help denote the order of magnitude, but not to specify the exact degree, of the public's knowledge of and sentiments toward the environment.[4]

Furthermore, due to the lack of sufficient longitudinal data, no clear pattern over time can be confidently established. The first known survey on public environmental attitudes in China was carried out in 1990, and only two nationwide surveys, undertaken three years apart in the mid-1990s, have been conducted. In fact, most regional and local surveys were conducted after 1994. These gaps in data make it very difficult to establish conclusively what trends, if any, there have been in public opinion on the environment in the PRC since 1994. Nevertheless, the data do allow us to delineate some overall baselines for an understanding of where China's public stands on the environment.

With these caveats in mind, we can proceed to examine the data on environmental opinions. First, researchers in China have been baffled by some extremely conflicting survey results pertaining to the public's perception of the degree of seriousness of environmental pollution problems. While the results gathered from two nationwide surveys conducted in 1995 and 1998 have shown that the majority of the respondents (69.9 percent and 56.7 percent respectively) considered China's environmental problems as "very serious" or "serious," a 1994 survey that focused on residents' environmental perceptions in Beijing and Shanghai showed that, in general,

Table 2.1

Surveys on Public Environmental Consciousness, 1990–2002

Year	Title	Survey organizer	Sample size
1990	A Social Survey on Environmental Pollution Problems[a]	State Environmental Protection Administration	1,600
1991	A Survey on Environmental Consciousness of Employees at Industrial Enterprises[a]	Research Center of the State Science Commission	1,734
1994	A Survey on the Environmental Consciousness of Secondary and Primary Students in China[a]	China Environment Newspaper Press	15,412
1994	A Survey on Public Environmental Consciousness in Qingdao[a,b]	Qingdao City Environmental Protection Bureau	1,143
1994	A Survey on Environmental Consciousness of Residents in Beijing and Shanghai[a]	Research Center of the State Science Commission	3,200
1995	A Survey on Global Environment (China)[a]	Beijing Lingdian Survey Company	1,050
1995	A Survey on the Environmental Consciousness of Residents in Cities of Beijing and Shanghai[a]	Gallop Consulting Company	822
1995	A Survey on the Nation's Public Environmental Consciousness[a]	China Environmental Protection Foundation and China People's University	3,662
1996	A Survey on Public Environmental Consciousness in Zhejiang Province[a]	Zhejiang Provincial Environmental Protection Bureau	9,367
1997	A Survey on Urban Residents' Environmental Awareness[c]	Research Center for Ecology and Environmental Economics, Chinese Academy of Social Sciences	7,276
1997	International Survey on Environmental Monitoring (China)[a]	Guangzhou Damun Information Services Company	1,850
1997	A Survey on Environmental Consciousness of Residents in Shanghai[a]	Shanghai Newspapers Society and Shanghai Shenzhou Survey Company	300
1997	A Survey on Public Environmental Consciousness in Beijing[a]	Beijing City Environmental Protection Bureau and City Environmental Protection Foundation	2,317
1997	A Survey on Environmental Consciousness of Residents in Lianyungang[a]	Lianyungang City Environmental Protection Bureau	7,396
1997	A Survey on Public Environmental Consciousness in Chongqing[a]	Chongqing City Environmental Protection Bureau	3,324

Year	Survey	Organization	Sample
1998	A Survey Report on the Nation's Public Environmental Consciousness[a]	State Environmental Protection Administration of China and Ministry of Education	10,495
1998	A Survey on Environmental Consciousness of Fuzhou's University Students[d]	Fujian Medical University	1,806
1998	A Survey on Students' Environmental Consciousness in Urumqi[e]	Urumqi City Environmental Protection Bureau	2,796
1998	A Survey on Students' Environmental Consciousness at Yunnan Normal University[f]	Yunnan Normal University	400
1998	A Survey on Environmental Consciousness of Residents in Panyu, Guangdong Province[g]	Panyu City Environmental Protection Bureau	1,746
1999	A Survey on Environmental Knowledge of Enterprise Staff[h]	Zhongyuan Oilfield Technology Safety Supervisory Department	26,038
1999	A Survey on Jianghan Plain's Peasants' Ecological and Environmental Consciousness[i]	China Youth Development Fund and World Wide Fund for Nature	66
1999	A Survey on Public Environmental Consciousness of Residents in Xinhua Zhen, Guangdong Province[j]	Guangzhou Environmental Protection Science Research Institute	*
1999	A Survey on Environmental Consciousness of Students at Hainan Normal University[k]	Hainan Normal University	564
2000	A Survey on Environmental Consciousness of Residents in Hangzhou[l]	Zhejiang University	1,000
2001	A Survey on Environmental Consciousness of University Students in Jiangxi Province[m]	Jiangxi Normal University	1,158
2001	A Survey on Environmental Consciousness of Residents in Huzhou Town, Zhejiang Province[n]	Huzhou Normal University	280
2002	A Survey on Environmental Consciousness of Residents in Fuzhou City[o]	Fujian Normal University	267

(continued)

Sources: [a]Guojia huanjing baohu zongju (State Environmental Protection Administration of China). "Quanguo gongzhong huanjing yishi diaocha baogao (Zhaiyao)" (A Survey on the Nation's Public Environmental Consciousness [Summary]). *Huanjing jiaoyu* (Environmental Education), no. 4, 1999, 27.
[b]Luan Xuezhu. "Qingdao shi gongzhong huanjing yishi diaocha yu jinhou duice yanjiu" (A Survey on Qingdao's Public Environmental Consciousness and Future Planning Study). *Shandong huanjing* (Shandong Environment), no. 4, 1995, 26–27.

Table 2.1 (*continued*)

cLi Zhou. "Chengshi huanjing zhuangkuang he jumin huanjing yishi diaocha baogao" (A Report on the State of the Urban Environment and Residents' Environmental Consciousness). *Yanjiu lunwen* (Research Dissertation), 1997, 2–4.

dZheng Zhenquan and Zhang Likang. "Fuzhou shi daxuesheng huanjing yishi diaocha" (A Survey on Environmental Consciousness of Fuzhou's University Students). *Huanjing jiaoyu* (Environmental Education), March 1999, 35–36.

eCui Yan and Chen Jianfeng. "Huanjing yishi diaocha shidian xuexiao xuesheng" (Students in Pilot Study Schools on Environmental Consciousness). *Huanjing jiaoyu* (Environmental Education), no. 1, 1999, 19, 34.

fChen Zhongnuan, Wang Xiafei, He Xiang, and Wang Jinliang. "Daxuesheng huanjing yishi diaocha yu huanjing jiaoyu chuyi" (An Investigation and Analysis on the Environmental Consciousness of College Students). *Yunnan huanjing kexue* (Yunnan Environmental Science), vol. 18, no. 4, 1999, 53–55.

gZhang Haiqing, Liu Gang, Wu Jianhong, Li Mincong, and Wu Kaiming. "Panyu shimin huanjing yishi diaocha yu pingjia yanjiu" (A Survey on Residents' Environmental Consciousness in Panyu and Evaluation Study). *Huanjing jishu* (Environmental Technique), no. 3, 2001, 38–42.

hZhou Songjing, Zheng Nan, and Guo Xuefeng. "Qiye liangong huanjing yishi diaocha fenxi ji jianyi" (An Investigation, Analysis, and Suggestion on Environmental Knowledge of the Enterprise Staff). *Guanli yu xinxi* (Management and Information), vol. 9, no. 4, 1999, 3.

iYu Ping. "Zhongguo: Youdai nongmin shengtai huanjing yishi de juexing–Jianghan pingyuan nonghu shengtai huanjing yishi diaocha" (China: Waiting for the Awakening of the Peasants' Ecological Consciousness–A Survey on Jianghan Plain's Peasants' Ecological and Environmental Consciousness). *Diaocha* (Survey and Research), no. 2, 2000, 27–29.

jYu Jican. "Guangdong sheng Xinhua zhen gongzhong huanjing yishi diaocha" (A Survey on Public Environmental Consciousness of Residents in Xinhua Zhen, Guangdong Province). *Huanjing wuran yu fangzhi* (Environmental Pollution and Prevention), vol. 23, no. 2, 2001, 77–78.

kGuo Lihua, Ma Wenru, Cheng Songlin, and Chen Haizhu. "Hainan shifan xueyuan xuesheng huanjing yishi diaocha" (A Survey on Environmental Consciousness of Students at Hainan Normal University). *Hainan shifan xueyuan xuebao (ziran kexue ban)* (Journal of Hainan Normal University: Natural Science Edition), vol. 14, no. 1, 2001, 98–104.

lQi Weifeng. "Chengshi shimin huanjing yishi diaocha yu pingjia–yi Zhejiang Hangzhou shi weili" (A Survey and an Evaluation on Urban Residents' Environmental Consciousness–Zhejiang, Hangzhou as an Example). *Guihua shi* (Planner), vol. 16, no. 3, 2000, 93–95.

mLuo Xiancheng and Zhong Yexi. "Jiangxi sheng gaoshi yuanxiao daxuesheng huanjing yishi diaocha" (A Survey on Environmental Consciousness of University Students in Jiangxi Province). *Jiangxi sheng tuanxiao xuebao* (Jiangxi Joint School Journal), no. 4, 2001, 21–22.

nWang Chunsheng. "Huzhou shi chengzhen jumin huanjing baohu yishi diaocha" (A Survey on Residents' Environmental Protection Consciousness in Huzhou). *Zhejiang yufang yixue* (Zhejiang Prevention Medicine), vol. 14, no. 12, 2002, 46–47.

oLi Lin, Huang Jin, Lu Wenhao, Wang Shunli, and Hu Qingqing. "Fuzhou shi gongzhong huanjing yishi diaocha fenxi" (An Analysis of Fuzhou Public Environmental Consciousness). *Fujian huanjing* (Fujian Environment), vol. 19, no. 5, 2002, 32–34.

*not available.

Table 2.2

Public Perception of the Environment

		% Response by year		
Location	Statement	1994	1995	1998
Beijing/ Shanghai	"Environmental pollution problems" as "very serious or serious"[a]	7.0–11.0		
Nationwide	"Overall environmental problems" as "very serious or serious"[b]		69.9	
Nationwide	"Environmental pollution problems" as "very serious or serious"[c]			56.7

Sources: [a]Xi Xiaolin, Fan Lihong, and Deng Xueming. "Zhongguo gongzhong huanjing yishi diaocha jieguo pouxi" (An Analysis of the Survey Results on Public Environmental Consciousness in China). In Xi Xiaolin and Xu Qinghua, eds., *Zhongguo gongzhong huanjing yishi diaocha* (A Survey on China's Public Environmental Consciousness). Beijing: Zhongguo huanjing kexue chubanshe [Beijing: China Environmental Science Press], 1999, 41.
[b]Hong Dayong. *Zhongguo gongzhong huanjing yishi chutan* (A Preliminary Study on China's Public Environmental Consciousness). Zhonghua huanjing baohu jijin hui (China Environmental Protection Foundation). Beijing: Zhongguo huanjing kexue chubanshe [Beijing: China Environmental Science Press], 1998, 74.
[c]Guojia huanjing baohu zongju (State Environmental Protection Administration of China) and Jiaoyubu (Ministry of Education). *Quanguo gongzhong huanjing yishi diaocha baogao* (A Survey Report on the Nation's Public Environmental Consciousness). Beijing: Zhongguo huanjing kexue chubanshe [Beijing: China Environmental Science Press], 1999, 6.

only 7 to 11 percent of the respondents in these two cities shared such a sentiment (Table 2.2).

In this bicity survey, the majority of the residents believed that the environmental problems that had an immediate impact on their health and living conditions—drinking water pollution, air pollution, noise pollution, and solid waste—were "not very serious" or "not serious" (Table 2.3). For other environmental problems that were spatially situated far beyond their immediate living environment—such as desertification, global warming, and depletion of the ozone layer—a substantial proportion (31.0 to 48.0 percent) of the respondents in these two cities admitted that they were "not sure" of the degree of seriousness of such national and international problems. A relatively small proportion (6 to 11 percent) of the respondents thought that such problems were "very serious" or "serious."

The generally positive opinions on the environment revealed by the respondents in Beijing and Shanghai may be related to the fact that most of them were quite happy, or at least satisfied, with their immediate living environments. For instance, when they were asked to consider how the conditions of their own

Table 2.3

Beijing and Shanghai Residents' Perception of the Nation's Environmental Problems (%)

Problem	Very serious/ serious	Neither serious nor not serious	Not very serious/ not serious	Not sure
Drinking water pollution	11.0	20.0	56.0	13.0
Air pollution	10.0	27.0	52.0	11.0
Noise pollution	7.0	19.0	68.0	6.0
Increase in solid waste	9.0	22.0	71.0	8.0
Chemical pollution	7.0	19.0	57.0	17.0
Food pollution	10.0	27.0	53.0	10.0
Reduction in green space	11.0	21.0	52.0	16.0
Desertification	13.0	15.0	26.0	46.0
Reduction in biodiversity	11.0	24.0	34.0	31.0
Global warming	6.0	15.0	31.0	48.0
Land pollution	11.0	25.0	30.0	34.0
Radiation pollution	19.0	17.0	19.0	45.0
Depletion of ozone layer	6.0	16.0	32.0	46.0

Source: Zhongguo guoji youhao lianluohui gailuopu zixun youxian gongsi (China International Friendly Network Association Gallop Consulting Company). "Beijing Shanghai chengshi jumin de huanjing yishi diaocha" (A Survey on the Environmental Consciousness of Residents in the Cities of Beijing and Shanghai). In Xi Xiaolin and Xu Qinghua, eds., *Zhongguo gongzhong huanjing yishi diaocha* (A Survey on China's Public Environmental Consciousness). Beijing: Zhongguo huanjing kexue chubanshe [Beijing: China Environmental Science Press], 1999, 135.

living environments had changed in the past five years, only a small fraction of the residents in Beijing and Shanghai—10 percent and 12 percent respectively— said that such conditions had worsened (Table 2.4).

Second, researchers are somewhat puzzled by another set of contradictory survey results on the public's environmental perceptions. For instance, 70 percent of the respondents in the 1995 nationwide survey believed that the environmental consciousness of people around them was "very weak" or "weak" (Xi, Fan, and Deng 1999, 51). In contrast, approximately three-quarters of the respondents in city-based surveys conducted in Beijing, Shanghai, and Qingdao, plus more than half of those in Lianyungang, said that the people around them showed a "very high" or "high" degree of concern for the environment (Table 2.5).

Third, to what extent has the environment become a "salient" issue for the public, that is, to what extent have citizens linked it to their immediate personal interests? Although developing a method to accurately measure the salience of an issue is problematic, many public opinion researchers have argued that "voluntary responses to 'most important problems' (MIP) ques-

Table 2.4

Beijing and Shanghai Residents' Perception of the Conditions of Their Own Living Environment

City	Conditions of living environment in the past five years			
	Improved	Remained unchanged	Worsened	Not sure
Beijing	48.0	40.0	10.0	1.0
Shanghai	38.0	49.0	12.0	1.0

Source: Yuan Fang. "Zhongguo shimin de huanjing yishi diaocha: Beijing he Shanghai" (A Survey on Chinese Residents' Environmental Consciousness in Beijing and Shanghai). In Xi Xiaolin and Xu Qinghua, eds., *Zhongguo gongzhong huanjing yishi diaocha* (A Survey on China's Public Environmental Consciousness). Beijing: Zhongguo huanjing kexue chubanshe [Beijing: China Environmental Science Press], 1999, 114.

Table 2.5

Public's Perception of the Degree of Concern for the Environment Shown by People Around Them (%)

Question: What is the degree of concern for the environment shown by people around you?

	Very high/high	Very low/low
Beijing/ Shanghai[a]	74.0	24.0
Qingdao[b]	73.0	27.0
Lianyungang[c]	57.0	43.0

Sources: [a] Xi Xiaolin, Fan Lihong, and Deng Xueming. "Zhongguo gongzhong huanjing yishi diaocha jieguo pouxi" (An Analysis of the Survey Results on Public Environmental Consciousness in China). In Xi Xiaolin and Xu Qinghua, eds., *Zhongguo gongzhong huanjing yishi diaocha* (A Survey on China's Public Environmental Consciousness). Beijing: Zhongguo huanjing kexue chubanshe [Beijing: China Environmental Science Press], 1999, 51.

[b] Li Yiming. "Qingdao shi gongzhong huanjing yishi diaocha" (A Survey on Public Environmental Consciousness in Qingdao). In Xi Xiaolin and Xu Qinghua, eds., *Zhongguo gongzhong huanjing yishi diaocha* (A Survey on China's Public Environmental Consciousness). Beijing: Zhongguo huanjing kexue chubanshe [Beijing: China Environmental Science Press], 1999, 169.

[c] Hong Shi and Wei Shantao. "Lianyungang shi gongmin huanjing yishi wenjuan diaocha" (A Survey on Public Environmental Consciousness in Lianyungang). In Xi Xiaolin and Xu Qinghua, eds., *Zhongguo gongzhong huanjing yishi diaocha* (A Survey on China's Public Environmental Consciousness). Beijing: Zhongguo huanjing kexue chubanshe [Beijing: China Environmental Science Press], 1999, 182.

tions . . . provide a good indicator of the salience of an issue" (Dunlap 1995, 74). Examples of MIP questions include open-ended questions that ask respondents what they perceive to be the most important problems in society and allow them to select any response they wish.

Table 2.6

Public's Rank-Ordered List of Various Problems at the National Scale

	Rank			
	1998 [a]		1995 [b]	
Problem	Adult	Youth	Overall*	Rural
Public order	1	4	3	3
Education	2	3	2	2
Population	3	2	4	4
Employment	4	5	10	9
Environmental protection	5	1	6	7
Social security	6	6	NM**	NM

Sources: [a] Hong Dayong. *Zhongguo gongzhong huanjing yishi chutan* (A Preliminary Study on China's Public Environmental Consciousness). Zhonghua huanjing baohu jijin hui (China Environmental Protection Foundation). Beijing: Zhongguo huanjing kexue chubanshe [Beijing: China Environmental Science Press], 1998, 77 (for overall figures) and 119 (for rural figures).

[b] Guojia huanjing baohu zongju (State Environmental Protection Administration of China) and Jiaoyubu (Ministry of Education). *Quanguo gongzhong huanjing yishi diaocha baogao* (A Survey Report on the Nation's Public Environmental Consciousness). Beijing: Zhongguo huanjing kexue chubanshe [Beijing: China Environmental Science Press], 1999, 17.

*In the 1995 survey, "inflation" was ranked as the number one concern among the public, with "public security" and "social morality" being considered the third and fifth most important public concerns respectively.

**NM = not mentioned.

Unfortunately, the issue of whether any MIP questions were asked in any of the surveys conducted on public environmental attitudes in China could not be ascertained by the information currently available to this author. Nevertheless, even without the benefit of a true salience test, a sufficient amount of evidence has been accumulated to show that the environment was ranked relatively low in the public mind in China. As shown in Tables 2.5 and 2.6, with the exception of the younger respondents—who consistently have regarded the environment as a problem of foremost concern for them—the adult population was always preoccupied with other matters that they considered more urgent than the environment at both the global and national levels.[5]

In both the 1995 and 1998 nationwide surveys, for instance, the environment was ranked overall by the respondents to be a problem of lesser importance than public order, education, population, and employment (Table 2.6). In fact, when asked to rate the priority of a given set of national development goals in the 1998 survey, respondents relegated environmental protection to the bottom of the list, with economic development accorded the top spot, followed by scientific research, population control, and the pursuit of social justice (Table 2.7).

Table 2.7

Public's Rank-Ordered List of National Development Goals

Development goal	Rank
Economic development	1
Scientific research	2
Population control	3
Social justice	4
Environmental protection	5

Source: Guojia huanjing baohu zongju (State Environmental Protection Administration of China) and Jiaoyubu (Ministry of Education). *Quanguo gongzhong huanjing yishi diaocha baogao* (A Survey Report on the Nation's Public Environmental Consciousness). Beijing: Zhongguo huanjing kexue chubanshe [Beijing: China Environmental Science Press], 1999, 9.

This finding at the national level is confirmed by similar patterns observed in several locality-based surveys (Table 2.8).

The rank-ordered lists of national development objectives and of problems at the global and national levels have thus indicated that several other issues have continued to hold higher priorities in the public's mind.[6] This observation is buttressed by the responses given by the public to several statements in the two nationwide surveys. While 45.5 percent of the respondents in the 1998 survey strongly agreed or agreed with the proposition that "economic development would inevitably damage the environment," only 36.3 percent of the same group strongly agreed or agreed that "economic development should slow down to help protect the environment." In fact, up to 45.3 percent of these respondents strongly disagreed or disagreed with the latter statement (Table 2.9). Moreover, unusually sizable proportions (18.5 to 23.6 percent) of the respondents answered "not sure" to both of these statements. High levels of "not sure" responses could simply reflect ignorance. In this case, however, these responses could also be interpreted as a sign that an ambivalent public was reluctant to trade the gains of economic growth for the benefits of environmental protection.

Nevertheless, once again, some evidence contradictory to these observations was produced by two other surveys. In two separate surveys conducted in the mid-1990s, 64.1 percent and 53.0 percent of the respondents strongly agreed or agreed that the "environment should be given higher priority, even if economic development has to slow down" (Table 2.9). These results demonstrated that the public gave a higher degree of preference to the environment than to economic development, contradicting the pro-growth proposition suggested by survey data generated from a different study.

Given conflicting observations that have been supported equally by evi-

Table 2.8

Public Perception of Environmental Problems in Relation to Other Problems

Rank	Qingdao (1995)	Gallop (1995)	Lingdian (1995)	Lingdian (1997)
1	Education	Education	Inflation	Unemployment
2	Economy	Public safety	Corruption	State-owned enterprise losses
3	Living standard	**Environmental protection**	Public safety	Corruption
4	Population growth	Scientific development	Education for children	**Environmental pollution**
5	**Environmental protection**	Economic development	Increase in income	Public safety
6	Scientific development	Population	Unemployment	Social security
7	National defense	*	**Environmental pollution**	Inflation
8	Energy	*	Drugs	External threats

Source: Xi Xiaolin, Fan Lihong, and Deng Xueming. "Zhongguo gongzhong huanjing yishi diaocha jieguo pouxi" (An Analysis of the Survey Results on Public Environmental Consciousness in China). In Xi Xiaolin and Xu Qinghua, eds., *Zhongguo gongzhong huanjing yishi diaocha* (A Survey on China's Public Environmental Consciousness). Beijing: Zhongguo huanjing kexue chubanshe [Beijing: China Environmental Science Press], 1999, 45.
   *no data available

dence drawn from a number of nationwide, regional, and local surveys purportedly conducted in a proper manner, it is apparent that no conclusive argument can be reached with great confidence at this stage as to whether or not the general public in China has shown a high level of concern for the environment. Nevertheless, early evidence from the surveys suggests that, from the perspective of the salience of the issue in the public's mind, the environment ranks relatively low in comparison with other concerns that have always captured the public's immediate interests.

What Does the Public Know About the Environment?

In a 1995 nationwide survey, approximately half of urban (54.1 percent) and four-fifths of rural (81.8 percent) residents indicated that they believed that the

Table 2.9

Public Attitudes Toward Environmental Protection and Economic Growth (%)

Statement	Strongly agree/ Agree	Strongly disagree/ Disagree	Not sure
"Economic development would inevitably damage the environment"	45.5[a]	31.0[a]	23.6[a]
"Economic development should slow down to help protect the environment"	36.3[a]	45.3[a]	18.5[a]
"Economic development should be given higher priority than the environment"	35.9[b]/46.0[b]	—	—
"Environment should be given higher priority, even if economic development has to slow down"	64.1[b]/53.0[b]/47.5[c]	—	—

Sources: [a] Guojia huanjing baohu zongju (State Environmental Protection Adminis-tration of China) and Jiaoyubu (Ministry of Education). *Quanguo gongzhong huanjing yishi diaocha baogao* (A Survey Report on the Nation's Public Environmental Con-sciousness). Beijing: Zhongguo huanjing kexue chubanshe [Beijing: China Environ-mental Science Press], 1999, 28.
[b] Xi Xiaolin, Fan Lihong, and Deng Xueming. "Zhongguo gongzhong huanjing yishi diaocha jieguo pouxi" (An Analysis of the Survey Results on Public Environmen-tal Consciousness in China). In Xi Xiaolin and Xu Qinghua, eds., *Zhongguo gongzhong huanjing yishi diaocha* (A Survey on China's Public Environmental Consciousness). Beijing: Zhongguo huanjing kexue chubanshe [Beijing: China Environmental Science Press], 1999, 46.
[c] Shen Hao and Ding Mai. "Zhongguo chengshi gongzhong de huanjing yishi" (The Environmental Consciousness of the Public in China's Cities). In Xi Xiaolin and Xu Qinghua, eds., *Zhongguo gongzhong huanjing yishi diaocha* (A Survey on China's Public Environmental Consciousness). Beijing: Zhongguo huanjing kexue chubanshe [Beijing: China Environmental Science Press], 1999, 105.

Table 2.10

Urban and Rural Residents' Perception of National Environmental Problems (%)

	Very serious	Serious	Not very serious	Not serious at all	Not sure
Rural residents	15.1	66.7	14.3	0.4	3.5
Urban residents	5.1	49.0	27.7	1.1	17.1

Source: Zhonghua huanjing baohu jijin hui (China Environmental Protection Founda-tion) and Zhongguo renmin daxue (China People's University). "Quanmin huanjing yishi diaocha" (A Survey on Public Environmental Consciousness). In XI Xiaolin and XU Qinghua, eds., *Zhongguo gongzhong huanjing yishi diaocha* (A Survey on China's Pub-lic Environmental Consciousness). Beijing: Zhongguo huanjing kexue chubanshe [Beijing: China Environmental Science Press], 1999, 73.

nation's environmental problems were "very serious" or "serious" (Table 2.10).

However, in the same survey, an even higher proportion of urban (78.1 percent) and rural residents (90.5 percent) confessed that their command of environmental knowledge could be regarded as "very little" or "relatively little" (Table 2.11).

These national statistics were replicated by figures taken from two 1997 city-based surveys: 64.8 percent and 67.0 percent of the respondents in Chongqing and Lianyungang, respectively, admitted that they commanded "very little" or "relatively little" knowledge on environmental issues.[7]

This set of statistics immediately leads one to wonder how and why a sizable proportion of the population who professed a poor command of environmental knowledge could conclude that the nation's environmental problems were "very serious" or "serious."[8] One likely explanation is that the general public's understanding of the nation's environmental problems was superficial at best, or based on partial (mis)information at worst. In China, much, if not all, of the public's knowledge of the state of the environment was acquired piecemeal through secondary sources such as mass media, which, despite recent relaxations on editorial stances, have remained a major tool of political propaganda and are tightly controlled by the state.[9]

The survey results also reveal a substantial gap between rural and urban residents' awareness of environmental issues (Tables 2.10, 2.11).[10] In fact, when both groups were presented with a set of global environmental problems, the knowledge gap between them was found to be even wider. For instance, only 8.7 percent of urban residents admitted that they had never heard of the problem of global warming, whereas up to 44.1 percent of their rural counterparts stated that they were ignorant of such an issue (Table 2.12). Indeed, up to 68.9 percent and 77.3 percent of rural respondents claimed that they had never heard of such global environmental problems as ozone layer depletion and acid rain, respectively.

Nevertheless, when they were asked to identify what they perceived to be the five most important environmental problems, the respective sets of responses given by urban and rural residents were not at all unexpected (Table 2.13). The problems that both groups perceived to be the most important were largely those that were commonly found in and near their respective immediate living and working environments. For example, water pollution was perceived by rural respondents as the most important environmental problem because it directly affected both their livelihood and health. In contrast, this same problem was perceived by urban residents as far less important than the more audible (noise) and visible (ambient air) pollution problems frequently found in more densely populated, built-up areas (Table 2.13).

Table 2.11

Public's Self-Assessment of Command of Environmental Knowledge (%)

Location	Very little/ none at all	Relatively little	Relatively more	Not sure
Nationwide (rural)[a]	27.3	63.2	9.5	*
Nationwide (urban)[a]	8.4	69.7	21.9	*
Chongqing[b]	1.3	63.5	23.6	11.7
Qingdao[c]	2.4	54.5	42.6	*
Lianyungang[d]	*	67.0	*	*

Sources: [a] Zhonghua huanjing baohu jijin hui (China Environmental Protection Foundation) and Zhongguo renmin daxue (China People's University). "Quanmin huanjing yishi diaocha" (A Survey on Public Environmental Consciousness). In Xi Xiaolin and Xu Qinghua, eds., *Zhongguo gongzhong huanjing yishi diaocha* (A Survey on China's Public Environmental Consciousness). Beijing: Zhongguo huanjing kexue chubanshe [Beijing: China Environmental Science Press], 1999, 71.

[b] Chongqing shi huanbao ju (Chongqing Environmental Protection Bureau). "Chongqing shi gongzhong huanjing yishi diaocha jieguo zongshu (A Discussion on the Results of the Survey on Public Environmental Consciousness in Chongqing). In Xi Xiaolin and Xu Qinghua, eds., *Zhongguo gongzhong huanjing yishi diaocha* (A Survey on China's Public Environmental Consciousness). Beijing: Zhongguo huanjing kexue chubanshe [Beijing: China Environmental Science Press], 1999, 155.

[c] Li Yiming. "Qingdao shi gongzhong huanjing yishi diaocha" (A Survey on Public Environmental Consciousness in Qingdao). In Xi Xiaolin and Xu Qinghua, eds., *Zhongguo gongzhong huanjing yishi diaocha* (A Survey on China's Public Environmental Consciousness). Beijing: Zhongguo huanjing kexue chubanshe [Beijing: China Environmental Science Press], 1999, 170.

[d] Hong Shi and Wei Shantao. "Lianyungang shi gongmin huanjing yishi wenjuan diaocha" (A Survey on Public Environmental Consciousness in Lianyungang). In Xi Xiaolin and Xu Qinghua, eds., *Zhongguo gongzhong huanjing yishi diaocha* (A Survey on China's Public Environmental Consciousness). Beijing: Zhongguo huanjing kexue chubanshe [Beijing: China Environmental Science Press], 1999, 183.

*Not available.

Due to rounding errors, totals do not add up to 100.0 percent.

What Are Citizens Themselves Willing To Do?

The available data on the public's willingness to take on certain responsibilities to contribute to environmental protection goals are as contradictory as those on the public's perceptions of the state of the environment. In the 1995 nationwide survey, up to 70 percent of the respondents reportedly were willing to pay an extra fee to help protect the environment (Zhonghua huanjing baohu jijin hui and Zhongguo renmin daxue 1999, 85). In the 1998 nationwide survey, up to 46.6 percent of the urban residents and 31.9 percent of the rural respondents said that they were willing to pay higher prices for environmentally friendly products and services (Table 2.14). In the bicity (Beijing and Shanghai) study,

Table 2.12

Public's Knowledge of Global Environmental Problems (%)

		Never heard of such problem	
Problem	Overall	Urban residents	Rural residents
Global warming	23.9	8.7	44.1
Ozone layer depletion	40.9	20.0	68.9
Acid rain	52.4	33.8	77.3
Fresh water shortage	26.0	11.9	44.8
Reduction of biodiversity	25.8	14.7	40.7

Source: Zhonghua huanjing baohu jijin hui (China Environmental Protection Foundation) and Zhongguo renmin daxue (China People's University). "Quanmin huanjing yishi diaocha" (A Survey on Public Environmental Consciousness). In Xi Xiaolin and Xu Qinghua, eds., *Zhongguo gongzhong huanjing yishi diaocha* (A Survey on China's Public Environmental Consciousness). Beijing: Zhongguo huanjing kexue chubanshe [Beijing: China Environmental Science Press], 1999, 77.

Table 2.13

Urban and Rural Residents' Perception of the Five Most Important Environmental Problems (%)

Five most important environmental problems			
Urban residents		Rural residents	
Pollution in public areas	(60.3)	Water pollution	(43.7)
Pollution from domestic waste	(60.0)	Depletion of wild plants and animals	(42.4)
Noise pollution	(58.3)	Pollution from pesticides	(38.1)
Ambient air pollution	(53.6)	Pollution from domestic waste	(36.8)
Water pollution	(51.0)	Pollution in public areas	(32.8)

Source: Xi Xiaolin, Fan Lihong, and Deng Xueming. "Zhongguo gongzhong huanjing yishi diaocha jieguo pouxi" (An Analysis of the Survey Results on Public Environmental Consciousness in China). In Xi Xiaolin and Xu Qinghua, eds., *Zhongguo gongzhong huanjing yishi diaocha* (A Survey on China's Public Environmental Consciousness). Beijing: Zhongguo huanjing kexue chubanshe [Beijing: China Environmental Science Press], 1999, 42.

however, the comparable figure dropped precipitously to 25 percent. In Lianyungang, only a meager 4 percent of those surveyed were willing to do so.

In other words, 96 percent of those surveyed in Lianyungang and 75 percent of those interviewed in Beijing and Shanghai either were not willing to, or were not sure whether they would, pay higher prices for environmentally friendly products and services. In fact, in the nationwide study, approximately one-quarter (24.3 percent) of the urban residents and three out of ten (29.8

Table 2.14

Willingness to Pay Higher Prices for Environmentally Friendly Products and Services (%)

Question: Are you willing to pay higher prices for environmentally friendly products and services?

	Willing	Not willing	Not sure
Urban (nationwide)[a]	46.6	29.0	24.3
Rural (nationwide)[a]	31.9	38.3	29.8
Beijing/Shanghai[b]	25.0	72.0	3.0
Lianyungang[c]	4.0	96.0 (Not willing + Not sure)	

Sources: [a]Guojia huanjing baohu zongju (State Environmental Protection Administration of China) and Jiaoyubu (Ministry of Education). *Quanguo gongzhong huanjing yishi diaocha baogao* (A Survey Report on the Nation's Public Environmental Consciousness). Beijing: Zhongguo huanjing kexue chubanshe [Beijing: China Environmental Science Press], 1999, 13.
[b]Xi Xiaolin, Fan Lihong, and Deng Xueming. "Zhongguo gongzhong huanjing yishi diaocha jieguo pouxi" (An Analysis of the Survey Results on Public Environmental Consciousness in China). In Xi Xiaolin and Xu Qinghua, eds., *Zhongguo gongzhong huanjing yishi diaocha* (A Survey on China's Public Environmental Consciousness). Beijing: Zhongguo huanjing kexue chubanshe [Beijing: China Environmental Science Press], 1999, 49.
[c]Hong Shi and Wei Shantao. "Lianyungang shi gongmin huanjing yishi wenjuan diaocha" (A Survey on Public Environmental Consciousness in Lianyungang). In Xi Xiaolin and Xu Qinghua, eds., *Zhongguo gongzhong huanjing yishi diaocha* (A Survey on China's Public Environmental Consciousness). Beijing: Zhongguo huanjing kexue chubanshe [Beijing: China Environmental Science Press], 1999, 182.

percent) rural respondents acknowledged that they were not sure whether they were willing to pay higher prices. Such unusually high proportions of "not sure" responses suggest that, when called upon to make a choice that would incur some personal sacrifice, a substantial proportion of the public apparently was not fully committed to environmental protection.[11]

Thus, two questions have emerged:

1. Why did the nationwide and city-based surveys produce two sets of results totally at odds with each other?
2. Why did an overwhelming majority of the residents in Beijing, Shanghai, and Lianyungang indicate that they were unwilling to pay higher prices for environmentally friendly products and services?

As for question 1, in the absence of greater detail on how the city-based surveys were designed and conducted, we can only speculate on the reasons for the differing results between the nationwide and city-based surveys. However, some empirical data gathered in the 1995 nationwide survey will help answer the second question. Among those who said that they were not willing to pay extra fees to protect the environment, their primary concern, as expressed by 46.4 percent of the respondents, centered on the issue of whether the collected fees would actually be spent on environmental protection projects (Zhonghua huanjing baohu jijin hui and Zhongguo renmin daxue 1999, 87).

A clue to the reason behind such a concern is suggested by the subsequent 1998 nationwide survey, in which up to one-third of the public believed that the local government had not undertaken any protection measures to address pollution problems, with another one-third saying that they were "not sure" on this matter (Guojia huanjing baohu zongju and Jiaoyubu 1999, 23). The reason also may stem from the public's lack of trust in government officials' commitment on matters pertaining to the environment.[12] In the 1995 nationwide survey, 46.6 percent of the respondents asserted that they "strongly disagreed" or "disagreed" with the view that officials at various government levels were highly committed to environmental protection (Table 2.15).

To What Extent Is the Public Committed?

The evidence accumulated thus far is full of conflicting views on the public's environmental perceptions, attitudes, and values. Contradictory survey data supporting opposing propositions, albeit not in abundant supply, have prevented us from reaching conclusions with a high degree of confidence regarding whether the public perceives the country's environmental problems as serious and the degree to which the public is committed to the cause of environmental protection.

Nevertheless, a sufficient amount of largely consistent evidence generated by the surveys has revealed that the public's immediate attention, except for that of teenagers, has always been captured by issues other than the environment.[13] In short, this finding essentially replicates findings elsewhere in the world: that although the public may express a considerable amount of concern over the environment, it is not, in and of itself, a salient issue in the public mind. The public is not yet convinced to fully commit to the cause of environmental protection.

What then are the major factors underlying the Chinese public's reservations toward committing themselves to the environmental agenda? Several propositions can be discerned. First, a substantial proportion of the public is quite optimistic about the future trends of environmental conditions, at both the local and national levels (Table 2.16). For instance, at the national level, only 7.1 percent of the respondents in the 1998 survey believed that the country's environmental conditions would suffer a significant deterioration. With regard to the local environment, the comparable figure dropped lower, to 3.2 percent. In fact, more than 40 percent of the respondents expected to

Table 2.15

Public Perception of the Level of Commitment for Environmental Protection Shown by Government Officials (%)

Statement: Officials at various governmental levels are highly committed to environmental protection.

Location	Strongly agree/agree	Strongly disagree/disagree
Nationwide[a]	53.4	46.6
Nationwide (urban)[a]	46.8	53.2
Nationwide (rural)[a]	62.1	37.9
Lianyungang[b]	90.0	10.0

Sources: [a] Zhonghua huanjing baohu jijin hui (China Environmental Protection Foundation) and Zhongguo renmin daxue (China People's University). "Quanmin huanjing yishi diaocha" (A Survey on Public Environmental Consciousness). In Xi Xiaolin and Xu Qinghua, eds., *Zhongguo gongzhong huanjing yishi diaocha* (A Survey on China's Public Environmental Consciousness). Beijing: Zhongguo huanjing kexue chubanshe [Beijing: China Environmental Science Press], 1999, 92.
[b] Hong Shi and Wei Shantao. "Lianyungang shi gongmin huanjing yishi wenjuan diaocha" (A Survey on Public Environmental Consciousness in Lianyungang). In Xi Xiaolin and Xu Qinghua, eds., *Zhongguo gongzhong huanjing yishi diaocha* (A Survey on China's Public Environmental Consciousness). Beijing: Zhongguo huanjing kexue chubanshe [Beijing: China Environmental Science Press], 1999, 181.

Table 2.16

Public Perception of the Future Trends of Environmental Conditions in the Next Five Years (%)

	Nationwide	Locality
Major improvement	10.4	13.2
Some improvement	32.9	33.6
Remain unchanged	23.0	13.8
Some deterioration	17.8	8.4
Significant deterioration	7.1	3.2
Not sure	8.8	27.8

Source: Guojia huanjing baohu zongju (State Environmental Protection Administration of China) and Jiaoyubu (Ministry of Education). *Quanguo gongzhong huanjing yishi diaocha baogao* (A Survey Report on the Nation's Public Environmental Consciousness). Beijing: Zhongguo huanjing kexue chubanshe [Beijing: China Environmental Science Press], 1999, 7.

see major improvements or some improvements in environmental conditions at both the national and local levels in the next five years. Furthermore, this widely shared optimism may have led the public to become complacent and to disregard calls from various quarters for a gradual and fundamental change in values and behaviors more pro-environment than the prevailing norms.

However, this optimistic outlook that China's environmental conditions will continue to improve has been betrayed by empirical evidence. Statistics reported by central government authorities have shown that the country's overall environmental conditions have been deteriorating over the past several decades and will continue to degenerate for the foreseeable future (Zheng 2002, 13–14; Guojia huanjing baohu zongju and Jiaoyubu 1999, 7). As alluded to earlier, until the early 1990s, the public's access to environmental information was so tightly controlled by the state that it has been postulated that the public may easily have been swayed into believing what the state prescribed (Stockholm Environment Institute 2002). What is certain, however, is that partly because of a lack of full access to official environmental data and partly as a result of being supplied with incomplete, if not distorted, information by the media, the Chinese public has become overly optimistic about the future prospect of the country's environmental conditions. To correct such misplaced optimism, a more transparent process and system need to be established to allow the public ready access to and scrutiny of easily understood environmental data at the local level.

Second, the public's halfhearted commitment toward the environment may stem from citizens' varying views of what constitutes the "environment." In principle, some of them might agree that the overall environment in China indeed has deteriorated. However, they may claim that their own cities and their own neighborhoods—which are observable and familiar and perhaps perceived as being able to be affected by some kind of local corrective actions—are in much better shape than the country at large. Results from several surveys have shown that a substantial proportion of citizens have rated the environmental quality of their own districts or cities at higher levels than that of the country at large. For instance, while 44 percent of the respondents surveyed in Qingdao considered the nation's environmental pollution problems as "very serious" or "serious," only 27 percent of them would assign their city's pollution problems to these same categories (Table 2.17).

Indeed, when these respondents were asked to assess the degree of seriousness of specific environmental problems at both the district level—in which the respondents reside—and the national level, they invariably said that each of these environmental problems was much less serious at the district level than at the national level (Table 2.18).[14]

Conclusion

Needless to say, a full evaluation of the validity of the above conjectures will have to await additional survey data that appraises the continuously changing

Table 2.17

Public Perception of Environmental Pollution Problems in Residing City and of the Country as a Whole (%)

Environmental pollution considered as "serious" or "very serious"	Residing city	Nationwide
Chongqing	60.0	75.0
Qingdao	27.0	44.0
Lianyungang	48.0	54.0

Source: Xi Xiaolin, Fan Lihong, and Deng Xueming. "Zhongguo gongzhong huanjing yishi diaocha jieguo pouxi" (An Analysis of the Survey Results on Public Environmental Consciousness in China). In Xi Xiaolin and Xu Qinghua, eds., *Zhongguo gongzhong huanjing yishi diaocha* (A Survey on China's Public Environmental Consciousness). Beijing: Zhongguo huanjing kexue chubanshe [Beijing: China Environmental Science Press], 1999, 39.

Table 2.18

Public Perception of Environmental Quality of Residing District and of the Country as a Whole (%)

Environmental problems considered as "serious" or "very serious"	Residing district	Nationwide
Air pollution	53.6	76.9
Water pollution	51.0	74.1
Noise pollution	58.3	65.1
Dust storms	26.1	51.0
Solid waste pollution	60.0	63.6
Insufficient greening	43.7	61.3
Forest destruction	14.7	72.3
Public area pollution	60.3	66.1
Pesticide pollution	27.3	55.9
Desertification	6.1	50.2
Industrial waste pollution	48.8	72.0
Marine pollution	0.5	49.7
Reduction of wild animals and plants	36.1	75.8

Source: Hong Dayong. *Zhongguo gongzhong huanjing yishi chutan* (A Preliminary Study on China's Public Environmental Consciousness). Zhonghua huanjing baohu jijin hui (China Environmental Protection Foundation). Beijing: Zhongguo huanjing kexue chubanshe [Beijing: China Environmental Science Press], 1998, 95–96.

configurations of the Chinese public's environmentalism. Nevertheless, two overall observations can be drawn, which have implications for methodology.

First, one of the major weaknesses of surveys with an explicit emphasis on environmental issues is that they very likely will elicit responses that reflect prevailing social norms rather than the respondents' personal beliefs and convictions. The results from this type of survey have consistently shown that the public cares deeply about the environment, in keeping with an emerging conventional wisdom that informs the public that showing support for environmental protection is a politically correct posture. However, the actual *degree* of public support for environmental protection may be much lower, particularly when the public is confronted with hard choices.

For instance, the 1994 bicity survey conducted in Beijing and Shanghai produced empirical evidence that demonstrated that the degree of public commitment toward environmental protection was somewhat lower when respondents were asked to pay extra fees for environmentally friendly products and services. Furthermore, that degree of commitment dropped a great deal further if respondents were asked to make major adjustments in their consumption behavior that might compromise their quality of life (Yuan 1999, 119). These types of questions, which are designed to help improve our understanding of how much people are actually willing to do themselves to support environmental protection, are much more useful for policy purposes than questions that ask people to reconfirm their endorsement of a core value— the importance of the environment—that has become more or less a prevailing social norm in China. The former types of questions should be combined with similarly structured questions that test the public's degree of support for the environment and are asked regularly over a long period.

Second, a test of the strength of public opinion for environmental quality is to look at the degree to which pro-environmental opinions translate into actual political impact (Dunlap 1995). Although not much research has been conducted on this particular aspect of environmentalism in China, cursory observations made by some researchers, both domestic and foreign, strongly suggest that public opinion on the environment has *not* been a major force shaping environmental policies (Yuan 1999; Stockholm Environment Institute 2002). Instead of policies being informed or influenced by public opinion, it is the public's own environmental perceptions of the environment that are being shaped by state policies propagated by the media. Although awareness of the environment is on the rise in China, the basic understanding of the nature of many issues by the public has remained elementary. As a result, members of the public are not able to push for any viable alternatives—and are not particularly interested in doing so.[15]

Hence, in addition to the fact that the political climate is not responsive to public pressures, local government officials simply do not have a high regard for public awareness of environmental issues because they consider the public's awareness inconsequential (Stockholm Environment Institute 2002). As revealed in several recent studies (Chan and Wong 1994; Tong 2002;

Wong and Chan 1996; Wu 1999), when it comes to evaluating the actual impact of pro-environment opinion, instead of public concern, it is actually the concern of local government officials entrusted with the responsibility for environmental management that matters. Instead of following the conventional approach and studying the public's environmental attitudes, perhaps a somewhat different research strategy is needed to help us gain a better understanding of how pro-environment opinion, or the lack of it, on the part of the local bureaucrats has impacted China's environment.

Notes

The author would like to thank two anonymous referees for their helpful comments and suggestions on an earlier draft of this chapter. I am indebted to Hong Dayong for providing a copy of several major works on the topic in the early stage of this research project. The author also would like to thank Wan Sau-chi for her able research assistance as well as Meimei Wong and Zhao Tao for their assistance in preparing the references.

1. This heightened public concern for the environment has been attributed in part to a significant increase in news media coverage of environmental issues, particularly on the lack of enforcement of environmental regulations, since the late 1980s (Xi, Fan, and Deng 1999, 58). However, the extent to which international actors, such as the environmental education program run by the U.S. Peace Corps, have played a role in elevating public concern for the environment has not been examined.

2. By one account, the concept of "environmental consciousness" started to gain public recognition in China in the early 1980s. This term was referred to in government documents for the first time in 1983 in association with the organization of the Second National Conference on the Environment (Yang 1999, 10). Ho (2001) provides a rather comprehensive account of the development of environmentalism in China, examining its origins as well as political and social implications at both the national and local levels.

3. The fact that quite a number of surveys on public environmental consciousness were conducted by local environmental protection bureaus themselves or local government officials raises a legitimate concern among the research community over the validity of such survey results because this practice amounts to the bureaus/officials evaluating their own performance and constitutes some degree of conflict of interest. The results gathered through such surveys also could have been biased methodologically, either by the way the questions were phrased or the manner in which the survey was administered at the street level. For instance, some researchers have pointed out that some responses from rural interviewees might have been biased in favor of the government because the interviews were conducted in the presence of local government officials (Zhonghua huanjing baohu jijin hui and Zhongguo renmin daxue 1999, 92).

4. Nisihira (1997), who conducted a comparative study on public environmental attitudes in China and Thailand, cautioned against reading too much into the survey results because "opinion surveys are intended to obtain rather shallow but broad-based information," 41.

5. Chung and Poon (1999) have found out from their own survey conducted in Guangzhou in 1997 that the younger generation (i.e., below the age of 17) was one of the groups most receptive to the appeal of the New Environment Paradigm.

6. Interestingly, a similar pattern of public opinion on the environment has been observed in the United States. For instance, Dunlap (1995, 77) noted that "despite the relatively strong consensus in support of environmental protection and the increased salience of environmental problems in 1970, the state of the environment was viewed by

only a minority of the public as one of the nation's most important problems."

7. The level of environmental illiteracy in China is, generally speaking, higher than that in more developed countries such as the United Kingdom, in which, in a 1995 survey, about half of the public (45 percent) admitted that they did not fully understand environmental issues (Worcester 1997, 167).

8. The author finds this surprising because one would expect the average person to refrain from arriving at a conclusive stance on a subject that he or she does not fully understand or about which he or she is not fully informed. How interviewees responded to such questions on environmental knowledge depended on what they meant by being "informed." It is not clear from the literature what yardstick the interviewees used to evaluate their level of environmental knowledge. Their knowledge could be interpreted to range from a full understanding of the underlying mechanism of global climate change to the simple recognition that this issue has been defined as a problem by the authorities. The author is grateful to one of the anonymous referees for raising this point.

9. For instance, in one nationwide and three city-level (Qingdao, Lianyungang, and Chongqing) surveys, more than 70 percent of the respondents reported that the news media were their predominant source of information on environmental issues (Xi, Fan, and Deng 1999, 58).

10. The differences in environmental perception between rural and urban populations in China have been examined by Chung and Poon (2001) through the application of the New Environmental Paradigm concept in an environmental attitude survey. They found that such differences may reflect "the stronger desire of the rural population to get economically developed" (7).

11. Willingness to pay studies are particularly problematic, especially in low-income countries. Surveys conducted in low-income countries in which the respondents were asked to pay for environmental protection efforts with time rather than money have shown they were much more willing to do so than their wealthier counterparts. Thus, "reluctance to pay by people in some of the poorer countries reflects extreme economic hardship, not a lack of environmental values" because "few people [in poorer countries] would offer monetary payment for anything, even for values they hold highly" (Brechin and Kempton 1994, 258).

12. Such a skeptical concern on the part of the public is probably justified. Enforcement actions against environmental violators are rarely taken by local environmental protection bureau officials, who generally have come to regard fees and fines as a major source of income to pay their own salaries rather than to pay for actual environmental clean-up activities (Ma and Ortolano 2000).

13. As Chen and Porter (2000, 62) have pointed out, "For most Chinese, a washing machine, a fridge (with or without CFCs), and perhaps ultimately a car are, along with peace and stability, the highest personal objectives."

14. Dunlap (1995, 80) has observed a similar pattern in the West: "respondents were so much less likely to see pollution as a community problem to begin with."

15. The low level of active participation in environmental activities by the general public, and the underlying reasons for it, have been discussed and analyzed by Ren (2002).

English-Language References

Ash, Robert F., and Richard L. Edmonds. 2000. "China's Land Resources, Environment and Agricultural Production." In Richard L. Edmonds, ed., *Managing the Chinese Environment*, 112–155. Oxford and New York: Oxford University Press.

Brechin, Steven R., and Wilett Kempton. 1994. "Global Environmentalism: A Challenge to the Postmaterialism Thesis?" *Social Science Quarterly* 75, no. 2: 245–269.

Cannon, Terry. 2000. "Introduction–The Economic Reforms, Demographic Processes and Environmental Problems." In Terry Cannon, ed., *China's Economic Growth: The Im-*

pact on Regions, Migration and the Environment, 1–32. New York: Palgrave.
Chan, Hon S., and K.K. Kenneth Wong. 1994. "Environmental Attitudes and Concerns of the Environmental Protection Bureaucrats in Guangzhou, People's Republic of China: Implications for Environmental Policy Implementation." *International Journal of Public Administration* 17, no. 8: 1523–1554.
Chan, Y.K. Ricky. 1999. "Environmental Attitudes and Behavior of Consumers in China: Survey Findings and Implications." *Journal of International Consumer Marketing* 11, no. 4: 25–52.
Chen, Zhicheng, and Robin Porter. 2000. "Energy Management and Environmental Awareness in China's Enterprises." *Energy Policy* 28: 49–63.
Chung, Shan-shan, and C.S. 1999. "The Attitudes of Guangzhou Citizens on Waste Reduction and Environmental Issues." *Resources, Conservation and Recycling* 25: 35–59.
_____. 2001. "A Comparison of Waste-Reduction Practices and New Environmental Paradigm of Rural and Urban Chinese Citizens." *Journal of Environmental Management* 62: 3–19.
Dunlap, Riley E. 1995. "Public Opinion and Environmental Policy." In James P. Lester, ed., *Environmental Politics and Policy, Theories and Evidence*, 63–114. Durham, NC: Duke University Press, 1995.
Edmonds, Richard L. 1994. *Patterns of China's Lost Harmony: A Survey of the Country's Environmental Degradation and Protection*. London: Routledge.
Feng, Zhenmin, and Xiaohua Wang. 2002. "Survey and Evaluation on Residents' Environmental Awareness in Jiangsu Province China." *International Journal of Environment and Pollution* 17, no. 4: 312–322.
Ho, Peter. 2001. "Greening Without Conflict? Environmentalism, NGOs and Civil Society in China." *Development and Change* 32: 893–921.
Ma, Xiaoying, and Leonard Ortolano. 2000. *Environmental Regulation in China: Institutions, Enforcement, and Compliance*. Lanham, MD: Rowman & Littlefield Publishers.
McElroy, Michael B. 1998. "Industrial Growth, Air Pollution, and Environmental Damage: Complex Challenges for China." In Michael B. McElroy, Chris P. Nielsen, and Peter Lydon, eds., *Energizing China: Reconciling Environmental Protection and Economic Growth*, 241–266. Cambridge, MA: Harvard University Committee on Environment.
Murray, Geoffrey, and Ian G. Cook. 2002. *Green China: Seeking Ecological Alternatives*. London and New York: Routledge Curzon.
Nisihira, Sigeki. 1997. "Survey on Environmental Awareness in China and Thailand." In Sigeki Nisihira, Reeitsu Kojima, Hideo Okamoto, and Shigeaki Fujisaki, eds., *Environmental Awareness in Developing Countries: The Cases of China and Thailand*, 29–45. Tokyo: Institute of Developing Economies.
Shapiro, Judith. 2001. *Mao's War Against Nature: Politics and the Environment in Revolutionary China*. New York, NY: Cambridge University Press.
Smil, Vaclav. 1984. *The Bad Earth: Environmental Degradation in China*. Armonk, NY: M.E. Sharpe.
———. 1993. *China's Environmental Crisis: An Inquiry into the Limits of National Development*. Armonk, NY: M.E. Sharpe.
Stockholm Environment Institute. 2002. *Making Green Development a Choice: China Human Development Report 2002*. Oxford: Oxford University Press.
Wong, Koon-Kwai, and Hon S. Chan. 1996. "The Environmental Awareness of Environmental Protection Bureaucrats in the People's Republic of China." *The Environmentalist* 16: 213–219.
Worcester, Robert. 1997. "Public Opinion and the Environment." In Michael Jacobs, ed., *Greening the Millennium? The New Politics of the Environment*, 160–73. Oxford: Blackwell Publishers.
World Bank. 2001. *China: Air, Land, and Water: Environmental Priorities for a New Millennium*. Washington, DC.

Chinese-Language References

Beijing lingdian diaocha gongsi (Beijing Lingdian Survey Company). 1999. "Huanjing riyi wei shiren guanzhu" (Public's Increasing Concern for the Environment). In Xi Xiaolin and Xu Qinghua, eds., *Zhongguo gongzhong huanjing yishi diaocha* (A Survey on China's Public Environmental Consciousness), 94–99. Beijing: Zhongguo huanjing kexue chubanshe [China Environmental Science Press].

北京零點調查公司。1999年. "環境日益爲世人關注"。中國公眾環境意識調查,郗小林、徐慶華主編。北京:中國環境科學出版社,94–99頁。

Chen Zhongnuan, Wang Xiafei, He Xiang, and Wang Jinliang. 1999. "Daxuesheng huanjing yishi diaocha yu huanjing jiaoyu chuyi" (An Investigation and Analysis on the Environmental Consciousness of College Students). *Yunnan huanjing kexue* (Yunnan Environmental Science) 18, no. 4: 53–55.

陳忠暖、王霞斐、何祥、王金亮。"大學生環境意識調查與環境教育芻議"。雲南環境科學,1999年,第18卷,第4期,53–55頁。

Chongqing shi huanbao ju (Chongqing Environmental Protection Bureau). 1999. "Chongqing shi gongzhong huanjing yishi diaocha jieguo zongshu" (A Discussion on the Results of the Survey on Public Environmental Consciousness in Chongqing). In Xi Xiaolin and Xu Qinghua, eds., *Zhongguo gongzhong huanjing yishi diaocha* (A Survey on China's Public Environmental Consciousness), 154–157. Beijing: Zhongguo huanjing kexue chubanshe [China Environmental Science Press].

重慶市環保局。"重慶市公眾環境意識調查結果綜述"。中國公眾環境意識調查,郗小林、徐慶華主編。北京:中國環境科學出版社,1999年,154–157頁。

Cui Yan, and Chen Jianfeng. 1999. "Huanjing yishi diaocha shidian xuexiao xuesheng" (Students in Pilot Study Schools on Environmental Consciousness). *Huanjing jiaoyu* (Environmental Education) 1: 33–34.

崔雁、陳建峰。"環境意識調查試點學校學生"。環境教育,1999年,第1期,33–34頁。

Guo Lihua, Ma Wenru, Cheng Songlin, and Chen Haizhu. 2001. "Hainan shifan xueyuan xuesheng huanjing yishi diaocha" (A Survey on Environmental Consciousness of Students at Hainan Normal University). *Hainan shifan xueyuan xuebao (ziran kexue ban)* (Journal of Hainan Normal University: Natural Science Edition) 14, no. 1: 98–104.

郭力華、馬文儒、程松林、陳海珠。"海南師範學院學生環境意識調查"。海南師範學院學報(自然科學版),2001年,第14卷,第1期,98–104頁。

Guojia huanjing baohu zongju (State Environmental Protection Administration of China). 1999. "Quanguo gongzhong huanjing yishi diaocha baogao (Zhaiyao)" (A Survey on the Nation's Public Environmental Consciousness [Summary]). *Huanjing jiaoyu* (Environmental Education), no. 4: 25–27.

國家環保總局。"全國公眾環境意識調查報告(摘要)"。環境教育,1999年,第4期, 25–27頁。

Guojia huanjing baohu zongju (State Environmental Protection Administration of China) and Jiaoyubu (Ministry of Education). 1999. *Quanguo gongzhong huanjing yishi diaocha baogao* (A Survey Report on the Nation's Public Environmental Consciousness). Beijing: Zhongguo huanjing kexue chubanshe [China Environmental Science Press].

國家環境保護總局、教育部。全國公眾環境意識調查報告。北京:中國環境科學出版社。1999年。

Hong Dayong. 1997. "Woguo gongzhong huanjing baohu yishi de diaocha yu fenxi" (An Investigation and Analysis of Our Country's Public Environmental Protection Consciousness). *Zhongguo renkou, ziyuan yu huanjing* (China Population, Resources, and Environment) 7, no. 2: 27–31.

洪大用。"我國公眾環境保護意識的調查與分析",中國人口、資源與環境,第7卷,
第2期,1997年,27–31頁。

———. 1998. *Zhongguo gongzhong huanjing yishi chutan* (A Preliminary Study on
China's Public Environmental Consciousness). Zhonghua huanjing baohu jijin hui
(China Environmental Protection Foundation). Beijing: Zhongguo huanjing kexue
chubanshe [China Environmental Science Press].

洪大用。中國公眾環境意識初探。中華環境保護基金會。北京:中國環境科學出
版社,1998年。

Hong Shi and Wei Shantao. 1999. "Lianyungang shi gongmin huanjing yishi wenjuan diaocha" (A Survey on Public Environmental Consciousness in Lianyungang). In Xiaolin
Xi and Qinghua Xu, eds., *Zhongguo gongzhong huanjing yishi diaocha* (A Survey on
China's Public Environmental Consciousness), 179–187. Beijing: Zhongguo huanjing
kexue chubanshe [China Environmental Science Press].

洪石、魏善濤。"連雲港市公民環境意識問卷調查"。中國公眾環境意識調查,郗小
林、徐慶華主編。北京:中國環境科學出版社,1999年,179–187頁。

Huang Tianxiang. 1999. "Beijing shi gongzhong huanjing yishi diaocha qianxi" (An Investigation and Analysis on Public Environmental Consciousness in Beijing). In Xiaolin
Xi and Qinghua Xu, eds., *Zhongguo gongzhong huanjing yishi diaocha* (A Survey on
China's Public Environmental Consciousness), 144–148. Beijing: Zhongguo huanjing
kexue chubanshe [China Environmental Science Press].

黃天祥。"北京市公眾環境意識調查淺析"。中國公眾環境意識調查,郗小林、徐
慶華主編。北京:中國環境科學出版社,1999年,144–148頁。

Ji Xiaoxiong, Fan Weida, and Luo Xinzhong. 1999. "Shanghai shimin huanjing yishi
diaocha" (A Survey on the Environmental Consciousness of Residents in Shanghai).
In Xiaolin Xi and Qinghua Xu, eds., *Zhongguo gongzhong huanjing yishi diaocha* (A
Survey on China's Public Environmental Consciousness), 149–153. Beijing: Zhongguo
huanjing kexue chubanshe [China Environmental Science Press].

稽曉雄、范偉達、羅心中。"上海市民環境意識調查"。中國公眾環境意識調查,郗
小林、徐慶華主編。北京:中國環境科學出版社,1999年,149–153頁。

Li Lin, Huang Jin, Lu Wenhao, Wang Shunü, and Hu Qingqing. 2002. "Fuzhou shi
gongzhong huanjing yishi diaocha fenxi" (An Analysis of Fuzhou Public Environmental
Consciousness). *Fujian huanjing* (Fujian Environment), 19, no. 5: 32–34.

李林、黃謹、盧文浩、王淑女、胡慶慶。"福州市公眾環境意識調查分析"。福建環
境,2002年,第19卷,第5期,32–34頁。

Li Yiming. 1999. "Qingdao shi gongzhong huanjing yishi diaocha" (A Survey on Public
Environmental Consciousness in Qingdao). In Xiaolin Xi and Qinghua Xu, eds., *Zhongguo gongzhong huanjing yishi diaocha* (A Survey on China's Public Environmental
Consciousness), 167–78. Beijing: Zhongguo huanjing kexue chubanshe [China Environmental Science Press].

李亦明。"青島市公眾環境意識調查"。中國公眾環境意識調查,郗小林、徐慶華
主編。北京:中國環境科學出版社,1999年,167–178頁。

Li Zhou. 1997. "Chengshi huanjing zhuangkuang he jumin huanjing yishi diaocha baogao"
(A Report on the State of the Urban Environment and Residents' Environmental
Consciousness). Yanjiu lunwen (Research Dissertation): 2–4.

李周。"城市環境狀況和居民環境意識調查報告"。研究論文,1997,2–4頁。

Lu Jianhua. 1999. "Huanjing yishi yu huanjing yishi diaocha" (Environmental Conscious-
ness and Investigation on Environmental Consciousness). In Xiaolin Xi and Qinghua
Xu, eds., *Zhongguo gongzhong huanjing yishi diaocha* (A Survey on China's Public
Environmental Consciousness), 19–26. Beijing: Zhongguo huanjing kexue chubanshe
[China Environmental Science Press].

陸建華。"環境意識與環境意識調查"。中國公眾環境意識調查,郗小林、徐慶華主
編。北京:中國環境科學出版社,1999年,1926頁。

Luan Xuezhu. 1995. "Qingdao shi gongzhong huanjing yishi diaocha yu jinhou duice yanjiu" (A Survey on Qingdao's Public Environmental Consciousness and Future Planning Study). *Shandong huanjing* (Shandong Environment), no. 4: 26–27.

栾學朱。"青島市公眾環境意識調查與今後對策研究"。山東環境，1995年，第4期，26–27頁。

Luo Xiancheng, and Zhong Yexi. 2001. "Jiangxi sheng gaoshi yuanxiao daxuesheng huanjing yishi diaocha" (A Survey on the Environmental Consciousness of University Students in Jiangxi Province). *Jiangxi sheng tuanxiao xuebao* (Jiangxi Joint School Journal), no. 4: 21–22.

羅先誠、鐘業喜。"江西省高師院校大學生環境意識調查"。江西省團校學報，2001年，第4期，21–22頁。

Pan Linping. 1999. "Zhejiang sheng gongzhong huanjing yishi wanjuan diaocha" (A Survey of 10,000 Residents' Public Environmental Consciousness in Zhejiang Province). In Xiaolin Xi and Qinghua Xu, eds., *Zhongguo gongzhong huanjing yishi diaocha* (A Survey on China's Public Environmental Consciousness), 158–616. Beijing: Zhongguo huanjing kexue chubanshe [China Environmental Science Press].

潘林平。"浙江省公眾環境意識萬卷調查"。中國公眾環境意識調查，郗小林、徐慶華主編。北京：中國環境科學出版社，1999年，158–166頁。

Peng Jinxin. 2002. "Dangdai Zhongguo huanjing baohu chenggong zhilu he tiaozhan jiexi" (An Analysis of the Success and Challenge of Contemporary China's Environmental Protection). In Ming Yang, ed., *Huanjing wenti yu huanjing yishi* (Environmental Problem and Environmental Consciousness), 1–11. Beijing: Huaxia chubanshe [Huaxia Press].

彭近新。"當代中國環境保護成功之路和挑戰解析"。環境問題與環境意識，楊明主編，北京：華夏出版社，2002年，1–11頁。

Qi Weifeng. 2000. "Chengshi shimin huanjing yishi diaocha yu pingjia yi Zhejiang Hangzhou shi weili" (A Survey and an Evaluation on Urban Residents' Environmental Consciousness–Zhejiang, Hangzhou as an Example). *Guihua shi* (Planner) 16, no. 3: 93–95.

祁巍鋒。"城市市民環境意識調查與評價以浙江杭州市為例"。規劃師，2000年，第16卷，第3期，93–95頁。

Ren Liying. 2002. "Huanjing baohu zhong de gongzhong canyu" (Public Participation in Environmental Protection). In Ming Yang, ed., *Huanjing wenti yu huanjing yishi* (Environmental Problem and Environmental Consciousness), 89–113. Beijing: Huaxia chubanshe [Huaxia Press].

任莉穎。"環境保護中的公眾參與"。環境問題與環境意識，楊明主編，北京：華夏出版社，2002年，89–113頁。

Shen Hao and Ding Mai. 1999. "Zhongguo chengshi gongzhong de huanjing yishi" (The Environmental Consciousness of the Public in China's Cities). In Xiaolin Xi and Qinghua Xu, eds., *Zhongguo gongzhong huanjing yishi diaocha* (A Survey on China's Public Environmental Consciousness), 100–108. Beijing: Zhongguo huanjing kexue chubanshe [China Environmental Science Press].

沈浩、丁邁。"中國城市公眾的環境意識"。中國公眾環境意識調查，郗小林、徐慶華主編。北京：中國環境科學出版社，1999年，100–108頁。

Tong Yanqi. 2002. "Huanjing yishi yu huanjing baohu zhengce de quxiang" (Environmental Consciousness and the Orientation of Environmental Protection Policy). In Ming Yang, ed., *Huanjing wenti yu huanjing yishi* (Environmental Problem and Environmental Consciousness), 56–75. Beijing: Huaxia chubanshe [Beijing: Huaxia Press].

童燕齊。"環境意識與環境保護政策的取向"。環境問題與環境意識，楊明主編，北京：華夏出版社，2002年，56–75頁。

Wang Chunsheng. 2002. "Huzhou shi chengzhen jumin huanjing baohu yishi diaocha" (A

Survey on Residents' Environmental Protection Consciousness in Huzhou). *Zhejiang yufang yixue* (Zhejiang prevention medicine) 14, no. 12: 46–47.

王春生。"湖州市城鎮居民環境保護意識調查"。浙江預防醫學，2002年，
第14卷，第12期，46–47頁。

Wang Yuqing. 1999. "Tigao quanminzu huanjing yishi cujin woguo huanbao shiye fazhan" (Raising the Nation's Environmental Consciousness and Promoting the Development of Environmental Protection Activities). In Xiaolin Xi and Qinghua Xu, eds., *Zhongguo gongzhong huanjing yishi diaocha* (A Survey on China's Public Environmental Consciousness), 1–4. Beijing: Zhongguo huanjing kexue chubanshe [China Environmental Science Press].

王玉慶。"提高全民族環境意識促進我國環保事業發展"。中國公眾環境意識調查，
郗小林、徐慶華主編。北京：中國環境科學出版社，1999年，1–4頁。

Wu Baozhong. 1999. "Tigao huanbao gongzuozhe he youguan bumen gaoceng juecezhe de huanjing yishi zhi guan zhongyao" (The Significance of Raising the Environmental Consciousness of Officials Working on Environmental Protection Matters and Senior Policymakers). In Xiaolin Xi and Qinghua Xu, eds., *Zhongguo gongzhong huanjing yishi diaocha* (A Survey on China's Public Environmental Consciousness), 7–9. Beijing: Zhongguo huanjing kexue chubanshe [China Environmental Science Press].

吳報中。"提高環保工作者和有關部門高層決策者的環境意識至關重要"。中國公
眾環境意識調查，郗小林、徐慶華主編。北京：中國環境科學出版社，1999年，
7–9頁。

Wu Xinxin, Wang Fenyu, and Deng Xueming. 1999. "Zhongguo gongye qiye zhigong huanjing yishi diaocha" (A Survey on Environmental Consciousness of the Staff in China's Industrial Enterprises). In Xiaolin Xi and Qinghua Xu, eds., *Zhongguo gong-zhong huanjing yishi diaocha* (A Survey on China's Public Environmental Conscious-ness), 241–253. Beijing: Zhongguo huanjing kexue chubanshe [China Environmental Science Press].

武欣欣、王奮宇、鄧雪明。"中國工業企業職工環境意識調查"。中國公眾環境
意識調查，郗小林、徐慶華主編。北京：中國環境科學出版社，1999年，
241–253頁。

Xi Xiaolin, Fan Lihong, and Deng Xueming. 1999. "Zhongguo gongzhong huanjing yishi diaocha jieguo pouxi" (An Analysis of the Survey Results on Public Environmental Consciousness in China). In Xi Xiaolin and Xu Qinghua, eds., *Zhongguo gongzhong huanjing yishi diaocha* (A Survey on China's Public Environmental Consciousness), 27–67. Beijing: Zhongguo huanjing kexue chubanshe [China Environmental Science Press].

郗小林、樊立宏、鄧雪明。"中國公眾環境意識調查結果剖析"。中國公眾環境
意識調查，郗小林、徐慶華主編。北京：中國環境科學出版社，1999年，
27–67頁。

Xi Xiaolin, and Xu Qinghua, eds. 1999. *Zhongguo gongzhong huanjing yishi diaocha* (A Survey on China's Public Environmental Consciousness). Beijing: Zhongguo huanjing kexue chubanshe [China Environmental Science Press].

郗小林、徐慶華。中國公眾環境意識調查。北京：中國環境科學出版社，1999年。

Xu Qinghua. 1999. "Renzhen zongjie jingyan gaohao gongzhong huanjing yishi diaocha" (Seriously Draw Up the Lessons and Enhance the Research Work on Public Environmental Consciousness). In Xiaolin Xi and Qinghua Xu, eds., *Zhongguo gongzhong huanjing yishi diaocha* (A Survey on China's Public Environmental Consciousness), 5–6. Beijing: Zhongguo huanjing kexue chubanshe [China Environmental Science Press].

徐慶華。"認真總結經驗 搞好公眾環境意識調查"。中國公眾環境意識調查，郗小
林、徐慶華主編。北京：中國環境科學出版社，1999年，5–6頁。

Yang Dongping, and Wang Lixiong. 1999. "Zhongguo baozhi huanjing yishi 1997" (The

Environmental Consciousness of China's Newspapers in 1997). In Xi Xiaolin and Xu Qinghua, eds., *Zhongguo gongzhong huanjing yishi diaocha* (A Survey on China's Public Environmental Consciousness), 188–223. Beijing: Zhongguo huanjing kexue chubanshe [China Environmental Science Press].

楊東平、王力雄。"中國報紙環境意識1997"。中國公眾環境意識調查，郗小林、徐慶華主編。北京：中國環境科學出版社，1999年，188–223頁。

Yang Ming, ed. 2002. *Huanjing wenti yu huanjing yishi* (Environmental Problem and Environmental Consciousness). Beijing: Huaxia chubanshe [Huaxia Press].

楊明。環境問題與環境意識。北京：華夏出版社，2002年。

———. 2002. "Zhongguo gongzhong huanjing yishi de tezheng" (The Characteristics of Public Environmental Consciousness in China). In Ming Yang, ed., *Huanjing wenti yu huanjing yishi* (Environmental Problem and Environmental Consciousness), 76–88. Beijing: Huaxia chubanshe [Huaxia Press].

楊明。"中國公眾環境意識的特徵"。環境問題與環境意識，楊明主編，北京：華夏出版社，2002年，76–88頁。

Yang Zhaofei. 1999. "Genghao de kaizhan huanjing xuanchuan jiaoyu tigao quanminzu huanjing yishi" (Expending a Better Effort to Start the Environmental Education Campaign: Raising the Nation's Environmental Consciousness). In Xi Xiaolin and Xu Qinghua, eds., *Zhongguo gongzhong huanjing yishi diaocha* (A Survey on China's Public Environmental Consciousness), 10–18. Beijing: Zhongguo huanjing kexue chubanshe [China Environmental Science Press].

楊朝飛。"更好地開展環境宣傳教育 提高全民族環境意識"。中國公眾環境意識調查，郗小林、徐慶華主編。北京：中國環境科學出版社，1999年，10–18頁。

Yu Jican. 2001. "Guangdong sheng Xinhua zhen gongzhong huanjing yishi diaocha" (A Survey on Public Environmental Consciousness of Residents in Xinhua Zhen, Guangdong Province). *Huanjing wuran yu fangzhi* (Environmental Pollution and Prevention) 23, no. 2: 77–78.

俞繼燦。"廣東省新華鎮公眾環境意識調查"。環境污染與防治，2001年，第23卷，第2期，77–78頁。

Yu Ping. 2000. "Zhongguo: Youdai nongmin shengtai huanjing yishi de juexing—Jianghan pingyuan nonghu shengtai huanjing yishi diaocha" (China: Waiting for the Awakening of the Peasants' Ecological Consciousness—A Survey on Jianghan Plain's Peasants' Ecological and Environmental Consciousness). *Diaocha* (Survey and Research), no. 2: 27–29.

喻萍。"中國：有待農民生態環境意識的覺醒—江漢平原農戶生態環境意識調查"。調查，2000年，第2期，27–29頁。

Yuan Fang. 1999. "Zhongguo shimin de huanjing yishi diaocha: Beijing he Shanghai" (A Survey on Chinese Residents' Environmental Consciousness in Beijing and Shanghai). In Xi Xiaolin and Xu Qinghua, eds., *Zhongguo gongzhong huanjing yishi diaocha* (A Survey on China's Public Environmental Consciousness), 109–130. Beijing: Zhongguo huanjing kexue chubanshe [China Environmental Science Press].

袁方。"中國市民的環境意識調查：北京和上海"。中國公眾環境意識調查，郗小林，徐慶華主編。北京：中國環境科學出版社，1999年，109–130頁。

Zhang Haiqing, Liu Gang, Wu Jianhong, Li Mincong, and Wu Kaiming. 2001. "Panyu shimin huanjing yishi diaocha yu pingjia yanjiu" (A Survey on Residents' Environmental Consciousness in Panyu and Evaluation Study). *Huanjing jishu* (Environmental Technique), no. 3: 38–42.

張海清、劉鋼、吳劍紅、黎敏聰、吳凱明。"番禺市民環境意識調查與評價研究"。環境技術，2001年，第3期，38–42頁。

Zheng Yisheng. 2002. "Zhongguo huanjing yu fazhan zonglun" (A Discussion on China's Environment and Development). In Ming Zang, ed., *Huanjing wenti yu huanjing yishi*

(Environmental Problem and Environmental Consciousness), 13–36. Beijing: Huaxia chubanshe [Huaxia Press].

鄭易生。"中國環境與發展綜論"。環境問題與環境意識，楊明主編，北京：華夏出版社，2002年，13–36頁。

Zheng Zhenquan, and Zhang Likang. 1999. "Fuzhou shi daxuesheng huanjing yishi diaocha" (A Survey on Environmental Consciousness of Fuzhou's University Students). *Huanjing jiaoyu* (Environmental Education), March: 35–36.

鄭振佺、張立康。"福州市大學生環境意識調查"。環境教育，1999年3月，35–36頁。

Zhongguo guoji youhao lianluohui gailuopu zixun youxian gongsi (China International Friendship Network Association Gallop Consulting Company). 1999. "Beijing Shanghai chengshi jumin de huanjing yishi diaocha" (A Survey on the Environmental Consciousness of Residents in the Cities of Beijing and Shanghai). In Xi Xiaolin and Xu Qinghua, eds., *Zhongguo gongzhong huanjing yishi diaocha* (A Survey on China's Public Environmental Consciousness), 131–143. Beijing: Zhongguo huanjing kexue chubanshe [China Environmental Science Press].

中國國際友好聯絡會蓋洛普咨詢有限公司。"北京、上海城市居民的環境意識調查"。中國公眾環境意識調查，郗小林、徐慶華主編。北京：中國環境科學出版社，1999年，131–143頁。

Zhongguo huanjing baoshe (China Environment Newspaper Press). 1999. "Zhongguo zhong xiao xuesheng huanjing yishi diaocha" (A Survey on the Environmental Consciousness of Primary and Secondary Students in China). In Xi Xiaolin and Xu Qinghua, eds., *Zhongguo gongzhong huanjing yishi diaocha* (A Survey on China's Public Environmental Consciousness), 224–240. Beijing: Zhongguo huanjing kexue chubanshe [China Environmental Science Press].

中國環境報社。"中國中小學生環境意識調查"。中國公眾環境意識調查，郗小林、徐慶華主編。北京：中國環境科學出版社，1999年，224–240頁。

Zhonghua huanjing baohu jijin hui (China Environmental Protection Foundation) and Zhongguo renmin daxue (China People's University). 1999. "Quanmin huanjing yishi diaocha" (A Survey on Public Environmental Consciousness). In Xi Xiaolin and Xu Qinghua, eds., *Zhongguo gongzhong huanjing yishi diaocha* (A Survey on China's Public Environmental Consciousness), 68–93. Beijing: Zhongguo huanjing kexue chubanshe [China Environmental Science Press].

中華環境保護基金會、中國人民大學。"全民環境意識調查"。中國公眾環境意識調查，郗小林、徐慶華主編。北京：中國環境科學出版社，1999年，68–93頁。

Zhou Songjing, Zheng Nan, and Guo Xuefeng. 1999. "Qiye liangong huanjing yishi diaocha fenxi ji jianyi" (An Investigation, Analysis and Suggestion on Environmental Knowledge of the Enterprise Staff). *Guanli yu xinxi* (Management and Information) 9, no. 4: 3.

周松景、鄭楠、郭學峰。"企業聯工環境意識調查分析及建議"。管理與信息，1999年，第9卷，第4期，3頁。

—— Chapter 3 ——

Environmental Law in the People's Republic of China

An Overview Describing Challenges and Providing Insights for Good Governance

Richard J. Ferris Jr. and Hongjun Zhang

During our recent project team meeting with officials and advisers working on a proposal for changes in China's environmental regulatory system, one fundamental question underscored for the team the importance of our deliberations.[1] What form and scope of environmental legal system can realistically support China's role as the host of the world's manufacturing operations?

Much of the global attention that China has received centers on the extent and nature of the burden that this role demands. This attention has resulted in numerous accounts that paint a very bleak picture of China's environmental challenges. These accounts have been reinforced by similarly somber descriptions of China's recent efforts to build a legal culture and system to address these challenges.[2]

Progress toward addressing China's environmental protection and related legal challenges is sometimes obscured by a legal culture that does not yet readily divulge or disseminate information that can be helpful to members of the regulatory and regulated communities alike.[3] With these issues in mind, the authors have prepared this chapter to provide readers with an introductory baseline of information on China's environmental regulatory system. This baseline serves to underscore the significant amount of positive work

Portions of this chapter were first published in Richard J. Ferris Jr. and Hongjun Zhang, "Reaching Out to the Rule of Law: China's Continuing Efforts to Develop an Effective Environmental Law Regime," *William and Mary Bill of Rights Journal* 11 (February 2003): 569–602.

underway toward a more robust environmental protection regime in China. It also describes the current status of China's environmental regulatory system and highlights for readers the productive and dynamic aspects of the system. Perhaps most importantly, the chapter provides examples of compliance challenges for investors and insights on approaches to address these challenges. For this discussion, the authors draw from their more than two decades of experience counseling transnational corporations, governments, and multilateral development organizations on China's regulatory system.

In particular, Part I of this chapter provides readers with a sense of the scope and characteristics of China's increasingly multifaceted and acute environmental problems. Part II provides background on China's environmental law framework, including descriptions of key national and local legal norms and lawmaking institutions. Part III discusses key government environmental law implementation approaches, including baseline information on the development and prosecution of environmental enforcement actions. Part IV recounts examples of compliance challenges and insights into approaches to such challenges based on the authors' observations in representing foreign investors and working or negotiating with Chinese government authorities.

China's Environment

Recent examples of environmental pollution and natural resource degradation issues faced by the investment community, government, and private citizens in China highlight the broad spectrum of China's environmental and related health challenges. These challenges include drinking water shortages, such as those arising from the massive industrial accident in Chongqing municipality in December 2003.[4] They also include harmful children's health situations, such as the high congenital birth defect rates recently recorded in places such as Heshun County in Shanxi Province.[5] In fact, at any moment in contemporary China, company managers, government officials, and ordinary citizens are dealing with situations as diverse as environmental impact assessment approvals,[6] product ecolabeling procedures,[7] genetically modified organism (GMO) imports and exports,[8] or toxic chemical exposures.[9]

Additionally, it is apparent that international environmental issues are inexorably tied to China's domestic environmental burdens. Klaus Toepfer, executive director of the United Nations Environment Programme, has commented that "[w]ith 1.3 billion people and an official goal to quadruple economic growth by 2020, China's environmental performance will not only determine the well-being of its own people but will have consequences for the whole planet."[10] This statement is supported by recent and growing evidence of the transboundary environmental implications of China's development boom. In 2002, environmental monitoring stations located at the peak of Hawaii's Mount Loa reportedly identified the presence of five-to-ten-day-old arsenic, copper, and zinc in emissions from Chinese smelting operations.[11] Furthermore, increasingly severe dust storms resulting, in large part, from desertification occurring throughout China have played havoc with air quality and transportation in China and neighboring countries such as Japan and the Republic of Korea.[12] Plumes of dust from these storms have been identified even in the mainland United States, reportedly transported via the jet stream.[13]

One positive aspect of these environmental developments is that they, in large part, have motivated meetings between high-level government officials in the affected countries to discuss possible solutions to China's progressive environmental problems. For example, the environmental ministers of China, Japan, and South Korea met in Beijing for the Fifth Tripartite Environment Ministers Meeting (TEMM) on December 13–15, 2003.[14] The ministers' discussions were focused largely on the problem of transboundary "dust" emanating from China.

The environmental implications of China's rapid development have also led to the inclusion of environmental issues on the diplomatic agendas of other countries and regions, such as the European Community. On November 12, 2003, the European Union (EU) and China signed a political agreement on strengthening environmental cooperation. The agreement outlined a number of ongoing and proposed areas of environmental support, including general cooperation on the implementation of environmental treaties and specific programs on climate change, biodiversity, water, clean production, energy efficiency, automobile emissions standards, and law enforcement.[15]

Despite the welcome infusion of political and technical support from foreign governments and their high-level officials, meaningful advancements in China's environmental law regime often are founded on political will and hard work "on the ground" in China. These advancements involve the efforts of individuals who undertake the actual law-drafting, implementation, and compliance-assurance work on a day-to-day basis. Similarly, lasting improvements in China's environmental legal system require that these individuals are actively and positively engaged by members of the regulated community. The need for a truly collaborative approach to improving the environmental legal system is underscored by the complexity of China's legal system and culture, as described in the subsequent sections.

China's Environmental Law Framework

Key Aspects of China's Environmental Lawmaking System

The principal institutions responsible for the enactment or promulgation of laws or legal norm-creating documents are identified in China's constitution.[16]

National People's Congress

The Constitution provides that the National People's Congress (NPC) is the highest legislative body in China. The NPC is empowered by the Constitution to enact and amend "fundamental" national statutes,[17] including statutes related to the establishment and organization of certain government institutions (that is, "organic statutes").[18]

The Standing Committee within the NPC is authorized to enact and amend all national laws (including statutes and other legal norm-setting instruments in the areas of environmental protection and natural resource conservation) with the exception of fundamental national statutes. Nonetheless, during times when the NPC is not in session,[19] the Standing Committee may supplement and amend laws enacted by the NPC, but only insofar as these supplements and amendments do not contravene the laws' "fundamental principles." Significantly, the NPC may revise or annul inappropriate decisions made by its Standing Committee.[20] In turn, the Standing Committee may revise or annul inappropriate national administrative regulations or local regulations that are promulgated by lower-level national and local administrative bodies.

The General Office of the NPC gathers input from specialized NPC committees and the State Council to put together a Five-Year Legislative Plan, which guides the legislative work of the NPC in five-year periods. The current NPC Five-Year Legislative Plan covers the term 2003–8. The current version of this plan (as of this writing) contains a number of proposals to draft environmental protection and natural resource conservation statutes. These include proposals to develop a Renewable Energy Development and Use Promotion Law (*Ke zai sheng nengyuan kaifa liyong cujin fa*), an amendment to the Land Administration Law (*Tudi guanli fa*), and an amendment to the Law on the Prevention of Environmental Pollution from Solid Waste (*Guti feiwu wuran huanjing fangzhi fa*).

NPC Legislative Committees

As mentioned above, the NPC has established a number of specialized advisory committees with responsibility for drafting national laws and overseeing implementation of these laws at the national and local levels. These committees, which currently number nine, address specific areas of law and are composed of congressional representatives with expertise and background relevant to their committees.[21]

The committee with primary responsibility for environmental protection, including issues related to the management of natural resources, is the Environmental Protection and Natural Resources Conservation Committee. Currently, there are twenty-eight members of this committee. While many of these committees were established as part of the Chinese government's attempt to streamline and reinforce the lawmaking process, they do not have the authority to override the power of the State Council and its administrative departments to propose draft legislation.[22] Other NPC objectives behind the formation of these committees include (1) concentrating expertise in specific subject areas to inform and improve the lawmaking process, and (2) expanding NPC influence over the development of national and local law (Figure 3.1).

State Council and State Council Administrative Departments

Below the NPC is the State Council. The State Council is China's highest administrative organ and the executive authority of the NPC. The council's functions and powers include the authority to (1) approve and promulgate national administrative regulations, (2) issue decisions and orders in accordance with the Constitution and other laws, (3) review legislative proposals for referral to the NPC or its Standing Committee, and (4) oversee the work of its underlying ministries and commissions.[23] In the area of oversight, it is generally true that the State Council may alter or annul inappropriate regulations of its underlying ministries and commissions.[24] The State Council includes a special office in charge of legal issues: the Office of Legislative Affairs. This office prepares the State Council's annual and five-year legislative drafting plans. These plans are an important indicator of which legal initiatives will likely be the foci of Chinese government and international resources in the near term (Figure 3.2).[25]

Under the State Council are its various ministries and other administrative departments.[26] In addition to the State Environmental Protection Agency (SEPA), these include numerous other government authorities with responsibilities that include or affect environmental protection.

An exhaustive list of the State Council's administrative departments with responsibilities involving environmental protection issues is beyond the scope of this chapter. Nevertheless, it is worth noting—if only to underscore the complexity of navigating multiple and sometimes overlapping or inconsistent

Figure 3.1 **Schematic Overview of the Modern Statute-making Process in China**

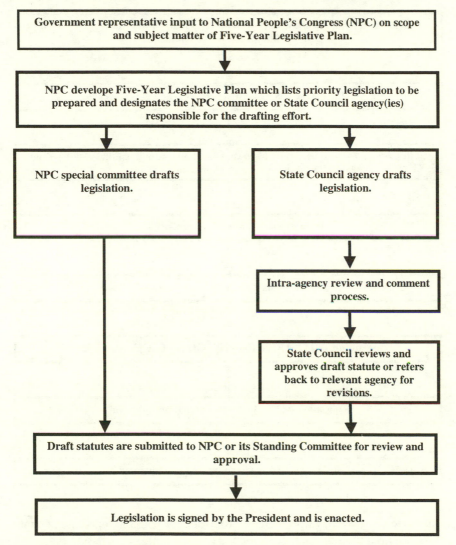

administrative agency requirements—key State Council administrative departments with environmental responsibilities (Box 3.1).

These and other administrative departments, akin to executive agencies in the United States, are authorized to make "ministerial regulations" within their areas of competence (that is, pollution control for SEPA and agricultural management for the Ministry of Agriculture). Administrative departments under

Figure 3.2 **Schematic Overview of the State-Council Rulemaking Process in China**

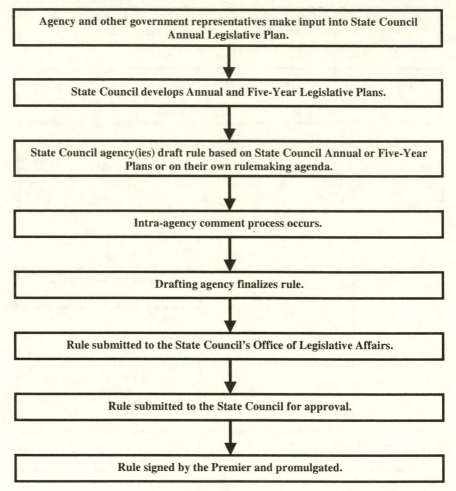

Agency and other government representatives make input into State Council Annual Legislative Plan.

State Council develops Annual and Five-Year Legislative Plans.

State Council agency(ies) draft rule based on State Council Annual or Five-Year Plans or on their own rulemaking agenda.

Intra-agency comment process occurs.

Drafting agency finalizes rule.

Rule submitted to the State Council's Office of Legislative Affairs.

Rule submitted to the State Council for approval.

Rule signed by the Premier and promulgated.

the State Council may also prepare proposals for national legislation ("statutes") within their areas of competence (Figure 3.3).

When completed, these legislative proposals typically are forwarded to the State Council for review and approval, and then are referred to the NPC for review and possible adoption. Drafts of regulations promulgated by the State Council constitute administrative regulations of the State Council. However, drafts of regulations prepared by ministries and administrative departments alone (that is, ministerial regulations) typically do not need to pass State Council review before the drafting ministries/administrative departments

---

Box 3.1

China's Key State Council Administrative Departments with Environmental Responsibilities

- General Customs Administration
- Ministry of Agriculture
- Ministry of Commerce
- Ministry of Communications
- Ministry of Construction
- Ministry of Education
- Ministry of Finance
- Ministry of Foreign Affairs
- Ministry of Information Industry
- Ministry of Justice
- Ministry of Land and Resources
- Ministry of Public Health
- Ministry of Public Security
- Ministry of Railways
- Ministry of Science and Technology
- Ministry of Water Resources
- National Forestry Agency
- State Administration of Quality Supervision, Inspection, and Quarantine
- State Development and Reform Commission
- State Environmental Protection Administration
- State Industry and Commerce Administration

---

promulgate the regulations. Nonetheless, the drafting departments often try to obtain comments from other agencies.

Provincial and Municipal Governments

At the provincial level, provincial people's congresses (and their standing committees) may issue local regulations, provided the latter do not contravene the Constitution, applicable national laws, and administrative and ministerial regulations. Provincial people's governments also may issue local regulations, provided the latter do not contravene regulations issued by the provincial people's congresses. In general, the lawmaking powers described in this section are provided under Section 5 of the Constitution (*Xianfa*).

Figure 3.3 Schematic Overview of the State-Council Agency Rulemaking Process in China

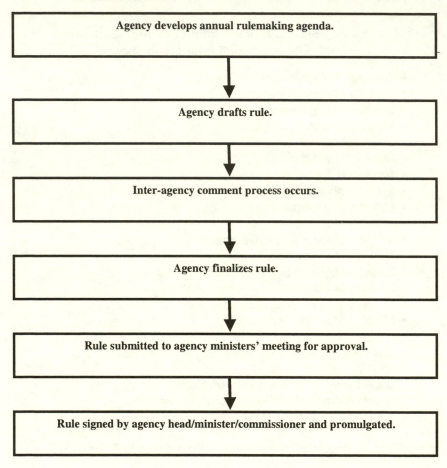

Four of China's municipalities, commonly referred to as "municipalities directly under the central government" or "special municipalities," have lawmaking powers corresponding to those of provincial governments. These municipalities are Beijing, Chongqing, Shanghai, and Tianjin. China's autonomous regions, including Inner Mongolia, Guangxi, Ningxia, Xizang (Tibet), and Xinjiang, also possess lawmaking powers similar to those of the provinces.

At the local government level, municipal people's congresses may promulgate local regulations to supplement or implement national and provincial laws and administrative regulations. These laws serve the same functions as provincial laws and are subject to restrictions similar to those at the provincial level, except that these regulations also must not contravene regulations issued by the people's congress of the province in which the municipal government is situated.[27] Municipal people's congresses must receive approval from their provincial people's congress of draft municipal regulations before promulgating them.[28] Increasingly, local governments are the "trendsetters" in China with respect to the development of influential legal measures, particularly for protection of the environment.

Special Economic Zones

Special Economic Zones (SEZs) serve a unique function in China.[29] Chinese national and local governments have established thousands of SEZs throughout the country over the past ten years.[30] This rapid proliferation has aroused concern and increased scrutiny at the national government level. Subnational governments have established these zones at the provincial, municipal, and even county levels. Located predominately in the eastern and southern coastal regions of China, SEZs are granted authority to offer special tax and other incentives to attract foreign investment. Generally, the laws of the municipality in which the SEZ is located apply to activities within the SEZ. For example, in 1992 the NPC authorized the Shenzhen Municipal People's Congress (with jurisdiction over the Shenzhen SEZ at the border with Hong Kong) to promulgate local regulations that would apply specifically to the Shenzhen SEZ.[31]

While a municipality typically would not be permitted to differentially regulate separate areas of the municipality, it can legitimately regulate an SEZ differently so long as (1) it receives NPC authorization and (2) the regulations applying to the SEZ do not contravene the Constitution, national and provincial laws, and administrative and ministerial regulations. In this context, it is important to emphasize that the national government can issue laws that address specific jurisdictions. In fact, the national government, via the central environmental agency, has issued environmental regulations that apply to foreign economic development regions. These include the *Dui wai jingji kaifang diqu huanjing guanli zanxing guiding* (Interim Regulations on Environmental Management for Economic Regions Open to Foreign Investment), promulgated by the National Environmental Protection Agency (now SEPA) on March 15, 1986, effective the same date.

Key National and Local Environmental Laws

Largely as a response to the country's environmental challenges, China's law- and policymakers are developing one of the region's most dynamic environmental law frameworks. At present, this framework includes roughly twenty statutes, more than forty State Council regulations, approximately 500 standards, and more than 600 other legal-norm-creating documents addressing primarily pollution control, natural resource conservation, and the management of the environmental aspects of consumer products (Figure 3.4).[32] Our recent count indicates that environmental laws at the provincial and municipal levels alone likely total more than 1,000.

In recent years, the number of compilations and databases of Chinese laws has increased significantly. The increase is due, in part, to the fact that many Chinese administrative agencies do not yet have a publicly available "official gazette" or other central publication for their administrative laws. Thus, members of the regulatory and regulated communities are relying largely on internal or external efforts to produce compilations and databases of Chinese laws.[33] One distinct problem with this procedure is that it often makes it very difficult to be sure that a particular compilation or database of laws is comprehensive and accurate.

Adding to this regime are China's obligations under more than eighty bilateral and multilateral environmental treaties.[34] Former premier Zhu Rongji reinforced China's commitment to assume responsibilities to reduce greenhouse gases when, on September 3, 2002, at the World Summit on Sustainable Development, he announced that China was moving forward to ratify the Kyoto Protocol to the Framework Convention on Climate Change (FCCC).[35] These accords often provide needed financial and other support to develop and implement domestic environmental laws by the institutions indicated above.[36]

National Environmental Laws

In 1979, the NPC Standing Committee enacted China's first environmental statute, the Environmental Protection Law (EPL).[37] Essentially, the EPL establishes fundamental concepts for environmental protection that often are reflected in subsequently adopted laws. Some of these concepts are described in Box 3.2.

The EPL was prepared as a general environmental law focusing on pollution control. Thus, the law is potentially applicable to all pollution-generating activities. Natural resource issues are addressed in the law only as they relate to pollution-control management. In his previous capacity as legislative director with the NPC Environmental Protection and Natural Resource Conservation Committee, one author of this chapter, Hongjun Zhang was involved in recent NPC discussions regarding the pollution-control focus of the EPL. A draft Natural Resource Conservation Law also was discussed. However, this draft has been tabled for possible discussion at a later, undetermined date.

Figure 3.4 **Schematic Overview of the Hierarchy of Laws in China**

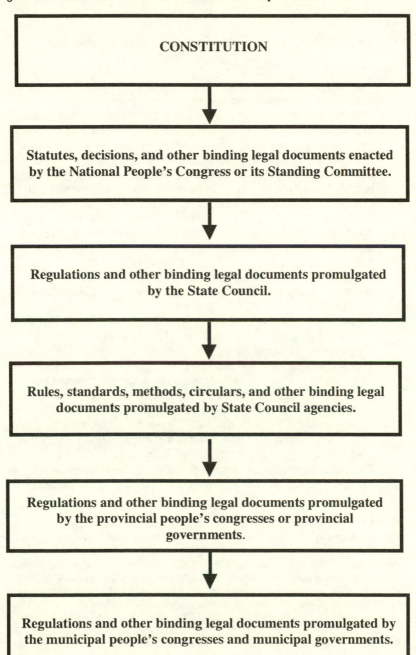

Box 3.2

Key Principles Set Forth in China's Environmental Protection Law*

- Individuals may report or file charges against those who cause pollution or otherwise damage the environment (art. 6);
- People's governments of provinces, autonomous regions, and municipalities directly under the Central Government may establish local pollutant discharge standards for activities not specified in national standards; for those items that are already indicated in national standards, these people's governments may establish local standards that are more stringent than those at the national government level and report these standards to SEPA (art. 10);
- Those who construct facilities that cause pollution must observe laws addressing environmental protection for such projects (art. 13);
- Measures must be undertaken to protect the ecological environment during the development or use of natural resources (art. 19);
- Technologies for the prevention and control of pollution at a facility/construction project must be (1) designed, (2) built, and (3) engaged concurrently with the principal part of the facility or construction project (art. 26);**
- Enterprises or institutions that cause severe environmental pollution will be required to eliminate and control such pollution within a specified time period (art. 29);
- Technologies or facilities that fail to meet the requirements set forth in environmental protection laws shall be banned (art. 30); and
- Entities shall not transfer facilities that cause severe pollution to entities that are unable to prevent and control such pollution (art. 34).

Notes: *For an English translation of the Environmental Protection Law of the People's Republic of China, see www.zhb.gov.cn/english/law_detail.php3?id=3.

**This concept often is referred to as the "three synchronizations" or "three simultaneities" principle. More simply put, this principle requires that pollution control equipment design, construction, and operation are undertaken at the same time as design, construction, and operation of the associated facility or construction project. *Guanyu ru he rending jianshe xiangmu weifan "san tong shi" zhidu wenti de fuhan* (Interpretive Letter on the Question of How to Identify Whether a Construction Project Has Violated the "Three Simultaneities" System) (Nat'l Envtl. Prot. Agency, Mar. 17, 1994). *Law Information System.* As noted earlier in this chapter, the National Environmental Protection Agency is the precursor to SEPA.

Box 3.3

Key Chinese Environmental Statutes

- The Air Pollution Prevention and Control Law (*Daqi wuran fangzhi fa*, 1987, amended 1995, 2000)
- The Clean Production Promotion Law (*Qingjie shengchan cujin fa*, 2002)
- The Desertification Prevention Law (*Fang shazhi sha fa*, 2001)
- The Energy Conservation Law (*Jieyue nengyuan fa*, 1997)
- The Environmental Impact Assessment Law (*Huanjing yingxiang pingjia fa*, 2002)
- The Environmental Noise Pollution Control Law (*Huanjing zaosheng wuran kongzhi fa*, 1996)
- The Fisheries Law (*Yu ye fa*, 1986)
- The Flood Prevention Law (*Fang hong fa*, 1997)
- The Forestry Law (*Senlin fa*, 1984, amended 1998)
- The Grasslands Law (*Caoyuan fa*, 1985)
- The Land Administration Law (*Tudi guanli fa*, 1986, amended 1998)
- The Law on the Prevention of Environmental Pollution Caused by Solid Waste (*Guti feiwu wuran huanjing fangzhi fa*, 1995)
- The Marine Environmental Protection Law (*Haiyang huanjing baohu fa*, 1982, amended 1999)
- The Radioactive Pollution Prevention and Control Law (*Fangshexing wuran fangzhi fa*, 2003)
- The Mineral Resource Law (*Kuangzhan ziyuan fa*, 1986, amended 1996)
- The Water and Soil Conservation Law (*Shuitu baochi fa*, 1991)
- The Water Law (*Shui fa*, 1988, amended 2002)
- The Water Pollution Prevention and Control Law (*Shui wuran fangzhi fa*, 1984, amended 1996)
- The Wildlife Protection Law (*Yesheng dongwu baohu fa*, 1988)

Since the enactment of the EPL, the NPC has adopted approximately twenty statutes primarily addressing pollution control, natural resource conservation, and product stewardship. Because an increasing number of nonenvironment-specific statutes include provisions related to the environment, it is difficult to determine with accuracy the exact number of pollution control, natural resource conservation, and product stewardship statutes. A list of key statutes in these areas appears in Box 3.3.

At lower levels of authority, beneath the statutes, are the State Council regulations and other legal-norm-creating documents issued by the State

Council and State Council administrative departments. As mentioned earlier, the State Council has issued roughly forty regulations that specifically address pollution control, natural resource conservation, and product stewardship. However, if the standards and other legal-norm-creating documents (for example, documents whose English translations are "catalogs," "interpretive letters," "circulars," "decisions," "methods," "measures," and "penalty procedures") are added to this number, the count may far exceed 1,000. Thus, while there may be areas of environmental law not yet addressed by national statutes, most subjects or activities generally considered to be within the purview of environmental law are addressed to some extent in China by one or more legal-norm-creating documents. This growing coverage in itself attests to the increasing complexity of this area of the law in China. What remains is to consider whether and how these statutes are being implemented.

Given the breadth of topical coverage at this level, members of the regulated community are well advised to look beyond statutory provisions when these provisions (1) do not address a particular activity or product or (2) address a particular product or activity in ambiguous terms. Notwithstanding the legal research hurdles that individuals concerned with understanding environmental requirements may face in China, these individuals are advised to assume that legal measures to address a particular environmental issue *do* exist—unless the results of extensive research and information received from government authorities prove otherwise.[38] Particular legal research challenges include a lack of agency rulemaking transparency, information access, and a general legal culture that still favors reliance on the instructions of authority figures over the texts of laws.

Local Environmental Laws

As noted above, local (provincial and lower-level government) environmental laws may exceed 1,000 pieces of legislation. Given the information-access challenges in China that are daunting even at the national government level, it is easy to imagine that a clear understanding of the scope and nature of local environmental laws is a complex task.

Local people's congresses and governments are required by Chinese law to submit newly adopted legal measures to the national government for the record. For instance, China's Constitution provides that "[t]he people's congresses of provinces and municipalities directly under the Central Government and their standing committees . . . shall report . . . local regulations to the Standing Committee of the National People's Congress" (art. 100). Information on the level of compliance with this requirement is inadequate to determine clearly the likely percentage of local environmental laws actually recorded with the national government.

However, through our day-to-day discussions with national government officials in China, we found that local governments periodically but inconsistently report new legal measures to their national counterparts. Local government agencies often do not have financial and personnel resources to devote to such tasks. However, national government authorities responsible for overseeing local environmental law development and implementation believe that more complete access to local laws is essential for them to fulfill their job responsibilities. Without such access, the national officials do not have the resources they need to determine whether local government authorities are complying with the fundamental legal standards set forth in national laws.

Against this backdrop, the authors note that local environmental laws typically address subjects covered in the majority of national environmental laws. For example, numerous provincial, autonomous region, and municipal laws essentially give local effect to national statutes covering general environmental protection and water and air pollution prevention and control issues (Box 3.4).

However, increasingly, local lawmaking activities move beyond the topical parameters set by national law and are helpful indicators of trends.[39] The NPC Environmental Protection and Natural Resource Conservation Committee, SEPA, and other national governmental bodies with environmental agendas monitor such local activities to identify similar or divergent approaches to environmental protection issues that may signal appropriate subjects for national laws. Recent examples of growing lawmaking trends at the local level include substance bans and waste minimization and recycling measures addressing the control of single-use or "throw-away" utensils and bags. For instance, the following local laws in these areas have attracted national government attention:

- Jiangsu Province Management Measures on the Prevention of Pollution from Single-Use Plastic Food Utensils and Plastic Bags (*Jiangsu sheng yicixing suliao canju he suliaodai wuran fangzhi guanli banfa*, issued September 22, 2000)
- Beijing Municipal Management Measures Limiting the Sale and Use of Plastic Bags and Single-Use Plastic Food Utensils (*Beijing shi xianzhi xiaoshou shiyong suliadai he yicixing suliao canju guanli banfa*, promulgated May 1, 1999)
- Guangzhou Municipal Rules Prohibiting the Manufacture, Distribution, and Sale of Single-Use, Non-Biodegradable Plastic Food Utensils (*Guangzhou shi jinzhi shengchan jingxiao shiyong yicixing bu ke jiang jie suliao canju guiding*, promulgated June 16, 1997)

Box 3.4

Examples of Key Provincial-Level and Municipal Laws

Provincial, Special Municipality, and Autonomous Region (Provincial-Level) Laws

- Beijing Implementing Measures for the "Water Pollution Prevention and Control Law of the People's Republic of China" (*Beijing shi shi shi "Zhonghua renmin gong he guo shui wuran fangzhi fa" banfa*, promulgated May 15, 2002)
- Hunan Province Measures on the Prevention of Pollution from Vehicle Emissions (*Hunan sheng jidong chepai qi wuran fangzhi banfa*, promulgated Feb. 12, 2001)
- Guangxi Zhuang Autonomous Region Environmental Protection Regulations (*Guangxi zhuang zizhiqu huanjing baohu tiaoli*, promulgated Mar. 26, 1999)
- Tianjin Municipal Air Pollution Prevention Regulations (*Tianjin shi daqi wuran fangzhi tiaoli*, promulgated July 18, 2002)

Municipal Laws

- Changchun Municipal Management Measures on the Prevention of Air Pollution (*Changchun shi daqi wuran fangzhi guanli banfa*, issued Sept. 11, 1993)
- Dalian Municipal People's Government Circular on Further Control of Air Pollution (*Dalian shi renmin zhengfu guanyu jinyibu kongzhi daqi wuran de tongzhi*, promulgated Aug. 17, 2000)
- Harbin Municipal Management Measures on the Prevention of Water Pollution (*Harbin shi shui wuran fangzhi guanli banfa*, promulgated Nov. 1, 2000)
- Suzhou Municipal Implementing Details on Rewarding and Reporting Violations of Environmental Protection Laws (*Suzhou shi jubao weifan huanjing baohu fa xin wei jiangli shishi xize*, issued Feb. 1, 2001)

- Xiamen Municipal Management Regulations Prohibiting the Sale and Use of Detergents Containing Phosphorous (*Xiamen shi jinzhi xiaoshou shiyong hanlin xi di ji guanli guiding*, issued December 29, 1999).

These laws often reflect environmental priorities for the localities. National environmental authorities such as SEPA generally favor independent local lawmaking initiatives addressing such priorities, particularly if the national authorities believe that national action on such issues may be premature. On the other hand, if particular issues, such as waste minimization or materials restrictions, are being viewed as priority issues by an expanding number of local governments, SEPA or other national authorities may determine that the time is appropriate for the national government to address the issue and set a national legal "baseline" for that issue. Furthermore, for certain issues viewed locally as priorities, national authorities may promote joint "pilot projects" with local governments to test the efficacy of certain legal approaches before developing the national rules. For example, SEPA piloted locally a number of projects in the areas of discharge fee collection and use prior to promulgating a national law governing this issue.

Implementation of China's Environmental Laws

Legal Underpinnings and Enforcement Procedures

China's environmental law enforcement system is based largely on internal protocols and longstanding practice at the national and local government levels. The general lack of publicly available documentation of enforcement practices and procedures increases the regulated community's feelings of unpredictability, unfairness, and helplessness concerning, in particular, law enforcement in the environmental sector in China.

Calls from within and without China for increased access to environmental enforcement procedures have led to recent efforts to publicly record procedures that formerly were embedded in internal protocols or simply based on agency practice. These efforts include the SEPA Administrative Penalty Procedures (*Xingzheng chu fa gongzuo chengxu*, promulgated February 2, 2001). These procedures set forth guidelines that national and local enforcement staff must follow to establish, investigate, and implement the penalty phase of enforcement actions for violations of national and local environmental law in China.[40] The procedures also record case-management requirements to protect the integrity of case evidence. SEPA promulgated these procedures and reportedly transmitted them to provincial environmental authorities as guidelines for environmental enforcement actions.

Increasingly, Chinese national government authorities are also focusing on legal provisions that expand on the general penalties indicated in environmental statutes and related measures. These provisions make available to enforcement officers added information on available enforcement options for various environmental violations. Furthermore, more specialized measures provide regulators and regulated community members with additional clarity concerning the range of available enforcement options. Nevertheless, these measures share with other environmental laws attributes such as insufficient definitions that limit their efficacy and increase regulated communities' uncertainty concerning the possible legal ramifications of particular national environmental law violations. Examples of penalty measures include the Measures on Administrative Penalties for Environmental Protection (*Huanjing baohu xingzheng chufa banfa*) (promulgated August 6, 1999).

Despite the growth in legal instruments that publicly describe procedures and penalties to guide enforcement actions, unwritten protocols and practices and written internal communications still guide a significant amount of environmental activities. In this respect, the authors offer the following observations concerning processing enforcement actions. These observations address three principal stages of enforcement: case initiation, investigation, and penalty assessment.

Case Initiation

The requirements for establishing a case are described in the Administrative Penalty Procedures mentioned above. However, national and local environmental authorities often base their decisions to launch an enforcement action on widely varying factors. Typically, cases are initiated based on findings from scheduled or spot inspection programs or visits; citizen complaints received by national and local officials via letter or phone calls, including calls to environmental "hotlines"; media reports; and information received from day-to-day communications among national and local environmental and other government authorities. Of course, not all information on environmental infractions or problems results in enforcement actions. Chinese environmental authorities at the national and local levels commonly face inspection and enforcement staff and budget limitations. Therefore, these authorities often proceed based on "firefighting": addressing first those cases they deem most serious. Based on our discussions with local and national inspection and enforcement staff, they consider a number of factors, any of which may influence their decision to initiate an enforcement case. Such factors include whether the:

- Violation presents potential or actual serious harm to human health and/or the environment
- Matter falls within agency or national government enforcement priority areas
- Incident occurred in an environmentally sensitive location or zone
- Violation involves fraud or withholding information from government authorities

- Agency is receiving political pressure to act on the matter
- Media attention on the matter has identified or called for urgent official action
- Violator has an exemplary or notorious environmental record
- Violation potentially or clearly involves criminal infractions
- Violation involves violations of nonenvironmental laws and requires coordination with other government authorities
- Staff or budgetary limitations require alternative approaches to enforcement.

Based on our experiences in these matters involving national government officials, the following criteria are key factors in their decisions whether to intervene in local enforcement matters. These include whether the:

- Violation involves jurisdictional questions such as whether national or local government authorities have the responsibility for environmental approvals at the violation site
- National authorities believe local authorities have insufficiently or inappropriately handled an inspection or enforcement matter
- Public outcry concerning a local enforcement matter is such that national authorities believe that formal national intervention or informal support in the matter is warranted
- Violation involves provincial requests to transfer the case to national authorities
- Violation involves transprovincial environmental issues, regardless of the existence of transfer requests
- National government leaders instructed national authorities to intervene
- Violation has received international community attention.

Case Investigation

After government authorities decide to initiate an environmental enforcement action, they begin or expand the investigation of the specific facts surrounding the case. Typical investigations include site inspections; reviews of compliance and violation records; interviews with management teams and plant employees, victims, witnesses, and local residents; and review of plant environmental control technology; as well as tests of wastewater discharges, groundwater, air, and other media in the area surrounding the incident or violation.

The investigations are generally conducted by the relevant environmental authorities in the jurisdictions in which the violations occur. However, depending on the above limitations and considerations, a case may be deemed of national significance requiring the intervention of national authorities in the investigation process. SEPA is increasingly proactive in its involvement in local enforcement matters. For instance, from December 26 to 28, 2003, SEPA Vice Minister Pan Yue led a group of national enforcement officials to conduct, with local officials, surprise inspections of more than forty facilities suspected of serious environmental infractions in the border regions of Shanxi, Shaanxi, and Inner Mongolia provinces.[41]

Penalty Assessment

Penalties for violations are specified in environmental statutes, related implementing measures, and in specialized "penalty" provisions. Depending on the seriousness of the violations, typical penalties that enforcement officers may assess include warnings, corrective action orders (with or without specific deadlines for correction), orders to report or publish specific company information, orders for victim compensation, fines, withholding of operational or import licenses, and facility shut-down orders. A significant number of environmental law violators in China are state-owned enterprises. Consequently, many Chinese local and national environmental authorities and their enforcement partners "negotiate" with state-owned violators, whereby the ultimate penalty assessments involve considerations such as the potential impacts of penalties on economic development and local employment. Other such considerations, more generally applied to the penalty phase, can include whether the:

- Violator has the capacity to pay a particular fine or compensation amount
- Violator is a state-owned enterprise (SOE) and therefore may simply pass on the cost of the penalty to the government or local economy
- Violation involves contamination of natural resources that will need to be remediated/recovered
- Case involves multiple violations.

In some instances, local enforcement officer discretion over whether a violator has the capacity to pay a particular fine or compensation amount can lead to differential enforcement treatment of foreign and local members of the regulated community. For example, the local enforcement officer's perception that a particular multinational has unlimited capacity to pay fines or compensation may result in the assessment of the highest fines for a specific violation. Whereas, the perception that a local company has limited financial capacity may lead to the assessment of the lowest, or no, fines for the same infraction. It is noteworthy that, outside the administrative penalty process, the Chinese judicial system may impose civil and criminal penalties on environmental law violators.

Enforcement Resources

As part of China's longstanding goal to improve the implementation of environmental laws, in April 2002 SEPA announced its plans to open the Environmental Emergency and Incident Investigation Center (EEIIC). According to the Circular on the Establishment of the SEPA Environmental Emergency and Incident Investigation Center (*Guanyu zujian guojia huanjing baohu zongju huanjing ying ji yushi gu diaocha zhongxin de tongzhi*, 2002) and our conversations with SEPA officials, the EEIIC is charged with fulfilling the following responsibilities:

- Investigating and supervising violations of Chinese law involving environmental pollution and ecological degradation
- Coordinating resolution of "transboundary environmental disputes" (involving more than one provincial jurisdiction)
- Inspecting environmentally polluted sites for possible evidence concerning violations of environmental laws
- Assisting SEPA to formulate policies and standards applicable to the enforcement of environmental laws.

Under the limits imposed by the circular, the EEIIC has the authority to hire a maximum of forty-five enforcement officers. While the addition of this many officers dedicated to investigation and enforcement issues is a boon to SEPA's environmental law implementation capacity, by no means will they suffice over the long term. Not including the individuals retained pursuant to the above circular nor individuals from other agencies that support SEPA enforcement activities, SEPA's present personnel-hiring authority is limited to 200 officers by State Council regulation.[42]

The establishment of the EEIIC represents SEPA's institutional response to repeated calls from the regulated and regulating communities alike for enhanced resources to implement environmental laws in China. In their discussions with us on enforcement issues, SEPA officials communicated the hope that this new institution will be the first in a series of capacity-building initiatives aimed at reinforcing the links between China's environmental laws and on-the-ground compliance with them. To this end, in 2003, SEPA converted the EEIIC into a full-fledged bureau within SEPA, named the "Supervision and Enforcement Bureau."

Another initiative that reaches beyond, but may reinforce, the implementation of environmental laws in China is the State Economic and Trade Commission's (SETC) establishment in 2002 of general counsel positions within "key state-owned enterprises."[43] According to this initiative, every "key state-owned enterprise" (SOE) designated by the SETC (or its successor) is required to establish the position of general counsel with overall responsibility for ensuring the SOE's compliance with China's laws.

It is still too early to predict whether the added enforcement and compliance resources discussed above will be successful. They serve, however, as evidence of China's acknowledgment of the need to bolster the existing environmental law implementation regime. They also represent a belief on the part of the Chinese government, however transient at this point, in mechanisms that give force to China's multitude of legal texts. This manifestation of the government's confidence in the legal system may serve as sufficient incentive to China's experienced and new generations of regulatory officials to encourage such initiatives further.

Compliance Challenges and Approaches

The following are examples of compliance challenges associated with China's modern environmental legal system. At the beginning of each section, the authors pose a question aimed at providing insights into approaches to address the particular compliance challenge. The authors draw from their experiences counseling multinational and other clients in the environmental sector in China. While these examples are particularly applicable to the corporate context, they also provide insights for other stakeholders in China's legal system.

Ambiguity of Legal Measures

When ambiguities in the legal text arise, do you seek verbal or written interpretations from the government authority responsible for interpreting the legal text?

Generally speaking, the officials responsible for interpreting national laws (and local laws implementing national laws) are based at the national government level (SEPA, for example). Ambiguities in legal measures include undefined terms in key laws, such as the Regulation on Mercury Content Limitation for Batteries (*Guanyu xianzhi dianchi chanpin gonghanling de guiding*), jointly issued by nine government agencies on December 31, 1997.[44] This regulation specifies requirements for a mercury-content label but does not indicate how the label should appear or what text should be placed in the label. This omission leaves open the question of whether symbols or Chinese characters would satisfy the requirement to indicate the mercury content on the label.

Without specificity in the laws, recourse is often made to the interpretive authorities. For members of the regulated community, the risk in this approach is that different authorities may have different verbal interpretations of the legal measures in question. Compliance risk could be minimized if the interpretations were compiled in a published guidance document and made available to the authorities, if not the public, to help prevent conflicting interpretations.

Chinese authorities generally are reluctant to issue written interpretations, particularly when members of the regulated community request the interpretation. This practice is changing, however, at certain agencies such as SEPA. Requests for written interpretations, reliance on existing written interpretations,[45] and exchanges of letters confirming that a compliance approach described by the company or other stakeholder is acceptable to authorities are increasing at certain agencies in China. Very gradually, these practices are reducing the ambiguity and resultant riskiness of broadly drafted Chinese laws.

Limited Rulemaking Notice and Opportunities for Comment and Related Advocacy

In situations in which you learn of an opportunity to comment on a proposed rule, or learn that a proposed rule will pose significant problems for your interests, how do you undertake government advocacy?

Many investors in China bring expectations regarding rulemaking notice and comment derived from their nations' more participatory legal regimes. Notice and comment on proposed laws, despite the focus that this practice has received in association with China's accession to the World Trade Organization (WTO) in 2001, is evolving at an inconsistent pace among Chinese agencies. Even so, a number of agencies are becoming increasingly receptive to outside input on draft measures. Nevertheless, while laws may refer to comment opportunities, China currently has no official administrative procedure for notice of draft measures or outside input on draft laws.

This lack is evident from recent lawmaking practiced in the environmental sector. For example, with respect to biological safety issues, the State Council issued the Management Regulation on Transgenic Agricultural Organism Safety (*Nongye zhuan jiyin shengwu anquan guanli tiaoli*) on May

23, 2001. The regulation entered into effect on the same day; however, it was not released to the public until June 5, 2001. On June 17, 2002, the Ministry of Health (MOH) released for public comment a package of three draft documents concerning genetically modified food evaluation and approval procedures. However, highlighting the need for a more robust understanding of effective notice and comment practices, the deadline for receipt of public comments on these documents was June 24, 2002 (only one week later).

To assess beneficial government advocacy approaches in situations in which comment on draft measures is possible and critical, it is helpful to understand the stringent resource capacities of Chinese agencies, including those in the environmental sector. While many Chinese agencies are under pressure to increase comment opportunities, few agencies have increased the staff responsible for effecting and responding to outside comment on proposed laws. As a result, agency officials may respond very negatively to massive stakeholder input on proposed measures. Essentially, the few officials responsible for drafting new laws are the same individuals who must respond to stakeholder comments and questions. Indeed, there may be only one individual with primary responsibility for a particular rulemaking initiative. If this law affects thousands of companies, this individual may face thousands of phone calls, e-mails, and visits. In this context, at least until more agency resources are allocated to respond to notice and comment issues, government authorities may prefer to engage on rulemaking issues with organizations representing multiple stakeholders rather than with individual stakeholders.

On matters unrelated to rulemaking per se, there is also an expanding amount of day-to-day lobbying activities that serve a critical role in acclimating government decision makers to more participatory policymaking. The significant number of Chinese participants in this type of government advocacy, which increasingly involves Chinese companies alone or in partnership with foreign organizations, also plays an important part in underscoring with Chinese officials the importance of building consensus with stakeholders on national laws and policies. What remains is to subject this process to written, meaningful, and public rules.

Gradual Implementation of Environmental Laws

When you learn of a new environmental law, do you assume that compliance is possible or necessary as of the law's effective date?

Chinese authorities often devote limited lawmaking resources to develop a new legal measure. When these measures are promulgated, they indicate a date for "entry into force." On its face, it would appear that this date refers to the time when compliance with the law is necessary. However, ambiguities in the law aside, it is likely that key implementing rules, lists, application forms, and other documents may not be available as of the date of the law's entry into force. For instance, China's Management Regulations on the Registration of Dangerous Chemicals (*Weixian huaxuepin dengji guanli banfa*) and Management Regulations on Licensing for Business and Sale of Dangerous Chemicals (*Weixian huaxuepin jingying xukezheng guanli banfa*) entered into force on November 15, 2002. However, the implementing rules for these regulations were not issued until November 21, 2002. Additionally, the registration/licensing application forms for these regulations were not published until January 2003. Generally speaking, key measures are issued at different times because the officials responsible for preparing the laws face significant time and other resource restraints. Hence, it is rare that laws are issued simultaneously with their implementing measures and supporting documents, in a single "package."

With this reality in mind, being accustomed to compliance landmarks is helpful. "Compliance landmarks" refer to phases during the Chinese law implementation process at which companies can undertake particular activities aimed at fulfilling legal requirements. Using the above example in the dangerous chemicals area, developing a "compliance landmark" approach in China would involve a "first phase" of compliance upon the entry into force of the regulations, a "second phase" at the issuance of the rules implementing the regulations, and a third phase involving completion of the application forms. If companies are involved, this approach would involve educating local company units about the need to establish phased compliance goals and educating company headquarters about the realities of phased compliance in China.

Agency Disharmony and Overlap

When you meet with Chinese officials to resolve environmental compliance or related issues, do you meet with all government agencies concerned, rely on key agencies to pass the word, or employ another approach?

The number of Chinese agencies involved in environmental issues is growing. However, this was not always the case. Until the mid-1990s, when agencies faced issues that could be characterized as "environmental," these agencies tended to refer the issues to the central environmental authority. Today, the situation is markedly different. Most Chinese agencies now willingly carry a "green flag" and actively engage in environmental matters. SEPA has viewed this "green mission creep" with increasing alarm. Behind this mission creep is an agency tendency to view new regulatory areas, including areas involving environmental protection, as having the potential to enhance agency visibility, resource needs, and therefore resource allocations from the central government. In a time of increased Chinese and global hand-wringing over environmental issues, agencies with an environmental agenda are more likely to receive national and international financial and other support.

While the increasing attention that Chinese agencies give environmental issues may signal improved environmental awareness among agency leaders, it also creates fertile ground for overlapping and inconsistent rulemaking efforts. One example is in the area of chemicals management. SEPA has overall management authority for environmental issues involving chemicals, including new chemical substance management. However, in preparing its rules, agency protocol encourages SEPA to consult with the State Administration of Quality Supervision, Inspection, and Quarantine (AQSIQ) and other agencies in matters involving chemical standard-setting and import and export management. Despite the tendency for Chinese agencies to engage in consultations with their peers on rulemaking activities, these consultations often do not resolve inconsistencies between or overlap among similar measures issued by different agencies. For example, AQSIQ can lawfully promulgate its own measures on chemical import and export inspection, which may indeed include registration provisions that overlap with SEPA requirements.

At present, there is no coordinating body charged with addressing regulatory overlap and inconsistency in the environmental area. This vacuum leaves stakeholders with the burden of proactively facilitating coordinated agency responses to particular environmental issues. This approach involves group meetings or successive meetings with relevant agencies. If there is a lead agency (for example, SEPA), this approach could employ the lead agency as a "door opener" in meetings with other agencies.

This coordination can be time consuming and require a more complex approach to government relations and advocacy. However, this approach can also increase the likelihood that a particular environmental issue will be resolved by numerous relevant agencies at one time. The alternative would require that stakeholders address a particular environmental issue with different agencies at different times, with each agency possibly less open to pursuing a coordinated approach.

Lack of Technical Infrastructure for Compliance

In light of the sore lack of sound technical infrastructure for compliance with China's environmental laws, how do you fulfill Chinese and internal compliance requirements and minimize long-term liability risks?

Many companies face situations such as the lack of environmentally sound disposal facilities for hazardous waste generated at the company site. The alternatives present significant challenges for investors in China. Alternatives include:

- Stockpiling wastes on site (awaiting the development of environmentally sound disposal options)
- Pursuing transboundary transport of the wastes to locations hosting more environmentally sound disposal facilities
- Constructing on-site treatment and disposal facilities
- Conducting exhaustive audits and other activities aimed at minimizing risks associated with the use of Chinese hazardous waste treatment and disposal options.

Each of these alternatives presents very significant work-site safety, administrative, financial, legal, and technical burdens. In this situation, a number of approaches are helpful, including the following.

- Obtain interpretations and guidance on waste management from national authorities. These interpretations may minimize legal risks otherwise associated with conducting waste-management activities in potential contravention of Chinese laws that specify "cradle to grave" management of hazardous waste (for cases in which such management is impracticable at present or in a particular situation).
- Investigate available disposal or treatment options, including government or industry-group-sponsored schedules for development of accessible and more advanced in-country disposal facilities. The Severe Acute Respiratory Syndrome (SARS) epidemic focused the national government's attention on hazardous waste disposal issues, particularly the need for sound facilities to dispose of hazardous medical wastes. As a result, the national government plans to allocate RMB 15 billion (roughly US$2 billion) to establish a nationwide system of hazardous waste treatment facilities.
- Educate company managers on the situation in China and the best environmental practices of long-term investors in China.

Risk of Historical Liability for Soil and Groundwater Contamination

Do you face long-term legal risks for historical contamination of soil and groundwater, even though China does not have in place legal measures requiring cleanup of this contamination?

China's neighboring jurisdictions are considering and enacting legislation establishing historical liability for soil and groundwater contamination.[46] China itself has been considering the question of how to encourage cleanup of contaminated land and subsurface water resources. In 1989–90, the National Environmental Protection Agency (now SEPA) established an ad hoc research group to conduct a feasibility study on the development of legislation similar to the U.S. Comprehensive Environmental Response, Compensation and Liability Act of 1980 ("Superfund"). Hongjun Zhang was a member of this group.

In the ad hoc group's final report, the members were divided on whether conditions in China were appropriate for the success of such an initiative. Proponents of Superfund-type legislation indicated that China would eventually need to clean up contaminated sites and that such legislation would provide the necessary legal underpinnings for such efforts. Furthermore, proponents argued that the creation of a Superfund was critical for ensuring financial capacity to clean up China's likely numerous contaminated sites. Opponents of the legislation at that time cited the fact that China faces many more pressing environmental problems—for example, urban air and water pollution—to indicate that historical contamination liability legislation was not a priority. Furthermore, opponents indicated that the Superfund program in the United States encouraged approaches that emphasize enforcement and the potential for litigation. These approaches, they argued, were not necessarily suitable for China's legal system. Furthermore, they underscored the substantial effort required to develop a national registry of contaminated sites and other practical issues as reasons to pursue further research before moving on the actual development of such legislation.

Since 1990, the debate has continued concerning whether or not to develop legislation or regulations imposing historical liability for contamination of soil and groundwater. NPC and SEPA officials are increasingly clear that contaminated soil and groundwater issues cannot be ignored. Recent policy initiatives call for enhanced waste management and disposal infrastructure and a national regime imposing disposal fees for hazardous wastes. Efforts are also underway to revamp China's solid waste laws. In the meantime, guidelines and a notice to local environmental authorities have been issued as Chinese government authorities and their technical advisers address issues such as soil and groundwater risk management. The Guidelines include the Environmental Quality Risk Assessment Criteria for Soil at Manufacturing Facilities (*Gongye qiye tu rang huanjing zhiliang fengxian pingjia ji jun*, HJ/T 25-1999, promulgated June 9, 1999). The notice is in the form of SEPA's Circular on Earnestly Accomplishing Environmental Pollution Prevention Work in the Enterprise Relocation Process (*Guanyu qieshi zuohao*

qiye banqian guocheng zhong huanjing wuran fangzhi gongzuo de tongzhi),
promulgated June 1, 2004. This Circular comprises a one-page document
that sets forth fundamental soil and groundwater testing requirements, among
other activities, to be addressed by local government authorities. While the
Circular does not provide details concerning clean-up standards, liabilities,
and other issues, it is clear that this document is a "signal" of legal developments to come in the area of historical liability for soil and groundwater
contamination in China.

Against this backdrop, investors should not turn a blind eye to the potential for contamination at target acquisition sites; the destinations of wastes
generated at their sites; venture partners' statements concerning waste treatment and disposal practices; opportunities for more aggressive monitoring
and treatment of solid, liquid, and gaseous wastes; and innovations in "closed-
loop" manufacturing facilities that promise limited or no waste output.

Conclusion

The legal, economic, and societal changes that China has initiated or hosted
over the past three decades have been striking. Among these changes are
developments that defy superficial characterizations of China's environmental legal system.[47] Such surface characterizations include that the:

- Lawmakers and regulatory authorities lack the political will to improve
  the system
- Environmental legal system is simplistic
- Regulated community lacks active supporters of a stronger and more
  predictable system
- Enforcement regime is moribund and lacks legal underpinnings.

Indeed, as this chapter underscores, China's modern environmental legal
system is increasingly typified by detailed legal measures, engaged and more
sophisticated regulatory personnel, and active and committed citizens and
members of the regulated community.

Nevertheless, there remain substantial challenges for these participants in
China's environmental legal system. These challenges involve lawmaking
ambiguity, the unavailability of notice and comment rulemaking, gradual
implementation of laws, agency disharmony and overlap, the lack of technical infrastructure for compliance, and the looming risk of historical liability
for soil and groundwater contamination. Perhaps the greatest challenge that
remains is that the evolution of China's legal regime is closely tied to sweeping changes in the political and administrative system. Dramatic changes to

China's existing political and administrative system will require protracted and concerted efforts by all members of Chinese society.[48]

Sweeping changes are not confined to the environmental law area. Propelled by China's development successes, they include the Chinese government's proactive involvement in global diplomacy and day-to-day discussions with foreign investors.[49] While China's role as host to much of the world's manufacturing base represents a substantial environmental challenge, this factor also increases the domestic and international scrutiny to which the country's environmental legal system is exposed. Similarly, this scrutiny fosters practices that are already helping to address important issues, such as the need for increased government receptivity to stakeholder advocacy, in China's environmental legal system.

As a case in point, the practice of engaging outside resources to assist with background research, training, and other matters conducive to better lawmaking no longer even raises eyebrows within the NPC legislative body, the NPC committees, the State Council, and many agencies under the State Council. Indeed, for many senior environmental lawmakers, the ability to indicate that a law-drafting effort benefited from the consideration of international models or experience is now seen to add weight to a legislative proposal that may help persuade other legislators to support the law.

Practices such as this represent a sea change in the formerly authoritarian and isolated approach to lawmaking in the Chinese government. Yes, the current system may allow only limited outside input into lawmaking activities, but input is now possible, whereas it was previously resisted.

Correspondingly, the same ambiguities that seem to frustrate the regulated community regarding the requirements of Chinese laws also represent opportunities to engage Chinese authorities in innovative approaches to compliance. Furthermore, ambiguous legal measures do not prevent proactive participants in the legal system from actively working with their Chinese government counterparts to identify, engage in, and benefit from corporate social responsibility (CSR) initiatives, such as programs aimed at environmental, health, and safety audits of company suppliers based in China.[50]

Ultimately, perhaps it is more useful to characterize these changes as opportunities for good governance approaches rather than challenges along China's legal path to sustainable development.

Notes

The authors thank Benjamin Liebman, director of the Center for Chinese Legal Studies at Columbia University Law School, for his valuable comments.
  1. These deliberations took place during the Technical Assistance (TA) project

sponsored by the International Bank for Reconstruction and Development (World Bank). This TA project supported efforts by China's State Environmental Protection Administration (SEPA) to develop administrative reform proposals in advance of China's government reorganizations scheduled for March 2003.

2. Much of this literature focuses on the many tensions that exist between the demands for effective controls on harmful behavior and the limits of China's current legal system and culture to provide such controls. See, for example, Patricia Pattison, "The Mountains Are High and the Emperor Is Far Away: Sanctity of Contract in China," *American Business Law Journal* 40 (2003): 459; Teemu Ruskola, "Law Without Law, or Is 'Chinese Law' an Oxymoron?" *William and Mary Bill of Rights Law Journal* 11 (2003): 655; William P. Alford and Yuanyuan Shen, "The Limits of the Law in Addressing China's Environmental Dilemma," in Michael B. McElroy, Chris P. Nielsen, and Peter Lydon, eds., *Energizing China: Reconciling Environmental Protection and Economic Growth* (Cambridge, MA: Harvard University Press, 1998), 405; and Richard J. Ferris Jr. and Hongjun Zhang, "The Challenges of Reforming an Environmental Legal Culture: Assessing the Status Quo and Looking at Post-WTO Admission Challenges for the People's Republic of China," *Georgetown International Law Review* 14 (2002): 429.

3. Aspects of China's regulatory culture that have reinforced nontransparent or adverse information-access practices in the environmental sector are discussed in Ferris and Zhang, "The Challenges of Reforming an Environmental Legal Culture," 439–41. This practice is by no means solely a characteristic of China's legal culture. For an early overview of issues associated with access to environmental data in Asia, see Jamie Allen, "Oranges in the Apple Cart: Gathering Environmental Data in Asia," *Asian Journal of Environmental Management* 1 (1993): 7. Furthermore, information-access challenges in China are not unique to the environmental sector. Paradoxically, China's rapid growth and increasing "openness" to the outside world have spurred the development of government Web sites and other information resources, but have also increased government sensitivities to the potential administrative burdens and government secrecy implications of such efforts. See, for example, Chris Yeung and Linda Choy, "China Steps Up 'Openness' Attack," *South China Morning Post*, June 18, 1994; see also Ferris and Zhang, "The Challenges of Reforming an Environmental Legal Culture," 443–47.

4. "On Buses, on Foot—Returning to an Uncertain Future: Warning on Water Shortages as Thousands of Evacuated Villagers Head Back Home," *South China Morning Post*, Dec. 30, 2003, 1.

5. Xinhua News Agency, "China Strives to Control High Congenital Birth Defect Rate," Dec. 30, 2003.

6. Xinhua News Agency, "Hot Sectors Cooled by Green Limits," Dec. 15, 2003, recounts that the central government is considering a massive enforcement campaign targeting environmental impact assessment of the overheating steel, aluminum, and cement industries.

7. Xinhua News Agency, "Environmental Labeling to Promote China's Green Economy," Dec. 3, 2003.

8. Xinhua News Agency, "China Steps up Efforts to Ensure Biosafety," Oct. 29, 2003.

9. Xinhua News Agency, "First Hospital-Based Centre to Treat Victims of Toxic Chemicals," Oct. 27, 2003.

10. Vanessa Houlder, "Companies Pressed to Adopt Higher Standards: Many De-

veloping Countries Are Making Progress on Pollution, but Controversy Still Rages," *Financial Times*, Oct. 16, 2003, 2.

11. Andrew Bridges, "Dirty Air Has Gone Global," *Toronto Star*, June 1, 2002, J5.

12. Howard W. French, "China's Growing Deserts are Suffocating Korea," *New York Times*, Apr. 14, 2002, depicts how dust from China's deserts is increasingly making life difficult in Japan and South Korea and is reportedly binding with the toxic by-products of certain industrial operations in China.

13. Ibid.

14. "Environment Ministers will Meet in Beijing," *Korea Times*, Dec. 12, 2003.

15. Delegation of the European Commission to China, Press Release, EU-China Agreement on Strengthened Environmental Cooperation, Beijing, Nov. 12, 2003, www.delchn.cec.eu.int/en/index.htm.

16. *Xianfa* (Constitution), arts. 58, 62, 64, 67, 89, 100, 116 (1982) (amended 1999).

17. For example, "fundamental" national statutes generally address issues such as the establishment, organization, and responsibilities of the NPC, people's governments, people's courts, civil and criminal liabilities, government prosecutory functions, and issues related to special administrative and autonomous regions. *Zhonghua renmin gong he guo lifa fa* (Law of the People's Republic of China on Legislation), art. 8 (2000). See *Law Information System* CD-ROM available from Information Center of the National People's Congress, 2 Xi Huang Chen Gen Bei Jie, Beijing, 100034. Thus far, no environmental protection and natural resource conservation statutes have been designated "fundamental" national statutes.

18. "Organic statutes" refer to the laws establishing the NPC, the State Council, and the people's government, people's courts, and people's procuratorate at national and local levels. See, for example, *Quan guo renmin daibiao dahui zuzhi fa* (The Organizational Law of the National People's Congress) (1982). *Law Information System.*

19. The NPC is generally in session only two weeks per year, normally in March.

20. As a practical matter, the NPC and its Standing Committee have thus far never exercised this authority.

21. Current committees are: Agriculture and Rural Area Committee (established 1998); Education, Science, Culture, and Health Committee (established 1983); Environmental Protection and Natural Resource Conservation Committee (established 1993); Finance and Economy Committee (established 1983); Foreign Affairs Committee (established 1983); Internal Affairs and Justice Committee (established 1988); Law Committee (established 1954); Nationality Committee (established 1959); and Overseas Chinese Committee (established 1983).

22. For more information on the role of this committee and State Council administrative agencies in the environmental lawmaking process and the roles of the NPC committees in this system, see Richard J. Ferris Jr. and Hongjun ZHANG, "The Development of the Rule of Law in China: Observations on the Environmental Lawmaking Process," *Metropolitan Corporate Counsel* (Mid-Atlantic ed.) 8 (Oct. 2000): 4.

23. *Xianfa* (Constitution), art. 89.

24. The State Council is required to refer inconsistencies between local and State Council regulations to the NPC Standing Committee for review and decision.

25. The term of the State Council's current Five-Year Legislative Drafting Plan is 2003–8. At the State Council, the Annual Legislative Drafting Plan generally is treated as being more authoritative, given the detailed nature of the work undertaken at the State Council level. The Annual Legislative Drafting Plan currently includes a number of environmental regulatory proposals, including the Management Regulations

for Household Electronic Product Recycling (*Jia yong dianqi huishou guanli banfa*).

26. These organizations were largely restructured during government administrative reforms undertaken in March 1998. Further government reorganization was initiated during the administrative restructuring that took place after the NPC meeting in March 2003.

27. Organic Law of the Local People's Congresses and Local People's Governments of the People's Republic of China, art. 7 (1979) (amended 1995). *Law Information System.*

28. Ibid.

29. Also referred to by names such as "Special Economic Development Zone," "Economic Development Zone," or "Free Trade Zone."

30. Daiva Marija Zedonis, ed., *Countries of the World and Their Leaders Yearbook 2003*, vol. 1 (Detroit, MI: Gale Research Co, Inc., 2002), 410, notes the introduction of more than 2,000 SEZs since 1993; Mary Rose Bonk, ed., *Worldmark Yearbook 2000,* vol. 1 (Detroit, MI: Gale Group, 2000), 586, details the economic successes of SEZs in recent years.

31. *Quan guo renmin daibiao dahui chang wu weiyuanhui guanyu shou quan Shenzhen shi renmin daibiao dahui ji qi chang wu weiyuanhui he Shenzhen shi renmin zhengfu fenbie zhiding fagui he gui zhang de yi an de jueding* (Decision of the Standing Committee of the NPC on Authorizing the People's Congress of Shenzhen Municipality and Its Standing Committee and the People's Government of Shenzhen Municipality to Formulate Regulations and Rules Respectively for Implementation in the Shenzhen SEZ) (July 1, 1992). See *Law Information System* CD-ROM.

32. The "other legal norm-creating documents" refer to the wide variety of documents, of various nomenclature, that reinforce, augment, or interpret the measures set forth in national and local environmental statutes, regulations, and standards.

33. While private publishers have undertaken to fill some of these information gaps, their law compilations typically do not provide an agency specific or comprehensive coverage of particular regulatory areas. Where good compilations are published, a limited number are made available at a limited number of locations. The result is that the practitioner often relies on a range of resources to achieve a comprehensive understanding of the legal requirements that exist on a particular subject. Electronic databases are increasing and may eventually help satisfy the informational needs of practitioners. However, when they are made available to the general public, access to such systems generally requires application and payment. Furthermore, these databases typically are not focused on a particular legal subject area, such as environmental protection. One database that government officials and private-sector companies use is the "Law Information System," developed by the Information Center of the National People's Congress and indexed in "Dublin Core" format (DC.Format) by KYInfo Technology Co., Ltd., Beijing.

34. For a fairly comprehensive, if not up-to-date, compilation of environmental treaties that China has concluded or signed, see *Zhongguo dijie he qianshu de guoji huanjing tiaoyue ji* (Compilation of International Environmental Treaties Concluded or Signed by China) (Beijing: Xueyuan, 1999).

35. Chen Ming, "World Hails China's Approval of Kyoto Protocol at Earth Summit," *Xinhua News Agency*, Sept. 3, 2002. China provided its instrument of ratification to the United Nations Secretary General on Aug. 30, 2002. See also "Kyoto Protocol on the United Nations Framework Convention on Climate Change," *International Legal Materials* 37 (1998): 22.

36. An example of a multilateral environmental treaty that addresses financial and other treaty implementation support for developing countries such as China is the "Stockholm Convention on Persistent Organic Pollutants," *International Legal Materials* 40 (2001): 532. China signed the Convention on May 23, 2001. See United Nations Environment Programme (UNEP), List of Signatories and Parties to the Stockholm Convention, www.pops.int/documents/signature/signstatus.htm.

37. *Huanjing baohu fa* (Environmental Protection Law) (1979), www.sepa.gov.cn/649645345759821824/19891226/1022930.shtml. The law originally was enacted on Sept. 13, 1979, "for trial implementation" and later abrogated by implementation of the Environmental Protection Law of the People's Republic of China, adopted Dec. 26, 1989. "For trial implementation" is a phrase that Chinese law drafters use to refer to laws that they perceive may be subject to repeal or other significant changes, or are untried at the time of passage. Synonyms for similar situations may be translated as "interim," "temporary," and "trial." The use of such terms is not consistent. Many laws that are subject to change do not include these terms in their titles or enactment/ promulgation notices.

38. To elucidate this point, we provide a sampling of legal measures covering the subject of environmental and organic labeling, subjects that are not addressed in specialized national statutes: *Guanyu fabu wo guo huanjing biaozhi tuxing de tongzhi* (Circular Announcing the Design of the China Environmental Label) (issued Aug. 25, 1993); *Huanjing biaozhi chanpin renzheng guanli banfa* (Measures on the Certification Management of Products Bearing Environmental Labels) (promulgated July 28, 1994); and *Youji shipin renzheng guanli banfa* (Measures for the Management of Organic Foods Certification) (promulgated June 19, 2001).

39. For a helpful, but hardly comprehensive, compilation of key local government environmental laws, see *Difang huanjing baohu fagui xuan bian (1999–2003)* (Collection of Local Environmental Protection Laws [1999–2003]) (Beijing: Huaxue gongye chubanshe [Chemical Industry Publishers], 2003).

40. A translation of the procedures is provided in Richard J. Ferris Jr. and Hongjun Zhang, "Reaching Out to the Rule of Law: China's Continuing Efforts to Develop an Effective Environmental Law Regime," *William and Mary Bill of Rights Law Journal* 11 (2003): 590–93.

41. "Guojia huanbao zongju fujuzhang Pan Yue shuai dui tu cha jin shan meng jiao jie 'Wuran hei sanjiao'" (Vice Minister Pan Yue of the State Environmental Protection Administration Leads Group to Undertake Surprise Inspections in the 'Black Triangle Areas' of Shanxi, Shaanxi, and Inner Mongolia), Jan. 2, 2004, www.sepa.gov.cn/649094490434306048/20040102/1044594.shtml.

42. *Guojia huanjing baohu zongju zhi neng she zhi nei she jigou he renyuan bianzhi guiding* (Regulation on Responsibility Allocation, Organizational Structure, and Personnel Limitations of the State Environmental Protection Administration) (State Council, June 23, 1998). See *Law Information System* CD-ROM.

43. *Guanyu zai guojia zhongdian qiye kai zhuan qiye zong falu guwen zhi du shi dian gongzuo de zhidao yijian* (Guiding Opinions on Pilot Work to Establish an Enterprise General Counsel System Within Key State-Owned Enterprises), jointly promulgated by the State Economic and Trade Commission, Party Organization Department, Party Enterprise Committee, Party Finance Committee, Ministry of Personnel, Ministry of Justice, and State Council Office of Legal Affairs, July 18, 2002, effective the same date. *Law Information System.* The responsibility for overseeing this initiative passed to the State Development Reform Commission after the March 2003 disbanding of the State Economic and Trade Commission.

44. These agencies were: the Light Industry General Bureau, State Economic and Trade Commission, Ministry of Internal Trade, Ministry of Foreign Trade and Economic Cooperation, State Administration for Industry and Commerce, State Environmental Protection Administration, General Customs Administration, State Technical Supervision Bureau, and State Import and Export Product Inspection Bureau.

45. SEPA has published a volume of regulatory interpretations, largely issued at the request of local government authorities. This publication brings to the public sphere volumes of interpretive guidance letters that were previously considered "internal" agency documents. *Zhongguo huanjing baohu zhifa jie shi daquan* (1982–2001) (China Environmental Protection Law Enforcement Interpretation Compilation) (Beijing: Xuefan Publishing Company, 2001).

46. These jurisdictions include Taiwan (Soil and Groundwater Pollution Remediation Act, 2000) and Japan (Soil Contamination Countermeasures Law, 2002).

47. Characterizations of the Chinese legal system, superficial or not, are not readily apparent. Attempts to generalize and discuss the system in terms of "rule of law" versus "rule of authority" (or human beings) are perhaps also too simplistic to accurately portray the complex traditions and cultural forces at work. (Ruskola, "Law Without Law," 655).

48. For instance, there is a "consensus mentality" among China's agencies that hinders any one agency from "going far beyond" the boundaries of politically and administratively acceptable conduct on a particular subject, such as rulemaking transparency. Thus, meaningful progress in this area must be supported by significant pressure from within and without the agencies. In this way, conduct that otherwise would be deemed risky or problematic due to lack of precedent may be considered to be politically expedient.

49. See David Hale and Lyric Hughes Hale, "China Takes Off," *Foreign Affairs* 82 (2003): 36–53, which describes China's recent more active role in global politics.

50. World Environment Center, "Applying Corporate Social Responsibility (CSR) to Global Supply Chain Management," 2003, gives the example of Ashland's efforts to green its supply chain in China, www.wec.org/eval/ashland1.htm.

—— Chapter 4 ——

Environmental Enforcement in China

Elizabeth Economy

China's spectacular rate of economic development over the past two decades has elevated hundreds of millions of Chinese out of poverty and propelled China into a position of significant stature within the global economy. Yet, as the Chinese leadership focused most immediately on ensuring the continuation of this rapid economic growth, it largely ignored the environmental consequences, leaving behind a legacy of pollution and destruction.

Of the world's ten most polluted cities, eight are located in China.[1] China ranks as the world's largest consumer of coal, and its consumption is estimated to be rising at more than 10 percent per year.[2] China also boasts the world's fastest growing automobile market and is home to twenty million vehicles.[3] As a result, the air in almost one-third of China's major cities is barely breathable. More than 50 percent of China's major waterways are heavily polluted,[4] forcing some seventy million people to drink water from substandard underground sources.[5] One-quarter of China's land is desert, and desertification is proceeding at a pace of more than 1,300 square miles per year.[6] In its current state, China's environment poses a serious threat to both human health and economic prosperity: China has the world's highest rate of chronic respiratory disease,[7] and the price tag for China's environmental degradation and pollution is estimated to be the equivalent of 8 percent to 12 percent of its annual gross domestic product (GDP). No aspect of China's environment, from air to land to water to biodiversity, remains untouched by this process of development.

In recent years, the Chinese leadership has recognized the gravity of China's environmental challenges and has taken steps toward a significant cleanup. During the tenth Five-Year Plan (2001–5), China pledged to spend

1.3 percent of its GDP on the environment sector, with the majority of this money focused on pollution treatment and prevention.[8] Beijing has also passed numerous laws and regulations and established an extensive central infrastructure for environmental protection, which has brought a measure of relief. At the same time, in keeping with its overall decentralization of authority for fiscal decision making, the state continues to devolve authority over environmental issues away from the center, delegating enforcement of both central and local government laws and regulations to local officials. Increasingly, international and domestic nongovernmental organizations (NGOs), the media, independent activists, and multinationals also are playing a role in ensuring the implementation of government policies. In some cases, local environmental protection efforts have achieved remarkable results; in others the environmental situation has continued to deteriorate. This chapter focuses on how and why this patchwork of environmental protection has emerged in China. It explores the politics, rather than the legal mechanisms, of environmental enforcement; assesses the successes and shortcomings of China's approach; and discusses the prospects for an overall improvement in enforcement efforts.

Enforcement Challenges

Beijing's strategy for environmental enforcement rests on three legs: inspections by the central government; local environmental protection bureau (EPB) regulations and enforcement; and reliance on the broader domestic and international community through the media, NGOs, individual activists, and multinationals. Above all, it is the local environmental protection authorities who are primarily responsible for:

- Overseeing environmental impact assessments for new development projects and enterprises (although some demand national-level approval)
- Monitoring emissions from factories
- Assessing fees for pollution discharges that exceed state standards
- If necessary, following through with legal action against firms that consistently fail to meet pollution standards.

EPBs also maintain critical links with the general populace through Web sites, hotlines, and educational programs.

In some cities with significant resources, strong ties to the international community, and proactive leaders, this devolution of authority has resulted in a marked improvement in environmental protection. On the other hand, over the past decade, it has become increasingly clear that, in many regions, environmental governance at the local level has had difficulty keeping up with the challenges of China's rapidly developing economy. In fall 2003, Wang Yuqing, deputy director of the State Environmental Protection Administration (SEPA), commented that environmental protection could not keep pace with economic development, further noting that "Some local officials are short-sighted by giving priority only to development, turning a blind eye to violation of environmental laws by some enterprises. . . . That is one of the important reasons why the incidence of environmental law offenses remains high."[9] Similarly, in 2001, Jiang Yandong, director of law enforcement within SEPA, noted that 10,000 cases against polluting enterprises had yet to be resolved because local governments were afraid that punishment would hurt economic growth.[10]

Environmental enforcement may also suffer from poor communication and follow-through on central mandates to local levels. Overwhelmingly, as Xiaoying Ma and Leonard Ortolano point out in their study of environmental regulation in China, there is a critical divide between formal and informal rules. Formal rules are the "pollution-control requirements detailed in laws and regulations," while informal rules are "derived from customs and unwritten codes of conduct [that] affect how environmental laws are implemented."[11] The embedded nature of the local environmental protection bureaus in the local governments, along with weak funding, poor training, and insufficient resources for local environmental authorities, further complicate environmental protection efforts. While the central government has attempted to buttress the efforts of local environmental officials through periodic inspections by central officials, these inspections are also often inadequate to the task at hand.

Responsibility of the Center

Beijing is primarily responsible for policy guidance; drafting laws and regulations; monitoring the overall state of China's natural environment; initiating countrywide campaigns to address problems such as deforestation and the cleanup of major water resources, including the "three rivers, three lakes" (*san he san hu*) campaign; and developing policies for participation in international conventions.

In terms of addressing issues of enforcement, SEPA is responsible for overseeing implementation of national laws at the national level, but implementation is overwhelmingly a local issue. Therefore, Beijing's most important role rests in the inspections that it undertakes at local levels. Typically, several ministries—often SEPA in conjunction with other agencies—contribute officials to these inspection teams. On some occasions, the inspection teams also include members of the media.

These inspections vary in scope and scale. Some span many provinces and review general enforcement of pollution regulations over a period of several months. During summer 2001, for example, SEPA launched a three-month pollution prevention campaign that inspected almost 1.5 million enterprises. Of these, approximately 9,000 were punished. The majority were fined, but others were ordered to suspend production until further investigation, or even shut down. This inspection sweep also contributed to additional policy changes in some of the localities. In Beijing and Chongqing, officials developed a set of new regulations to better define the responsibilities of local enterprises and officials in managing pollution problems. Other cities, for example, Dalian in northeast China, initiated pollution hotlines for the public to report pollution-related problems.[12] In September 2003, SEPA and the State Development and Reform Commission, Ministry of Supervision, Ministry of Justice, Ministry of Commerce, and Ministry of Public Security conducted a month-long inspection campaign of 360,000 enterprises that led to the temporary closure of 6,849 companies. Unless these companies improve their practices, they risk being permanently shut down.[13]

In other instances, inspections by central authorities are prompted by specific pollution issues or environmental disasters. Throughout the 1980s and early 1990s, only 25 percent of the water in the Huai River—one of China's seven major river systems—met state standards. Despite local pleas for help, the central government did not take action to improve the situation. In 1994, however, there was a major pollution disaster in which almost twenty-six million pounds of fish were killed; cropland was polluted; and thousands of people became ill with dysentery, diarrhea, and vomiting. Beijing then dispatched an inspection team, including top officials such as the then head of the State Science and Technology Commission, Song Jian. The central government followed through by initiating a three-year campaign to clean up the Huai, which was followed by a second three-year campaign during 1997–2000, the "Zero Hour Campaign." Specific targets were set for water quality, factories were ordered to improve their practices or be shuttered, and a number of wastewater plants were to be built.[14]

SEPA also frequently taps the media to participate in these campaigns, as a means both to increase pressure on local enterprises and officials and to inform other regions of SEPA's activities and the results of the inspection. In May 2002, for example, SEPA broadcast a television program that addressed the issue of violations of environmental protection laws and regulations. It followed up by sending seven inspection and supervision teams, which included reporters, to twelve provinces, autonomous regions, and municipalities to review the performance of thousands of factories and projects. After the inspection, 800 heavily polluting companies across the country were shut down. In addition, 283 people, including twelve officials, were punished for violating environmental regulations.[15]

This type of inspection effort is valuable in signaling high-level attention to local enforcement problems. However, such inspection sweeps fail to address the essence of the problem, which resides in the nature of the local political and economic situations. Officials in Beijing are clearly aware of this problem. As Tian Weiyong, then a SEPA division chief in charge of supervising environmental pollution cases, stated in an interview in 2002, "Some local governments refused to cooperate in punishing those factories, which [makes] our work very difficult."[16] China's official English-language daily, *China Daily*, also noted the specific challenge of the central inspection approach. It reported on a set of inspections SEPA undertook in 2000, in which five inspection teams were dispatched around the country to inspect pollution discharges from industrial companies. The article noted that firms that failed to meet the pollution standards would address the problem while the inspections teams were there. However, once the inspectors left the site, the firms often did not continue to employ their pollution control technologies and continued to fail to meet state standards. As the article commented, "This offers some proof of the inability of the infrequent inspection mechanism."[17]

There is little evidence to suggest that the inspection method can be modified to make it more effective: SEPA is already stretched to the limits of its capacity. With its wide range of environmental management responsibilities, SEPA cannot expend more capital or require more personnel to undertake more inspections. It also is unlikely that SEPA's capacity will be greatly expanded in the near future. To maintain a small central environmental bureaucracy is not an accident but rather a conscious decision by China's top leaders. According to current SEPA director Xie Zhenhua, in 1998, as part of a broader bureaucratic reform, SEPA's staff was cut in half, although its status within the overall bureaucracy was raised to that of other ministries.[18] At the same time, for more than a decade, primary responsibility for environmental protection has rested with local officials. Thus, *if China's environmental enforcement is to improve significantly, it will have to arise largely from local officials.*

Locals Call the Shots

Devolution of authority for environmental protection to local officials was formally enshrined in the 1989 environmental responsibility system (*huanjing baohu mubiao zerenzhi*). This system emulated the grain responsibility system, making local officials responsible for the environmental health of their regions in the same way that they were responsible for grain production. A contractual system was also developed along the same lines of the grain responsibility system. Local environmental protection bureaus were expected to review performance for the past year, establish goals for the forthcoming year, and help mayors define the terms of their contracts with provincial governors. In one set of interviews with local EPB officials in eight major cities across China, only in Dalian did a local EPB official indicate awareness of the contract responsibility system.[19] However, in his study of environmental policymaking in China and Taiwan, Michael Rock reports that Nanjing has employed the system to good effect. In Nanjing, people had long complained about the pollution and smell emanating from Xuanwu Lake. In the 1990s, the mayor formed a task force to study the problem, and the group recommended a set of steps to bring the water quality of the lake to grade 5, the lowest quality of water ranked by SEPA. The mayor then included the cleanup of the lake in his environmental contract with the governor. Since then, the city invested well over US$1 million to clean up the lake[20] and, by 2001, the water had attained grade 5 quality.[21]

In theory, the contract responsibility system permits close coordination among all the relevant actors: local environmental officials, officials from economic and planning bureaus, the mayor, and the governor. Yet, even if contracts are signed, which remains an uncertainty in many areas of China, local enforcement of national laws remains a significant challenge.

There are several reasons for this. First, environmental protection at the local level is spread quite thinly across the country. There are only 2,000 environmental protection bureaus, with approximately 60,000 employees.[22] Given China's geographic and population size, such a force is quite limited. In some provinces and cities, there have been significant problems with the quality of the environmental protection force. In summer 2003, nine environment and industrial officials in Hunan were fired or punished for neglecting their duty.[23] According to Jonathan Schwartz's study of China's state environmental capacity, the quality of environmental officials is now on the rise. With increasing opportunities for formal training in environmental studies, many officials in the larger environmental protection bureaus hold master's degrees or doctorates. Moreover, there are regular mandated training courses and skills testing.[24]

However, even as skills increase, the number of environmental protection officials with responsibility for enforcement remains woefully inadequate. Even in Shanghai, which has received national recognition for its environmental leadership, environmental protection officials feel unable to meet the environmental needs of the municipality. In 1999 Shanghai's EPB employed only 100 environmental inspectors, who had responsibility for well over 20,000 factories.[25]

In some cases, it is not the EPBs that fail, but rather the institutions hired by the environmental protection bureaus to undertake environmental impact assessments. In June 2002, for example, SEPA punished forty-one institutions licensed to carry out environmental impact assessments for failing to meet SEPA standards.[26]

Even when local environmental protection officials do attempt to enforce environmental regulations, they often encounter political and social obstacles. EPBs are embedded within the local governments. While they must follow the laws and regulations that emanate from the center or from their local governments and participate in programs directed by SEPA, EPB officials' salaries, office space, and cars are all determined by the local governments. Because of this, EPB officials are particularly susceptible to pressure from senior officials within the local government. In some cases, these local officials have personal ties with enterprise directors and try to broker lower discharge fees for the polluting enterprises. In other cases, local officials may pressure EPB officials to limit or ignore the fees because of concerns for social stability. The central government has reported that it typically collects about 30 percent of the total fees actually owed.[27]

On the other hand, EPB officials themselves are not always blameless. Blatant abuse of the discharge fee system prevails. In 2001 the central government audited almost fifty cities and found that more than US$70 million had been misappropriated and used for such things as purchasing houses and cars.[28] As a result of widespread abuse, EPBs reportedly will not be allowed to collect fees in the future; rather fee collection will fall under the purview of the Ministry of Finance.[29]

When the first round of enforcement fails, a second effort is often pursued through the court system. Increasingly, Chinese citizens are seeking restitution for their pollution-related economic losses or health problems through the legal system. Environmental legal activists such as WANG Canfa in Beijing have been leading the charge to pursue environmental lawsuits on behalf of clients throughout the country who otherwise would have no recourse. Some cases result in significant fines and/or prison sentences for factory managers and environmental protection officials, although the cases can take a long time to be resolved.

In one case in Guangxi Autonomous Region, a family's mango groves were devastated by a strange disease four years after coming to fruition. The family filed a claim with the Yulin EPB in Guangxi, which sent an inspection team to the site, including an expert on mango research and development from the local university. The team determined that the disease stemmed from the air pollution produced by nearby cement plants, and the EPB ordered the cement plants to compensate the family. Neither side agreed with the settlement so the case went to trial. While the family won their case at the first trial, the cement factories then induced the local party leadership to support their case and won the second round. In the end, after six years of hearings and appeals in various courts, the Chen family was finally compensated at the level it desired.[30]

More recently, in January 2003, forty-seven farmers in Jiaxing, Zhejiang Province, received RMB $7.5 million (approximately US$915,000) for enduring more than a decade of destruction to their fisheries and decline in water quality due to factories discharging their wastewater.[31] In another case, an individual won a lawsuit against an automobile manufacturer because the car he had just purchased emitted a foul smell due to high levels of benzene and formaldehyde.[32]

Environmental lawsuits also arise when pollution damages the public's health. In one such case, an interior design company paid a family approximately US$15,000 for incurring health problems due to the company's use of poisonous levels of formaldehyde. The family's ills included colds, persistent fever, one tumor, and frequent vomiting.[33] Moreover, in 2002 two EPB officials in Yangcheng County, Shanxi Province, were sentenced to jail for failing to stop a chemical plant from discharging toxic waste into the drinking-water system. The villagers had filed a lawsuit against the environmental protection officials for "dereliction of duty" when they ignored reports that showed that the town's water system had been poisoned. Seventy-nine people were hospitalized, forty-nine with serious conditions. In the end, the EPB officials were punished for not properly overseeing the siting of the company as well as permitting it to operate in a dangerous manner.[34]

Nevertheless, barriers to successful resolution of cases remain. As with the system of EPBs, courts are beholden to local government. The local government controls both the personnel and the budget of the courts, making political intervention in the legal system a common problem. As a prominent China legal activist, Wang Canfa, has stated, "If people in the provinces try and sue these companies, they come up against courts which are not very independent because they are influenced by local governments. Even if the peasants are right, they often lose the case."[35]

Difficulties may also arise if the source of the pollution is located in one jurisdiction and the plaintiff in another. For example, a local court ordered a factory producing arsenic in Guangxi to stop production because of arsenic's highly polluting nature. The arsenic caused skin disorders, among other problems. Yet, the factory continues to operate. The owner has paid only half the reparations promised. Much of the difficulty in collecting the rest of the money is due to the fact that the factory owner lives in Hunan, a neighboring province.[36]

In addition, rather than adhere strictly to the letter of the law, courts often take into account external factors in processing their cases or making their rulings. In one case, in Beijing, for example, three families won a pollution case against two factories for noise and air pollution. While the plaintiffs sued for $20,000 for impaired health, hearing loss, and lack of sleep, in the end, they were awarded a total of $4,200. The award was significantly lower than that sought because the two enterprises were "key" enterprises—those considered essential to the local economy—and the court feared social unrest if the enterprises were closed down or fined significantly.[37] Similarly, when one environmental lawyer attempted to file suit on behalf of seventy-one villagers against a polluting coal mine outside Beijing,[38] the court demanded that, to collect fees for each suit, the lawyer had to file seventy-one separate suits.[39]

There have also been negative repercussions to the courts' newfound willingness to hold environmental protection officials liable for some pollution problems. In 2001, then Vice Premier Wen Jiabao stated that the central government should "harshly penalize incompetent local officials whose responsibility is to safeguard the environment, as well as those enterprises involved in serious pollution cases."[40] The result is that some EPB officials have been reluctant to assist in cases for fear that they will be found negligent.[41]

Enforcement at the local level is also assisted by the occasional alliance between the courts and the banking system. If a firm refuses to pay its fines, even after receiving a court order to do so, a local bank may freeze the firm's assets and deduct the money from its accounts. Even such efforts, however, may fall prey to political intervention. In one case in Shanxi Province, forestry officials attempted to seek US$530,000 in damages from a highway construction company for destruction of forests along a highway. Although the court ruled in favor of the forest department and ordered the assets of the company frozen, a senior government official intervened just days later to release the company's assets.[42]

In addition to the bureaucratic impediments to effective enforcement of environmental regulations, in many instances localities have not put in place the appropriate incentives for compliance. Fees for pollution are set too low to encourage compliance. Companies simply prefer to pay the fees rather than shift their production processes to decrease their emissions.

Still, there are signs of hope. Devolution of authority for environmental protection also has permitted some municipalities to be more aggressive about environmental protection and enforcement. For example, during the late 1990s, Dalian, Shanghai, and Zhongshan all moved to ratchet up their environmental enforcement efforts. All have demonstrated impressive improvements in air and water quality and have been recognized as model environmental cities in China. Guangzhou also is working hard to achieve such status. In 2002 Shanghai published the first local environmental yearbook in China. In the same year, the Shanghai environment online home page had nearly three million hits, and districts strove to meet the designation of a national model environmental district.[43] In recent years, as a result of its preparation for hosting the 2008 Olympics, Beijing, too, has demonstrated a remarkable capacity to turn its environmental protection effort around, promising to devote 4 percent—approximately US$1.5 billion annually—of its city revenues to environmental protection in the coming years.[44] One of the city's major initiatives is to convert all of Beijing to natural gas before the Olympics.[45]

In contrast to other less environmentally proactive regions, these cities—and the others that rank at the top of China's environmental protection efforts—share several characteristics. First, and most important, the mayor is a strong, independent supporter of environmental protection. This support translates directly into an enhanced status within the local bureaucracy for the local EPB. These environmental model cities also share strong ties to the international community, which allow them easy access to the best environmental training, technologies, and policy approaches. In Dalian, for example, Japanese companies raised the standard of environmental technology in the city, and the Japanese Environment Ministry provided assistance and capacity building for Dalian EPB officials. Finally, these model cities typically rank in the upper tier of China's localities in GDP per capita. Not surprisingly, this wealth gives local leaders the financial wherewithal to devote more of the city's revenues to environmental protection. In Guangdong Province, for example, the provincial EPB is installing an electronic sulfur dioxide monitoring system in the facilities of 300 of the largest polluters in the province; this system will save 75 percent of the labor costs that typically are involved in pollution monitoring.[46] (One important caveat is that the data cannot be used as the basis of prosecution. Nevertheless, the information will provide important signals to EPB officials as to which enterprises to target for inspection.)

In contrast, poorer regions within China often find themselves unable to make improvements in their environment due to lack of resources. In Qinghai, a significant lack of funds has stymied local efforts to fulfill the central government's mandate to restore grasslands. Qinghai receives only US$24 million or so in central funds, and most of that must support infrastructure development or poverty alleviation.[47]

International NGOs and multinationals can also play significant roles in enhancing the capacity of local environmental protection actors and advancing new policy initiatives that will promote enforcement. In Shenyang, for example, with assistance from the American Bar Association, the municipal government passed a regulation in 2003 that sets out the requirements for public participation and citizen access to information. This regulation was scheduled to go into law in 2004. Ordinary citizens even participated in drafting the law by sending in comments after a draft law was published in a local newspaper.[48] Included in the draft was a regulation requiring that the local government publicize construction projects that will have significant impact on the environment (except in cases in which secrecy is required by state regulations). Other international NGOs, such as Environmental Defense, have also played a critical role in promoting market-based policy approaches to the enforcement of environmental regulations, for example, allowing tradable permits to regulate pollutants such as sulfur dioxide.[49] Finally, multinationals may exert a significant influence on local enforcement capacity, by either using state-of-the-art waste management technologies in their enterprises or insisting that their Chinese partners (or potential partners) adhere to a higher standard of environmental practice. Royal Dutch/Shell, for instance, hired an outside environmental consulting firm as well as the United Nations Development Programme (UNDP) to conduct a social impact assessment during its negotiations with PetroChina to complete a joint venture deal on the West–East Gas Pipeline Project.[50]

Change from the Outside In

Given the significant potential of environmental enforcement to be undermined by political intervention at the local level, Beijing has sought to use forces outside the government to pressure local enterprises and officials to improve implementation of environmental laws and regulations. These external forces include formally registered NGOs, grassroots public participation, and the media. These actors have had some notable successes in their efforts, yet their impact overall remains marginal. Their numbers are small and their capacities limited.

Environmental NGOs: Their Influence and Limits

The establishment in 1994 of China's first environmental NGO, Friends of Nature, resulted from a confluence of events. In the wake of the 1992 United Nations Conference on Environment and Development (UNCED) in Rio de Janeiro, Brazil, China's leaders concluded that NGOs could play a significant role in environmental protection. During the conference, the formal negotiations among the participating countries' delegations occurred side by side with an NGO conference, unprecedented in its size. The NGOs were a powerful force, attracting significant media attention. China's participation in the NGO conference, however, was limited because it did not have genuine environmental NGOs. Rather, it brought government-organized NGOs to the table. Their inability to participate in a meaningful way was a source of embarrassment within the Chinese leadership. At the same time, there was clear recognition that the stepped-up scale of China's commitment to environmental protection would require the participation of the Chinese people. Thus, not only would genuine NGOs enhance the government's limited capacity to improve the environment, but such NGOs also would improve China's international image.

Concurrently, a small group of Beijing-based Chinese scholars and environmentalists had been exploring the possibility of establishing an environmental NGO. When one of the founding members of this small group, Liang Congjie, spoke with a top Chinese environmental protection official following UNCED to gauge the government's potential support, he was encouraged by the official to try to register his group as an NGO. With the support and advice of many other scholars and environmentalists, Liang registered Friends of Nature in 1994. Since that time, environmental NGOs have flourished quietly in China, gradually expanding the scope of their activities.

In the mid to late 1990s, the rallying cries of China's nascent NGOs were to enforce the protection of China's increasingly endangered biodiversity, in particular, the Tibetan antelope in China's far west and the snub-nosed monkey in Yunnan. The first environmental activists rallied students and intellectuals to draw attention to the plight of these animals. They also tapped personal connections at the highest level of the government to begin to focus the attention of central officials on the failure of local officials to protect these endangered species. In both cases, officials in Beijing exerted intense pressure on local officials to improve the situation. In the case of the Tibetan antelope, the NGOs also offered financial and material support to local herdsmen-turned-enforcers, who were increasingly successful at preventing poachers from killing off the antelope. While these large-scale campaigns captured the attention of the Chinese central leadership and media, the fear among some NGO leaders now is that both problems are resurfacing, since high-level attention has shifted elsewhere.[51]

Many subsequent efforts to assist in environmental protection are much smaller in scope. For example, Friends of Nature supports an environmental education van that travels with experts from Beijing to remote areas of China to help educate the local people about their particular environmental challenges and potential response measures. Still other NGOs have been quite daring in their approach, going undercover to expose illegal logging and official corruption, occasionally receiving death threats in the process.

NGOs have also sprouted up to tackle urban environmental issues. With the support of SEPA, for example, the NGO Global Village Beijing has established green communities that recycle, employ energy-efficient technologies, and generally undertake conservation-oriented work.

There is some evidence that NGO leaders are becoming bolder over time, seeking to hold accountable not only local governments but also Beijing. In 1998 China launched the Go West Campaign (*Xibu da kaifa*) to develop the interior provinces of the country. While official pronouncements included "ecological construction" as one of the five major tenets of the campaign, many NGO leaders remained skeptical of the government's commitment to practice environmentally sustainable development. They first attempted to persuade the central government to include SEPA among the twenty or so ministries in charge of overseeing the development program. Although unsuccessful, one renowned environmental leader, Liao Xiaoyi, has attempted to keep up the pressure, calling on Beijing to ensure that promises it had made concerning the centrality of environmental protection in the campaign would be fulfilled. Liao's comments suggest that, as the campaign progresses, she is prepared to act as a watchdog on local governments as well as on Beijing.[52]

One case that has attracted substantial publicity is the Nujiang River hydropower project. The Nujiang passes through Tibet, Yunnan, and Myanmar, and then flows into the Indian Ocean. The project has prompted significant objections not only from Chinese experts but also from environmental protection advocates, including scientists, writers, journalists, singers, and movie stars, sixty-two of whom signed a petition against the project in October 2003. Beijing has yet to decide the outcome.[53]

Despite its essential interest in encouraging environmental NGOs to act as watchdogs at the local level, Beijing carefully circumscribed the activities of NGOs through a set of regulations promulgated in 1998. Beijing is concerned that, by opening the political space for NGOs, it risks the development of organizations whose interests may not be aligned with those of China's Communist Party. These organizations could attempt to broaden their mandate, for example, by insisting on governmental transparency and accountability in environmental protection, to a push for broader political reform. For instance, the Regulations for Registration and Management of Social Organizations demand that NGOs (1) register with a governmental oversight agency, (2) refrain from establishing local offices in other parts of the country, and (3) maintain a certain level of funding. In addition, the oversight agency or "mother-in-law" of each NGO keeps close tabs on the membership of the NGOs. In one recent case, one of the founding members of Friends of Nature, Wang Lixiong, became active in protesting the treatment of Tibetan dissidents. Friends of Nature was informed that if it did not remove him from the membership list, the organization's license would not be renewed. While Wang Lixiong protested the move, in the end Friends of Nature succumbed to the government's pressure.[54]

Much of the success of environmental NGOs is due to their linkages with the media. The Chinese government has, in fact, encouraged the media to raise general awareness of environmental protection issues, inform the Chinese public, and act as the eyes and ears of the central government in ferreting out environmental wrongdoing.

Media's Effect on Environmental Protection

The media have had a profound impact in all of these areas. In terms of environmental awareness, for example, the media triggered a number of grassroots efforts to establish local battery recycling centers. During the late 1990s, having spent time in Germany researching how that country had responded to the challenge, one television producer aired a program on battery recycling. After they saw the television report, people were struck by the degree to which their health could be endangered by batteries leaking into the soil. The result was that battery recycling efforts sprouted up in various parts of China well before SEPA had any guidelines in place. In Dalian, in China's northeast, physician Geng Haiying independently asked department stores to serve as battery depositories. After they were persuaded that Geng was not attempting to profit personally from the effort, three department stores signed on to the program. The Dalian EPB also offered moral support; without formal guidelines it did not feel that it could play a more substantial role. The media, too, took an interest in publicizing Geng's program, which received official support from SEPA through the publication of formal guidelines just a few months later. In this case, the media and public led the government in policymaking. Today, enforcement of the new regulations has become the issue. Local EPBs complain about "battery phobia." Most cities don't possess adequate recycling facilities for all the batteries people are bringing to them.[55]

With regard to local enforcement of central regulations, the media also play a critical role in warning Beijing officials that their mandates are not being heeded. Former premier Zhu Rongji often requested tapes from news programs that had reported on the failure of local officials to implement central directives on afforestation and logging bans. Most famously, in 2000, in the aftermath of the two campaigns to clean up the Huai River, SEPA director Xie Zhenhua declared the campaigns a success. Yet one scientist at a local university, Su Kaisheng, performed his own analysis of the water quality and disputed the government's claims. Three newspapers followed up with their own independent investigations: two wrote articles in support of the scientist and only the *People's Daily* supported the government. Television news programs also investigated the Huai River cleanup and found it lacking.[56] Three years later, Xinhuanet.com ran a program on the Internet featuring a discussion by Yang Shuqing, a hydrologist, discussing his views on the flooding and pollution of the Huai. More than 1,000 Chinese participated in a spirited online debate on the content of the program.[57]

Finally, the media can play an important role in bringing polluting enterprises and their officials to justice. In one case in the mid-1990s, a restaurant owner in Shanghai agreed to pay his fine to the local EPB only after a local television station reported his dereliction.[58] In some cases, such media investigations can be dangerous work. In 2003 in Shanxi Province, the director of the Xuanbo Joint Cokeoven Plant ordered his workers to attack a television reporter from CCTV who was investigating pollution at the plant. The reporter was rescued by a SEPA delegation that arrived shortly thereafter, which then ordered the local environmental enforcement group in Baode County to protect his right to investigate.[59]

The Public as Environmental Protector

As the battery recycling effort demonstrates, one of the most important sources for improving China's environment is the Chinese public. Over the past decade, there has been a dramatic upsurge in both the level of interest and the level of involvement among the Chinese public in improving the environment. While formal involvement by the public in NGOs or mass-based environmental activities such as battery recycling or tree planting remains relatively limited, the public also acts as a watchdog through its complaints to local officials. In 1996 Chinese environmental officials received more than 67,000 letters complaining about environmental pollution.[60] Just two years later, that number had increased dramatically to 241,321.[61] The Dalian hotline alone received a few thousand phone calls in just several months. Perhaps not surprisingly, the evidence suggests that the more educated the populace becomes, the more likely it is to lodge a complaint.[62] Local environmental officials state that many of their best tips for polluting enterprises come from such letters and phone calls. When such complaints remain unaddressed, legal recourse is one option, as discussed above. At the same time, the Chinese public also has resorted to violent demonstrations to persuade enterprise officials or environmental officials to take action to address local pollution issues.[63] Certainly, the Chinese government recognizes the threat posed by environmental pollution for social unrest. In the mid-1990s, one senior official commented that environmental pollution and degradation was one of the four major sources of social unrest in the country.[64]

Conclusion

Similar to all rapidly developing economies, China faces significant environmental challenges. In addition, China's system of environmental protection, which combines a well-defined formal structure and set of laws with an underdeveloped environmental bureaucratic apparatus and still-developing set of behavioral norms, faces great obstacles in protecting its environment.

The Chinese government has clearly relegated the bulk of environmental protection to local governments, giving them formal responsibility for meeting the environmental needs of their citizens and the national and local laws and regulations. However, there are too few local environmental officials with too much responsibility. In some cases, they are not well trained, although this is gradually changing. These environmental officials' responsibility to the local governments means that nonenvironmental criteria are often brought to bear in deciding how the breach of a law or regulation ought to be managed. Personal ties between local officials and enterprise managers, local leaders' concerns over layoffs and the potential for social instability, lack of trained local workers, and corruption all have undermined the efficacy of China's environmental protection laws at the local level. Even if an environmental case is brought to trial locally, the same set of political considerations are often brought into play, diminishing the likelihood of a resolution that adheres strictly to the letter of the law.

As Beijing looks to engage other entities in the fight to protect the environment, central government officials have opened the door to NGOs, grassroots participation, the media, and the international community. All of these actors have played important roles with regard to various issues at various times. Nevertheless, their impact is felt primarily at the margins, in part because they are still in a nascent stage and in part because the government limits the range of their activities.

Looking to the future, China's best environmental hope appears to rest with the regions in which the mayors are environmentally proactive, have substantial financial resources, and boast strong ties to the international community. Cities such as Dalian, Shanghai, and Zhongshan are recognized environmental leaders in China and set a positive example for the rest of the country. Slowly but surely, other cities are following. Yet, for many of them, such a confluence of factors may be decades away. Until then, environmental enforcement will continue to rely on a highly imperfect, idiosyncratic system in which the law is only one among numerous factors that determine how well China's environmental laws and regulations will be implemented.

Notes

The author would like to thank Laura Geller for her excellent research assistance.

1. Shiqiu Zhang and Shumin An, "Poverty and Environment in China: Can We Make a Change?" www.epe.be/objective2002/2ndconference/presentations/zsq-poverty.pdf, 13.

2. Keith Bradsher, "China's Boom Adds to Global Warming Problems," *New York Times,* Oct. 22, 2003, A1.

3. Australian Broadcasting Corporation, "Feature on Car Sales in China," July 9, 2003, www.abc.net.au/abcasiapacific/focus/stories/s940621.htm.

4. Dexter Roberts, "The Greening of China," *Business Week* (Oct. 27, 2003): 53.

5. New China News Agency, "Chinese Ministry Says Water in Many Urban Areas Unfit for Drinking," BBC Monitoring International Reports, Oct. 30, 2003.

6. *China Daily,* "Desert Still Poses Great Threat," June 18, 2003.

7. Roberts, "The Greening of China," 53.

8. "China: The Most Attractive Environmental Market," China International Environment Protection Exhibition and Conference 2003, Beijing, Dec. 15–18, 2003, www.Chinaenvironment.com/ciepec2003/c3/en2003chinamarket.htm.

9. Xinhua General News Service, "China Punishes 12,000 Firms for Environmental Offenses," Nov. 22, 2003.

10. *People's Daily,* "Clean Progress Sought on Pollution Fight," Oct. 10, 2001.

11. Xiaoying Ma and Leonard Ortolano, *Environmental Regulation in China* (Lanham, MD: Rowman and Littlefield, 2000), 10.

12. Yong Zhang, "Tough Campaign Clears Air," *China Daily,* Sept. 26, 2001.

13. *South China Morning Post,* "6,800 Polluting Companies Told to Clean Up or Close," Sept. 25, 2003, 8.

14. Xinhua News Agency, English, Jan. 1, 1998.

15. *China Daily,* "800 Polluting Companies Get the Boot," July 12, 2002.

16. Aibing Guo, "Some 16,000 Polluting Enterprises Get Punished," *China Daily,* Oct. 7, 2002.

17. *China Daily,* "More Effort Needed to Stop Pollution," Oct. 27, 2000.

18. Conversation with SEPA director Xie Zhenhua, New York, Spring 1998.

19. Elizabeth Economy, *The River Runs Black: The Environmental Challenge to China's Future* (Ithaca, NY: Cornell University Press, 2004).

20. Michael T. Rock, "Integrating Environmental and Economic Policy Making in China and Taiwan," *American Behavioral Scientist* 45(9) (May 2000).

21. State Environmental Protection Administration, *2001 Report on the State of the Environment in China* (Beijing: 2001).

22. Abigail Jahiel, "The Organization of Environmental Protection in China," *China Quarterly* (Dec. 1998): 772.

23. New China News Agency, "China Punishes Nine Officials for Pollution of River by Unprocessed Waste Water," July 15, 2003.

24. Jonathan Schwartz, "Understanding Enforcement: Environment and State Capacity in China," *Sinosphere* 3(4) (Fall 2000): 14.

25. Interview with Shanghai Environmental Protection Bureau official, Shanghai, September 1999.

26. *China Daily,* "Environmental Impact Consultants Punished," June 21, 2002.

27. Hua Wang, Mamingi Mlandu, Benoit Laplante, and Susmita Dasgupta, "Incomplete Enforcement of Pollution Regulation: Bargaining Power of Chinese Factories," World Bank Working Paper Series: Environment, Pollution, Biodiversity, Air Quality, no. 2756 (Washington, DC), 6 (Apr. 2002), http://wbln0018.worldbank.org/research/workpapers.nsf/. econ.worldbank.org/files/3605_wps2756.pdf.

28. Shengwen Zou, "Wo guo huanjing jigou jiang bu zai chi pai wu fei" (China's Environment Protection Apparatus Will No Longer Be Able to Pocket Waste Discharge Fees), 2002, www.china.org.cn/chinese/2002/Jan/973539.htm.

29. *Ming Pao* (Hong Kong), "State Council Strips Environmental Protection Agency of Right to Use Sewage Charges," trans. *FBIS Daily Report China,* Mar. 30, 2001.

30. Kezhu Xu, "A Case of Air Pollution Damage by Cement Plants in Yulin City, Guangxi Province," in Canfa Wang, Jing Hu, Tadayoshi Terao, Kenji Otsuka, Min Liu, and Kezhu Xu, *Studies on Environmental Pollution Disputes in East Asia: Cases from Mainland China and Taiwan,* Joint Research Program Series 128 (Chiba, Japan: Institute of Developing Economies, 2001), 93–108.

31. "Zhejiang Peasants Compensated for Pollution," Jan. 13, 2003, www.cenews.com.cn/english/2003-01-13/201.php.

32. Ya Wang, "Car Owner Wins Pollution Suit," Apr. 14, 2003, www.cenews.com.cn/english/2003-04-14/287.php .

33. Mark O'Neill, "Decorator Pays for Using Toxic Chemicals," *South China Morning Post,* Jan. 2, 2003.

34. *China Daily,* "Two Officials Imprisoned for Neglect of Their Duties," Aug. 6, 2002.

35. Tamora Vidaillet, "Chinese Turn to Law to Right Pollution Wrongs," Reuters, Feb. 5, 2002.

36. Jize Qin, "Villagers Speak Out on Arsenic," *China Daily,* Dec. 17, 2002.

37. U.S. Embassy-Beijing, "Environment, Science and Technology Update," Jan. 31, 2003, www.usembassy-china.org.cn/sandt/estnews013103.htm.

38. Interview with Chinese environmental lawyer at the Council on Foreign Relations, New York, Oct. 2002.

39. " . . . many countries have legal procedures stipulating 'class action' and 'representative action.' Although Chinese civil law procedure also stipulates such a system, the court [sic] there also have [sic] the judicial power to decide whether to try lawsuits as class actions." Source: Canfa Wang, Kezhu Xu, and Min Liu, "A Summary of Policy and Legal Analysis on Dealing with Environmental Disputes in China," in Wang et al., *Studies on Environmental Pollution Disputes in East Asia,* 20.

40. "Clean Progress Sought on Pollution Fight," *People's Daily,* Oct. 10, 2001.

41. Interview with Chinese environmental lawyer at the Council on Foreign Relations, New York, Oct. 2002.

42. *China Environment News,* Dec. 18, 2001.

43. Shanghai Environmental Protection Bureau, "2003 Shanghai Environmental Bulletin," www.sepb.gov.cn/english/2003.htm.

44. Roberts, "The Greening of China," 53.

45. Ibid.

46. *China Daily,* "Electronic Eyes to Watch Polluters," Nov. 20, 2003.

47. U.S. Embassy-Beijing, "Defending China's 'Water Tower': Environmental Protection in Qinghai Province," April 2003, www.usembassy-china.org.cn/sandt/ptr/Water-Tower-prt.htm.

48. Brian Rohan, "Clearing the Air: The Human Rights and Legal Dimensions of China's Environmental Dilemma," [US] Congressional/Executive Commission on China Issues Roundtable, Jan. 27, 2003. Available as written testimony at www.cecc.gov/pages/roundtables/012703/rohanStmt.php.

49. Tradable permits is a system by which pollution caps are set and the rights to pollute are bought and sold among participating factories or other actors.

50. Economy, *The River Runs Black*, p. 216.

51. Interview with Chinese environmental NGO official, Council on Foreign Relations, New York, April 2002.

52. Allen T. Cheng, "Western Province Projects Get $122b Injection," *South China Morning Post*, Mar. 26, 2003.

53. *China Daily*, "Take Environment into Account," Nov. 6, 2003, www.china.org.cn/english/environment/79320.htm.

54. Human Rights in China, press release, "Activist Writer Wang Lixiong Dismissed from Environmental Group," Feb. 14, 2003, http://iso.hrichina.org/iso/news_item.adp?news_id=1235.

55. Jun Liu and Qian Zeng, "Public Take Recycling into Their Own Hands," *China Daily*, Sept. 8, 2000.

56. Jasper Becker, "Clean Up of River a Sham," *South China Morning Post*, Feb. 26, 2001, 8; *Far Eastern Economic Review*, "Intelligence" (Mar. 1, 2001): 10.

57. Xinhua News Agency, "Ordinary Chinese People Contribute Ideas to Harness Huaihe River," Aug. 9, 2003, www.China.org.cn/english/MATERIAL/72035.htm.

58. *China Environment News*, May 15, 1995, 13.

59. New China News Agency, "Chinese TV Reporter 'Attacked' by Factory Workers During Investigation," Nov. 13, 2003.

60. *1997 China Statistical Yearbook* (Beijing: China Statistical Publishing House, 1997), 770.

61. Anna Brettell, "Bounded Accountability: The Environmental Complaints System," *China Rights Forum Journal* 4 (2002).

62. Susmita Dasgupta and David Wheeler, "Citizen Complaints as Environmental Indicators: Evidence from China," *Sinosphere* 3(4) (fall 2000): 27–28.

63. Jun Jing, "Environmental Protests in Rural China," in Elizabeth S. Perry and Mark Seldon, eds., *Chinese Society: Change, Conflicts and Resistance* (New York: Routledge, 2000), 144.

64. *Inside China Mainland* 19, no. 3 (1997): 94, cited in Lisa Eileen Husmann, "Falling Lands, Rising Nations: Environmental Nationalism in China and Central Asia," Ph.D. diss., University of California, Berkeley, 1997, 150.

—— Chapter 5 ——

Beyond the Bureaucracy

Changing China's Policymaking Environment

Eric Zusman and Jennifer L. Turner

China is a country under severe environmental stress. Development and population pressures threaten China's forests, deserts, and coastal ecosystems. Escalating pollution levels poison China's air, water, and soil. Until recently, China's reputation for developing ineffective environmental policies made these environmental problems seem unsolvable. In recent years, China has developed air pollution regulations and supported resource conservation projects that promise to put its past reputation to rest. Domestically, environmental awareness has grown, and China's younger generation of leaders is better educated and more capable of absorbing new policy concepts and management tools than their predecessors. While these internal factors clearly played a role in China's environmental policy improvements, this chapter explores the significant influence of international organizations on strengthening environmental policy design and implementation in China.

Many theories on policymaking in China emphasize interbureaucratic obstacles to policy reform. In contrast, this chapter emphasizes the extrabureaucratic influences that international NGOs and multilateral organizations have had on policy innovation. As interest in protecting China's environment has spread, international organizations (bilateral, multilateral, and nongovernmental) have increased their activities inside China. These international organizations have enhanced communication and coordination among China's bureaucracies and empowered nonstate actors in the environmental policy sphere—highlighting how considerable policy change can be initiated beyond China's bureaucracy. Before illustrating the extent of external influence on environmental policies and projects in China, we begin with a discussion of perspectives on Chinese policymaking.

Bureaucratic Fragmentation in the Environmental Policymaking Sector

In 1979 Deng Xiaoping initiated internal economic, legal, and political reforms that decentralized considerable power within China's political system and opened the country to the global economy. The growing openness of the Chinese polity sparked an explosion of economic growth. It also gave rise to new theories on policymaking. Prior to Deng's reforms, most scholars argued that Chinese elites used policy decisions to strengthen their personal power bases, or that the subordinates of elites designed "rational" solutions to meet perceived policy problems. In the Deng era, the traditionally accepted "power" and "rationality" approach gave way to a third approach: bureaucratic fragmentation.

Bureaucratic fragmentation focuses on organizations within the state—chiefly regional governments and functional ministries—as the actors with the most pull in the policymaking process. Because these organizations typically have narrowly conceived sectoral interests and responsibilities, they tend to develop competing visions of the appropriate course of policy action. Consensus-building institutions in Beijing are either too overburdened or uninformed to resolve the myriad disputes that arise out of such a system. Thus, bureaucracies are forced to bargain over the substance of policy. The result is policy outcomes vague enough to appease bureaucratic stakeholders but often so ineffective that policy problems remain unsettled (Lampton 1987, Lieberthal and Lampton 1992, Lieberthal and Oksenberg 1988).

A related set of bureaucratic obstacles frustrates policy implementation. In China, central government ministries oversee lower-level agencies through tight vertical lines of authority (*xitong*). These vertical lines obstruct horizontal coordination among local government agencies, particularly when resource management issues cut across jurisdictional boundaries. For example, if one county receives pollution dumped downstream by a county upstream, water pollution and water management laws mandate that the provincial government mediate the conflict. Sometimes, however, the central government's Ministry of Water Resources intercedes because provincial governments are unable to manage conflicts between counties (Turner 1997).[1] To get a firmer handle on the key actors involved in environmental policymaking, we outline organizations that play a key role in environmental policymaking.

Competing Environmental Policy Bureaucracies

China's State Environmental Protection Administration (SEPA) is the chief architect of national environmental protection standards, regulations, and laws.[2] Promoted to the level of State Council ministry in 1998, SEPA shares this responsibility with the Natural Resource and Environmental Protection Committee of the National People's Congress and numerous central government bureaucracies with interests in issues related to environmental protection (such as the Ministry of Science and Technology, Ministry of Water Resources, and Forestry Bureau).

While the influence of these other organizations varies greatly depending on the issue, SEPA is involved in most facets of environmental policymaking and standard setting. The environmental protection system (*huanbao xitong*) also consists of more than 16,000 local environmental protection bureaus (EPBs) (*difang huanbaoju*) affiliated with and falling below SEPA at the provincial, municipal, county, and township levels. The local EPBs are tasked with implementing regulations and tailoring national ordinances to meet local conditions.[3] The EPBs hold a dual allegiance to SEPA and their local government.

The State Council sits atop the organizational hierarchy.[4] The State Council is charged with coordinating bureaucratic interests and reconciling bureaucratic conflicts. The Environmental Protection Commission, a nonadministrative, interministerial coordination mechanism, was established in 1993 to assist the State Council with these responsibilities.

SEPA shares the same official rank as other functional line ministries in the central government, China's thirty-two provincial governments, and the newly formed National Development and Reform Commission (NDRC). In 2002 NDRC merged the functions of the former State Development Planning Commission and the State Economic Trade Commission (SETC). Therefore, SEPA and EPBs are nested in a matrix of authority relationships that hamper the development and implementation of environmental policies when interests conflict—as frequently occurred in Deng's progrowth era (Jahiel 1998, Xue et al. 2000) (Figure 5.1).

Weak Enforcement of Environmental Policies

Over the past twenty years, economic bureaucracies as well as provincial and lower-level regional governments have been SEPA's chief organizational rivals because they believed that harsher environmental regulations would force coal mines to shut down, power plants to reduce energy production, logging industries to lay off workers, and, most importantly, localities to slow economic growth. In fact, central government ministries often used the last rationale—that environmental protection and economic development were inherently contradictory—as a foil against SEPA's advocacy of more stringent environmental regulations. Local governments also used this logic to

Figure 5.1 **Bureaucratic Fragmentation**

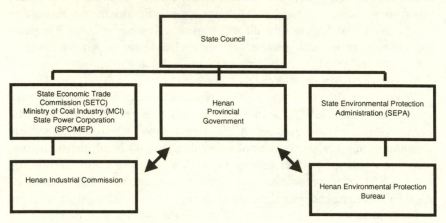

Source: This model is adapted from Ma and Ortolano 2000, 39.

justify actions that blunted the EPBs' implementation of environmental regulations (Jahliel 1998).

Thus, through the early 1990s, the widely held belief that proenvironmental and progrowth objectives were mutually exclusive reinforced a systemic propensity to produce weak environmental regulations and stymie their implementation. If the story ended here, this chapter would resemble many previous analyses that associated policy weakness with bureaucratic fragmentation. However, China's efforts to mitigate one of its most intractable air pollution problems—acid rain—and to address complex biodiversity conservation challenges present a wrinkle in the standard plot line. Namely, international involvement in these areas has introduced new policy dynamics and facilitated cooperation among government agencies and nonstate actors. The accounts of international involvement in acid rain control policies and projects promoting energy efficiency and biodiversity differ from past bureaucratic fragmentation analyses of China's environmental protection history and offer a more optimistic prediction about the country's future policy development (Shen 1999, Wang and Luo et al. 2001, Zusman 2001).

Air Pollution Inside and Outside China

Air pollution problems are not unique to China. Many areas in the developed world still struggle with local air pollution in excess of standards, while much of the industrializing world is just beginning to assess the social and ecological impacts of poor air quality. Instead, it is the cause of air pollution that distinguishes China from other regions. More than any other country, China depends on the combustion of coal for power generation and industrial production. Although the percentage of coal use has declined since its peak of 1.4 billion metric tons in 1996, it still accounts for nearly 70 percent of all power generated in China (Zhang and Wen 2000). As the common refrain in China's energy sector makes clear, for many years to come "coal will be taken first" (*yi meitan wei zhu*) (Zusman 2001).

Incinerating coal releases sulfur oxides, nitrous oxides, carbon oxides, ash, and other impurities into the atmosphere. Locally, coal smoke and particulate matter pose a direct threat to respiration, raising morbidity and mortality rates. Regionally, sulfur oxides and nitrous oxides react with other elements in the atmosphere to create acid precipitation, leveling a costly toll on the natural environment, reducing agricultural output, and damaging buildings and industrial infrastructure.

Measuring the impacts of acid precipitation is still an inexact science, and cost estimates vary widely, but most assessments are not encouraging. Some studies find that acid deposition has already reduced Chinese agricultural production by 5 to 10 percent (Zhang and Wen 2000, 47–50). Cross-sectoral figures place the total losses due to acid precipitation in China between 2 percent and 0.7 percent of gross domestic product (GDP) (Wang 2001). The best cost-benefit analysis to date predicts that in the areas in which acid precipitation hits China the hardest, the benefits of remedial action outweigh the costs by at least a ratio of 1.25 to 1 and at most by a ratio of 2.51 to 1 (Wang et al. 2001).

Although these figures are striking, they offer little insight into the expanding scope of China's acid rain problems. In the 1980s, acid deposition was most severe in the southwestern part of the country. The region with the most damage covered an area north of the Pearl River Delta, south of the Yangtze River Basin, and west of the Sichuan Plateau. Coal in the southwest has China's highest average level of sulfur concentration and was chiefly responsible for the previously localized problem. In the early 1990s, acidification became more acute in central China, with regions as far north as Liaoning and Shandong provinces confronting rising levels of acid deposition. These regions suffered from local pockets of high-sulfur coal as well as the interprovincial transport of sulfur emissions (Yang et al. 2001).

The discovery of the interprovincial transport of emissions came at roughly the same time that researchers discovered that China's air pollution problems were not confined to China. The prevailing winds that carried sulfur emissions among provinces also were to blame for acid deposition on the southern tip of Japan and the Korean peninsula.[5] In addition to this regional spreading, scientific studies launched in the mid-1990s predicted that China's coal-burning plants were discharging enough greenhouse gases (carbon dioxide [CO_2]) to place China on a trajectory that would surpass the United States as the chief contributor to global warming within two decades (Logan et al. 1999). China was becoming an environmental threat to both its domestic atmospheric commons and the regional and global commons.

A consequence of these discoveries has been that some regions in China that receive a disproportionate share of the damage from emissions have complained that regions that receive a disproportionate share of the benefits from those emissions should curb heavily polluting power plants (Zusman 2001). However, since most localities are not fully cognizant of the interregional transport of emissions, objections among Chinese regions have not been as pronounced as international calls for China to reduce its emissions.

Domestically, the battle over sulfur dioxide (SO_2) policy has been fought between environmental protection bureaucracies and opponents within local government agencies and industries that see stronger regulations as running counter to development priorities. Internationally, foreign governments and multilateral lending institutions have supported projects and research that advocates greater regulatory coordination and policy change. The evidence suggests that these international calls for better bureaucratic coordination have begun to be answered. The earliest evidence that an effective policy solution to China's acid rain problems might be on the horizon can be found in the second version of the Atmospheric Pollution Control Law (APCL) (*Daqi wuran fangzhi fa*).[6]

The second version of the APCL was passed in 1995. It states that, based on the recommendation of the chief environmental bureaucracy (in this case, SEPA), the State Council could cordon off regions in which acid rain or sulfur emissions are most serious and in which the sternest emissions reduction measures need to be implemented. Following up on this provision, in January 1998 the State Council ratified a plan that created the Acid Rain Control Zone and the Sulfur Dioxide Control Zone, commonly referred to as "the two control zones."

The two control zones cover 175 cities that contribute disproportionately to the total level of SO_2 emissions. These cities make up 11 percent of China's landmass and generate 60 percent of China's total emissions. Regions that receive precipitation below 4.5 pH, have rainfalls in excess of critical acid precipitation loads, and have relatively high SO_2 emissions qualify for classification in the Acid Rain Control Zone. Regions that have ambient air quality above national class 2 standards, daily emissions concentrations that surpass national class 3 standards, and relatively high SO_2 emissions qualify for classification in the Sulfur Dioxide Control Zone[7] (Yang et al. 2001) (Tables 5.1 and 5.2, Map 5.1).

The 1998 plan that created the two control zones was significant not only

Table 5.1

Details on the Two Control Zones

| Item | Two control zones | Broken down by zone | |
		Acid rain control zone	Sulfur dioxide control zone
Number of cities and/or areas	175	112	63
Area km²	105	78	27
1995 population (millions)	491	374	117
1995 GNP (billions of renminbi)	363.639	257.6157	106.0233
1995 total sulfur dioxide emissions (10,000 tons)	1395	793.4	601.6
2000 total sulfur dioxide emissions (10,000 tons)	1179	719	460

Source: Yang et al. 2001.

Table 5.2

Emission Allowances Across the Two Control Zones
(figures in the million of tons)

Year	2000	2005
National	19.95	17.95
The two control zones	11.79	9.40
SO$_2$ control zone	4.60	3.66
Acid rain control zone	7.19	5.73

Source: Yang et al. 2001.

in drawing regional borders around the problem but also in allowing central regulators in SEPA to set *quantity-based* emissions targets within that jurisdiction over subsequent five-year plans.[8] Codified in the third version of the APCL passed in 2000, the setting of quantity or total emissions control standards (*zongliang kongzhi zhibiao*) was a notable departure from regulations that had been much maligned for relying solely on concentration-based standards (*nongdu kongzhi zhibiao*) (Ma and Dudek 1999). Concentration-based standards allow enterprises and EPBs to focus on pollution concentrations in individual discharges without regard for the total amount of emissions from sources or regional emissions caps. At one time, this now-closed regulatory loophole had led to high compliance with standards and permitted an escalation in absolute quantities of emissions at the source and regional and interregional levels (Panayotou 1998, Wang, Ge, and Yang 2000).

The final addition to the recent air pollution regulations is the legal backing

Map 5.1   **The Two Control Zones**

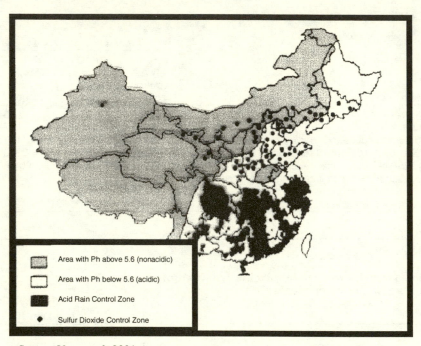

Source: Yang et al. 2001.

in the APCL 2000 for the total emissions control permits (*paifang wuran xukezheng*), which will allow EPBs to hold individual sources to agreed total emissions targets. Permits have been used on wastewater discharges in China since 1988 and were piloted for air pollutants in sixteen cities in 1992. The mention of permits in the APCL 2000 gives EPBs a legal justification for devolving emissions caps down to individual sources. For the time being, the permit system is still in a developmental phase, as most EPBs fill in emissions totals on their permits after pollution sources report them (Zusman 2001).

The two control zones, the total emissions control standards, and the permit system authorize SEPA and its subordinates to define quantifiable emissions loads and coordinate emissions targets at the source, regional and interregional levels. Allowing a central regulator to pass down emissions quotas and granting local regulators the statutory power to enforce these quotas are necessary elements of a comprehensive regulatory regime. More generally, the two control zones, the total emissions control standards, and the permit system illustrate an effort to integrate regulatory objectives in recent environmental legislation.

In being interviewed for this chapter, representatives from the central level and eight EPBs consistently emphasized that putting these new regulations into law marked a substantial step forward in reducing China's SO_2 levels. Seven of the eight EPB officials reinforced this sentiment when they indicated their offices were working hard to meet the new quantity-based total emissions control targets (Zusman 2001).[9] An international environmental management consultant shared this perspective in arguing that good-faith efforts to reach the new total control standards and having the necessary mechanisms in place to do so are more important than the immediate attainment of emissions control goals (Zusman 2001).

While these comments highlight recent advancements, they say little about the forces that brought them to fruition. The obvious question is, How did the environmental protection sector score the gains outlined above? This chapter argues that an important source of policy change resides beyond China's bureaucracy within international organizations. The next section turns to these external catalysts for policy change.

Multilateral and Bilateral Aid

As China's environmental problems have spread outside China, the World Bank, the Asian Development Bank (ADB), and foreign governments increasingly have leveraged their resources to offer new approaches to environmental management. Many of the techniques they support assume that economic development requires a healthy environment. They also presume that policies that effectively protect the environment require bureaucratic coordination. China's interaction with multilateral and bilateral agencies is illustrative of how the nature of international environmental cooperation has evolved.

For seventeen years, the World Bank has provided more than $7 billion to China for thirty-nine ongoing or completed energy-related projects. The World Bank's relationship with China began with energy-capacity building efforts and has since shifted to a more ecofriendly portfolio that ranges from energy conservation to heating district conversion to renewable energy development (Hildebrandt and Turner 2002, World Bank 2000). In the 1990s, the World Bank also published three major studies on Chinese environmental policy and contemplated reorienting its funding approach so that the bank could have greater influence on national and local environmental policy decisions.[10]

Since the mid-1990s, the ADB and foreign governments have followed and, in some senses, taken over the World Bank's lead in China. Since 1995, the ADB has offered low-interest loans for forty-seven projects with environmental or natural resource preservation as primary or secondary objectives (Asian Development Bank 2004).[11] Between 1995 and 1999, Japanese environment-related yen loans issued under official developmental assistance (ODA) increased fiftyfold (from 252 billion yen to 125 trillion yen) (Forrest, Turner, and Qin 2001).[12] Even though U.S. government agencies are constrained by congressional restrictions on aid and assistance to China, in 2001 and 2002 U.S. government agencies undertook 199 environmental and energy conservation initiatives in China—primarily scientific and policy training exchanges or joint research projects (Turner 2002, 2003).

China's Ministry of Foreign Trade and Economic Cooperation (MOFTEC) must approve all foreign aid projects in China (Baldinger 2000, Zusman 2001). While having a central ministry determine the suitability of projects has slowed environmental aid, it also has ensured that, when projects are approved, they generally offer benefits to China. The significant growth in China's level of international environmental assistance over the past decade indicates that not only are domestic agencies becoming better at proposing projects in which Chinese interests are served but also international actors have become more willing to fund projects that seek to remedy nominally domestic concerns.

It is important to keep in mind the qualification "nominally domestic" when thinking about the international organizations' motivations for these projects. Recent evidence suggests that there is a growing recognition among the foreign development community that projects aimed at domestic environmental concerns in China will have positive spillover effects for the regional and global environmental commons. In other words, the dividing line between China's domestic and international problems has begun to fade (Nielsen 2000). Examples of international aid's targeting international and domestic air quality concerns include:

- World Bank and Japan have grassland protection initiatives in northern and western China to halt desertification and mitigate sandstorms that plague northern China, Japan, and Korea.
- European Union and Japanese bilateral aid programs are beginning to investigate the potential of Clean Development Mechanism (CDM) pilot projects to improve local air quality and limit CO_2 emissions.
- Japanese bilateral model city programs often include investments and new municipal regulations of electricity plants to decrease SO_2 emissions that damage forests and crops in China, Japan, and Korea.
- The Japanese and Korean governments have been active in bringing China into regional cooperative organizations (such as Korean, Chinese, and Japanese tripartite environmental ministerial meetings and the Acid Deposition Monitoring Network in East Asia) to promote projects and policy research to decrease SO_2 emissions from China.

- The ADB, Resources for the Future, U.S. EPA, and Norwegian Institute for Air Research are working with the Shanxi provincial government and the Taiyuan municipal government to develop a workable SO_2 emissions trading system in Taiyuan.
- Environmental Defense, a U.S.-based NGO, is working with the Chinese NGO, Beijing Environment and Development Institute; SEPA; and EPBs in Shandong, Shanxi, Jiangsu, and Henan provinces to study and set up market-based emissions trading instruments to reduce SO_2 pollution.

The last two projects—the tradable SO_2 emissions projects—are particularly noteworthy because they have brought together Chinese government agencies with domestic and international research institutes and NGOs to address China's acid rain problems. Participants in these projects begin by setting a regional cap on emissions over a stipulated time period, allocating permits to individual sources in that region, and determining which sources can purchase and sell permits (at market-determined prices). The process of setting emissions caps, allocating permits, and determining the rules for trades had the effect of enhancing regulatory coordination.

To have their intended effects, tradable permit projects require that central and local government agencies, legal experts, and research institutes define quantity-based standards and distribute pollution permits. Once again, the quantity-based standards and pollution permits only recently were codified in the amended Air Pollution Control Law (APCL). While the veiled nature of decision making in China makes it impossible to link the tradable emissions and pollution taxes to the APCL reforms, it is clear that the pilot projects on emissions trading and pollution taxes have brought together a diverse collection of international and domestic environmental policy experts and, in so doing, strengthened the legal basis for coordination between regional and functional bureaucracies. The next section highlights how international environmental NGOs similarly have sparked policy networks and cooperation among Chinese state and nonstate actors in the energy-efficiency and biodiversity spheres.

International NGOs Building New Policy Networks

International assistance to address environmental issues has not been confined to large-scale investments from multilateral or bilateral agencies. The Ford Foundation and World Wildlife Fund (WWF) have maintained offices and funded environment-related projects in China since the mid-1980s.[13] Shortly thereafter, the International Crane Foundation (ICF) began conducting research in China. These early efforts set the stage for a sharp increase in NGO assistance during the late 1990s.

The recent surge in both domestic and international NGO activity reflects a greater awareness of China's impact on the global environment. Three issues currently top the international NGO agenda: reducing greenhouse gas emissions, maintaining biodiversity, and promoting "green" civil society. This section begins with a discussion of international (primarily U.S.-based) NGO involvement in energy-related projects. It then segues into international NGOs' involvement in resource conservation and biodiversity projects. A recurring theme in this section is that the most successful NGO projects take into account the need to communicate and coordinate between affected parties— especially Chinese bureaucracies.

NGOs and Energy Projects in China

Energy-related projects have been one of the most dynamic areas of NGO activity in China. The confluence of interests among private, public, national, and international interests is the primary reason that these projects have flourished. From China's perspective, energy-efficient technologies and management techniques provide obvious benefits to industry, while less obviously reducing the effects of pollution on crops, forests, and inland fisheries.

From the perspective of NGOs, the transfer of energy-efficient technologies and management techniques to China improves air quality and stabilizes energy sources for Chinese citizens as well as reducing greenhouse gas emissions and other regionally harmful pollutants. Moreover, promotion of energy efficiency and energy conservation in China could be crucial for future world energy markets, in which China is already a major player.

Yet, the confluence of interests does not end there. In fact, international NGOs have been particularly resourceful at identifying mutually beneficial opportunities for cooperation. Between 2000 and 2002, thirteen international NGOs and four U.S.-university-affiliated research centers launched thirty-nine energy-related projects in China. These projects cover everything from energy policy development to energy-efficiency technology standard-setting to market construction for energy-efficiency technologies (Table 5.3).

International Institute for Energy Conservation (IIEC)

From 2000 to 2002, IIEC's collaboration with the Chinese motor industry, the Ministry of Finance, and central agencies responsible for motor production yielded energy-efficiency standards to regulate motor manufacturers in China (Hildebrandt and Turner 2002). Since the motor project's completion,

Table 5.3

U.S. Nongovernmental Organization Energy Projects, 2002

Organization	Project title	Partners
Alliance to Save Energy	Energy Efficiency Seminars	Municipal government offices
The Atlantic Council	Clean Air for China and India	Committee for Energy Policy Promotion of Japan, Confederation of Indian Industry, South-North Institute for Sustainable Development (SNISD, Chinese NGO)
American Council for an Energy Efficient Economy	• Green Lights Program • U.S.-Sino Energy Efficiency Teams	SETC, Global Environmental Facility, Beijing Energy Efficiency Center (BECon, Chinese NGO), State Development Planning Commission (SDPC), UN Industrial Development Organization, U.S. DOE, Lawrence Berkeley National Laboratory (LBLN), local Chinese partners
Center for Energy and Environment Policy	Renewable Energy for Rural Electrification in Western China	Chinese Ministry of Agriculture, Chinese Academy of Sciences, U.S. DOE, U.S. National Renewable Energy Laboratory (NREL)
Center for Resource Solution	Two Energy Policy Assistance Projects	Lawrence Berkeley National Laboratory (LBNL)
Environmental Defense	Two SO_2 Emissions Trading Pilot Projects	Beijing Environmental Development Institute (Chinese NGO) and Chinese State Environmental Protection Administration
Natural Resources Defense Council	• Two Energy Efficient Building Codes Projects • Fertilizer Industry Project • Energy Policy Project • Fuel Cell Scooter Technology Development • Controlling Power Plant Emissions	U.S. DOE, Chinese Ministry of Science and Technology, LBNL, Chongqing City Economic Commission, State Power Company, Energy Research Institute (China), BECon, SNISD, Taiwan Institute for Economic Research, China Research Academy for Environmental Sciences (CRAES), Regulatory Assistance Project, and Massachusetts Department of Environmental Protection

(continued)

Table 5.3 (*continued*)

Organization	Project title	Partners
Joint Institute for Energy and Environment	• Renewable Energy for Rural China, Global Climate Change • Reform of the Pollution Levy System	SEPA, Chinese Research Academy of Environmental Science
WWF-China	Evaluation of Wind Power Development in China China Air Conditioner Energy Efficiency Standards	BECon, Jikedian Renewable Energy Development Center
Export Council for Energy Efficiency	International Energy Efficiency MTechnology Assistance Program (directs grants from U.S. DOE to various energy NGOs to do work in China)	Alliance to Save Energy, IIEC, National Association of Energy Service Companies, National Association of State Energy Officials, Solar Energy Research and Education Foundation, China Energy Conservation Association, Shanghai Energy Conservation Center, China State Power
Massachusetts Institute of Technology	Sustainable Urban Housing, Coalwashing Study of Japan's Green Aid in China	
International Institute for Energy Conservation	• Appliance Standards, Labeling, and Market Transformation • Compressed Natural Gas Transportation Project • Energy Efficient Transformers • CFC/Copper Energy Efficiency Program in China for Energy-Efficient Industrial Motors and Motor Systems	State Development and Planning Commission, State Economic and Trade Commission, China State Bureau of Quality and Technology Supervision, Small and Medium Electrical Motor Association, German GTZ, NREL, LBNL, U.S. DOE, City of Xiamen, numerous other Chinese research institutes
National Research Council	Future of Personal Transport in China	Chinese Academy of Engineers

Resources for the Future	Air Quality Improvement in Shanxi (SO_2 emissions trading from electricity utilities)	Norwegian Institute for Air Research, RCA Associates, CRAES, Shanxi Provincial Government, Taiyuan Municipal Government, U.S. EPA
Renewables for Development	Large-Scale Rural Electrification Through Renewable Energy	IN-SHP (Chinese NGO)
U.S.-China Energy and Environment Technology Center, Tulane University	• Energy Conversion System Optimization for Steel Mills • Health Effects of Clean Coal Technology Transfer • Integrated Resource Planning for Major Cities in China • U.S.-China Clean Coal Technology Center • Feasibility Study for Marketing Gasification Technology in China	BaoSteel and Ma-An-Shan Steel Mills, Center for Bio-environmental Research, MIT, Tsinghua University, LBNL, NREL, Chinese city governments, Chinese Institute for Gas Technology, Shanghai Coking Corporation and other Chinese energy industries, China Clean Coal Research Center
Harvard University Center for the Environment, China Project	Dynamic Economy-Energy-Environment Model Total Damages of Energy-Related Air Pollution to Human Health and the Economy in China	John F. Kennedy School of Government and Department of Economics at Harvard University, Chinese Academy of Social Sciences, Chinese Institute of Quantitative and Technical Economics
Total: Seventeen organizations (four of which are university research centers)	Thirty-nine projects	

Source: Turner, ed. 2002. "Inventory of Environmental Work in China," 137–89.

other industries in China have requested IIEC's assistance with the development of energy-efficiency markets for their own technologies.

Among the numerous factors underlying IIEC's success, a few stand out as particularly noteworthy. IIEC operates an office in China and employs a small Chinese staff. It also places a premium on networking with the government and industry officials prior to initiating a project. In the early stages of the motor project, for instance, IIEC interviewed government and industry stakeholders interested in promoting energy-efficiency technology in China. Through these discussions, IIEC staff discovered that government regulators and industrial participants felt that the motor sector had a need that foreign expertise could fill. Hence, local buy-in for the project existed before it formally began.

Natural Resources Defense Council (NRDC)

In the late 1990s, one innovative NRDC lawyer, with support from the Energy Foundation and the W. Alton Jones Foundation, created the China Clean Energy Program within NRDC. This energy program has been exemplary in creating diverse and effective networks within China. NRDC's China Clean Energy Program aims to promote energy efficiency, renewable energy technologies, and tighter emissions standards in China in the construction, utility, and transportation sectors.

One of the most innovative projects within this NRDC program has been the Initiative for Taipei-Shanghai Cooperation on Fuel Cell Vehicles and Sustainable Transportation. The W. Alton Jones Foundation supported this initiative both to introduce clean scooter technology to mainland China and to build cross-strait environmental cooperation to reduce political tensions. In this project, NRDC has created a tripartite partnership of mainland Chinese, Taiwanese, and U.S. institutions to promote the diffusion of fuel-cell-powered vehicles, especially motor scooters, in mainland China. NRDC has patiently built trust with one Beijing-based NGO (South-North Institute for Sustainable Development) and the Taiwan Institute for Economic Research. Together with these two partner organizations, NRDC explored bringing together business partners and the municipal governments of Taipei and Shanghai. As a U.S. environmental NGO, NRDC would have found it nearly impossible to gain access to the Shanghai and Taipei governments, but the local partners helped initiate these contacts. NRDC was a skillful manager of building the state and nonstate partnerships for this scooter project, which continues to move ahead with the support of its partners.

NRDC has built similarly diverse partnerships between state and nonstate organizations in their efficient buildings projects. The most successful has been an energy-saving building codes project, supported by the U.S. Department of Energy (DOE) and the Energy Foundation. NRDC has been working with China's Ministries of Science and Technology and of Construction and the Lawrence Berkeley National Laboratory to reduce energy consumption in Chinese buildings by setting standards. NRDC succeeded in pulling Chinese private-sector participants (for example, developers of materials and equipment manufacturers) into this standard-setting process.

Moreover, the Chongqing city government agreed to allow NRDC to assemble a team of experts to review the city's draft building-code legislation—the first of its kind in China. While the city government initially was nervous about showing the draft legislation to foreigners, the Chinese officials did use the advice to craft detailed building-codes management and implementation regulations. The city officials were so pleased with the resulting building codes that NRDC has been invited to continue to help them in the implementation stages (Watson and Finamore 2002).

The NRDC and IIEC have helped to build bridges between usually uncooperative government bureaucracies. Both Chinese government and industries are beginning to recognize the economic benefits of energy-efficiency savings and therefore have been willing to work with international energy NGOs and adopt innovative new policies and management mechanisms. While younger bureaucrats in China are much better trained than their predecessors, the leaders of their agencies are not always open to new ideas from those below them. However, international environmental NGOs sometimes are able to empower younger bureaucrats, who can point to advice from the foreign experts as justification to introduce new ideas.

Funders Supporting NGO Energy Projects in China

The W. Alton Jones Foundation, the Energy Foundation, and the U.S. DOE (directly and indirectly through U.S. national energy laboratories) have been the chief funding sources for NGO energy projects in China. The U.S. DOE, for example, has provided support for eleven of the seventeen NGOs and research centers engaged in energy work in China. The two foundations have been active in increasing international and domestic NGO energy projects and research in China as well.

In the late 1990s, the Energy Foundation began the Sustainable Energy Program, through which it provided grants to Chinese organizations. The program opened doors for U.S. NGOs hoping to gain footholds in China, since many of the Chinese grantees chose U.S. NGOs as their project partners.

The Energy Foundation also created the U.S.-China Policy Advisory Council to promote the exchange of ideas and information about energy problems among Chinese and foreign governments, NGOs, and research communities. This council is composed of Chinese and U.S. energy scholars and former policymakers and has gained access to high-level Chinese officials.[14]

Most energy NGOs have built strong partnerships with Chinese energy research centers. In a unique case, Battelle, a research center affiliated with the U.S. Pacific Northwest National Laboratory, helped create an energy technology and policy research center in China: The Beijing Energy Efficiency Center (BECon). Battelle and other international NGOs and energy research institutes conduct joint research with BECon researchers, making their center a major player in Chinese energy policy circles.

Biodiversity and Conservation

In 1998 a series of floods struck the Yangtze River, resulting in thousands of casualties and approximately US$20 billion in property losses. These floods represent the most vivid example in recent memory of the tremendous strains placed on China's natural resources and biologically diverse regions. The floods were a symptom of problems that run deeper than a single incident. An inestimable but growing percentage of forests and grasslands in western China have been denuded, which was one of the primary causes of the Yangtze floods (Sun 2001). Development is encroaching on many of China's nature reserves and threatening animal and plant species—between 15 and 20 percent of which are endangered in China (Glacy 2002, Huang 2003). Damage to nature reserves and growing forest and water degradation—particularly in the southwest, which is the country's most biodiverse region—have drawn the attention of international NGOs.

In fact, next to energy, biodiversity and resource conservation became the second largest area of NGO project activity in the 1990s. In 2001 alone, twelve international NGOs and one U.S. university were responsible for thirty-two conservation and biodiversity protection projects in China (Table 5.4). Similar to NGO energy initiatives, conservation projects have been most effective when they involved relationships with multiple partners and opened channels of communication among local state and nonstate actors. In contrast to the energy projects, international conservation NGOs have found it more challenging to establish these relationships and open these channels.

World Wildlife Fund (WWF)

WWF arguably has had the most success in implementing projects and sparking environmental policy change in China, due, in no small measure, to the

Table 5.4

U.S. Nongovernmental Organization Biodiversity and Conservation Projects, 2002

Organization	Project title	Partners
The Nature	Yunnan Great Rivers Project	Yunnan Provincial Government (and Yunnan Provincial Planning Commission, Conservancy Department of Forestry, and other provincial bureaus), Institute of Forest Planning and Design, SW College of Forestry, Kunming Institutes of Biology and Zoology, Yunnan University Institute of Ecology
University of Wisconsin	Community-based Management of Natural Resources	Inter-Agency Consortium of Yunnan Province, Chiangmai University (Thailand), U.S.-China Environmental Fund, Global Environment Facility, UN Development Programme
WWF-China	• Panda Program • Integrated Conservation and Development in Pingwu County • Pilot Projects in Wetland Restoration and Use	Local governments and communities in project areas
International Snow Leopard Trust	Snow Leopard Management Plan	Mountain Institute, Office of Working Commission and Management Bureau of the QNNP
Pesticide Action Network North America	World Bank Accountability Project–China Case Study	Center for Community Development Studies (Yunnan-based Chinese NGO)
World Resources Ecological Institute	Resources Policy Support Initiative	Center for Biodiversity and Indigenous Knowledge, Research Center for Ecological and Environmental Economics, Yunnan Academy of Social Sciences, Yunnan Institute of Geography

(continued)

Table 5.4 *(continued)*

Organization	Project title	Partners
Rural Development Institute	Dongfang County Rural Land Tenure Reform Pilot Project
Legal and Policy Approaches to Land Tenure on Grassland and Forest land
Rural Land Tenure System
Legal and Policy Reform Initiative
Land Management Law
Monitoring Survey Project	China Institute for Reform and Development, Dongfang County Government (Hainan Province), Center for Community Development Studies, Development Research Center of the State Council, World and Forest Land Bank, Renmin University
Conservation International	Two Hot Spot Conservation Projects (Hengduan Mountains in Sichuan and an area that overlaps into Sichuan and Yunnan provinces)	Sichuan Provincial Government and several county governments, Sichuan provincial research institutes
Missouri Botanical Garden	Flora of China Project	Harvard University; California Academy of Sciences; Botanical Institutes of Beijing, Guangzhou, Kunming, and Nanjing; The Smithsonian Institution
International Crane Foundation	Integrating Conservation with Rural Development at Caohai Nature Reserve
Protection of Black-Necked Cranes in Tibet
Studies of Waterbirds and Water Levels for Conservation of Threatened Wetlands at Poyang Lake Environmental Summer Camp Exchange between Russia and China Conservation of Globally Significant Wetlands Used by Siberian Cranes
Coordinated Crane County on the Yunnan/Guizhou Plateau	Chinese State Forestry Admin. Forest Bureaus of Heilongjiang, Jilin, Yunnan, Tibet, and Jiangxi Provinces; Caohai Nature Reserve; Guizhou Environmental Protection Agency; Trickle-up Program; Tibet Plateau Institute of Biology; Agro-Environmental Protection Institute; Poyang Lake Nature Reserve; Jiangxi Nature Reserve Management Office; Muraviovka Park (Russia); Changlindao Nature Reserve (China)

Organization	Project	Partners
International Fund for Animal Welfare	China Bear Campaign Asian Elephant Habitat Conservation and Community Development Project Tibetan Antelope Campaign CITES Education and Awareness Beijing Raptor Rescue Center Pet Rescue Doctor Dog Humane Education	State Forestry Administration, China Wildlife Conservation Association, CITES China, Beijing University of Traditional Medicine, Animals Asia Foundation (Hong Kong), Wildlife Division of Simao Prefecture, Beijing and Yunnan Forestry Departments, Institute of Ecology at Beijing Normal University, GreenRiver (Chinese NGO), Wildlife Trust of India, Longon Metropolitan Police, Yunnan CITES office, SEPA, Nature Reserves in Qiang Tang, Kekexili, and Arjin Shan, International Bird Rescue and Research Center (California), California Rapter Center, Kadoorie Farm and Botanic Garden (HK), Beijing Zoo, Friends of Nature (Chinese NGO), Beijing Man and Animal Environment Education Center
Ford Foundation (as funder)	Indigenous Innovations and Alter-natives to Swidden-Fallow Agroforestry Systems in Xishuangbanna Ecotourism and Eco-Cultural Tourism	Grantee: Center for Biodiversity and Indigenous Knowledge
World Resources Institute (as funder)	Watershed Management Project	
Total: Thirteen organizations	Thirty-two projects	

Source: Turner, ed. 2002. "Inventory of Environmental Work in China," 137–89.

organization's demonstrated commitment to the country. Since the mid-1980s, WWF has gone from a staff of one to thirty and funded more projects than any international environmental NGO in China. As one might anticipate from its logo, WWF has focused much of its energy on researching panda populations and working with provincial and subprovincial forestry bureaus, research institutes, and local communities to protect these populations. As one might not anticipate from its logo, these collaborative efforts have aimed to help both pandas and people. Poverty alleviation initiatives, nature reserve manager training, community participation, and natural resource management decisions have been just a few areas reflecting WWF's focus, which is increasingly interconnected.

The goodwill that WWF has accumulated over the years has enabled it to expand the scope, depth, and efficacy of its projects far beyond what was initially expected in the 1980s. For instance, WWF staff is involved in projects that include conservation planning for forests in the upper Yangtze, nature reserve management training throughout Tibet, and a "Living Yangtze" program to better manage the Poyang wetland reserve in the lower reaches of the river. WWF also has begun to tackle energy conservation. For example, in a particularly inventive arrangement, WWF brought together Chinese government officials, scientists, and industry to develop an energy-efficiency standard for air conditioners.

International Crane Foundation (ICF)

Whereas WWF has expanded the range of its interests over time, the International Crane Foundation (ICF) has limited its activities to nature reserve management. For example, in 1993 nearly a decade of studying China's nature reserves culminated in an ambitious nature reserve project in Guizhou Province's Cao Hai Nature Reserve. When it ended, ICF's work in Cao Hai was one of the longest running natural resources interventions in China.

The Cao Hai project focused on designing a management strategy for a fragile wetland habitat in the reserve. The most distinctive aspect of the project was financing. Project administrators set up microfinance mechanisms (small grants and revolving loan funds) for local communities to develop sustainable farming and other business activities in and around the nature reserve. Because of these financing mechanisms, the Cao Hai reserve has become a model for other nature reserves in China. Managers from other reserves in China have visited Cao Hai, hoping to apply lessons learned to their own reserve. Cao Hai therefore has continued to be a place in which international organizations and foundations, local governments, and community groups can convene, cooperate, and learn about balancing biodiversity conservation and development.

The Nature Conservancy

The Nature Conservancy (TNC) began working with the Yunnan provincial government on conservation in northwest Yunnan in 1998. The first two-and-a-half years of this cooperative effort—known as the Yunnan Great Rivers Project—consisted of Chinese and U.S. researchers, NGOs, and government agencies studying the culture, history, and ecology of an area in northwest Yunnan. The studies allowed TNC staff to become familiar with local government officials, government-organized nongovernmental organizations (GONGOs), NGOs, local research centers, and community groups.

The more than forty partners in the project then participated in drafting a master plan for conservation in the area. The plan was completed in 2001 and incorporated in the Yunnan provincial government's tenth Five-Year Plan. It is unusual for community and NGO groups to draft plans with government agencies, but with TNC as the "glue," productive dialogues brought to realization this otherwise improbable outcome.

Similar to WWF, TNC has built a large staff of forty bilingual Chinese and U.S. citizens who are helping TNC set up demonstration projects in various areas of northwest Yunnan to implement the 2001 master plan. Since 2003, TNC and its governmental, scientific, and community partners have been working at five sites in northwestern Yunnan (covering 66,000 km^2) to introduce alternative energy systems and reduce the threat of fuel wood collection to forest ecosystems. TNC also brought in China's Tsinghua University and the U.S. Park Service to develop conservation area plans that integrate resource and tourism management for each of the five sites.

Despite the master plan, the Yunnan provincial government has been slow to expand its cooperation with TNC. The reason may be that TNC has spent more time constructing relationships with local governments than with the provincial government. It also may be that some Chinese partners find the concept of an NGO elusive or consider an NGO operating in a predominantly minority area suspicious. TNC officials are working to overcome these challenges by strengthening ties with provincial levels and creating a new process of local planning, involving local groups in the implementation of demonstration projects.

During the process of setting up the energy-efficiency and biodiversity projects, some of the U.S. NGOs created cooperative networks among government and nongovernmental organizations in China. Building such networks is quite an accomplishment and has helped provide models for better policy implementation in energy and conservation sectors in China. As highlighted in the SO_2 discussion, Chinese government agencies both within and between jurisdictions traditionally have encountered problems cooperating on environmental and energy issues. These problems are not confined to competing missions and turf battles but also include the lack of coordinating institutions or catalysts for cooperation—a role that some international organizations have come to play.

China's Changing Policymaking Environment

Research on the relationship between international environmental politics and China's domestic policies typically employs a bureaucratic fragmentation approach, faulting bureaucratic obstacles for sidetracking negotiations on international environmental treaties (Economy 1997, Oksenberg and Economy 1998). While compelling, this research focuses on the failure of diplomatic negotiations to alter behavior that may or may not be in Chinese actors' interest to change. As a result, the studies overlook the fact that some international cooperation has been more effective in creating opportunities to discover where mutual interests lie and, once mutual interests are located, facilitating communication and coordination among invested parties.

Research on "epistemic communities" and "policy moods" has influenced our thinking on these matters. Epistemic communities are made up of a group of experts who share a normative commitment and empirical solution to remedying a set of policy problems (Finnemore and Sikkink 1998, Haas 1992). Policy moods are a more diffuse set of ideas and norms that originate within China's leadership ranks and provide bureaucrats with cues to the types of policies acceptable to leaders (Tanner 1995). Although different in origin and agency, both epistemic communities and policy moods highlight how ideas and individuals can help overcome bureaucratic obstacles to policymaking.

In policy areas in which there is a high degree of uncertainty and a growing incentive for international cooperation—such as the environment—these moods and communities are likely to be increasingly influential.[15] The approach offered in this chapter takes this influence a step beyond moods and communities, making it both similar and different to a bureaucratic fragmentation approach. It is similar in that it stresses organizations, but different in that it stresses international organizations. It is similar in that it recognizes fragmented interests, but different in that it recognizes that these interests can be integrated. These differences raise two points concerning the changing nature of the environmental policymaking beginning outside and ending inside China.

First, from a purely structural standpoint, by virtue of their position outside the Chinese bureaucracy, multilateral, bilateral, and nongovernmental organizations are not subject to the same structural constraints that frustrate domestic agencies. Although it is true that aid projects require governmental approval, the more than 250 projects that have been initiated and the more than fifty Chinese cosponsors illustrate another truism: the exchange of knowledge and the development of relationships through these international cooperative efforts have forged a denser network of overlapping interests than can be envisioned in the bureaucentric view of the Chinese policymaking system.

Second, the rising frequency with which environmental projects have been approved in recent years underscores that the internationalization of China's "domestic" environmental problems has also induced an internationalization of the forces that impinge on policymaking. Chinese agencies interested in preserving the domestic environment and international agencies interested in preserving the global environment have capitalized on the growing domestic and international concern over China's environmental problems to boost the frequency and efficacy of their collaborative efforts within China.

Conclusion

This chapter argues that reforms in China's air pollution laws and the formation of the new policy networks of state and nonstate actors to implement energy and conservation projects have been influenced and promoted by multilateral, bilateral, and NGO aid and technical assistance. By navigating the bureaucracy and working with it, international organizations are helping to transmit international environmental norms and create avenues for future cooperation and coordination.

Although international organizations are the focus of this chapter, clearly their influence is not an all-inclusive explanation for China's recent progress in environmental policy. The current generation of policymakers and regulators in China unquestionably is more receptive to proenvironmental regulations than those occupying their positions even a decade ago. Moreover, the severity of China's pollution problems has increased public pressure on domestic officials to tighten laws and regulations. Yet, because China lacks democratic institutions, officials have been less sensitive to public pressures for policy change than pressures from international organizations.

In a China that is increasingly receptive to the global marketplace, international organizations are critical to understand the why, who, when, and how of policymaking. Such an approach might be not only applicable to explaining the sources of environmental policy, but also useful in other policy areas in which international cooperation plays a more prominent role. A possible direction for future research might compare different policy areas to determine the ways in which international organizations vary in their influence and why.

Notes

The SO_2 and multilateral organization sections of this study are based on interviews Eric Zusman conducted in the PRC during 2000 and 2001. Much of the data was obtained through research internships at the Chinese Research Academy of Environmental Sciences (CRAES) in Beijing. The author thanks the National Security Education Program and the University of California Institute of Global Conflict and Cooperation for funding these internships as well as for their logistical support. In particular, the author wishes to acknowledge Cao Dong, Wang Jinnan, and Yang Jintian at CRAES and Mao Xianqiang at Beijing Normal University for the insights that helped shape this study, and Richard Baum, Barbara Geddes, Linda Hasunuma-Choi, Michael Johnston, Michael Ross, Miranda Schreurs, Hiroki Takeuchi, James Tong, Yanqi Tong, and Richard Zusman for comments on earlier drafts. Errors of fact or interpretation are the author's alone.

The international NGO information in this chapter is drawn from the yearly inventory of U.S. NGO environmental and energy projects in China compiled by Jennifer Turner and Tim Hildebrandt and their interns at the Woodrow Wilson Center's China Environment Forum. Information also was drawn from monthly China Environment Forum meetings, which include a broad range of NGO representatives, government officials, and academics active in environmental work in China (www. wilsoncenter.org/cef/).

1. One extreme recent case involving two provinces occurred when tannery factories in Jiangsu Province emitted toxic pollutants into a river flowing into Zhejiang Province. Rural residents in Zhejiang became ill, and crops were poisoned. Because local and provincial governments in Zhejiang were unwilling or unable to help resolve the conflict, local residents in Zhejiang filled ten boats with stones and sank them at the provincial border to create a dam, which flooded and contaminated agricultural fields and villages in Jiangsu. Not surprisingly, violence ensued among border villages. The Ministry of Water Resources had to step in to resolve the conflict.

2. The institutional leverage of SEPA has increased over the past four years. In 1998 SEPA was promoted to ministerial status and given a vote at State Council meetings. It simultaneously received a cutback in personnel. While a cutback may not seem like an endorsement, it actually was much smaller than the personnel reductions suffered in many other ministries. SEPA does not have the same connections as some of the older ministries such as the Ministry of Water Resources, but SEPA is well situated in the organizational hierarchy because of its extensive connections outside of China. In recent years, SEPA has become better at using international support and the attention of the international community to advance its institutional goals.

3. Due to the sheer number of EPBs, it is impossible to assess the institutional leverage of these agencies. Their leverage tends to vary greatly from one region to another. Based on author interviews, EPBs tend to hold the most sway in the richer coastal provinces and in areas in which pollution has gotten so bad that it has attracted attention beyond the region.

4.—ED.: A detailed discussion of the structure of China's environmental law regime is contained in the chapter by Ferris and Zhang, this volume.

5. For instance, see the long-range transport and deposition study by Arndt and Carmichael (1995), which presents findings from the Regional Air Pollution Information System (RAINS-Asia) project, patterned after a similar system used in Europe to project the damage done from transboundary deposition.

6. This section borrows heavily from Ellerman, "Considerations for Designing a Tradable Permit System to Control SO_2 Emissions in China."

7. Class 2 standards are greater than .06 mg/m^3; class 3 standards are greater than 0.25 mg/m^3. *Source:* www.zhb.gov.cn/english/standards-search.php3?var=a&case_code=find_category.

8. The first plan to contain quantity-based SO_2 emissions targets was the ninth Five-Year Plan. The first plan to contain targets for the two control zones was the tenth Five-Year Plan.

9. One municipal EPB official who indicated in an interview that his city was not using the mass-loading standards was from Shanghai.

10. For instance, the World Bank initiated a project in Zhenjiang, Jiangsu Province, and Huhhot, Inner Mongolia, that would inform local residents of the pollution performance of local factories. The three major studies were *Environmental Strategy* (1992); *Clear Water, Blue Skies* (1997); and *China: Air, Land and Water* (1999).

11. The Asian Development Bank is working with Chinese policymakers to draft a Yellow River Basin Water Management Law. When completed, the law will mark the first time that China has ratified a law for a single river system.

12. Figures are available at *Japan's Annual ODA Report 1999,* www.mofa.go.jp/policy/oda/summary/1999/.

13. For superb coverage of various types of foreign NGOs and aid organizations operating in China, see the quarterly publication from Beijing "China Development Brief," www.chinadevelopmentbrief.com.

14. For example, a former head of China's Ministry of Energy, who also runs the China Research Society, heads the council.

15. For the difference in effectiveness between international and transnational organizational linkages, see Huntington 1973.

Bibliography

Arndt, Richard, and Gregory R. Carmichael. 1995. "Long-Range Transport and Deposition of Sulfur in Asia." *Water, Air and Soil Pollution* 85: 2283–88.

Asian Development Bank. 2004. "People's Republic of China: Project Profiles." www.adb.org/Documents/Profiles/ctry.asp?ctry=47.

Baldinger, Pamela. 2000. *Environmental Trends and Policies in China: Implications for Foreign Business.* Washington, DC: U.S.-China Business Council.

Economy, Elizabeth. 1997. "Chinese Policymaking and Global Climate Change: Two-Front Diplomacy and the International Community." In Schreurs and Economy 1997, 19–41.

Ellerman, A. Denny. 2001. "Designing a Tradable Permit System for the Control of SO_2 Emissions in China." Center for Energy and Environmental Policy Research, MIT Research Paper, web.mit.edu/ceepr/www/2001–009.pdf.

Finnemore, Martha, and Kathryn Sikkink. 1998. "International Norm Dynamics and Political Change." *International Organization* 52: 887–917.

Forrest, Richard, Jennifer Turner, and Xin Qin. 2001. "U.S.-Japan Environmental Cooperation: Promoting Sustainable Development in China." Draft report presented at the Woodrow Wilson Center Conference, Washington, DC, Nov. 20.

Glacy, Lawrence. 2002. "The Mismanagement of China's Nature Reserves." *China Environment Series* 5: 69–73.

Haas, Peter. 1992. "Introduction: Epistemic Communities and International Policy Coordination." *International Organization* (winter): 1–36.

Hildebrandt, Timothy, and Jennifer Turner. 2002. "Powering up the Dragon: World Bank and NGO Energy Efficiency Projects in China." *China Environment Series* 5: 12–15.

Hong Kong SAR Government, Environment, Transport and Works Bureau. 2003. "Emissions Trading." Paper to the Advisory Council on the Environment (ACE Paper 4/2003), www.etwb.gov.hk/boards_and_committees/ace/2003ace/paper042003/index.aspx?langno=1&nodeid=323.

Huang Liangbin. 2003. "The Zhangjiajie Phenomenon." *China Environment Series* 6: 132–35.

Huntington, Samuel. 1973. "Transnational Organizations in World Politics." *World Politics* 25: 333–68.

Jahiel, Abigail. 1998. "The Organization of Environmental Protection in China." *China Quarterly* no. 155 (Sept.): 756–87.

Lampton, David. 1987. "The Bargaining Treadmill." *Issues and Studies* (Mar.): 11–41.

Lieberthal, Kenneth, and David Lampton, eds. 1992. *Bureaucracy, Politics, Decision Making in Post-Mao China*. Berkeley: University of California Press.

Lieberthal, Kenneth, and Michel Oksenberg. 1988. *Policymaking in China: Leaders, Structures, and Processes*. Princeton: Princeton University Press.

Logan, Jeffrey, Aaron Frank, Jianwu Feng, and Indu John. 1999. "Climate Action in the United States and China." Environmental Change and Security Project. Woodrow Wilson Center, Washington, DC, May, www.pnl.gov/china/climactione.pdf.

Ma Xiaoying, and Leonard Ortolano. 2000. *Environmental Regulation in China: Institutions, Enforcement and Compliance*. Lanham, MD: Rowman and Littlefield.

Ma Zhong, and Daniel Dudek. 1999. *Zongliang kongzhi yu paiyu jiaoyi* (Total Emissions Control and Tradable Permits). Beijing: Zhongguo chubanshe.

Nielsen, Chris. 2000. "Perspectives on the Global and Chinese Environment." *China Environment Series* 3: 3–11.

Oksenberg, Michel, and Elizabeth Economy. 1998. "China: Implementation Economic Growth and Market Reform." In *Engaging Countries: Strengthening Compliance with International Environmental Accords,* ed. Edith Brown Weiss and Harold K. Jacobson. Cambridge: MIT Press.

Panayotou, Theodore. 1998. "The Effectiveness and Efficiency of Environmental Policy in China." In *Energizing China: Reconciling Environmental Protection and Economic Growth,* ed. by Michael B. McElroy, Chris P. Nielsen, and Peter Lydon. Cambridge: Harvard University Press.

Schreurs, Miranda A., and Elizabeth Economy, eds. 1997. *The Internationalization of Environmental Protection*. Cambridge: Cambridge University Press.

Shen Defu. 1999. "Huanjing jianli xianzhuang fenxi yu duice" (Analysis and Measurement of the State of Environmental Supervision). *Huanjing baohu kexue* (Environmental Protection Science) (Apr.): 46–48.

Sinkule, Barbara, and Leonard Ortolano. 1995. *Implementing Environmental Policy in China.* Westport, CT: Praeger.

Sinton, Jonathan, and David Fridley. 2001. "Hot Air and Cold Water: The Unexpected Fall in China's Energy Use." *China Environment Series* 4: 3–20.

Sun Changjin. 2001. "Paying for the Environment in China: The Growing Role of the Market." *China Environment Series* 4: 32–42.

Tanner, Murray Scot. 1995. "How a Bill Becomes a Law in China: Stages and Processes in Lawmaking." *China Quarterly* no. 141 (Mar.): 39–55.

Turner, Jennifer. 1997. "Authority Flowing Downwards? Local Government Water Policy Implementation in China." Ph.D. diss., Indiana University, Bloomington.

———. 2003. "Inventory of Environmental and Energy Work in China." *China Environment Series* 6: 199–280.

Turner, Jennifer, ed. 2002. "Inventory of Environmental Work in China 2002." *China Environment Series* 5: 137–89.

U.S. Embassy in China, Beijing. 2001. Environment, Science and Technology Section. "Translation of China's Year 2000 State of the Environment Report." www.usembassy-china.org.cn/sandt/SOTE4web.htm.

Wang Jinnan. 2001. "New Trends in Sulfur Dioxide Regulations." Presentation at State Environmental Protection Administration (SEPA)/Environmental Defense Meeting, Beijing, June 15.

Wang Jinnan, Chazhong Ge, and Jintian Yang. 2000. "Zhongguo de shui yu huanjing: shijian yu zhanwang" (China's Taxes and the Environment: Practice and Outlook). *Zhongguo huanjing zhengce* (Environmental Policy Research Series) (Mar. 1).

Wang Jinnan, Hong Luo, Ge Chachong, and Cac Dong. 2001. " 'Liang kongqu' suanyu he eryanghualiu wuran fangzhi 'shiwu' guihua shehui jingji yingxiang yu pinggu" (The Appraisal of Social and Economic Impacts of the Acid Rain and Sulfur Dioxide Control Program in the Total Control Area in the Tenth Five Year Plan). *Zhongguo huanjing zhengce* (Environmental Policy Research Series) (Apr. 20).

Watson, Robert, and Barbara Finamore. 2002. "Brick by Brick: Improving the Energy and Environmental Performance of China's Building." *China Environment Series* 5: 86–89.

World Bank. 2000. *The Bank's Assistance to China's Energy Sector: An OECD Country Sector Evaluation.* Washington, DC.

Xue Nanfa, Jingzhi Yang, Xueling Feng, and Shusong Cao. 2000. "Shichang jingji xingshi xia huanjing jiance gongzuo de sikao" (Considerations on Environmental Monitoring Under Circumstances of the Market Economy). *Sichuan huanjing* (Sichuan Environment) (Mar.): 73–75.

Yang Jintian, Dong Cao, Jinnan Wang, Shuting Gao, Hong Luo, Xiaoping Qian, Chazhong Ge, Wenhua Xiang, and Xinxin Qiu. 2001. "Sulfur Dioxide Trading Programs in China: A Feasibility Study." Chinese Research Academy of Environmental Science, Beijing.

Zhang Kunmin, and Zongguo Wen. 2000. "Nengyuan xiaolu: nengyuan duoyanghua he shixian kechixu fazhan" (Resource Efficiency: Resource Diversification and Realizing Sustainable Development). *Shanghai huanjing kexue* (Shanghai Environmental Science) (Feb.): 47–50.

—— Chapter 6 ——

Emissions Trading to Improve Air Quality in an Industrial City in the People's Republic of China

Richard D. Morgenstern, Piya Abeygunawardena, Robert Anderson, Ruth Greenspan Bell, Alan Krupnick, and Jeremy Schreifels

Can emissions trading or other instruments that harness the power of the market be effective tools for advancing sustainable development and improving environmental quality in the People's Republic of China (PRC)? Can such instruments reduce emissions at lower costs than conventional administrative approaches in a planned-market economy in which monitoring and enforcement systems are still in their infancy, and state-owned enterprises are the dominant polluters?

Studies by the Asian Development Bank (ADB) and others of the potential application of market-based instruments (MBIs) to enhance air quality in the PRC have been underway for more than a decade. Beginning in the early 1990s, the ADB encouraged a few one-off emissions trades in the PRC to offset air pollution from new coal-fired power plants.[1] The PRC's tenth Five-Year Plan (FYP) (2000–2005) calls for major emissions reductions, although it does not prescribe any specific ways to achieve them. This chapter reports on efforts, endorsed by a number of senior Chinese officials and supported by the ADB, to extend the pilot type of emissions trades to establish a demonstration of a cap and trade system to meet the goals of the tenth FYP. Cap and trade is a form of trading that sets a cap on emissions for enterprises in an area and lets them trade emissions authorizations (also called allowances or permits).

In spring 2001 the ADB awarded a contract to Resources for the Future (RFF) (based in Washington, DC), in cooperation with the Chinese Research

Academy of Environmental Sciences (CRAES) and the Norwegian Institute for Air Research (NILU), to strengthen the institutional capabilities of the provincial agencies to facilitate MBI implementation.[2] Demonstration of an emissions trading program in Taiyuan, the capital of Shanxi Province, was envisioned as a key step in the process.

With air quality that, at one time, had earned it the dubious distinction of being first on a World Bank list of the most polluted cities in the world, and significant pressure from the central government in Beijing to improve air quality, Taiyuan's municipal officials understandably were eager to participate in the study. The adage that "Rome wasn't built in a day" aptly describes the challenges involved in introducing a rigorous environmental management system, including emissions trading, in Taiyuan—an adage that would apply to most other environmental policy changes. Establishing a full-scale emissions trading system resembles assembling a complex mosaic through addressing a large number of technical issues, such as emissions monitoring, as well as policy-relevant and sometimes politically sensitive issues, such as designing and managing the trading system within the appropriate legal framework. The exercise is not merely a matter of mechanically assembling pieces into a working whole. In addition, a variety of stakeholders and constituents must understand how such a program works, agree that it is in their interests to be part of the effort, and be trained to do their shares in making it a reality.

To understand both the challenges and the proposed means of addressing them, a number of issues must be examined. Section II of this chapter explores the background for the project by addressing three questions: Why emissions trading? Why Taiyuan? and Why sulphur dioxide (SO_2)? Section III examines the institutional context for the emissions trading system. Section IV considers the rationale for the cap and trade type of program selected for the demonstration. Section V outlines the design of the proposed emissions trading system, and section VI offers a series of concluding observations.

Background

Heavy reliance on relatively uncontrolled coal combustion as a source of heat and power has created serious environmental problems in China. The toll on human health alone is estimated to cost approximately 2 percent of China's annual GDP.[3] Particulate matter (PM) and SO_2 are the major pollutants of concern, although with recent progress in reducing PM emissions, attention increasingly is shifting to the control of SO_2. In many urban areas, particularly the coal-rich northern provinces and heavily industrialized central and southern provinces, high SO_2 concentrations—along with fine particles created by the atmospheric transformation of SO_2 into sulfates—represent a serious public health threat.

The PRC shares in common with most of the developing world various challenges in implementing effective environmental protection. These include limited resources and regulatory experience, and a heavy national policy push toward economic development. Consequently, the Chinese government and its advisers lean heavily toward solutions that incorporate economic and administrative efficiency. In response to these concerns, the PRC has devoted considerable energy to developing frameworks for economic incentives. An early example is the pollution levy system. Piloted in 1978 and formally adopted in 1982, the pollution levy system is in use in most provinces. Under the theory of a levy system, firms facing high costs to reduce pollution would opt to pay the levy while firms facing lower costs would opt to treat the pollution until the point at which the additional cost of pollution abatement equaled the per-ton value of the levy.

Originally, the levy system was applied only to emissions concentrations that exceeded the national standards. The funds from the levy were used to finance the environmental protection bureaus (EPBs) and to create a mechanism for financing a portion of pollution control, not to enforce pollution standards. In 1993 the government initiated a pilot in two provinces and nine cities in which the levy rate was increased fivefold, and the levy was applied to total emissions. In 2000 the basis for calculating the levy nationwide was changed to total emissions.

However, even with recent increases, the levy still is estimated to be no more than half of typical marginal costs to abate emissions. The low rate, 80 percent of which is recycled back to enterprises for pollution control investment, creates only limited incentives to reduce emissions.[4] Enforcement is another issue. Although the emissions standards were set uniformly by the central government, local governments are in charge of collecting the fees. Revenue collections tend to be sensitive to local environmental and economic conditions.[5] Emissions fees in the late 1990s generally were collected only from profitable enterprises and, reportedly, the fee amount still could be negotiated with local EPBs.[6]

Why Emissions Trading?

One option that might facilitate reduced emissions could be to increase the levy as high as the estimated marginal abatement costs, if possible. A similar approach was recently announced in Beijing, which is undertaking a large number of reforms to reduce pollution prior to the 2008 Beijing Olympics. In fact, RFF explored this option with officials in both Shanxi Province and

Taiyuan. However, it soon became clear that reforming the current levy system while introducing large rate increases to encourage further pollution abatement would not be politically acceptable. In contrast, introducing emissions trading in tandem with the recently enshrined system for Total Emissions Control (TEC) (see below) was seen as more acceptable, particularly to the local enterprises, which feared the imposition of higher taxes via increased pollution levies.

Economic theory suggests that, from an efficiency point of view, augmenting the levy system with a strengthened command and control system is not likely to achieve maximal additional emissions reductions.[7] In general, command and control systems force firms to take on similar shares of the pollution control burden (that is, a uniform percentage reduction) or install specific technologies, regardless of cost. Even though such approaches may have some advantages—they may be easier for regulated firms to understand and more easily enforced (both contentious issues)—they can be quite expensive. Emissions trading has the potential to achieve the same objectives at a lower overall cost. Recent analyses have documented savings from the use of emissions trading to manage acid rain in the United States at 40 percent or more below the cost of conventional approaches.[8] In contrast to the levy system, which, in theory, relies on price signals to induce reductions in emissions, a trading system sets emissions quantity targets, distributes permits to the polluting firms, and allows the trading of the permits among the firms in the system.

Under emissions trading, sources with higher marginal abatement costs can pay sources with lower marginal abatement costs to clean up more than required. This has important efficiency and distribution implications. It provides benefits to society because low-cost sources achieve the required emissions reductions. High-cost sources benefit by saving money—they pay lower-cost sources less than it would cost to make the reductions on their own. Lower-cost sources benefit by receiving compensation from high-cost sources for their excess reductions. This compensation helps offset the costs of control technologies or process changes. Emissions trading also creates flexibility in the timing of compliance, smoothing out pollution control investment needs through emissions banking, a form of intertemporal trading. For all these reasons, emissions trading has the potential to be an attractive instrument for environmental management, particularly in a country like the PRC, which has set extremely high pollution reduction goals that would necessarily involve making major new pollution control investments as part of the tenth FYP and beyond.

Economic theory strongly supports using market solutions to address environmental problems. However, whether these solutions can work in countries in which legal and institutional arrangements to ensure compliance are still in their formative stages is an open question.[9] For example, it is not clear that state-owned enterprises (SOEs) have any real incentive to pursue cost-effective emissions reduction strategies such as emissions trading. SOEs are accustomed to negotiating their compliance with government agencies ad hoc and case-by-case and have not been subjected to aggressive enforcement.

Why Taiyuan?

Taiyuan, the capital of Shanxi Province, was selected by provincial officials as the site for this project. Taiyuan is a heavily industrialized area and one of the most polluted cities in Shanxi Province. Industry accounts for approximately 70 percent of provincial GDP, which is based largely on coal mining, coke production, iron and steel and other metallurgical industries, construction materials (cement), chemical manufacturing, and ceramics. The province produces approximately one-third of the nation's total coal. Approximately 70 percent of the annual production of energy resources in the form of coal, coke, and electrical power are exported outside the province for sale. State-owned enterprises account for approximately 70 percent of the industrial output, although a number of these enterprises are moving to privatize.

Taiyuan is located 500 kilometers (km) southwest of Beijing. It consists of the central city, the autonomous subcity Gujiao, three counties, and six districts. It has a population of 2.7 million and covers 6,909 square km. Approximately two-thirds of the population live in the 2 percent of the land area that comprises the city proper. Topographically, Taiyuan is surrounded by mountains on three sides, creating a Los Angeles–type of smog trap in which air pollutants tend to accumulate.

In 2002, reported annual daily SO_2 concentrations in Taiyuan averaged 0.2 mg/m^3, more than three times higher than the PRC's Class II annual standard (0.06mg/m^3). Although subject to considerable year-to-year variation, official figures suggest that the trend in SO_2 concentrations has been relatively flat over the past decade (Table 6.1). The local Taiyuan government has set emissions targets in response to China's national tenth FYP, which calls for dramatic reductions in SO_2 emissions by 2005. Given recent economic growth in the region averaging 10 percent per year and apparent reasonably stable air quality, the considerable effort already devoted by the government and regulated entities to environmental improvement appears to be paying off. At the same time, the relatively high SO_2 levels indicate the magnitude of the challenge that lies ahead as Shanxi strives to increase its

Table 6.1

Annual Average Daily SO_2 Concentrations in Taiyuan, 1991–2000 (mg/m^3)

1991	0.277
1992	0.303
1993	0.153
1994	0.169
1995	0.211
1996	0.212
1997	0.248
1998	0.276
1999	0.272
2000	0.200

Source: Taiyuan Environmental Protection Bureau.

economic output while meeting the major emissions reduction goals established in the tenth FYP.

In addition to its high SO_2 levels, Taiyuan was selected as the location of the demonstration for several other reasons.

- Since the ADB had just made a major loan to the province (and the city) for investments in air pollution control technologies, the pilot provided a unique opportunity to integrate these efforts in an improved air quality management system.
- Provincial and local officials expressed strong interest in participating in a demonstration.
- The local government and other local institutions have available a high degree of technical support.
- A number of large enterprises expressed interest in participating in a demonstration.
- A variety of technical factors made Taiyuan an attractive site, including the availability of extensive monitoring data, and ongoing research and modeling activities in the area.[10]
- There was good reason to believe that, by using a trading program, abatement cost savings would be significant because sources have what economists term "heterogeneity in abatement costs." This last reason requires some explanation.

The extent of heterogeneity of marginal abatement costs among enterprises and the presence of economies of scale in pollution abatement are critical determinants of the suitability of an emissions trading system to address a particular environmental problem in a particular area.[11] As noted, emissions trading has the potential to smooth out (or hydrogenize) differences among plants or locales in marginal abatement costs among emissions sources. Such cost heterogeneity may exist because of inherent differences in technical control options, fuel types, or other factors relevant to individual emissions sources. Cost heterogeneity also may exist—at least temporarily—because of the time-related variations in implementing reductions stipulated in the regulation. Thus, if the regulation calls for a 50 percent emissions reduction staged in 10 percent increments over five years, some sources may install a control technology yielding the full 50 percent reduction early in the five-year period while others may wait until the fourth or fifth year. In that case, there would be an opportunity for the two to engage in emissions trading during the five-year transition period.

Another rationale for emissions trading is associated with economies of scale in pollution abatement. Suppose there are two identical sources, and one has control technology that can achieve 100 percent reduction in emissions at the same cost as the second source, which can achieve only a 50 percent reduction. If both sources were required to reduce emissions by 50 percent, it would make sense for one of the sources to reduce its emissions completely and sell the excess reductions to the other source. While situations involving large economies of scale in pollution abatement are uncommon, they have been recorded in the literature.[12]

Researchers have documented considerable cost heterogeneity among different industrial sources of SO_2 emissions in the PRC. For example, a recent study in the neighboring province of Shaanxi estimated potential cost savings of 50 percent or more for SO_2 reductions from the use of market-based instruments compared to additional command and control regulations.[13]

A relatively manageable number of large sources make up most of Taiyuan's direct SO_2 emissions. These sources span several industries. Furthermore, according to a control cost survey administered by the RFF team (Table 6.2), there is considerable abatement cost heterogeneity among the sources. The Taiyuan government also considers the sources to have relatively strong management.

Why SO_2?

Researchers in China, Europe, and the United States have identified SO_2 emissions as a particularly potent air pollutant, both as a gas and as fine particulates (sulfates). To examine how a major reduction of SO_2 emissions could affect health in Taiyuan, we developed rough estimates of health benefits by:

Table 6.2

SO$_2$ Control Measures Planned or in Use in Taiyuan, 2001–2

Control measure	Status	Where applied	Cost-effectiveness (RMB/ton) (US$)
Close small boilers	Done	Citywide	Unknown
Wet method	In use	Taiyuan District Heating, Xishan thermal plant, Jinxi	500–1,100 ($60–130)*
Lower sulfur coal (~1.3%)	In use	Taiyuan #1, #2, Taiyuan Iron and Steel, others	667 ($85)
Add limestone to fuel	Planned	Coal gasification power plant	1,070 ($130)
Full FGD[1]	Planned	Taiyuan #1, #2	1,300–1,667 ($150–200)*
Simple FGD	In use	Taiyuan #1	2,000 ($240)**
Coal washing	Limited use	Coking plants	2,800 ($340)

Source: Project team.
Notes: [1]FGD = flue gas desulfurization
　　　* As estimated by plant officials.
　　　** Plus unspecified investment costs.

- Establishing the expected amount of SO$_2$ emissions reductions implied by a proposed cap on such emissions
- Identifying the key types of damages (morbidity, mortality, other)
- Establishing physical relationships between the pollutant emissions and the extent of different types of damages
- Identifying the responses by affected parties to mitigate some (or all) of the damages
- Placing a monetary value on physical damages, including damages to human health.

Our approach relies heavily on a concentration-response function developed by the Harvard Institute for International Development (HIID) in its analysis of health benefits in neighboring Shaanxi Province.[14] The calculations examine what would happen if Class II standards were to be met in Taiyuan. Overall, HIID estimated that attainment of the standards could avert between 402 and 1,886 premature deaths annually. In monetary terms, the

annual savings in health costs of such a reduction in air pollution are estimated at RMB 925 million to RMB 4.3 billion.[15]

Given the potentially sizable benefits to the community of attaining class
2 standards, can a practical mechanism be established and implemented to
bring about the required emissions reductions? The next section considers
the institutional arrangements for air pollution control in China, specifically
in Taiyuan.

Institutional Context

No environmental policy can exist in an institutional vacuum. Rather, environmental policies—like all others—operate in a context of laws, regulations, government and industry behavior, and even cultural norms. There has
been an explosion of environmental law drafting in the PRC over the past
decade and a great deal of experimentation with various policy approaches.
Of particular relevance to the current institutional context are the PRC Atmospheric Pollution Prevention and Control Law, the tenth FYP, regional and
local regulations, practices and targets for improving the air, and the structure and functioning of the local EPB in Taiyuan. This section describes national air pollution policies in the PRC; surveys the air pollution control context
for Shanxi, specifically for Taiyuan; and reviews the history of the pollution
permits system in Taiyuan.

National Policy

The basic mandate for air pollution control is contained in the PRC Law on
Atmospheric Pollution Prevention and Control (hereafter, Air Act).[16] Passed
in 2000, the Air Act is a "framework" environmental law. It provides in very
broad, general terms the outlines of the Chinese approach to controlling
emissions. It identifies "key cities for air pollution control," of which Taiyuan
is one. It requires the Taiyuan government to establish plans to control or
gradually reduce the total maximum annual load of air pollution emissions
for jurisdictions specified by the State Council.[17] The State Environmental
Protection Administration (SEPA) has the responsibility to prepare implementing regulations or sublaws, which it must submit to the State Council.
The implementing regulations are to include language encouraging the use
of emissions trading.

Total Emissions Control (TEC) and Two Control Zones (TCZ) are the two
basic state policies to control SO_2 emissions in the PRC. The TEC concept
was introduced in the ninth FYP (1996–2000) and formally enshrined in the
Air Act in 2000. The TEC plan caps total emissions of twelve air, water, and

solid waste pollutants (including SO_2) in key geographical areas. Selected cities are requested to establish rules for TEC to support targets for environmental improvement. The TEC plan also directs that, as industry restructures, it must consider cleaner production techniques and pay attention to the entire production process, not just end-of-pipe pollution. Certain backward production processes and obsolete equipment are targeted for replacement. Priority is to be given to measurement of emissions and enforcement of regulations. Automated air quality monitoring networks are planned for large and medium-sized cities, including Taiyuan, and continuous emissions monitors (CEMs) are mandated for new large emissions sources.

In January 1998, the State Council approved an ambitious plan originally proposed by SEPA to control acid rain and SO_2 emissions in the most seriously affected regions, designated as the "Two Control Zones." Together, the acid rain and SO_2 control zones cover approximately 11 percent of China's territory and are responsible for 60 percent of China's total SO_2 emissions. China's overall goals for these zones for the year 2010 are to bring all cities into compliance with ambient air quality standards. Shanxi was listed as one of the most seriously polluted SO_2 emissions control areas.

The tenth FYP establishes specific targets for pollution control at the regional and local levels. Overall, by 2005 the PRC aims to reduce SO_2 emissions nationwide to 10 percent below 2000 levels. For the two acid rain and SO_2 Control Zones, SO_2 emissions are targeted at 20 percent below 2000 levels by 2005. Provinces and autonomous municipalities also are allocated their own SO_2 emissions targets under the plan, with the goal of achieving reductions from 1.5 to 20.5 percent.

Air Pollution Control in Shanxi and Taiyuan

The Shanxi EPB estimated that, in the absence of additional policy initiatives, the total SO_2 emissions in Shanxi Province will reach 1.575 million tons by 2005. The goal set in the province's tenth FYP for the same period is 1.1 million tons of emissions. The specific targets for 2005 for major cities in Shanxi Province are shown in Table 6.3. By far, the largest reductions are slated for the SO_2 control zone of Taiyuan—a full 50 percent drop below 2000 levels.

In response to the demands of the tenth FYP, officials of Shanxi Province are engaged in extensive planning to reduce SO_2 and other pollutants. Power plants are required to upgrade their sulfur removal technologies, for example, through mixing limestone with the coal prior to combustion or by installing flue gas desulfurization (FGD). All boilers with thermal capacity greater than ten tons of steam per hour are required to use coal with sulfur content of 1

Table 6.3

SO$_2$ Emissions and Total Emissions Control Objectives for Major Cities in Shanxi in the Tenth FYP

Location	2000 emissions (tons)	2005 TEC level (tons)
Taiyuan (city plus 3 counties)	295,000	200,000
Taiyuan (SO$_2$ control zone)	258,000	125,100
Datong	160,000	150,000
Yangquan	140,000	130,000
Shanxi Province	1,575,000	1,100,000

Source: Taiyuan Environmental Protection Bureau.

percent or less. In addition, both of the large power plants in Taiyuan have closed several small boilers. The goals of the tenth FYP do not leave much room for adding new industries or sources. However, Shanxi officials expect that new sources will engage in emissions trading to offset their emissions.

Taiyuan's Early Efforts with Trading and Other Air Pollution Policies

The Taiyuan city government began experimenting with emissions permits and Total Emissions Control (TEC) in the mid-1980s. As early as 1985, Taiyuan City established a series of local laws and regulations, including "Total Emissions Control Standards for Air Pollutants." In the mid-1990s, following the principle of "increasing output without increasing pollution, and building new facilities to replace the old ones," the city conducted pilot experiments on emissions trading and emissions offsets. This experience encouraged enterprises to conduct various analyses of the cost-effectiveness of alternative types of emissions controls to examine the options that they had available for low-cost emissions reductions.[18]

In 1993 the Taiyuan city government issued a regulation entitled Rules on Environmental Offsets for Air Pollutants to serve as the legal basis for pilot emissions offsets. In 1998 the Taiyuan city government issued the Administrative Regulation for Total Emissions Control of Air Pollutants in Taiyuan City, which also included a provision for "permit exchange," a form of emissions permit trading. On the basis of this regulation, the Taiyuan EPB began to issue to large enterprises updated permits with TEC-based limits. In 1994 and 1997, forty key enterprises were issued air pollutant permits by the Taiyuan EPB. Unfortunately, these permits were defined for a limited period (two to three years), and all have expired. The current mechanism for establishing requirements is emissions "target responsibility agreements," which essentially are a series of written agreements or contracts detailing the responsibilities of city government and enterprises for environmental quality.

In 1999 the Taiyuan government announced new initiatives for air pollution control. These included requiring the reduction of coal use in the central urban area by means of fuel switching, closing small boilers, installing monitoring devices, and imposing emissions controls on larger boilers.[19] With assistance from the ADB, the urban gas supply system is being expanded, and the district heating system is slated for modernization using heat from the larger power stations in the city to replace community boilers. The heating sources are in place, but the local service area is still limited. A significant investment will be required to expand the local heat distribution network. The key legislative and regulatory developments pertaining to Taiyuan's emissions permit program are summarized in Table 6.4.

Rationale for a Cap and Trade System in Taiyuan

This section discusses the rationale for selecting a cap and trade form of emissions trading in Taiyuan, rather than emissions "offsets," or an open-market trading system, or even an increase in the levy. Three overall reasons underlie the selection of a cap and trade system:

1. Such a system provides greater environmental certainty than other approaches.
2. It is consistent with the already-announced TEC policy requiring local governments to set emissions targets, which then can serve as limits for the cap and trade policy.
3. There is growing interest at the national and provincial levels in introducing cap and trade systems throughout the PRC.

Forms of Emissions Trading

Initially, three different emissions trading approaches were considered by the project team, the ADB, and the Chinese officials involved in the Taiyuan demonstration: (1) emissions "offsets," (2) open-market trading system, and (3) cap and trade. Since structurally different emissions trading programs are often identified in different ways, the names alone are not sufficient to characterize the programs. Rather, it is important to identify their key attributes, such as whether emissions are capped or uncapped.

So long as permits, or "allowances," are given away (typically, grandfathered) rather than sold, industry retains more financial resources

Table 6.4

Major Policy and Regulatory Developments Related to Air Emissions Permits

Year	Activity
1985	Taiyuan government issues air emissions control management rule requiring facility modifications to meet emissions standards
1987	National Air Pollution Prevention and Control Law approved
1991–97	National pilot program for emissions permits supervised by SEPA
1993	Taiyuan city government issued Rules on Environmental Offsets for Air Pollutants, which started pilot emissions trading in Taiyuan
1995	National Air Pollution Law amended
1996	State Council issues Decision Regarding Several Issues of Environmental Protection (*Guofa* No. 31)
	State Council approves Total Emissions Control (TEC) Plan for Major Pollutants
1998	State Council approves National Acid Rain and SO_2 Control Zoning Plan
	Taiyuan city government issues Administrative Regulation for Total Emissions Control of Air Pollutants in Taiyuan City, including provision for "permit exchange"
1999	Taiyuan city government announces new initiatives for air pollution control and countermeasures
	New TEC-based permits issued for major pollution sources
2000	National Air Pollution Law amendments approved. Updated law includes more stringent enforcement provisions and provisions for emissions trading, but requires national implementing regulations to be effective.

than under policies involving levies (or taxes), because payments associated with buying and selling allowances flow from one enterprise to another, not to the government. Enterprises still must finance actions to control emissions but typically are not required to pay the government for those emissions. Moreover, in choosing emissions control activities, enterprises are free to use the emissions-reducing options that they believe to be most cost-effective, whether end-of-pipe or otherwise. They do not need to seek prior approval from government authorities, as in the case of recycled levy revenues in the PRC. Nor are environmental authorities required to make any calculations of marginal control costs for different enterprises, as they would in deciding on the appropriate size of an increased SO_2 levy.

The least-structured type of emissions trading system involves emissions "offsets." Under an offset program, emissions reductions are allowed in one place to compensate for increased emissions somewhere else. Offsets can be between different plants (an "external offset") or between sources of emissions within the same plant ("internal offsets"). Typically, offsets are approved and implemented on a case-by-case basis. Offsets may involve financial compensation, but this is not an essential element.

Emissions reductions from one source in excess of the proposed emissions increases at another may be required in order to provide for an overall net reduction in emissions. For example, a source may have to reduce two tons to offset one ton of increases at another source. Offsets can be particularly useful for allowing new or expanded sources of pollution to locate or produce in a region that is not meeting its ambient targets or standards. In these cases, new sources may have the responsibility for obtaining (or paying for) emissions reductions from existing sources. Emissions offsets were among the first market-based instruments used in the United States, in the early years of the U.S. air management program. As noted, the PRC has previously experimented with offset programs in a number of pilot projects, including in Taiyuan.

A more ambitious trading approach is the open-market trading system. A pollution source can earn marketable emissions credits by reducing its emissions to levels below a regulatory standard or by making reductions in advance of a prescribed deadline. For example, if an enterprise is subject to an emissions standard, and this standard exceeds its actual emissions, it may sell the amount of pollution reduction implied by the difference, depending on the rules of the particular system. The credits earned may be sold to other sources and used to offset an equal amount of excess emissions, and they may be resold as well; or they may be banked for future use. This approach institutionalizes the offset idea by permitting sources to trade without case-by-case approval. This approach also reduces transaction costs relative to an offset system. It has been implemented in a handful of states in the United States. The main difficulty with open-market trading systems is meeting an aggregate emissions reduction target, because it may be difficult to monitor all of the credit-generating activities, and no overall limit on emissions is built into the design.

Still more ambitious is a cap and trade system, of which the U.S. SO_2 allowance trading system under its Clean Air Act is the canonical example. Sources may trade pollution reduction responsibilities among themselves to meet an aggregate emissions cap set by the federal government in the given area. In this system, emissions credits (or allowances) are allocated without reference to a regulatory standard (although sources still *are* required to comply with certain standards regardless of the number of allowances they possess). Instead, the regulatory agency decides on the aggregate level of allowable emissions for all the parties participating in the program (the "cap"), and then it allocates to each party a portion of this amount in the form of "allowances" that can be traded. Each allowance gives a source the right to discharge one unit of the pollutant in question. The allocation may be made according to the parties' historical performance (for example, emissions, fuel use, output), by auction, or by other means. Once allowances are allocated, parties are prohibited from emitting more pollution than their allocation, unless they purchase additional allowances from another party.

National Policy Context for Emissions Trading

A cap and trade system for Taiyuan is consistent with national efforts already underway to introduce a market-based approach to controlling SO_2 emissions. As early as the 1980s, the PRC began discussing emissions trading pilots in combination with air quality management projects. For example, SEPA has carried out several academic case studies on the transfer of emissions allowances among enterprises. SEPA's next step was to conduct pilot experiments with emissions trading. SEPA's interest in emissions trading continued to grow in the 1990s as it began working with international partners to help build local capacity on emissions trading. The Total Emissions Control (TEC) approach was discussed extensively in the period of the ninth FYP.

In 1994 SEPA carried out emissions trading policy pilots in six cities: Baotou, Kaiyuan, Taiyuan, Liuzhou, Pingdingshan, and Guiyang. The pilots introduced flexibility into the emissions control requirements and enabled enterprises to transfer allowances within an enterprise, pay an environmental compensation fee to obtain additional emissions allowances, invest in non-point-source pollution controls to obtain additional emissions allowances, and sell surplus allowances to other sources that held insufficient allowances. In these pilots, the trading—in the form of offsets—was heavily influenced by institutional and political considerations and was not strictly market driven. Rather, it worked in combination with new, expansion, and technical innovation projects arranged by local EPBs.

SEPA also partnered with the U.S. Environmental Protection Agency (EPA) to increase the knowledge and understanding of emissions trading. In 1999 SEPA and the EPA initiated cooperation on a study to explore the feasibility of introducing nationwide SO_2 emissions trading in the Chinese power sector.[20] This study explored the theory, methods, legal bases, and conditions of emissions trading and considered special conditions in the PRC. Through workshops, training activities, and personnel exchanges, a number of Chinese management and research personnel studied emissions trading in depth.

Parallel to the Shanxi project, the U.S. nongovernmental organization (NGO) Environmental Defense has worked for five years on another trading effort. It has taken place in two industrial cities: in Benxi, to draft tougher air pollution legislation based on the U.S. acid rain model, and in Nantong, to develop a demonstration SO_2 trade whereby a light manufacturer can expand operations in exchange for contributing funds for pollution control to a local power plant. The Nantong trade is quite similar to an emissions offset. Environmental Defense is also working with the PRC's largest power generator, State Power of China, to develop a trade.

In 2002, to gain more experience and facilitate nationwide adoption of emissions trading, SEPA organized pilot programs in seven provinces. After one year of preparatory work, some provinces have already reported some initial success. For instance, two power plants in Jiangsu have reached an agreement to trade SO_2 allowances in order to meet TEC limits. SEPA expects to strengthen and expand these pilots. Finally, at the end of this process, SEPA endorsed the Taiyuan demonstration and clearly signaled the importance of this demonstration to the overall policy structure.

Design of a Cap and Trade System

Although the economic rationale for a cap and trade system—to reduce the costs of meeting SO_2 emissions goals—is compelling, it is certainly true that "the devil is in the details." For an emissions trading program to be successful, a number of policy and administrative issues must be sorted out.[21] Governmental decisions must address such matters as the overall pollution reduction to be achieved, the deadline to meet the goal, the actual sources of emissions to be included in the program, the initial permit allocation plan, and the creation of proper incentives for compliance. Administrative elements include designs for compliance, emissions measurement and monitoring, enforcement, emissions reporting, and allowance tracking systems. However, each of these also includes policy aspects. Table 6.5 summarizes the key design elements.

Policy Design

To develop its regulation on emissions trading—which was issued in October 2002—the Taiyuan city government had to make decisions on a wide

Table 6.5

Summary of Key Design Elements

Policy-level design elements

1. Environmental goals	Issues
Emissions level for cap	Maximum emissions limit or cap for the trading program
Timing (beginning year, target year, phase-in)	Timing of emissions reduction requirements
Capturing environmental impacts from emissions trading	Environmental implications to using emissions trading

2. Scope and applicability of trading program	
Affected sources	Source categories to include in trading program
Trading area	Geographic scope or area covered by trading program
New sources	Incorporating new sources

3. Allowance distribution vs. auction or sale	
How sources obtain allowances	Different avenues for obtaining allowances
Prices	Prices of the allowances
Banking	Whether sources will be allowed to save allowances for use in future compliance years

4. Policy interactions	
Relationship with discharge standards	Whether emissions trading system will interfere with other discharge standards
Relationship with pollution levy	Whether pollution levy will restrict or interfere with emissions trading system

Administrative design elements

1. Emissions quantification, reporting, and verification	
Emissions quantification	Standards for emissions measurement
Emissions reporting	Reporting standards for emissions data
Verification	Validating emissions data, including quality control checks of methods used and equipment (monitors)

2. Allocations and auctions	
Defining and allocating allowances	Define allowance
	Establish an allowance distribution method
	Allowance accounts
	Who can hold allowances
Auction	Annual auction procedures

(continued)

3. Legal authority and responsibility	
Authority and roles	Program administration
	Legal framework (within which emissions trading laws can be developed)
Compliance	Procedure for compliance determination
	Authority to enforce noncompliance at the source level
	Noncompliance penalty
4. Information systems	
Tracking systems	Emissions tracking
	Allowance tracking
	Allowance transfers

range of policy issues. One decision that was not within the city government's discretion was the SO_2 emissions goal; that had been set in the Economic Development Tenth FYP for Taiyuan. As noted above, that plan set the SO_2 emissions goal for 2005 at 125,100 tons, a 50 percent reduction from the 2000 emissions level.

It is notable that only smokestack emissions count in this exercise. Fugitive emissions (emissions from other parts of the plant that are not discharged through the stacks)—which can be a very large fraction of total emissions from coke plants, iron and steel plants, and other heavy industrial sources—were excluded from the emissions inventory. Counting them in the cap likely would have environmental benefits and result in a more realistic and comprehensive cap being set. However, because of the difficulty of accurately estimating fugitive emissions, it was decided not to include them in the program at this time.

A program could include one or a combination of the following: all sources, large industrial and other point sources, only the largest sources, and/or already permitted point sources. The Taiyuan EPB decided to include only the twenty-three coal combustion sources that had been given emissions quotas or targets for 2001. While Taiyuan has other large sources of SO_2 emissions (such as the glass company and some other users of sulfuric acid [H_2SO_4]), the EPB recommended initially limiting trading to combustion sources. Emissions from the twenty-three enterprises that were proposed for the demonstration account for approximately 50 percent of the total SO_2 inventory in Taiyuan (not counting fugitive emissions). As noted earlier, these twenty-three sources are also regarded as having relatively strong management.

The decision on the geographic scope of the trading area followed from the decision to include the twenty-three sources. The Taiyuan EPB decided to include just the city proper. They considered but rejected including the autonomous municipality of Gujiao as a part of the Taiyuan SO_2 control zone, because doing so would have required an additional level of administrative coordination.

Often, how allowances are distributed is one of the most controversial elements of a trading program. The reason is that the allowance represents a valuable economic asset to an enterprise. Allowances were given away in U.S. programs, but recent research suggests that they should be at least partly auctioned.[22] Alternatively, they could be sold at a predetermined price, although this method would not be as efficient and would, like auctions, likely invite resistance from the firms. These different options also imply different degrees of administrative complexity. In general, if the permits are given away, the receiving enterprises may reap benefits upon selling their permits. In contrast, if the permits are sold, the revenues may be generated for use by the government.

In discussions, most government officials felt that the sale of emissions permits at fixed prices or through an auction probably would not be a feasible allocation mechanism at this time. They noted that sources have limited financial resources due to relatively depressed economic conditions and low profit margins. Taiyuan EPB officials focused on the possibility of allocating most emissions allowances to sources in proportion to historic quotas, but reserving 10 percent to 15 percent of the allocation for new growth.

The RFF team and local officials engaged in extensive discussions and analyses to establish the following principles:

- In general, the 2005 SO_2 reduction goal for each source is 50 percent of its 2000 reported SO_2 emissions. A uniform annual reduction (equal percentage) is to be applied to each source from 2001 to 2005.
- If participating enterprises are SO_2 control point sources in Taiyuan's tenth FYP and their 2005 SO_2 emissions specified in the plan are already lower than 50 percent of their 2000 reported emissions, their planned 2005 SO_2 reduction goals are met.
- If sources are listed in the 2001 environmental responsibility contract system, their 2001 contract emissions are adopted as the baseline. A uniform annual reduction (equal percentage for each source) is applied to each source from 2002 to 2005.
- If sources' SO_2 emissions specified in their 2001 environmental responsibility contracts are already lower than 50 percent of their 2000 reported emissions, their 2005 reduction goals are set at 20 percent below 2001 permitted emissions. Each source is required to reduce 5 percent of its 2001 permitted SO_2 emissions every year, beginning in 2002.

Another key policy decision is whether sources can "bank" (save) unused allowances for future use or sale. Banking can provide firms needed flexibility in developing control strategies. The U.S. experience shows that banking can be done without environmental detriment. Indeed, experience with banking has shown that firms tend to bank, in the aggregate, a significant number of tons each year, resulting in fewer emissions than allowed by the cap, and, thus, correspondingly more rapid environmental improvement. Experience also shows that most firms will keep some emissions in the bank as insurance against future need, which is a pattern that tends to create additional environmental improvements.

Item 20 of the Administrative Regulation for Total Emissions Control of Air Pollutants in Taiyuan City allows banking so long as prior approval is obtained from the EPB. Although EPB and company representatives had varying views on this issue, it was ultimately decided to include a banking provision in the demonstration program.

Administrative Design

Parallel to handling the policy design issues, a wide range of administrative design issues were considered. The administrative elements cover important details of the trading system, including compliance, monitoring, enforcement, reporting elements, legal issues, and information systems. Many of these decisions, which are examined below, are needed for *any* emissions-based regulatory system to function properly, not merely an emissions trading system.

It is beyond dispute that regulators and the public must be assured that real, not imaginary, pollution reductions are being traded. Thus, it is essential that tight procedures be implemented for determining the quantity of emissions actually emitted. The best approach would be to have continuous emissions monitors (CEMs) installed in each emitting stack. Indeed, some major sources in Taiyuan already use CEMs to track their emissions, but these devices are used either for purposes internal to the plant or intermittently by EPB inspectors in their periodic inspections. Standards need to be developed to ensure that CEMs are installed, operating properly, and calibrated regularly.[23] There is, in fact, strong interest in improving monitoring capabilities in Taiyuan. Evidence of this commitment is the recent request by Chinese officials to the ADB to use recent loans to purchase additional CEMs.

Another improvement would be to ensure that the information obtained from monitoring is easily available to regulators. A central database for CEM data is under development by the Taiyuan EPB. It will include online data transfer. Alternately, other techniques, for example, direct or indirect measurement through fuel use and sulfur content calculations, could be used. However, the accuracy of periodic direct measurements depends on a number of assumptions, including operating conditions, production levels, and control equipment operation. The accuracy of indirect emissions measurement depends on the quality and quantity of fuel type information. Ensuring that data quality is high is an important task for any type of environmental program and could be challenging to governments with limited data collection experience and authority.

One government institution needs to take primary responsibility for the administration of the program. The obvious institution to do this is the Taiyuan EPB, because it is responsible for emissions regulation and already has in place the beginnings of the necessary monitoring and enforcement infrastructure. The role for the provincial EPB and the relationship between the provincial EPB and the Taiyuan EPB are critical issues. Unfortunately, neither EPB is an independent body and may not possess the requisite jurisdiction to act in case of violations. In particular, because power plants are regulated from a provincial (and even national) level, procedures and regulations for addressing power plant regulation need to be developed within the local permits exchange system.

No environmental regulatory program works without a system to ensure compliance. A strong compliance program has many aspects, all of which are designed to ensure that sources will play by the rules and be treated fairly through a set of procedures that are clear, transparent, and consistently applied. As part of the demonstration activities carried out in Taiyuan, a number of technical programs have been put in place to help manage disputes and to encourage enterprises to follow the rules.

- *Emissions Tracking System (ETS).* The EPB needs information to determine whether enterprises are operating within the parameters of the system, including whether their SO_2 emissions are less than or equal to the allowances they hold. The ETS was developed to integrate technical monitoring information collected by the Taiyuan EPB with additional data on coal purchases, new SO_2 control measures undertaken, enterprise-level output, and other factors. Enterprises will be able to submit their data in electronic (or paper) format, and the Taiyuan EPB will be able to generate reports specifically tailored to its regulatory needs.
- *Allowance Tracking System (ATS).* The ATS will ensure the functioning of the trading system. This system can report and verify trades.
- *Provision for reconciliation.* In the process of buying and selling allowances, enterprises normally will need to reconcile their emissions and permit holdings. Thus, they may need to buy additional allowances or

sell some to be sure that their emissions do not exceed the allowances held. Procedures for reconciliation were written into a "Procedures Guide" as part of the project.

- *Appeals process.* Disputes will arise in any environmental program. To resolve disputes, it was proposed that a mediation committee be established. The committee could consist of senior government officials and key enterprise managers, plus perhaps members of the academic community, the public, and the media.

To ensure that enterprises involved in emissions trading follow the rules, governments at all levels need to send a strong and consistent message about their commitment to enforcement. Putting this into an economic framework, the "cost" of violating an emissions limit must be higher than the "benefit" the violator gains by noncompliance. One way to manage this problem would be to impose cash penalties, for example, a fee on each unit of emissions exceeding the allowances held. The compliance penalty could be made at least as high as the cost of coal washing. Currently, coal washing costs approximately RMB 2,800 per ton of SO_2.[24] Setting the penalty at a slightly higher level than the cost of coal washing would ensure that compliance is less costly than paying the penalty for emissions in excess of one's quota. Another approach might be public disclosure and civil or criminal prosecution of violators.

Additional reforms are necessary. Penalties must be collected in a timely fashion to link the pain with the violation and ensure timely compliance. Enforcement officials must not be constrained by fears that they will run afoul of powerful interests or that, in taking an aggressive enforcement posture, they will endanger their own salaries and social benefits. This is a critical issue in the PRC, in which the EPBs are not independent of the local People's Congress and the political apparatus.[25]

Stakeholders widely acknowledged that penalties for noncompliance should be higher than the marginal cost of compliance. At the same time, they wanted penalties set at "realistic" levels. Although the Administrative Regulation on SO_2 Emissions Trading in Taiyuan City set sufficient penalties—RMB 3,000 (US$364) to RMB 8,000 (US$968) per ton—the regulation limits total penalties to no more than RMB 30,000 (US$3,630), which is undoubtedly too small to induce full compliance with the program, a fact pointed out in meetings by local industry.

The need for effective penalties raises the larger issue of the interface between the existing pollution levy system and the penalty system, as well as that between the pollution levy system and the emissions trading system. Levies are paid on every unit of SO_2 emissions, whether these emissions exceed the enterprise's quotas or not. However, these levies currently are too low relative to the cost of reducing SO_2 emissions to significantly discourage emissions.

As work proceeds on emissions trading, some difficult decisions must be made about the levy system. A small levy that is used for raising revenue, which now exists, presents no obstacle to the successful functioning of an emissions trading system.[26] However, technically, a levy system with a levy high enough to change polluting behavior duplicates a trading system. At any one time, either the price of a unit of emissions set in the market or the levy rate will be binding. The PRC could use one of the following options to address this problem:

1. Recognize that the levies are very low and allow the two systems to coexist
2. Eliminate the levy charge on SO_2 to all participating enterprises, but auction or sell SO_2 emissions allowances at an administered price and rely on penalty collections for paying EPB expenses
3. Give away allowances but impose a small surcharge for each allowance equal to the current levy rate. The difficulty, of course, is that it is not possible to discontinue the levy without prior approval from SEPA.

Another issue that the PRC must face is the integrity of a trading system. By its very nature, emissions trading allows different enterprises to emit different levels of pollution. For those who are not fully knowledgeable about the program, these differences may create misunderstandings about whether firms are being treated fairly and equitably. In addition, there must be confidence in the general population and among the regulated community that trades are legitimate; that the grant of discretion to a particular plant is not based on favoritism; and that the program does not enrich plant owners or operators, regulators, or other vested interests at the expense of the environment.

Perhaps the best way to examine this issue is to think about the United States' SO_2 emissions trading system. In the United States, decisions about allowance allocations, information on actual trades, and virtually the entire program are subject to public inspection. This helps ensure that there is no cheating, that everyone is treated fairly, and that interest groups (including neighborhood groups, NGOs, and competitors) have confidence in the program. A campaign to inform the public about the program may reduce suspicions that the program has been instituted to benefit favored units, enterprises, or individuals, or to punish others.

Transparency would also help the enforcement aspect of the program in China, for example, by establishing a disclosure system so that an informed public and environmental NGOs can, in effect, help keep the program honest. After the SARS epidemic of 2003, some PRC provinces, particularly those with the most negative publicity about SARS, began experimenting with limited transparency concerning government programs, but considerable improvements are needed to result in effective program enforcement.

An effort toward greater transparency would be consistent with China's current emphasis on increasing public environmental awareness and related efforts. Article 15 of the new Air Act has provisions calling for greater transparency in setting the TEC and issuing emissions permits.

With the assistance of CRAES, the World Bank is working on a system for the PRC using color coding and public disclosure as the means to channel public pressure for environmental compliance. A limited form of public disclosure is already being used in many PRC cities, whereby an air quality (ambient) index is being made available to the public on a "real-time" basis. Moreover, the Chinese media increasingly have been used to pressure polluting units to control their pollution through public disclosure. Many large cities have "green" newspapers and "green" reporters for television and radio. Last year the Taiyuan EPB reported in a newspaper the efforts that sources were making to reduce emissions. This year the EPB plans to prepare a report for the government and private enterprises that discusses emissions and facility utilization. Nevertheless, all these green newspapers and media outlets are owned and directed by the government, which clearly limits their ability to serve as independent observers.

Over the course of this project, stakeholders, including local officials and enterprise representatives, raised a number of additional issues: (1) emissions trading might not be feasible because of the high percentage of emissions emitted by a relatively small number of sources, (2) poor economic conditions may hinder trading, and (3) a stronger demonstration of high-level government support is necessary before emissions trading can proceed. Each of these issues is considered below.

1. A few large sources and many small sources might present significant challenges to an emissions trading system. In Taiyuan there are two very large sources and a small number of other sources with substantial emissions. The remaining sources, although numerous, are relatively small. Participants feared that this size distribution of the sources might create a problem for emissions trading. It is certainly possible that the "market" could be distorted by an attempt by one or two large firms to monopolize the emissions market. The RFF team suggested that the Taiyuan authorities monitor trades closely for such behavior. Size alone, however, is not the major factor in market distortion. Rather, the key measure is the difference between the number of allowances granted to a source and its current emissions. This differ-

ence need not be greater for large sources than for small sources. For instance, a skewed size distribution exists in Los Angeles. Nevertheless, monopoly behavior has not been an issue in the California-based Regional Clean Air Incentives Program (RECLAIM) program, in which a few power plants dominate in terms of quantity of emissions, although there may have been such an issue in New Jersey.[27]

2. Poor economic conditions within the firms might lead to resistance to emissions trading. Concern has been expressed about the economic health of the Taiyuan enterprises and whether this would affect their interest in participating in an emissions trading program. It is true that for an emissions trading program to be successful, clear regulatory goals for reduction of emissions and adequate enforcement must be present. The environmental authorities in Taiyuan and Shanxi Province must make it absolutely clear to sources that they will, in the aggregate, need to reduce emissions by specified amounts. If sources are not in actuality required to meet their regulatory requirements and the regulation is not effectively enforced, then neither emissions trading nor any other approach will succeed. However, if enterprises and firms are facing genuine regulatory requirements, a trading system can reduce compliance costs to below those that would be incurred if all sources were required to meet the same reduction goals in the same time frame. Thus, firms might be expected to support the trading program to the extent that the government is serious about reducing emissions.

3. It is clear that, for emissions trading to succeed in Taiyuan, there is a need for a stronger demonstration of high-level government support. Several workshop participants made the point that no environmental program, including an emissions trading program, can succeed in Taiyuan without explicit support from high levels of the city and provincial governments. It has been proposed that the Shanxi Planning Commission convene an advisory group of key government officials and industry managers in Taiyuan to assess the overall demonstration and a working group of technical staff to monitor the detailed operation of the demonstration.

Overall Conclusions

To put the Taiyuan effort into perspective, it is useful to review the experience of the highly successful SO_2 trading program in the United States. It is clear that it can take years for these programs to develop. The U.S. program was preceded by many years of theoretical and empirical analyses considering appropriate design features for a trading program, as well as more than ten years of experiments with less sophisticated market-based instruments.

While the experiments of the EPA with offsets and other forms of economic incentive mechanisms had only limited success, the lessons fed directly into a political debate over how to reduce SO_2 emissions of existing power plants—a debate that in 1990 led to the creation of the SO_2 Allowance Trading Program in the Clean Air Act amendments. This was followed by a four-year lead-in period in which the EPA wrote implementing regulations using notice-and-comment rulemaking procedures that required extensive solicitation of public views, followed by the formal establishment of the emissions trading program. The U.S. program was built on an existing, well-established regime for environmental enforcement. Such a regime does not yet exist in the PRC.

Interestingly, the target set in the United States was approximately a 50 percent reduction in SO_2 emissions from the baseline, similar to the cap established in Taiyuan (50 percent reduction from 2000 levels). However, in the case of the United States, the reduction was phased in over a longer period, with the majority of the reductions to be achieved in 2000—a full ten years after the Clean Air Act amendments were signed into law and five years after the program was implemented, rather than over the three to five year period contemplated in Taiyuan.

Current conditions in the PRC also are quite different from those that existed historically in the United States. Using law to manage social problems is a relatively new development in China. Generally, throughout Chinese history, personal responsibility has been a more important motivator than the law. However, in recent years, there has been a proliferation of laws, including the legal framework under which an emissions trading program could operate. Many of the laws are written in broad terms and lack detailed guidance, and they have not been tested in practice. Due in part to this lack of detail, local environmental regulators still are struggling with basic issues of how to ensure compliance with environmental requirements and how to achieve regulatory independence. Many of the inherent conflicts of interest in a system in which state-owned industry is overseen by another arm of the state structure are present in the PRC.[28] At the same time, the country has only limited experience with markets for intangible commodities—a category that includes pollution credits.

A major milestone achieved during the period of this demonstration project was the promulgation by the Taiyuan city government of a regulation for the emissions trading program (October 2002). Although some controversial issues remain, for example, the cap on penalties, Taiyuan's regulation is notable as the first comprehensive regulation of its kind in the PRC to support a cap and trade system on a citywide basis. The numerous other achievements of the project include:

- Education of government and industry leadership about the benefits of adopting emissions trading
- Establishment of an administrative framework to support the regulation
- Development and demonstration of various computer-based tools to facilitate emissions monitoring and verification, and to manage the allowances (Emissions Tracking and Allowance Tracking Systems)
- Capacity building and training on the theory, practice, and management of emissions trading systems for both government and industry, including training of senior officials and technical and managerial staff
- Initial simulation of emissions trading among selected facilities.

The PRC's growing concerns about environmental health, combined with its enhanced financial and technical abilities to address these problems, give hope for future progress. As cities such as Taiyuan increasingly look for options to enhance their environmental management systems and reduce emissions of SO_2 and other critical pollutants, emissions trading is a particularly attractive option. Overall, the participants in the Taiyuan project believe that this work has succeeded in developing the foundation for effective and efficient SO_2 control in Taiyuan, and in advancing the emissions trading model to a point that other areas of Shanxi Province can adopt it. At a public meeting in Taiyuan in September 2003 attended by high-level officials from Shanxi Province and representatives of the ADB, the officials expressed their support for the policy. They also indicated their intention to support continued development of the infrastructure for an effective emissions trading program. The latest indications are that the government is moving aggressively to assist enterprises with the acquisition of CEMs and certain control equipment— key features of an emissions trading program—with the assistance of international lenders. Whether and when this system becomes fully operational and how the inevitable "growing pains" of the system are resolved depend on the interplay of a complex set of local and national factors. What is clear, however, is that the seeds of change have been sown.[29]

Notes

1. See P.N. Fernando, Aminul Huq, Piya Abeygunawardena, Robert Anderson, and Ricardo Barba, *Emissions Trading in the Energy Sector: Opportunities for the People's Republic of China* (Manila: Asian Development Bank, 1999).
2. The U.S. Environmental Protection Agency (EPA) provided extensive assistance in training and capacity building on the design and implementation of emissions trading programs. Key individuals involved in the project, in addition to the authors, are Stephanie Benkovic (EPA), Shawei Chen (formerly RFF), Melanie Dean (EPA), Cao Dong (CRAES), Joe Kruger (EPA), Steinar Larsen (NILU), Wang Jinan

(CRAES), Yang Jintian (CRAES), and Xuehua Zhang (formerly RFF). We express special thanks to Dan Millison (ADB), who participated as a consultant in the early phases of the project. The activities described herein were carried out from Mar. 2001 to Sept. 2003.

3. See Xie Zhenhua, "Speech to the National Acid Rain and SO_2 Comprehensive Control Conference," *China Environment Yearbook* (Beijing: China Environment Yearbook Press, 1998).

4. A regulatory change in late 2002 phased in new requirements for the use of levy funds. No longer will EPBs be funded with levy collections nor will firms automatically receive a portion of their payments to use in financing pollution control projects. Rather, a competitive process will be used to allocate levy funds to firms.

5. Wang Hua and David Wheeler, "Endogenous Enforcement and the Effectiveness of China's Pollution Levy System," Development Research Group, World Bank, Washington, DC, 2001.

6. Barbara A. Finamore, "Taming the Dragon Heads: Controlling Air Emissions from Power Plants in China," National Resources Defense Council Report, Washington, DC (June 2000), www.efchina.org/documents/TamingtheDragonHeads.pdf.

7. For example, see the contrary argument in D. Cole and P. Grossman, "When Is Command and Control Efficient? Institutions, Technology, and the Comparative Efficiency of Alternative Regulatory Regimes for Environmental Protection," *Wisconsin Law Review* 5 (1999): 887, www.iulaw.indy.indiana.edu/instructors/cole/when is command and control efficient.pdf. See also D. Cole and P. Grossman, 2003. "Toward a Total Cost Approach to Environmental Instrument Choice," in R. Zerbe and T. Swanson, eds., *Research in Law and Economics* (Greenwich, CT: JAI Press, 2002).

8. Curtis Carlson, Dallas Burtraw, Maureen Cropper, and Karen Palmer, "SO_2 Control by Electric Utilities: What Are the Gains from Trade?" *Journal of Political Economy* 108 (6): 1292–1326. See also Alan Carlin, "The United States Experience with Economic Incentives to Control Environmental Pollution," *EPA Office of Policy Planning and Evaluation* (EE-0216, July 1992), http://yosemite1.epa.gov/ee/epa/eed.nsf/pages/USExepriceWithEconomic Incentives.html.

9. See, for example, Clifford S. Russell and William J. Vaughan, "The Choice of Pollution Control Policy Instruments in Developing Countries: Arguments, Evidence and Suggestions," in Henk Folmer and Tom Tietenberg, eds., *International Yearbook of Environmental and Resource Economics 2003/2004* (Cheltenham, UK: Edward Elgar, 2003); Ruth Greenspan Bell and Clifford Russell, "Ill-Considered Experiments: The Environmental Consensus and the Developing World," *Harvard International Review* (winter 2003); Ruth Greenspan Bell and Clifford Russell, "Environmental Policy for Developing Countries," *Issues in Science and Technology* (spring 2002), reprinted in e-journal "Failsafe," June 17, 2002, www.felsef.org/summer02.htm#4b, and also reprinted in Gloria E. Helfand and Peter Berck, eds., *The Theory and Practice of Command and Control in Environmental Policy,* International Library of Environmental Economics and Policy Series (Hampshire, UK: Ashgate Publishing, 2003). For an alternative view, see Joe Kruger, Katherine Grover, and Jeremy Schreifels, "Building Institutions to Address Air Pollution in Developing Countries: The Cap and Trade Approach," OECD paper CCNM/GF/SD/ENV(2003)15/FINAL, 2002, www.oecd.org/dataoecd/11/25/2957736.pdf. Also see Jintian Yang and Jeremy Schreifels, "Implementing SO_2 Emissions in China," OECD paper CCNM/GF/SD/ENV(2003)16/FINAL, 2002, www.oecd.org/dataoecd/11/23/2957744.pdf.

10. Air quality modeling is being conducted by the Norwegian Institute for Air Research, which also participated in this ADB-sponsored project.

11. In the formulation used here, these costs do not take into account the time of year that the emissions occur, the location of the source, stack height, or other parameters that might affect actual human exposures.

12. In the United States, for example, detailed engineering analysis of the control options available to one particular power plant revealed that the marginal abatement costs declined dramatically in the range of 70 to 80 percent reductions. See Leland Deck, "Visibility at the Grand Canyon and the Navajo Generating Station," *Economic Analyses at EPA: Assessing Regulatory Impact,* ed. Richard D. Morgenstern (Washington, DC: Resources for the Future, 1997), 267–302.

13. Harvard Institute for International Development, "Market-Based Instruments for Environmental Management in the People's Republic of China," paper submitted to the Asian Development Bank (TA No. 2951-PRC), May 1999.

14. Ibid.

15. One RMB (renminbi) or Chinese yuan (CNY) equals approximately US$0.12; RMB 8.28 equals US$1. The details of these calculations are available in Richard Morgenstern, "Inception Report for TA-3325," May 1999 (Contract No. COCS/00-685), submitted to the Asian Development Bank by Resources for the Future, June 2001.

16. The new Air Act was adopted at the fifteenth meeting of the Standing Committee of the Ninth National People's Congress on Apr. 29, 2000, promulgated by Order No. 32 of the President of the PRC on Apr. 29, 2000, effective Sept. 1, 2000.

17. See "Key Aspects of the 2000 Amendments to the Air Pollution Prevention and Control Law of the People's Republic of China, Briefing for Corporate Counsel and EHS Managers," Beveridge & Diamond, P.C., 2001, www.bdlaw.com/publications.asp. The coauthor of this briefing paper is the former chief environmental law drafter for the Chinese National People's Congress.

18. For example, the Taiyuan Coal Gasification Company planned to build a 26MW power station to burn low-quality coal (gangue) with three new 35-ton/hour fluidized furnaces. Even with dust removal treatment, an additional 660 tons/year of dust would be emitted, and the factory would exceed allowed emissions. Emissions exchange was required by Taiyuan to offset the new pollution. The new power station was required to supply heating to the Coal Separation Factory and the nearby Taiyuan Cement Factory, so that a 41-ton/hour boiler could be decommissioned, resulting in a 298-ton/year reduction in dust.

19. A survey of small boilers subject to the closure requirements indicates quite dramatic reductions in SO_2 emissions from these sources. See Richard Morgenstern, Alan Krupnick, and Xuehua Zhang, "The Ancillary Carbon Benefits of SO_2 Reductions from a Small-Boiler Policy in Taiyuan, PRC," *Journal of Environment and Development,* (June 2004): 140–55.

20. See Jinnan Wang, Jintian Yang, Stephanie Grumet, Jeremy Schreifels, and Zhong Ma, eds., *SO_2 Emissions Trading Program: A Feasibility Study for China* (Beijing: China Environment Press, 2002).

21. For a more complete discussion of the policy and administrative issues involved in designing the Taiyuan cap and trade system, see "Final Report of Shanxi Air Quality Improvement Project (TA-3325)" submitted to the Asian Development Bank by Resources for the Future, July 2003.

22. Dallas Burtraw, Karen L. Palmer, Ranjit Bharvirkar, and Anthony Paul, "The

Effects of Allowance Allocation on the Cost of Carbon Dioxide Emissions Trading," Discussion Paper 01-30 (Resources for the Future, Washington, DC, August 2001). www.rff.org/rff/Documents/RFF-DP-01-30.pdf.

23. The EPA and SEPA are working together to propose standards for the certification, installation, operation, maintenance, and calibration of CEMs.

24. See Table 6.2.

25. The chapter by Elizabeth Economy in this volume details China's environmental enforcement challenges.

26. For more information about the interaction between the pollution levy and emissions trading systems in China, see Denny A. Ellerman, "Designing an Emissions Trading System for the Control of SO_2 Emissions in China," in Wang Jinnan, Yang Jintian, Stephanie Benkovic, Jeremy Schreifels, and Zhong Ma, eds., *SO_2 Emissions Trading Program: A Feasibility Study for China* (Beijing: China Environment Press, 2002).

27. For details on RECLAIM, see www.aqmd.gov/reclaim/reclaim.html. Information concerning the New Jersey case can be accessed through the U.S. Justice Department, United States v. PSEG Fossil LLC, D. N.J., No. 02CV340, 1/24/02.

28. In similar economies, such as those of the countries formerly composing the Soviet bloc, environmental regulators' lack of independence while part of the Soviet bloc significantly lessened their ability to enforce environmental requirements, particularly when environmental goals collided with other important societal goals, such as production targets. The PRC has officially elevated the importance of environmental protection as a key component of its development strategy. The PRC has also demonstrated a willingness to invest state funds in pollution control projects and shut down unprofitable and polluting industries when necessary. Whether these efforts will be successful is yet to be seen.

29. For a debate on the prospects for emissions trading in the PRC in the foreseeable future, see Ruth Greenspan Bell, "Choosing Environmental Policy Instruments in the Real World," OECD paper CCNM/GF/SD/ENV(2003)10/FINAL, Aug. 23, 2003, www.oecd.org/dataoecd/11/9/2957706.pdf; and Joseph Kruger, Katherine Grover, and Jeremy Schreifels, "Building Institutions to Address Air Pollution in Developing Countries: The Cap and Trade Approach," OECD Paper CCNM/GF/SD/ENV(2003)/16/FINAL, 2003, www.oecd.org/dataoecd/11/25/2957736.pdf. Copies of the final report on the Shanxi Air Quality Improvement Project (TA-3325) can be obtained directly from the ADB, www.adb.org. A summary version is available from Resources for the Future, www.rff.org.

— Chapter 7 —

Environmental Implications of China's Energy Demands

An Overview

Frank Wang and Hongfei Li

Over two decades of rapid economic growth, energy demand in China has increased tremendously. In 1980 the total primary energy consumption in China was 17.3 quadrillion Btu, and in 2001 it increased to 39.7 quadrillion Btu.[1] Energy is the physical driving force behind industrialization. In developing countries, energy demand is closely correlated with economic growth. A robust economy, in turn, leads to prosperity. As living standards rise, people increase their spending on home appliances for air conditioning, refrigeration, cooking, and space and water heating, as well as on automobiles and other energy-intensive products. Energy consumption in China is expected to increase continuously. At an average annual rate of 3.5 percent, it is projected to reach 90.8 quadrillion Btu in 2025.[2] China is the world's most populous country, and its energy production and consumption give rise to significant health and environmental impacts both domestically and globally. Because production of energy generally is associated with adverse environmental impacts, this chapter examines the availability of energy sources in China in the future and assesses the environmental effects of increased energy consumption.

In the next section, we present an overview of China's current energy situation and its future prospects. We begin with a discussion of coal, China's primary source of energy. In 2001 coal constituted about 64 percent of China's energy consumption. This statistic reflects China's abundant reserves of coal and limited reserves of oil and natural gas. Many of China's energy-related environmental problems—particularly acid rain and air pollution—result from the country's reliance on coal. Another major contributor to air pollution is urban smog caused by automobiles. China's transportation sector is expected to grow significantly as a result of its admission to the World Trade Organization (WTO), and we will discuss China's efforts to address the resulting environmental impact through regulatory efforts and the use of clean fuel sources.

The future energy mix will be influenced by many (often mutually conflicting) factors, including economic growth, environmental concerns, regulatory changes, and technological progress. A consequence of improved personal wealth is a yearning for greater personal freedom. Therefore, an important factor in China's near future is the social impact of energy production—particularly the use of coal, nuclear power, and hydroelectric projects. In the third section, we identify several variables that could impact China's future energy consumption trends.

China's Energy Outlook

China has a population of 1.285 billion and had a gross domestic product (GDP) in 2001 of US$1.2 trillion, an increase of 7.3 percent over 2000.[3] With an enormous and still-growing population, and a strong desire to raise living standards, China's energy consumption is expected to double within the next two decades. Total primary energy consumption in China in 2001 was 39.7 quadrillion Btu, putting it second in the world. A breakdown of China's energy consumption by source is shown in Figure 7.1.

As indicated above, coal is the dominant source of energy in China, 64 percent, followed by oil, 26 percent. Hydroelectric power, 7 percent, and natural gas, 3 percent, contribute the rest of China's energy needs. The "others" category corresponds to merely 0.18 quadrillion Btu, which is essentially composed of nuclear power. We detail each source below.

Coal

China is the world's largest consumer and producer of coal. In 2001 China consumed 1.25 billion metric tons of coal, more than 26 percent of the world's total consumption.[4] The United States is another heavy coal user, with consumption comparable to China's: 0.96 billion metric tons in 2001. While most coal in the United States is used for electric power generation, which is subject to clean air standards, coal in China has been used primarily in the industrial sector, for steam and direct heat (mainly in the chemical, cement, and pulp and paper industries); and for the manufacture of coal coke for the steelmaking process. Coal is also used directly by households for heating and cooking. Because coal consumption is spread so broadly among a range

Figure 7.1 **China's Energy Consumption, 2001**

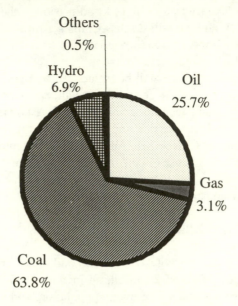

of end users, coal-related emissions in China traditionally have not been subject to clean air standards. This situation has impeded the enforcement of environmental regulations.

Coal combustion results in several types of emissions that adversely affect the environment, particularly ground-level air quality. The main emissions from coal combustion are carbon dioxide (CO_2), sulfur dioxide (SO_2), nitrogen oxides (NO_x), particulates, and mercury (Hg). SO_2 and soot caused by coal combustion are two major air pollutants, forming acid rain, which now falls on about 30 percent of China's total land mass. Industrial boilers and furnaces are the largest single-point sources of urban air pollution. Coal mining also has direct effects on the environment: strip mining affects land and causes subsidence; coal piles and slag heaps generate considerable quantities of pollutants. In addition, the coal mining process takes a high human toll. Over the past decade, nearly 10,000 mining deaths have been reported annually.[5]

China has limited reserves of oil and natural gas, as we will discuss later, and it has expressed a strong interest in coal liquefaction technology, particularly given the potential to apply such technology as a substitute for petroleum used in the transportation sector. The first pilot coal liquefaction plant became operational in coal-rich Shanxi Province in late 2001. In addition, Royal Dutch/Shell signed an agreement in late 2001 for a coal gasification project in Hunan Province that will be used to replace naphtha as a feedstock for a large fertilizer plant. Liquefaction and gasification require high temperature and pressure, and some of these processes emit toxic organic compounds such as polynuclear aromatic hydrocarbons, organonitrogen, and sulfur compounds. Widespread use of these technologies might result in significant environmental impacts due to the formation and dispersion of toxic substances into the air and water.[6]

The emission of CO_2 is another significant by-product of coal combustion. On a per-unit-of-energy basis, coal combustion produces more CO_2 than natural gas or most petroleum products; nearly 80 percent more than natural gas and approximately 20 percent more than residual fuel oil (the petroleum product most widely used for electricity generation). In 2001 the United States and China were the world's dominant coal consumers and also the two top emitters of CO_2, accounting for 24 percent and 13 percent, respectively, of the world's total emissions. Forecasts based on differing economic growth rates and shifting fuel mixes result in the prediction that by 2025, the United States' share of world CO_2 emissions will decline to 22 percent, while China's share will increase to 18 percent.

Furthermore, the common use of coal for household heat and energy has led to indoor air pollution. There are numerous accounts of coal-related health hazards.[7] Documented examples of health effects include numerous cases in Guizhou Province of cancerous skin lesions, deformed limbs, arsenic poisoning, and fluorosis, which can soften and disfigure teeth and bones. Only in the past few years have scientists determined the source of the arsenic and fluorine: coal. Damp and cool autumn weather makes it impossible to dry corn, chili peppers, and other crops outside, so families bring them indoors to dry over coal-burning heat sources. The coal used in Guizhou Province contains unusually high concentrations of arsenic and fluorine. Compounding the problem of the contaminated fuel is that most homes have no chimneys. As a result, volatilized elements from the coal collect indoors. While scientists now understand the source of the health problems, most residents have no alternative to using coal.

Although there is nearly universal agreement that China's coal pollution must be addressed, there is little doubt that coal will continue to play a dominant role in China's energy mix for the foreseeable future. As is the case for residents of Guizhou Province, much of China simply has no choice but to continue using coal despite the detrimental health and environmental consequences. While China's reserves of oil and natural gas are limited, it has coal in abundance, approximately 12 percent of the world's total. Therefore, coal demand is projected to rise significantly, at an annual rate of 3.2 percent. Consumption is projected to reach 2.65 billion metric tons in 2025, more than double current consumption levels. Although removal of pollutants such as SO_2 from flue gases is technically feasible, it is expensive. A twofold increase of coal consumption is likely to result in a significant increase in pollution.

Oil

China is the world's third largest oil consumer, behind the United States and Japan. Consumption of petroleum products totaled 0.68 million metric tons per day in 2001, up from 0.66 million metric tons per day in 2000.[8] Within the next decade, China is expected to surpass Japan as the second largest oil consumer, making the former a significant player in the international oil market. Figure 7.2 shows the current major players in the international oil market.

China's demand for oil has grown with increased motorization and switching from coal and traditional noncommercial fuels to oil in the residential and service sectors. In 2001, in the transportation sector, vehicle ownership in China was 13 per 1,000 people. This figure compares with 779 per 1,000 people in the United States. China's accession to the WTO in 2001 is expected to increase competition in China's automobile sector, stimulating passenger car sales and demand for fuel.[9]

With strong growth in its automobile industry, the Chinese government has become increasingly concerned about air quality issues, particularly in urban areas. Since 2000 China has banned leaded gasoline, and the country is moving toward national emissions standards. Beijing has led the way in many initiatives, in part to prepare for its role as host of the 2008 Olympic Games. This progress includes compliance with the Euro 2 Emission Standard by Beijing as of January 1, 2003, and expected compliance by 2005 for the rest of the country.[10] The target date for implementing the Euro 3 Emission Standard in Beijing was January 1, 2005, and possibly 2010 for the rest of China. To meet these standards, the Beijing municipal government is ordering city vehicles to convert to liquefied petroleum gas and natural gas, as discussed below.

At a projected annual growth rate of 3.3 percent, China's oil consumption will reach 1.47 million metric tons per day by 2025.[11] China has estimated oil reserves of 2.5 billion metric tons—less than 3 percent of the world's reserves for a country with 22 percent of the world's population.[12] China has been a net oil importer since 1993. Imported oil accounts for more than 30 percent of its current consumption, a dependence that is expected to grow over the next two decades (Figure 7.3).

China's leadership is concerned about the country's increased reliance on oil imports and has been taking measures to ensure its energy security. The

Figure 7.2   **Oil Consumption and Domestic Supply of Major Players in the International Oil Market, 2001**

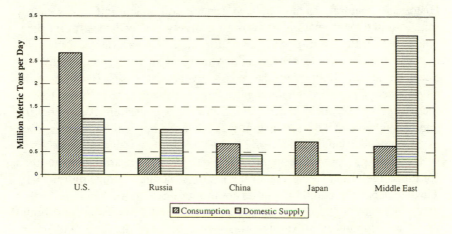

Figure 7.3   **China's Consumption and Production of Oil, 1990–2025**

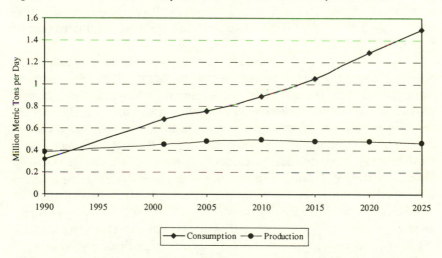

Chinese government regards oil imports as a strategic vulnerability that could be exploited by foreign powers seeking to influence China. China has been strengthening relationships with oil-exporting countries and fostering the development of oil reserves in and seeking the establishment of stronger economic, political, and possibly military ties with Central Asia and Russia.[13] Despite these efforts, China is fundamentally reluctant to deepen its reliance on foreign oil. So long as this reluctance persists, China is not likely to replace coal with cleaner fuels on a large scale.

Natural Gas

Historically, natural gas has not been a major component in China's energy mix. Until the 1990s, natural gas was used largely as a feedstock for fertilizer plants, with little use in power generation. In 2001 it accounted for only 3 percent of the country's energy mix. Among fossil fuels, natural gas produces the least pollution and the fewest greenhouse gases. Because of the environmental benefits of natural gas, China has made several moves toward increasing its use, including replacing polluting household-based cooking and heating coal stoves with natural gas stoves in major urban centers such as Beijing and Shanghai.

Handling gaseous fuels requires more sophisticated arrangements than for liquid fuels, and China's natural gas infrastructure remains rudimentary. Thus, transporting natural gas costs about four times more than transporting crude oil. Although natural gas can be cooled and compressed into liquid form for shipping by tanker, the conversion facilities are large and potentially dangerous. These challenges notwithstanding, China has been aggressively exploring its own natural gas resources. It has begun constructing liquefied natural gas (LNG) regasification terminals and has initiated several gas pipeline projects.

China has plans to increase natural gas supplies substantially and to expand its natural gas pipeline network despite the fact that it remains commercially unprofitable. The country's largest natural gas reserves are located in western and north-central China, necessitating a significant additional investment in pipeline infrastructure to carry it to densely populated eastern cities. The most ambitious of planned pipelines is the 4,184-kilometer (km) West–East Gas Pipeline under construction, which will connect gas fields in China's sparsely populated west to urban markets in the east. The pipeline will initially run from the Tarim Basin in Xinjiang Province to Shanghai and subsequently connect to Beijing through a 322-km link. This project represents a convergence of economic, political, domestic, and foreign policy interests and underscores the political and economic significance of Xinjiang.[14]

The share of natural gas used for power generation and residential cooking and heating is expected to increase significantly. The Chinese government anticipates that Beijing's natural gas infrastructure will be fully operational in time for the 2008 Olympic Games. Shanghai has announced that it will stop building coal-fired electric power plants and speed up the construction of natural-gas-fired plants. Guangdong Province has launched a project to build six 320-megawatt (MW) gas-fired power plants and to convert existing oil-fired plants with a capacity of 1,800 MW to liquefied natural gas.

To reduce air pollution, the Chinese government has been promoting the use of alternative fuel vehicles (AFVs). Many programs have been initiated in large cities, including Beijing, Shanghai, Tianjin, Chongqing, and Guangzhou. The Beijing municipal government is ordering city vehicles to convert to liquefied petroleum gas (LPG) and compressed natural gas (CNG). The capital's 5,100 buses and 32,000 taxis run on these alternative fuels, and seventy-five gas stations offer these two types of clean fuel. Similarly, Shanghai has 400 buses and 30,305 taxis that use alternative fuels and eighty-seven refueling stations to service these vehicles.[15]

It is expected that natural gas will gain market share from coal in the residential and commercial sectors. Consumption of natural gas is expected to increase more than sixfold by 2025, at a projected annual growth rate of 7.9 percent. Such growth requires increases in domestic production. Development of the natural gas industry is an element in China's quest for energy security, but China's natural gas supply is even more limited than its oil reserves. Its natural gas reserves are listed as 1.51 trillion cubic meters or 0.97 percent of the world's total.[16] Imports of natural gas to China, by pipeline and in liquefied form, will be necessary. China is projected to begin importing natural gas around 2005, and the share of imports in China's natural gas consumption is expected to reach 30 percent by 2020.[17]

Hydroelectric Power

Over the next decade, China has extensive plans to expand its hydroelectric capacity above the current 79,000 MW of installed capacity. The Three Gorges Dam project, currently under construction, remains the world's largest and most ambitious hydropower project. With the displacement of more than one million people living around the construction site and reservoir, and submersion of significant archeological sites, it continues as among the most controversial projects in the world today. In November 2002, work on the Three Gorges Dam project reached a significant milestone with the successful blocking of the Yangtze River. The river's waters are now being channeled through diversion holes in the partially completed dam. The dam's reservoir began to fill in June 2003.[18] By the end of 2003, it began generating electricity with the installation of the first four 700-MW generators. The project plans for a total of twenty-six generators, with a capacity of 18,200 MW, which are expected to become fully operational in 2009. The official cost of the Three Gorges Dam is set at US$25 billion, although the actual cost is likely to exceed this figure.

At present, few attempts have been made to address concerns regarding the accumulation of toxic materials and other pollutants from industrial sites that will be inundated after construction of the dam. Given China's scarcity of clean water, the extent to which dams and reservoirs improve or reduce water quality is a major concern. Despite criticism from the international community, the Chinese government argues that the dam is needed to provide electricity, claiming that it will replace ten large coal-fired power stations that otherwise would burn fifty million tons of coal, or the energy equivalent of twenty-six nuclear plants. By doing so, the government asserts, the dam will result in environmental benefits. In addition, the dam should reduce flooding on the Yangtze River.

In addition to the Three Gorges, the Chinese government has several other large-scale hydroelectric projects either under construction or in the planning stages. The Yellow River Water and Hydroelectric Power Development Corporation (YRWHDC) is developing twenty-five hydropower projects on the Yellow River with a combined 15,800 MW of installed electric capacity. In July 2001 construction began on the 5,400-MW Longtan project on the Hongshui River, which is expected to begin operating in 2007. Other large-scale projects under construction include the 1,350-MW Dachaoshan hydroelectric project, scheduled for completion by the end of 2003, and the 4,200-MW Xiaowan project, scheduled for completion in 2012. The last two are located on the Mekong River. Proposals have been submitted for the 14,000-MW Xiluodo project (on the upper portion of the Yangtze River, known locally as the Jinsha River); 6,000-MW Xiangjiaba project (Jinsha River); 5,000-MW Nuozhadu project (Mekong River); and 1,500-MW Jinghong project (Mekong River).

As with the Three Gorges Dam, information on the actual consequences of dams and other water-related infrastructure on China's natural systems is limited; there are few comprehensive reviews. Based on experience elsewhere, some of the main physical and ecological concerns center on the loss and fragmentation of land, habitat, and species and the loss or degradation of many of the ecosystem functions that natural rivers provide. These include wetlands functioning as carbon sinks, nutrient recycling, and water purification.

Nuclear Power

Although nuclear power represented just over 1 percent of total electricity generation in China in 2001, it has an important role in supplying the rapidly industrializing coastal provinces, which are remote from China's coalfields.

China's tenth Five-Year Plan (2001–5) incorporates the construction of nuclear power plants. New facilities under consideration include two additional 900-MW units at Lingao, and up to six 1,000-MW reactors at Yangjiang, Guangdong Province. Additional developments are to take place in Shandong

Province, with two 1,000-MW units planned for Haiyang. Also proposed are two 1,000-MW reactors at Hui An, Fujian Province and two 1,000-MW units at Sanmen, near Qinshan in Zhejiang Province.

In 2001 China had only three nuclear power units in operation: Guangdong 1 and 2 (944 MW each) and Qinshan 1 (279 MW). Four new units were opened in 2002, adding a total of 3,151 MW of nuclear capacity: Lingao 1 and 2 in Guangdong Province (938 MW each), Qinshan 2-A (610 MW), and Qinshan 3-A (665 MW) in Zhejiang Province. Four nuclear reactors are under construction: Qinshan 2-B (610 MW), Qinshan 3-B (665 MW), and Tianwan-1 and Tianwan-2 in Jiangsu Province (1,000 MW each). The last are scheduled to be completed in 2005. These projects involve Canadian, French, and Russian contractors.

Nuclear power is considered by some technically trained people to be the most benign of all energy sources in terms of environmental impact. However, nuclear waste is an extremely sensitive issue. Thus, projections of nuclear power capacity are fraught with economic and political uncertainty. If the projects outlined above come on line, China's nuclear capacity is projected to grow from 2,167 MW in 2001 to about 20,000 MW in 2025—the largest projected increase of any country in the world.

Nonhydroelectric Renewable Energy

In 2001 nonhydroelectric renewable energy contributed merely 0.01 quadrillion Btu, or 0.02 percent of China's energy mix. With assistance from international donors, China has undertaken a multimillion-dollar effort to develop wind and solar projects. One example is the Brightness Program, launched in 1996 to encourage the use of solar panels and wind turbines for electricity generation using low-cost loans. Pilot projects under the program have been set up in Gansu, Inner Mongolia, and Tibet. The ultimate goal of the program is to provide electricity to eight million people by 2005 and to twenty-three million people by 2010.

In an effort to boost interest in wind-powered power generation, the Chinese government has announced that it will cut the value-added tax on wind-generated electricity by half, reducing the average cost of wind generation by between US$6 and US$7 per MW hour. The Asian Development Bank (ADB) is providing loans worth some US$58 million to establish wind projects in Heilongjiang, Liaoning, and Xinjiang provinces. One of the projects is a 200-MW wind farm in Xinjiang, which is China's largest wind installation.

Current utilization of solar energy includes small-scale uses, such as household consumption, television relays, and communications. Solar energy consumption has been increasing steadily. For example, the number of solar kitchen ranges in use has been climbing, a significant fact considering the negative environmental and health effects of coal-burning stoves mentioned earlier.

In addition to these material developments, energy efficiency is often considered an energy resource. There is huge potential in China for energy efficiency. Based on World Bank estimates, 10 percent of total Chinese industrial energy demand can be met through energy efficiency efforts by 2010. China has made impressive progress in raising energy efficiencies in both production and end uses.

Environmental Policy

Over 90 percent of China's SO_2 emissions are attributable to coal-fired boilers. The government has been focusing on emissions from power generation and large industrial facilities, enacting a range of regulations and policies. In 1982, a SO_2 pollution levy was introduced, which became the cornerstone of national SO_2 control. The levy system proved only modestly successful at controlling emissions for two reasons: (1) the levy applied only to medium-sized and large sources and was set too low to encourage significant SO_2 abatement, and (2) the fee was rarely reinvested in new abatement activities. To improve the system, in 2000 the levy was changed from a fee based on excess emissions to a charge on total emissions. Moreover, in 2002 China implemented a new coal policy that increases the pollution levy to RMB 5 (US$0.604) per ton and requires power companies and large industrial facilities to install desulfurization equipment. It mandates that smaller facilities use low-sulfur coal or cleaner fuel alternatives. The new policy is expected to reduce SO_2 emissions nationwide by 10 percent from 2000 levels within five years, and by 20 percent within specified "control zones," including Beijing, Shanghai, Tianjin, and 197 other cities. The control zones account for 11.4 percent of China's land area but for 66 percent of the 20 million tons of SO_2 emitted each year.

In a parallel effort to encourage a switch to cleaner burning fuels, the government has introduced a tax on high-sulfur coals. In Beijing, officials aiming to phase out coal from the city center have established forty "coal-free zones" and have made plans to construct natural gas pipelines. Similar efforts are underway in other major Chinese cities. In addition, pilot SO_2 emissions trading programs are underway in Taiyuan, Shanxi Province; Benxi, Liaoning Province; and Nantong, Jiangsu Province.[19] In early 2002 the State Environmental Protection Administration (SEPA) announced that the provinces of Shandong, Shanxi, Henan, and Jiangsu; the special administrative regions of Macau and Hong Kong; and three cities (Shanghai, Tianjin, and Liuzhou) would pioneer China's first cross-provincial border emissions trading pilot. Rules and a timetable for the pilot emissions trading programs are being developed.

While the Chinese government is concerned with the country's environmental problems, it tends to prioritize issues that directly impact its population, such as particulate matter and SO_2 emissions, rather than long-term concerns such as global warming. It is undertaking initiatives to lessen emissions of pollutants such as SO_2 and nitrogen oxide through improved pollution controls on power plants as well as policies designed to increase the proportion of natural gas in the country's fuel mix. China is a non-Annex I country under the United Nations Framework Convention on Climate Change, meaning that it has not agreed to binding targets for reduction of CO_2 emissions under the Kyoto Protocol. China's contribution to world CO_2 emissions is expected to increase in the coming years, with some forecasts suggesting China's emissions may exceed those of the United States by 2025.[20] Thus, any effort to curb greenhouse gas emissions will be futile without China's involvement.

Projections

Figures 7.4 and 7.5 summarize the projections of China's primary energy consumption through 2025. The growth rate of hydroelectric power and oil is consistent with the growth rate of overall total energy usage. Hence, their projected share of China's energy mix remains unchanged at 7 percent and 26 percent respectively. The phenomenal growth in natural gas consumption results in a significant increase in its share in China's energy mix, from 3 percent in 2001 to 8 percent in 2025. Although the projected growth of China's nuclear capacity is no less spectacular if it materializes, its share in the energy mix increases from essentially zero in 2001 to just 1 percent in 2025. As a result, nuclear energy will do little to offset the anticipated rapid growth in electricity demand or CO_2 emissions. Increases in natural gas and nuclear energy result in a decline in the share of coal from 64 percent to 58 percent. On an absolute scale, however, coal consumption in China will increase tremendously. While the world's coal use has been in a period of slow growth since the 1980s due to environmental concerns, China is a key exception. China's share of the world's total consumption is projected to rise from 26 percent in 2001 to 39 percent in 2025.

China's Future Energy Sources

Based on the *International Energy Outlook 2003* (*IEO2003*) forecast, China's consumption of every primary energy source will increase over the next twenty-five years, but the basic structure of China's energy mix will not change

Figure 7.4 **China's Projected Energy Consumption, 2025**

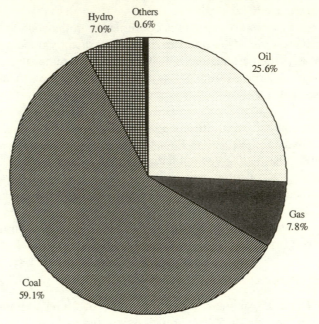

Figure 7.5 **China's Primary Energy Consumption, 1990–2025**

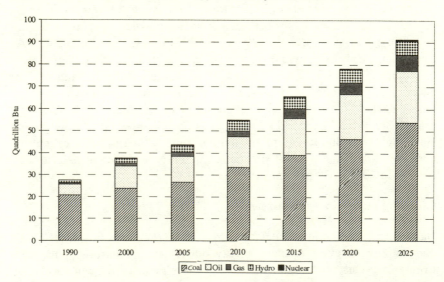

significantly. Much of the increase in its future energy demand is projected to be for fossil fuels, because it is expected that fossil fuel prices will remain relatively low and that the cost of generating energy from other fuels will not be competitive. Because the share of fossil fuels in China's overall energy consumption is expected to remain by far the greatest (more than 90 percent), CO_2 emissions will increase accordingly, from 832 million metric tons in 2001 to a projected 1,844 million metric tons in 2025. China is unlikely to place a high priority on efforts to reduce or stabilize CO_2 emissions.[21]

Among fossil fuels, coal will continue to play the dominant role, despite the resulting environmental damage. From the preceding discussion, it is apparent that a decline of coal's share in the energy mix, from 64 percent in 2001 to 58 percent in 2025, is more the result of high growth in other sources than a reduced reliance on coal per se. Because the *IEO 2003* projections are influenced by numerous variables, they are subject to considerable uncertainty. In the following section, we discuss issues that might lead to even heavier coal usage, and discuss the challenge posed by China's reliance on coal.

Future of Oil and Natural Gas

To develop a basis for understanding the future consumption of oil and gas in China, we can consider the historical trends of energy consumption in developed countries. Oil consumption increased sharply in the United States and Europe after World War II, in part as a response to environmental crises. For example, London suffered from "killer fogs" linked to coal burning. In response, "smokeless zones" were established, in which the burning of coal for home heating was banned, and in 1957 Parliament passed the Clean Air Act, which favored oil. Similarly, a smog crisis in New York City on Thanksgiving in 1966 precipitated passage of the Air Quality Act the following year.[22] Within two years, Consolidated Edison, the utility serving New York City, switched to oil.

In 1955 coal met 75 percent of Western Europe's energy needs, and oil 23 percent. By 1972, coal's share shrunk to 22 percent, while oil consumption rose to 60 percent, nearly a complete reversal.[23] The situation was not as dramatic in the United States, because the United States is rich in coal reserves. Nonetheless, the proportion of coal in the United States energy mix dropped from 37 percent in 1949 to 17 percent in 1972.[24] However, the major reason for the switch from coal to oil in Western Europe and the United States was *cost:* in the 1950s, with repeated price cuts, oil was more cost effective than coal. While Japan had a later start, inexpensive oil proved to be the fuel of choice, and it became the energy source that powered Japan's remarkable economic growth.

Unfortunately, cheap oil is not an option for China. As global consumption rises and oil supplies are restricted, economics dictate that oil prices will rise. Therefore, *cost* is a primary factor preventing China from substituting oil for coal. Oil price shocks in the 1970s sent the major economies into recession, highlighting the vulnerability of Western economies stemming from their reliance on oil. Today, a large and growing portion of the world's oil supplies comes from relatively unstable locations, including the Middle East and the former Soviet states surrounding the Caspian Sea. There are no guarantees of an uninterrupted oil supply, another factor that discourages China from shifting from coal to oil.

A more fundamental problem is that global oil supplies are finite. It is difficult to say with certainty how long supplies will last. A pessimistic prediction asserts that, at current rates of production and consumption, the world's oil will last another forty-five years; an optimistic projection asserts another 100 years.[25] As reserves diminish and become more costly to extract, it seems reasonable to assume that oil quantities will be severely restricted at some point within this time frame. The most feared potential consequence of declining oil supplies and rising prices is a long-term economic downturn. Projected to be the second largest oil consumer in the world, China must be prepared to deal with severely limited oil supplies and adjust to a post-oil economy.

Natural gas is part of China's energy diversification strategy to reduce its dependence on oil. Unlike oil, natural gas supplies are geographically dispersed, not concentrated in the Middle East. Natural gas, a clean-burning fuel, offers an attractive option for China. However, the high costs of exploration, development, and transportation hinder China's switch to natural gas. It is difficult to gauge supply needs, which are affected by economic cycles and weather patterns, and the lack of such information makes it difficult to forecast profitability and attract capital investment.

Technology may offer a partial solution. The industrial process used to convert natural gas to a liquefied form has improved. Today, natural gas can be converted to liquid fuels at prices that are only about 10 percent higher than crude oil. Modest technical improvements should broaden the exploitation of this commodity in coming years, and such developments will also provide remarkably clean fuels.[26] Experts say that the price per million Btu needed to justify new investment is in the range of US$3–4.50. In late 2003, the price hovered around US$6, although few expect it to stay that high.[27] Liquefied natural gas (LNG) can be used in place of petroleum to generate energy. The need for fuel for the transportation sector is the single most important factor driving China's increasing demand for oil. If advanced methods of producing liquid fuels from natural gas can be made profitable and scaled up quickly, natural gas may become the next major source of transportation fuel, thereby meeting some of China's vital energy needs.

Future of Nuclear Energy

Nuclear energy was once regarded as the realization of a dream for cheap, unlimited electric power. This attitude has changed significantly following the Three Mile Island and Chernobyl nuclear disasters. In recent years, efforts to curb CO_2 emissions have put nuclear power back in the spotlight.[28] A study suggests that the only reasonably sure way to cut emissions in China substantially over the next thirty years is through the massive construction of nuclear power plants.[29] However, under most economic assumptions, nuclear power is a relatively expensive option for electricity generation when compared with natural gas or coal, particularly given China's access to inexpensive coal.[30]

In addition, the fate of nuclear power is closely linked to public attitudes.[31] While the ability of people in China to protest may be limited, it is unrealistic to discount the possibility of popular opposition. It is worth noting that environmentalism was the most important rallying point for the democratic movement in some countries. Nuclear power plays a uniquely sensitive role in politics, and it is too soon to say whether China will fulfill its ambitious plans to increase its nuclear capacity as projected.

Future of Renewable Energy Sources

At a time when many countries throughout the world are dismantling hydroelectric dams, China has been making tremendous investments in hydroelectric power. While hydroelectric power can make a substantial contribution to China's energy supplies, it has limitations that make it a less attractive option. Constraints include the geographic concentration of dams (primarily in the center and southwest of the country), sizable capital investment required, and long lead time, as well as substantial social and environmental risks. As noted previously, more than one million people were displaced by the Three Gorges Dam project. A less publicized fact is that, since 1985, five large dam projects (supported by World Bank loans), with a total installed capacity of 7,040 MW, displaced approximately 343,000 people.[32] Many existing dams were built at a time when environmental and social standards were largely absent. However, based on reactions in recent years, it is almost certain that future large-scale projects will not proceed without strong opposition.

For the foreseeable future, renewable sources such as solar and wind power are not sufficiently technologically advanced to meet more than a fraction of China's needs. As discussed earlier, an array of international programs are promoting renewable energy in China, but the effect of these programs is largely symbolic. They are unlikely to make a significant impact on China's energy needs or its environment.

Future of Coal

Coal is the most plentiful fuel in China, and at present rates of consumption, China has sufficient reserves to last another 100 to 200 years. If energy development projects from other sources are not fulfilled, coal is likely to fill the gap. China has been researching converting coal to gas or liquid fuels to create a substitute for vehicle fuels. However, not only is this process expensive, but doing so on a significant scale would require enormous mining projects and create vast environmental damage. These actions could roll back China's commitment to adopting vehicular emissions standards.[33]

While there are claims that "switches to low-sulfur coal, scrubbers and other air-pollution control devices have today removed the vast part of sulfur dioxide and nitrogen dioxide emissions,"[34] it is important to read between the lines. Looking at the United States, for example, emissions of nitrogen oxides from coal-burning electric power plants were 6.1 million short tons in 1980 and 5.4 million short tons in 1998; emissions of SO_2 were 16.1 million short tons in 1980 and 12.4 million short tons in 1998. Although these modest reductions are welcome, they hardly qualify as the "vast part" of the emissions.[35] The improvements in the United States followed significant investments in pollution-reducing equipment. Plants in the United States had an incentive to invest in such technology: a plant owner faces fines of up to US$2,000 per ton of emissions.[36] By comparison, China's new pollution policy has increased the pollution levy to only RMB 5 (US$0.604) per ton of SO_2.

Therefore, even if China enforces its pollution policy effectively, it will generate limited funding for equipment upgrades. So long as China continues to rely on coal, it is unclear how the country will attain a clean air standard and mitigate the environmental impacts. In addition, China is grappling with the high human toll of coal mining. China's coal industry has an appalling record: Beijing's work safety bureau reported that at least 4,500 fatalities occurred in coal mines last year, although unofficial estimates put the figure as high as 10,000.[37] Less dramatic, but just as devastating, is the severe damage to human health by black lung disease. These problems are pressing social issues that the country must address.

Conclusion

As its economy continues to expand, China's energy needs escalate. To increase its energy production, China faces a range of unpleasant choices. There is no costless solution for energy production, and all energy sources create their own sets of issues. Coal is an undesirable yet unavoidable option. China's aggressive energy development projects in the areas of hydroelectric power, natural gas, and nuclear power tend to be risky. Some of these projects have been criticized as monumental environmental gambles.

Replacing dirty coal with cleaner oil has played a pivotal role in environmental preservation in the United States and Europe during their post–World War II economic expansions. At present, the high cost of oil has caused serious economic problems for all nations, but China suffers especially acutely because it must pay for imported energy supplies with precious foreign exchange. When the issues are presented starkly as "economic growth versus clean environment," the pressure on Chinese politicians to allow industry to defer pollution control measures seems irresistible. We can only hope that technological advancements provide affordable solutions to minimize energy-related environmental degradation.

On the brighter side, the coming of the 2008 "green" Olympic Games has increased China's awareness of the need for environmental protection, and this awareness has been reflected at the policy level. China's adoption of vehicular emissions standards is a positive first step. Coming at the dawn of an era of fast growth in automobile ownership, an early start is the most effective means of ensuring future air quality control.

Notes

The authors thank Chris Nielsen, director of the China Project, Harvard University Center for the Environment, and two anonymous reviewers for their valuable suggestions. Some information provided by them has been incorporated directly in the final version of this chapter, but any deficiency or inaccuracy remains the responsibility of the authors.

1. In comparison, total primary energy consumption in the United States in 2001 was 97.1 quadrillion Btu.

2. U.S. Energy Information Administration (EIA), *International Energy Outlook 2003 (IEO2003)* (Washington, DC: Government Printing Office, 2003), 181. The projection cited here is the reference case, which assumes the annual growth rate of gross domestic product (GDP) to be 6.2 percent.

3. Much material in this section is taken from *IEO2003*, published by the U.S. Energy Information Administration. All subsequent quotes and statistical data are assumed to be from this source unless otherwise indicated. Energy-related data and forecasts are difficult tasks and are the subjects of numerous studies and disagreements. Another authoritative, perhaps more commonly cited, source is the *World Energy Outlook* published by the International Energy Agency (IEA). We have adopted information from *IEO* due to its easy access over the Internet. A key omission in this chapter is the topic of biomass consumption. Biomass is composed chiefly of crop wastes, fuelwood, and dung. Because it is collected and used as fuel outside of formal markets, biomass is not reflected in official energy statistics. Although it is poorly understood, one estimate suggests that biomass accounts for about 15 percent of China's actual total energy consumption. This estimate reflects the general limitation on data relating to rural conditions in China—a major caveat, given that half of China's population, or 640 million people, still live a fundamentally rural existence.

4. We made a conversion of the *IEO2003* data using 1 short ton = 0.907 metric ton. In terms of energy, the gross heat content of coal depends on country and year. For China in 2001, the conversion factor is 18,512 thousand Btu per short ton (U.S. Energy Information Administration, *International Energy Annual 2003,* 146).

5. BBC News, "Scores Dead in China Mine Blast," Sept. 28, 2000.

6. Advanced coal gasification technology exists that will enable easier control of pollutants. See, e.g., Ni and Sze, "Energy Supply and Development in China." Economic viability remains a major concern.

7. E.g., Peng et al., "Indoor Air Pollution from Residential Energy Use in China." This paragraph closely follows Simpson, "Coal Control," 20.

8. A conversion of the *IEO2003* data using a factor 1 metric ton = 7.3 barrels is used; see *International Energy Annual 2003,* 137.

9. Bradsher, "China's Factories Aim to Fill the World's Garages," A8.

10. Under this standard, in the near future, nitrogen and oxygen compound emissions from light-duty vehicles should decrease about 55 percent, and particulates from heavy-duty vehicles should decrease by 55 percent. See *People's Daily*, "Beijing to Apply Euro 2 Emission Standard Next Year," July 29, 2002, english.peopledaily.com.cn/200207/29/eng20020729_100511.shtml.

11. In comparison, oil consumption by 2025 is projected to be 4.0 million metric tons per day in the United States and 0.89 million metric tons per day in Japan.

12. From the most recent estimates in PennWell Corp., *Oil and Gas Journal*, 52.

13. This subject has been studied by various groups, e.g., Downs, *China's Quest for Energy Security.*

14. Andrews-Speed, Liao, and Dannreuther, "Searching for Energy Security," 13–28.

15. Lun Jingguang, "Clean City Vehicles in China."

16. PennWell Corp., *Oil and Gas Journal*, 52.

17. Downs, *China's Quest for Energy Security*, 9. See also references therein.

18. Kahn, "A River Rises Through It, Washing Away the Past," 14.

19. Chapter 6 in this volume details the emissions trading program in Taiyuan.

20. Bradsher, "China's Boom Adds to Global Warming Problem," A1.

21. May, "Energy and Security in East Asia," 16–19.

22. "Smog Here Near the Danger Point," *New York Times,* Nov. 25, 1966, 1.

23. Yergin, *The Prize*, 545.

24. U.S. Energy Information Administration, *Annual Energy Review 2002*, www.eia.doe.gov/emeu/aer/txt/ptb1801b.html.

25. Campbell and Laherrère, "The End of Cheap Oil," 78; PennWell Corp., *Oil and Gas Journal*, 52; Smith, *Energy, the Environment, and Public Opinion*, 54–58.

26. Fouda, "Liquid Fuels from Natural Gas," 92.

27. Wald, "In Natural Gas's Future," C2.

28. Rhodes, "Nuclear Power's New Day."

29. Lu, "The Role of Nuclear Energy in the CO_2 Mitigation Strategy of the People's Republic of China," 20.

30. A Massachusetts Institute of Technology study suggests that the cost of nuclear power is 6.7 cents per kilowatt-hour, compared to 4.2 cents for coal and natural gas (*without* assigning a cost to CO_2 emissions); see Deutch and Moniz, "How to Prevent the Next Energy Crisis."

31. See, e.g., Nordhaus, *The Swedish Nuclear Dilemma.*

32. Fuggle and Smith, "Experience with Dams in Water and Energy Resource Development in the People's Republic of China," www.dams.org/report/.

33. There are potential merits to the coal gasification technology mentioned earlier. One major advantage is the possibility of CO_2 capture and geological sequestration. For additional information see www.fossil.energy.gov/programs/sequestration/geologic/.

34. Taken from Holdren, "Energy: Asking the Wrong Question," which quotes Lomborg, *The Skeptical Environmentalist,* and USEPA, *National Air Pollutant Emission Trends 1900–1998.*

35. Ibid.

36. Kubasek and Silverman, *Environmental Law,* 166.

37. BBC News, "Blast Hits China Mine," May 14, 2003.

Bibliography

Andrews-Speed, P., Liao Xuanli, and R. Dannreuther. "Searching for Energy Security: The Political Ramifications of China's International Energy Policy." *China Environment Series* 5 (2002): 13–28.

Baldinger, P., and Jennifer L. Turner. *Crouching Suspicions, Hidden Potential: United States Environmental and Energy Cooperation with China.* Washington, DC: Woodrow Wilson Center (June 2002).

BBC News. "Blast Hits China Mine," May 14, 2003. news.bbc.co.uk/2/hi/asia-pacific/3025981.stm.

———. "Scores Dead in China Mine Blast," Sept. 28, 2000. news.bbc.co.uk/2/hi/asia-pacific/945847.stm.

Bradsher, Keith. "China's Boom Adds to Global Warming Problem." *New York Times,* Oct. 22, 2003, A1.

———. "China's Factories Aim to Fill the World's Garages," *New York Times,* Nov. 2, 2003, A8.

Campbell, Colin J., and Jean H. Laherrère. "The End of Cheap Oil." *Scientific American* (March 1998): 78.

Deutch, John, and Ernest Moniz. "How to Prevent the Next Energy Crisis." *New York Times,* Aug. 14, 2003, A25.

Downs, Erica Strecker. *China's Quest for Energy Security.* RAND Report MR-1244-AF. Santa Monica: RAND, 2000.

Fouda, Safaa A. "Liquid Fuels from Natural Gas." *Scientific American* (March 1998): 92.

Fuggle, R., and W.T. Smith. "Experience with Dams in Water and Energy Resource Development in the People's Republic of China." *World Commission on Dams* (Nov. 2000). www.dams.org/report/.

Henry, J. Glynn, and Gary W. Heinke. *Environmental Science and Engineering,* 2d ed. Upper Saddle River, NJ: Prentice Hall, 1996.

Hessler, Peter. "Underwater: The World's Biggest Dam Floods the Past." *New Yorker* (July 7, 2003): 28.

Holdren, John P. "Energy: Asking the Wrong Question." *Scientific American* (January 2002): 65.

Kahn, Joseph. "A River Rises Through It, Washing Away the Past." *New York Times,* June 1, 2003, sec. 4, 14.

Kubasek, Nancy K., and Gary S. Silverman. *Environmental Law,* 4th ed. Upper Saddle River, NJ: Prentice Hall, 2002.

Lomberg, Bjørn. *The Skeptical Environmentalist.* New York: Cambridge University Press, 2001.

Lu Yingzhong. "The Role of Nuclear Energy in the CO_2 Mitigation Strategy of the People's Republic of China." *China Environment Series* 1 (1997): 20.

Lun Jingguang. "Clean City Vehicles in China." IEA Workshop on Clean City Vehicles with a Special Focus on Developing Countries. Paris, Sept. 24–25, 2002. www.iea.org/workshop/ccv/ccv1%201un.pdf.

May, Michael. "Energy and Security in East Asia." *China Environment Series* 1 (1997): 16–19.

McElroy, Michael B., Chris P. Nielsen, and Peter Lydon, eds. *Energizing China: Reconciling Environmental Protection and Economic Growth.* Cambridge, MA: Harvard University Press, 1998.

Ni Weidou, and Šze Nien Dak. "Energy Supply and Development in China." In McElroy, Nielsen, and Lydon, eds., *Energizing China,* 67.

Nordhaus, William D. *The Swedish Nuclear Dilemma.* Washington, DC: Resources for the Future, 1997.

OECD/NEA (Nuclear Energy Agency). *Nuclear Energy in a Sustainable Development Perspective.* Paris, 2001.

Peng Ruicong, Wang Lihua, Wang Hong, He Kebin, and Xu Xiping. "Indoor Air Pollution from Residential Energy Use in China." In McElroy, Nielsen, and Lydon, eds., *Energizing China,* 287.

PennWell Corporation. *Oil and Gas Journal* 100 (Dec. 23, 2002): 52.

People's Daily. "Beijing to Apply Euro 2 Emission Standard Next Year," July 29, 2002. http://english.peopledaily.com.cn/200207/29/eng20020729_100511.shtml.

Pomfret, John. "China's Monumental Gamble, River Halted by Dam That Will Bring Power, or Untold Destruction." *Washington Post,* June 2, 2003, A11.

Rhodes, Richard. "Nuclear Power's New Day." *New York Times*, May 7, 2001.

Simpson, Sarah. "Coal Control." *Scientific American* (February 2002): 20.

Smith, Eric R.A.N. *Energy, the Environment, and Public Opinion.* Lanham, MD: Rowman and Littlefield, 2002.

"Smog Here Near the Danger Point." *New York Times*, Nov. 25, 1966, 1.

U.S. Energy Information Administration. *Annual Energy Review 2002.* www.eia.doe.gov/emeu/aer/txt/ptb1801b.html.

———. *International Energy Annual 2001.* Washington, DC: Government Printing Office, 2003. www.eia.doe.gov.

———. *International Energy Outlook.* Washington, DC: Government Printing Office, 2003. www.eia.doe.gov.

U.S. Environmental Protection Agency. "National Air Pollutant Emission Trends: 1900–1998." Report EPA 454/R-00-002. Washington, DC: Government Printing Office, March 2000.

Wald, Matthew L. "In Natural Gas's Future, Experts See More High Prices and Growing Imports." *New York Times,* June 27, 2003, C2.

World Oil. 223 (8) (August 2002).

Yergin, Daniel. *The Prize: The Epic Quest for Oil, Money, and Power.* New York: Simon and Schuster, 1991.

Zou Ji, and Yuan Haiyo. "Air Pollution, Energy and Fiscal Policies in China: A Review." OECD Publication 119, 1997.

Zusman, Eric, and Jennifer L. Turner. "Beyond the Bureaucracy: Changing China's Policymaking Environment." This volume, chapter 5.

—— Chapter 8 ——

Reviving the Scorched Earth?

A Snapshot of China's Hazardous Waste Management and Cleaner Production Programs

Dan Millison

Industrial solid waste generation in China is estimated to be 0.5 ton per person per year. A total of 650 million tons was generated in 1995. This amount is projected to increase to one billion tons per year by 2005, of which 5 to 10 percent will be hazardous (Bromby 1997, Liu et al. 1999). These figures exclude wastes from township and village enterprises (TVEs), which may comprise an additional 100 million tons per year. Approximately 18 percent of this waste is treated (115 million tons), 3 to 4 percent is discharged without treatment (20 million tons, 2 million tons of which, for example, is coal ash discharged into rivers), and approximately 38 percent is stored for further treatment (247 million tons). At these rates, more than one billion tons of solid wastes will be stockpiled over a five-year period. The amount of hazardous waste is estimated to range from 2.2 to 8.3 million tons per year, of which 1.5 to 3 million tons per year are discharged into the environment without treatment (Liu et al. 1999, Zhuang 2003). Estimates vary due to uncertainties in applying waste definitions and whether TVEs are included.

Successfully managing these waste streams is a monumental challenge, with a potentially large market for waste treatment and disposal, as well as pollution prevention. China's tenth Five-Year Plan (FYP) for National Social and Economic Development (2001–5) calls for an investment in hazardous waste treatment of approximately US$8 billion of the US$26 billion allocated for all environmental programs. Investments in cleaner production (CP) are targeted to reach more than US$10 billion (PA Consulting 2003b). A key goal of the tenth FYP is to maintain hazardous waste generation at year 2000 levels via CP and industrial reform measures. Hazardous waste management

(HWM) and CP are critical elements in China's overall waste control and management strategy, yet neither is at a mature stage there.

The development of China's environmental management programs resembles that of most other countries: priority is given to immediate public-health-oriented problems, namely, air and water pollution and urban sanitation. After some progress with these initial challenges, HWM and CP programs have begun to develop in earnest, albeit with delays and limitations. Experience in developed and developing countries indicates that, to support successful programs, a variety of conditions must be present. Legislative, technical, institutional, and financial vectors must converge to create an enabling framework. Typically, ten to fifteen years elapse from the time that environmental problems are identified and a program is defined to the point that a functional regulatory program and infrastructure are put in place (Probst and Beirle 1999). While China's experience is consistent with that of most other countries, in some aspects it has lagged behind other East Asian countries, especially with respect to HWM infrastructure and financing CP. The slower pace is due in part to the perception that environmental issues have technological, rather than managerial, solutions (Clarke et al. 1997, Evans and Hamner 2003).

Linking Hazardous Waste Management and Cleaner Production: The CP Equation

Cleaner production can be defined as an industrial management process of maximizing resource and production efficiency and minimizing waste outputs. Industrial CP comprises principles of reformulation, replacement, reduction, and reuse (for background, see, for example, Luken and Freij 1994). In the Chinese context, CP can be defined more broadly to include:

- Eco-efficiency
- Pollution prevention
- Waste minimization, reuse, and recycling ("comprehensive utilization")
- Green productivity
- Industrial ecology/industrial metabolism ("eco-industrial partnerships").

In China, CP and HWM sometimes are thought of as distinctly different things, but the following equation clearly illustrates the link:

$$Energy + Raw\ Materials + Water = Products + Wastes$$

In the simplest terms, CP is an effort to make hazardous waste and other environmental pollution problems disappear through better management of inputs and production processes.

As China's economic development accelerated with the onset of economic reforms in the late 1970s, its environmental management programs emphasized end-of-pipe controls rather than CP. By the mid-1990s, China had become a net energy importer (requiring payment in foreign exchange), causing the economic benefits of CP in the form of energy efficiency to become painfully obvious. High energy costs, combined with pervasive ecological degradation due mainly to air and water pollution, have led to giving CP a prominent role in environmental management policy. HWM, the infrastructure development which might be seen as the epitome of Chinese "gradualism," also is maturing, in terms of the PRC implementing a more complete regulatory framework and a national program for safe treatment and disposal capacity.

Hazardous Waste Management and Cleaner Production in the Chinese Context

Since the onset of economic reforms, China has received substantial foreign technical and financial assistance to support its development objectives, including environmental programs. China's CP and HWM programs have enjoyed donor-funded support, foreign-sourced training and overseas study tours, technology transfer, and institutional strengthening. The pattern of donor-supported assistance has shifted from direct intervention—that is, sector-specific or one-off project investments to develop waste treatment capacity or fund prototype CP projects—to a more strategic, staged approach of policy support followed by targeted investment (Evans and Hamner 2003).

China's capacity to absorb foreign assistance and investment appears infinite. Yet, its development pattern is mixed:

- Economic growth has raced ahead in the coastal provinces and lagged significantly in the western regions.
- Environmental management was not a serious factor in national government planning until the 1990s (Clarke et al. 1997).
- By the standards of developing countries, China is heavily polluted (Newfarmer and Johnson 1997).

Like many other developing countries, China has emphasized the need for technology transfer and financial assistance rather than management and human resource development. Bilateral donor support has promoted primarily technology transfer via hardware exports. Multilateral donors have emphasized policy intervention for management and institutional strengthening, with mixed success.

Some key external legislative developments that have affected China's CP and HWM programs are: (1) two key U.S. legislative developments in the 1980s,[1] and (2) the Basel Convention for the Control of Transboundary Shipments of Hazardous and Dangerous Wastes. China adapted many aspects of the U.S. HWM system, a policy reinforced by China's accession to the Basel Convention.

In the United States, the CP-HWM link became pronounced throughout the late 1980s as regulatory and market forces prompted industrial enterprises to reduce the amount of hazardous and toxic wastes generated and disposed off-site and to shift their emphasis to reducing the amount of such materials used in production processes. Two major legislative developments created the U.S. regulatory framework: the Hazardous and Solid Waste Amendments to the Resource Conservation and Recovery Act (RCRA, passed in 1984), and the Superfund Amendments and Reauthorization Act (SARA, passed in 1987), which included community-right-to-know provisions, especially those provisions for public disclosure of hazardous and toxic materials use included in the Toxic Release Inventory (TRI) program.

The 1984 RCRA amendments imposed the current regulatory requirements for HWM, including operating regulations for treatment, storage, and disposal facilities (TSDFs). The technical requirements specified in RCRA are de facto the world standards for TSDFs. The TRI program was designed to incorporate greater public awareness concerning hazardous and toxic materials use, with the expectation that public pressure would cause industries to clean up their production processes. While extensive literature exists on the role of public participation in environmental management, TRI and similar programs have caused industries to systematically review their operations, resulting in widespread waste minimization efforts and a general shift to CP processes and technologies.[2]

Roughly coincident with the phased implementation of the RCRA amendments (1984–88) was the adoption of the Basel Convention in 1988, developed in response to several cases of transnational dumping of hazardous wastes. The Basel Convention defined waste classifications in a manner not unlike RCRA and other developed-country systems, established a protocol and limitations for transboundary waste transfers, and specified technical guidelines for appropriate waste management facilities. While the convention afforded some protection from illegal waste exports to developing country signatories, it also obligated signatories to build the necessary infrastructure to control hazardous wastes within their own borders. Thus, the Basel Convention effectively provided an enabling policy framework for international environmental technology transfer. Within this framework, various bilateral and multilateral agencies funded a variety of HWM projects in Asia from the late 1980s through the mid-1990s.

As a signatory to the Basel Convention, China began its HWM program in the late 1980s, yet did not approve national definitions of hazardous waste until 1998, did not have a modern TSDF operating until the late 1990s, and did not publish national standards for key TSDF operations until 2001. Basel signatories face the practical necessity of harmonizing their national laws with Basel Convention definitions and stipulations, and this requirement has been a significant factor retarding China's HWM programs.

Historical Development of Treatment, Storage, and Disposal Facilities in East Asia

Beginning in the 1970s and 1980s, countries in East Asia began systematically developing environmental control programs, including solid and hazardous waste management. Various factors affected the outcomes of HWM programs, particularly regarding developing centralized treatment capacity. These programs followed a typical pattern, with major development issues summarized in Box 8.1.[3]

By the late 1980s, legislation and regulatory programs were fairly well developed, preliminary waste surveys and siting studies had been conducted, and extensive multilateral and bilateral donor support had been mobilized to support national environmental program development. The TSDF development programs were to some extent "kick-started" by donor-funded technical assistance for feasibility studies. The U.S. Trade Development Agency (USTDA) and other donor agencies, World Bank and Asian Development Bank (ADB), provided a series of grants for feasibility studies in China, Indonesia, and Malaysia. World Bank and ADB assistance included proposed project loans to finance a handful of TSDFs. During the 1990s, several TSDFs opened in the region. Table 8.1 summarizes the chronology of HWM program and TSDF project development in East Asia.

In the late 1980s, these initial USTDA-funded feasibility studies generally concluded that a potentially large market existed (for example, in most cases, well over 100,000 metric tons per year [T/y]) and that a commercially viable TSDF would require a minimum of 10,000 T/y delivered to a centralized facility from a 200-kilometer (km) market radius. At these throughputs, the cost of processing and disposal was estimated to range from US$100 to $200/ton for secure landfill (in late 1980s dollars), with much higher treatment costs for dedicated incineration. The feasibility studies paid some attention to facility financing, ownership, and operations, but were not intended to fully resolve those issues. However, fur-

Box 8.1

Hazardous Waste Management Program and
Treatment, Storage, and Disposal Facilities Project
Development Issues

HWM Program Development Issues
- Define problems and develop legislative approaches
- Designate a lead agency
- Promulgate implementing regulations, rules, and operating guidelines
- Develop treatment and disposal infrastructure
- Create a mature enforcement and compliance regime

TSDF Project Development Issues

Regulatory requirements and operating guidance. What are the facility siting criteria? How will permits be defined and issued? What companies and government agencies will be subject to the regulations? What criteria will apply to facility operations? What requirements will be imposed on waste transportation? What level of enforcement will be exercised that in effect creates the market for commercial TSDFs?

Waste definitions and prediction of waste volumes. What wastes will be regulated? Will small generators be exempted from management requirements?

Management strategies, disposal options, and treatment technologies. What management options will be allowed? What treatment technologies will be permitted? What are the waste acceptance procedures? Will codisposal of municipal and industrial wastes be allowed?* Dedicated incineration? Deep-well disposal?

Ownership, financing, and economics. Who will own and operate the facilities? How will construction be financed? How will tariffs and fees be calculated or regulated? What parameters will be used to determine whether centralized facilities are economically beneficial?

Operations and human resource management. Who will actually manage and operate the facilities? What worker training and

certifications will be required? Waste manifest system? Disposal
documentation? Emergency response plans?

Note: *In the United States, several landfill sites that allowed codisposal of
industrial and municipal wastes prior to the 1984 RCRA regulations have been
included in the Superfund cleanup program. Biodegradation of chlorinated solvents resulted in generation of vinyl chloride gas (an intermediate degradation
product), a compound more toxic than the original substance. Thus, while
codisposal may appear to be an attractive management option, without careful
operating controls, the cure will be worse than the disease.

---

ther progress in TSDF development depended largely on which business
model was adopted for specific projects. In the early and mid-1990s, the
ADB and World Bank funded more detailed development and design studies, which included resolution of ownership and other operational issues.
Outside of China, public-private partnerships with majority private financing emerged as the most common model of TSDF ownership and
operations. In China, World Bank loans financed the first commercial-
scale TSDF at Shenyang. More recent projects, however, are adopting
public-private partnership arrangements.

Technology transfer has been a minor issue. Most Chinese facilities have
a combination of stabilization/solidification, secure landfill, and incineration
in cement kilns or dedicated incinerators. The Hong Kong Chemical Waste
Treatment Center (CWTC) is a notable exception because it was required to
accept all hazardous wastes collected in the territory. Waste-specific technologies generally have been limited to on-site treatment. Despite its attractive-
ness as a "permanent destruction" solution, incineration is limited to
high-heating-value wastes (for example, in the United States, only approximately 2 percent of hazardous waste is incinerated).

TSDF Status in China

China's path to modern TSDF development began in earnest with the USTDA-
funded feasibility study beginning in 1988 for a facility near Shenyang,
Liaoning Province. In addition, the World Bank provided a series of loans for
environmental protection and waste treatment projects in Liaoning Province,
including design and construction of a modern TSDF that began operating in
1999. The landfill is reported to be experiencing operational difficulties, due in
part to lack of revenue. At the time of this writing, run-on water, possibly
contaminated by contact with waste, was not being pumped and treated (Van

Table 8.1

East Asia Hazardous Waste Management Chronology

Year	Country	Milestone
1974	Malaysia	Environmental Quality Act passed
1975	Malaysia	Department of Environment formed
1980	Hong Kong (SAR)	Waste Disposal Ordinance passed
1981	Hong Kong (SAR)	Environmental Protection Administration formed
	Malaysia	Twelve candidate TSDF sites identified
1982	Hong Kong (SAR)	Preliminary TSDF siting efforts
	Indonesia	Basic Environment Law passed; Ministry of Environment (KLH) formed
1983	Indonesia	Initial surveys and siting studies for 10 TSDFs
1984	Malaysia	Draft HWM regulations
1986	Hong Kong (SAR)	Department of Environment formed
	Indonesia	USTDA FS for Cileungsi site TSDF
1987	Hong Kong (SAR)	FS for Tsing Yi Island Chemical Waste Treatment Center
	Malaysia	USTDA FS for Kualita Alam TSDF
1988	China	USTDA FS for Shenyang TSDF
	Thailand	Ministry of Industry industrial waste regulations developed and promulgated
1989	Malaysia	HWM regulations promulgated; fifteen proposals submitted for TSDF development
1991	Indonesia	Environmental Impact Management Agency ("BAPEDAL") formed
1992	China	WB FS for Beijing TSDF
1992	Hong Kong (SAR)	HWM regulations promulgated
	Indonesia	WB FS for Cileungsi site TSDF; USTDA FS for East Java TSDF
	Malaysia	MOU for Kualita Alam operations
	Thailand	Hazardous Substance Act passed; Pollution Control Department formed; Samae Dam TSDF opens
1993	China	WB-loan-funded development of Shenyang TSDF
	Hong Kong (SAR)	Tsing Yi Island Chemical Waste Treatment Center opens
	Indonesia	MOU for Cileungsi TSDF operations
	Thailand	Ratchaburi landfill opens
1994	China	Private sector FS for Tianjin TSDF; ADB FS for Beijing TSDF (proposed loan)
	Indonesia	HWM regulations become effective; Cileungsi TSDF opens
	Thailand	TSDF operating company created
1995	China	WB FS for Shanghai TSDF; Solid Waste Law amended
	Indonesia	HWM regulations amended; MOU for East Java TSDF; ADB FS for Aceh and E. Kalimantan (proposed loan)
1996	China	Shenzhen secure landfill pilot project
1997	China	Suzhou-Singapore Industrial Park FS
	Indonesia	Basic Environment Law amended
	Thailand	Rayong TSDF opens
1998	China	SEPA hazardous wastes catalogue
	Hong Kong (SAR)	Subsidies removed on HWM collection and treatment
	Malaysia	Kualita Alam opens

(continued)

1999	China	Shenyang TSDF (secure landfill) opens
	Indonesia	HWM regulations amended
2000	China	Shanghai TSDF operational
2001	China	TSDF operational standards published; tenth FYP
		identifies eight TSDF projects for priority development
2003	China	Tianjin TSDF opened; new HWM program
		guidelines and regulations published

Sources: Authors' notes, Wong and Lai (2002, 2003), Zhuang (2002, 2003), Probst and Beirle (1999).

Notes: Acronyms: ADB = Asian Development Bank; FS = feasibility study; HWM = hazardous waste management; MOU = memorandum of understanding; SAR = Special Administrative Region; SEPA = State Environmental Protection Administration; TSDF = treatment, storage, and disposal facility; USTDA = United States Trade Development Agency; WB = World Bank.

Epp 2003). Two rotary kiln incinerators are under construction, and there is adequate space for additional treatment units at the kiln site. New treatment units may use plasma arc technology.

While progress was slow and sure in Liaoning, the relatively early commissioning of the Hong Kong CWTC set high design and operational standards for TSDFs in China. The technology-intensive approach in Hong Kong is unique to the region, if not the world, but was necessary to accommodate the local conditions and waste characteristics associated with a very large number of small and diverse waste generators. The early operations of the Hong Kong facility were successful and may have fed mainland perceptions that technology was "the answer" and that management and institutional aspects of TSDF development were unimportant.

Development of several other facilities began in the early 1990s, targeting primarily the large urban/industrial areas of Beijing, Tianjin, Shanghai, and Shenzhen. Beijing and Shanghai received World Bank support for feasibility studies in the early and mid-1990s, respectively. A homegrown pilot project facility was developed in Shenzhen with technical support from Qinghua University; the pilot later was scaled up to commercial operations. The facility currently has extensive liquids treatment capacity and uses solidification prior to landfill. Planned expansion includes a third secure landfill cell, rotary kiln incinerator, and recycling unit. In 1997 the Suzhou Singapore Industrial Park commissioned a feasibility study focusing on incineration technology. A comprehensive TSDF is being planned that will include secure landfill and incinerators using rotary kiln and possible plasma arc technologies (Van Epp 2003).

Shanghai's strategy was to construct a new hazardous waste disposal cell at an existing solid waste landfill and retrofit cement kilns for certain organic wastes. The Shanghai landfill site was not consistent with the regional and international standards already set in Hong Kong and Indonesia, due primarily to high flood risk, but was selected as an acceptable option for early development. In Beijing, after the initial feasibility study funded by the World Bank, the ADB provided project preparation technical assistance in anticipation of financing facility construction and startup. Ultimately, the original Beijing TSDF project was scrapped due to changes in the potential market and possibly unrealistic business expectations of the local government. New initiatives are underway to develop facilities for the Beijing and Tianjin areas.

Development of a TSDF for the Tianjin municipality began in 1994, following China's aggressive adoption in 1992 of its Agenda 21 program for sustainable development, which included a national hazardous waste strategy. A U.S.-based consulting firm conducted a pro bono feasibility study for Tianjin from 1994–96. The firm also proposed a prepayment financing scheme that enabled calculation of a lower unit treatment cost than that for any other proposed facility in the region (approximately RMB 600, or US$75, per ton).[4] Although there was considerable private-sector interest in the TSDF project in 1996, it took several years to resolve the issues of risk guarantees and treatment cost versus treatment tariffs (Tianjin 1998; Zorn 1998, 1999). A new facility with 40,000 T/y treatment capacity was to be commissioned in 2003 (Wong and Lai 2002, 2003).

In Zhejiang Province, the Dadi Environmental Protection Co., Ltd. (Dadi) was established in 1998 to provide industrial waste management services. The Hangzhou Industry Solid Waste Disposal Facility, owned by Dadi, was the first demonstration project authorized by the State Environmental Protection Agency (SEPA) for provincial hazardous waste disposal. The service area covers most of Zhejiang Province and they are allowed to accept special wastes from outside the province. The facility reportedly is in early operational status as of mid-2004, with liquids treatment capabilities and a rotary kiln incinerator undergoing test operations. Facility plans include rotary kiln and possibly plasma arc technology; secure landfill; and recycling units for tires, electronics, and fluorescent lights (Van Epp 2003, Zhuang 2003). As of mid-2004, USTDA is providing a grant through SEPA for further facility development. Dadi has submitted a proposal for funding to ADB's Private Sector Operations Department, which is considering possible financial support, pending the participation of additional investors.

Table 8.2 summarizes TSDF status in China.

Why Has China Lagged on TSDF Development?

Despite the apparent availability of technology and financing, the PRC has

Table 8.2

Current Treatment, Storage, and Disposal Facilities' Status in China

Facility location	Facility type	Treatment capacity	Operational status*	Ownership structure	Approximate investment
Shenyang	L	20,000 T/y**	1999	GOGO	$15 million
Shanghai	L, CK	25,000 T/y (Phase 1) 25,000 T/y (Phase 2)	1997 (Phase 1) 2003 (Phase 2)	GOCO	> $10 million
Tianjin	L, DI	12,000 T/y (initial)	2003	JV	$16 million
Shenzhen	L	5,000 T/y pilot 20,000 T/y commercial	1995	GOGO	$18 million
Beijing	L, DI	10,000 T/y	—	GOGO	—
Fuzhou	L, DI	20,000 T/y (Phase 1) 40,000 T/y (Phase 2)	2003 (under construction)	?	$14 million $6 million
Nanchang	DI	5,500 T/y (medical waste)	2003	?	RMB 11 million
Nanning	DI	7,000 T/y (medical waste)	2002	?	RMB 6.3 million
Hubei	L, DI, CK	20,000 T/y	2004	GOCO	$15 million
Hangzhou	L, DI, CK	100,000 T/y	2003	JV	$18.8 million

Sources: Authors' notes, SEPA tenth FYP, Wong and Lai (2002, 2003), Zhuang (2002, 2003).

Notes: The order corresponds to approximate date of original feasibility studies, but for simplicity those dates were not included. Several other projects are in the planning and feasibility study stages and are not listed here.

Acronyms: CK = cement kiln; DI = dedicated incinerator; GOCO = government owned, contractor operated transfer; GOGO = government owned, government operated transfer; JV = joint venture; L = landfill.

*Operational status = year of commercial operations.

**T/y = metric tons per year.

lagged in developing a centralized TSDF infrastructure relative to Southeast Asia. Many factors explain China's lag in development, although seven reasons stand out:

1. Low priority for environmental programs in general, and hazardous waste in particular
2. Inadequate funding of environmental programs and limited development of commercial markets for centralized waste treatment operations
3. Lack of appropriate legislation and regulations to implement an effective program
4. Weak enforcement of environmental regulations and standards, and minimal culture of compliance
5. Emphasis on technological solutions vs. management controls
6. Limited business models and markets for waste treatment services
7. Lack of an integrated approach to environmental management.

Development Priorities

In the scheme of overall infrastructure development, hazardous waste treatment has received a lower priority than electric power, water supply, municipal wastewater treatment, urban sanitation, and solid waste management.[5] This low status is not surprising, as it is similar to regulatory priorities that have been established in other countries.

Lack of Early Financial Commitment

As noted above, the right combination of legal, institutional, social, financial, and technological factors all must be present for a successful program. This necessity, not emphasized in earlier five-year plans, is well recognized in the tenth FYP (2001–5), which calls for overall environmental investments of 1.5 percent of GDP and identifies eight national-scale TSDFs to be developed and more than 100 additional facilities for HWM.

Regulatory Framework

Despite an early endorsement of the Basel Convention and external funding for various pilot projects, national legislation for HWM programs—especially regulatory waste definitions—has been slow to appear. TSDF development has not been aggressively coordinated by SEPA. The PRC and Indonesia have both enjoyed extensive, donor-funded technical assistance; yet, China is fully five years behind Indonesia in promulgating waste definitions.[6] With little history of a rule of law to support a modern regulatory program, this is not surprising (for a more in-depth analysis of legal and regulatory compliance issues see Alford and Shen 1998).

Enforcement and Compliance Regime

Enforcement of environmental regulations in China has been weak. Although there are several well-defined regulatory instruments, most "enforcement" occurs through the Pollution Levy System (PLS), generally in the form of opaque negotiations between regulators and the regulated. Without including hazardous waste in the PLS operating equation (due to a lack of national standards and definitions to be followed), basic waste control regulations cannot be enforced by local environmental protection bureaus (EPBs). At the national level, political leaders of different stripes have argued over the need for large investments in environmental protection. One of the most serious enforcement actions initiated from the highest levels of government was not issued until fifteen years into the development of modern-day regulatory programs.[7] Attention to transboundary waste shipments has also stretched regulatory resources (Box 8.2).

Technological Solutions Versus Practical Management

When regulatory programs bring pressure on government and enterprises alike, the natural response is to find the easiest apparent solution. With respect to HWM, high-technology solutions often appear attractive (and such solutions have been actively promoted by vendors and some bilateral programs). Technology options are often seized upon as "The Solution" without recognition of the practical limitations.

For example, incineration always appears attractive at first glance, especially in densely populated regions with intense land pressure, since it holds the promise of total waste destruction. However, as noted above, incineration is limited to high heating-value wastes; dedicated incinerators require substantial operator training and expertise; and incinerators capable of destroying a wide variety of wastes are expensive to build, operate, and maintain. As noted above, incineration accounts for only approximately 2 percent of total hazardous waste treatment in the United States, despite being prescribed in federal regulations as the best available technology to handle many wastes. If treatment technologies were the answer, export credit agencies quickly could have underwritten the sale of several large incinerators and other treatment systems and the problem would have been solved in short order. In effect, *technologies* have been available, but *applications* have not been viable. Essentially,

Box 8.2

"Basel and the Beast": Protecting the Environment or Distracting the Public?

The Basel Convention is a worthy piece of international law. However, pursuing well-publicized transboundary cases can strain the limited human resources of regulatory agencies at the expense of domestic enforcement and compliance obligations. Assigning several regulatory staff to police a single case involving one or two containers of alleged hazardous waste legitimately may be questioned when there may only be a handful of people assigned to the national program. On the other hand, from the public relations perspective, it is impossible to ignore such cases. A widely publicized incident in Guangdong Province in 2002 highlights this management quandary.

That year several media reports documented improper disposal of waste electronics and computers in Guangdong Province. Much of this waste—perhaps as much as ten million pieces of electronics scrap per year—was alleged to originate from the United States (e.g., see Pontoniere 2002). Earlier in 2002, the National People's Congress had urged more stringent legislation to control electronic waste management, including imports. The Congress noted that 150 million pieces of electronics scrap per year were being generated in China ("NPC Representatives" 2002), suggesting that most of the waste at the Guangdong site had originated in China. Whatever the origin, the pictures of the "reclamation" operation in Guangdong showed appalling conditions.

Several questions arise: (1) How much of the waste is originating in China and how much from overseas? (2) Would supplier take-back regulations prevent such exports from developed countries? (3) What is the extent of public health and environmental damage caused by this improper waste management? (4) What is the most cost-effective method of controlling improper disposal as observed in Guangdong (e.g., developing a modern demanufacturing and recovery system)? (5) Would a stricter enforcement regime have prevented the illegal import and disposal activity?

The broader context of imports to China from the United States appears less alarming. For example, approximately 99 percent of hazardous waste exports from the United States go to Canada and Mexico. In 1995, the United States generated 276 million tons of hazardous waste, of which approximately 266,000 tons (less than 1/10 of 1 percent) were legally exported, while 60 percent was intended for reclamation or recovery (www.epa.gov/ wastes/international trade/ 2003). Although China currently has about 80,000 tons/year of treatment capacity available, as much as two million tons are inadequately treated or disposed of illegally (CERNET 2000). If all U.S. hazardous waste exports were dumped directly into China—which is most certainly not the case—they would represent less than 15 percent of the total waste stream being generated from domestic sources. Some multinational corporations in China actually ship waste back to the United States for proper treatment (Bromby 1997).

Bottom line. The Basel Convention obligates its signatories to (1) develop the management capacity to handle their own wastes plus wastes imported legally for reclamation, and (2) prevent import of illegal waste shipments. China is struggling to meet its treaty obligations.

China Environmental Review 4, Issue 13. 2002. "NPC Representatives Call for Legislation on Household Electronics Recycling." Information attributed to Richard Ferris and Zhang Hongjun.

HWM is an extension of and advancement over urban waste collection and processing, and not rocket science.[8]

Limited Business Models and Markets for Commercial Waste Treatment

Ostensibly, HWM has been a government-led initiative, with significant donor support but a limited role for private-sector participation. World Bank and ADB-funded assistance was intended in part to eliminate policy barriers, strengthen the regulatory system, build human resource capacity to build and operate facilities, and finance a small number of prototype TSDF projects. By helping create an enabling framework, the initial capital infusions were expected to have some leverage and accelerate broader HWM infrastructure development. Compared to the pace of TSDF development in other Asian countries, the high-priority projects in Liaoning, Beijing, and Shanghai did not engender immediate, rapid growth in HWM facilities beyond the pilot project in Shenzhen and some private-sector-led feasibility studies in Tianjin and Suzhou. By the late 1990s, this situation had begun to change, as evidenced by the Hangzhou Dadi example noted above.

Lack of enforcement and limited government funding translated into lack of facility development and weak markets for environmental services and commercial waste management services. Without direct government funding, treatment capacity theoretically was to be developed with substantial private-sector participation; however, there has been no clear legal framework for private participation.

Private-sector firms have been marketing products and services in China since the 1980s, and many have been willing to finance large-scale infrastructure projects. Despite this availability of financing, lack of a predictable legal framework and government unwillingness to provide risk guarantees prevented or delayed new business models from flourishing in all sectors of the infrastructure.

Compartmentalization Versus Integrated Environmental Management

China has not taken an integrated, holistic approach to pollution control and waste management. The country has had a tendency to compartmentalize environmental problems according to medium (air, water, solid waste), and to deal with them in a sequence roughly proportional to infrastructure development priorities. In other words, cleaner air will come with modernization and expansion of heavy industries and the power sector, cleaner water will come with renewed investment in water supply systems and wastewater control, and hazardous waste will be dealt with after those problems have been brought under control.

In addition, cultural and intellectual factors have had some effect. A common intellectual barrier in China and other developing countries is stated succinctly as "all we need is money and technology," without acknowledging the need for management skills.[9] A "culture of compliance" is still evolving as the rule of law takes hold. Polluting enterprises in China are maturing and are moving toward the point at which they take proactive responsibility for pollution control and waste management.

Cleaner Production in China: Beyond Industrial Modernization

The industrial response to environmental management has been characterized in four phases:

1. Environmental consciousness and pollution control
2. Pollution prevention and productivity

3. Environmental performance and competitive advantage
4. Sustainable development (SD) (Rao 2000).

Broadly considered, China began tackling the first phase in the 1980s; the second phase in the 1990s; and, with accession to the WTO at the turn of the twenty-first century, entered the third phase. The fourth phase also was addressed beginning in the 1990s, with the quick adoption of SD principles and preparation of the Agenda 21 sustainable development program. Nevertheless, China's industrial development cannot yet be classified as sustainable.

If the waste volumes noted earlier are correct, then hazardous waste is the proverbial tip of the iceberg and, compared to the considerable effort already devoted to HWM, a much larger effort is called for in the context of CP.[10]

Recalling the CP equation . . .

$$Energy + Raw\ Materials + Water = Products + Wastes$$

. . . the potential scope of CP activities is quite broad, comprising energy efficiency, water conservation, raw-materials management and substitution, industrial process efficiency and process changes, product quality, and waste minimization (Box 8.3). CP now is being defined broadly and applied to the enterprise level and the public utility level, and as a concept in urban planning and city management.[11]

Key Drivers of Cleaner Production

When driven by purely financial and economic considerations, industrial CP is just another name for industrial modernization. A successful CP program requires both a market pull and a regulatory push. Experience indicates that the regulatory push creates an enabling environment that forces new CP-oriented thinking onto enterprise management. An effective regulatory push causes pollution control costs to increase from zero to a range that impacts profitability. Making the cost of compliance cheaper than the cost of non-compliance is the job of both regulators and enterprise managers. Making noncompliance unattractive by other means (for example, legal penalties, such as revocation of operating licenses) is the job of regulators, consumers, and civil society. This combination of factors created the CP market in the United States and is emerging now in China.

"Creating the market" for CP sounds like a simple prescription, but it is not easy in practice. Government awareness and support are required to create the appropriate policy framework to foster market evolution. A comparison of wind power development in China and India illustrates this point.

Box 8.3

Typical Cleaner Production Applications

Energy + Raw Materials + Water = Products + Wastes

Energy efficiency
- Replace coal-fired power generating units with natural-gas-fired units to improve thermal efficiencies from 30 percent to well over 80 percent.
- Use inside-the-fence cogeneration (combined heat/steam and power) to replace dedicated boilers and power generation units.

Raw-material changes
- Reformulate production process to use environmentally benign materials, e.g., use citric acid-based cleaners instead of chlorinated solvents in electronics manufacturing.

Water conservation
- Recycle up to 80 to 90 percent of cooling water in power generation and other industry sectors.
- Reuse secondary sewage treatment effluent as industrial process cooling water to reduce total water consumption and water pollution loads.

Solid waste minimization and reuse
- Use calcium sulfate residue from power plant desulfurization as an input for gypsum wallboard production.
- Reuse power plant ash as additive in cement manufacturing and as construction fill supplement.
- Reuse shredded tires as an additive in road surfacing.
- Cocompost municipal sewage treatment sludge and biodegradable solid wastes.

Comprehensive redesign of major production processes
- Replace obsolete process technologies with more efficient and environmentally friendly technologies, e.g., replace mercury cells with ion-exchange or diaphragm technology to manufacture caustic soda.
- Replace traditional steelmaking technologies, e.g., blast furnaces, with granular coal injection, minimills, or the direct reduced-iron process.

Both are developing economies, but neither would be considered an advanced market economy, due to trade barriers, protection of state-owned enterprises, and immature capital markets. However, since the early 1990s, while the world watched in awe at the economic growth of China, India has developed three times as much installed wind power capacity. The relative mix of policy incentives, financing options, and regulatory frameworks accounts for the difference (Lew 2001).

At the enterprise or production facility level, it is useful to think of CP in terms of two factories: the visible factory that manufactures products, employs people, and contributes to economic development; and the other factory—not always visible to management—that causes pollution, creates public health problems, and detracts from economic progress. The manager's aim should be to improve efficiency, minimize operating costs, maximize profits, and not pollute the environment. The typical cycle of CP implementation begins with no-cost/low-cost changes (mainly housekeeping), then medium-cost modifications (equipment improvements), progressing to capital-intensive process modification or replacement. The financial return on investment is inversely related to the cost of the CP effort, i.e., the no-cost and low-cost CP options typically yield the highest relative returns. Table 8.3 presents examples of CP efforts in China.

China's CP programs have been largely donor-driven, with substantial support from the United Nations Development Programme (UNDP), United Nations Environment Programme (UNEP), World Bank, ADB, and various bilateral agencies. Typical donor-funded projects have targeted specific industry sectors (for example, construction materials or chemical manufacturing), provided audits and assessment, prepared feasibility studies, and proposed specific implementation projects. Donor support in the 1980s and 1990s was primarily in the form of prototype projects: one-off, sector-specific (for example, construction materials or chemical manufacturing) or project investments (covering selected enterprises from a few sectors) intended to demonstrate practical, commercial aspects of CP. The CP knowledge base now is extensive, with CP centers having been established in several cities. Applying a broad definition of CP, donor support, including grant-funded technical assistance and loan-funded projects, is well over US$1 billion (for example, see Evans and Hamner 2003 for a summary of ADB assistance).

In the context of industrial CP, the situation in China might be described as "long on audits and assessment, short on implementation." There is little documentation of projects that have been self-financed or supported solely by government funding (for a notable exception of CP technology transfer in the electronics sector, see Bersin et al. 2001). The leverage sought by donors

Table 8.3

Examples of Cleaner Production Measures in Chinese Enterprises

Cost category	Target	Type	Industrial sector	Outline of CP measures
Low-cost measures (high ROI)	Operation	Good house-keeping	Fertilizer plant	Cover fertilizer bags to prevent rainfall from washing out ammonia and contaminating surface runoff.
		Waste segregation	Fertilizer plant	Recover spent lubricants before they get to sewer.
		Simple recycling	PVC plant	Reuse noncontact cooling water/ water conservation.
Medium-cost measures (medium ROI)	Equipment	Equipment modification	Pulp and paper mill	Install screw press to improve black liquor extraction, thus reducing BOD discharge.
		Equipment modification	Pulp and paper mill	Install nozzles to increase water pressure for washing pulp, thus reducing water consumption.
		Source treatment	Fertilizer plant	Treat excess scrubbing liquor ["liquor" is industry terminology for specific wastewater stream] at gas desulfurization area in order to recover sulfur.
		Source pretreatment and recycling	PVC plant	Pretreat and recycle liquid stream at the acetylene reactor.
High-cost measures (low ROI)	Process	Process change	Chlor-alkali plant	Replace diaphragm electrolysis technology by membrane electrolysis technology/energy conservation.
		Complex recycling	Fertilizer plant	Install distillation unit to purify and recycle spent lubricants/ reduce pollution by oily waters.

Source: PA Consulting Co. 2002.
Notes: Acronyms: BOD = biochemical oxygen demand, ROI = return on investment, PVC = polyvinyl chloride.

on externally funded projects has not yet been realized (as is the case with the HWM program). Obviously, the market for CP is still developing in the PRC. Unlike the United States, where the increasing cost of hazardous waste disposal and ever-tightening regulatory pressure forced industries to minimize wastes, similar compliance pressures are virtually nonexistent in China. Despite the limited regulatory pressure and weak economic drivers for waste minimization, from the enterprise viewpoint, CP is becoming a more obvious option for achieving compliance with environmental discharge and emissions standards (PA Consulting Co. 2003a).

While the PRC was developing stronger legislation and more stringent standards in the 1990s, regulated industries complained that they could not afford to comply with the standards. Their reaction contrasted with that in other developing countries, in which typical environmental compliance costs have been 3 to 5 percent of total capital and operating costs (Ecology and Environment 1998). The conclusion is that the Chinese enterprises that cannot afford to comply with discharge standards are operating with very slim profit margins or are inherently unprofitable. At the same time, various barriers have prevented the enterprises' making the capital investments to upgrade process efficiency, become profitable, and achieve compliance. "Clean and green" was not a centerpiece of official Chinese industrial policy until recently (PA Consulting Co. 2003a, b). China's accession to the WTO is expected to rapidly increase market pressures that will drive enterprise reforms, including CP.

Barriers to CP Implementation

Why do CP implementation and investment appear to be so slow relative to the level of donor support? As is the case with HWM, a learning curve must be surmounted, and a similar set of several factors must converge to support CP implementation. At least six barriers to widespread CP implementation are discussed briefly below (PA Consulting Co. 2002, 2003a, b).

Policy and Intellectual Framework

Although several ministries have been involved in CP activities, national leadership has come primarily from the erstwhile State Economic Trade Commission (SETC) and SEPA.[12] CP has been a component of the eighth and ninth environmental five-year plans but was not incorporated in the overall national plan until the current tenth FYP (2001–5) was prepared. SETC and SEPA both have had limited influence over enterprise behavior. There is a latent tendency for policymakers and enterprise managers to view any "environmentally beneficial" expenses as dead-load cost with no possible economic or financial benefits.

Lack of Information and Knowledge About Cleaner Production

Most planners and managers do not have any working knowledge of CP concepts and options. Internet access, electronic communications, and e-business, which can facilitate the exchange of CP knowledge, are in early stages of evolution and have not been widely adopted, especially in small- and medium-scale enterprises (SMEs).

Management Leadership and Market Incentives

Without working knowledge of CP concepts, managers cannot effectively lead CP audits or promote implementation of recommended CP options. High transaction costs also inhibit CP adoption at the enterprise level: while the payback for specific CP alternatives may be fast, as short as six months, the initial capital costs may be high and the overall savings may represent a very small percentage of total operating costs. The economic incentives that have driven CP in other countries are just beginning to emerge in China. Immature market conditions, including cross-subsidies and continued policy lending (directed credits and soft loans based on government directives rather than financial credit-worthiness), do not generate sufficient market forces to promote CP adoption.

Technology Transfer

Some CP options may require foreign-sourced technology, the availability of which is limited by intellectual property concerns. There is a tendency for Chinese managers to pursue high technology rather than "appropriate technology" solutions.

Legislative Framework and Regulatory Pressure

The environmental regulatory framework does not provide adequate incentives or disincentives to clean up pollution. A culture of compliance is just beginning to emerge.

Financing

Ongoing banking-sector problems, continued policy lending practices, limited credit made available to market-oriented enterprises, and the generally poor credit history of enterprises have resulted in limited capital for CP projects. Typically, enterprises that have ready access to financing have no real incentive to clean up, while enterprises with sound CP proposals but limited political influence are not able to obtain needed capital.

Under today's market conditions, an enterprise or facility manager who recognizes the benefits of CP may not have a clear understanding of management options, knowledge of hardware sources, or the capability to prepare a detailed investment proposal, much less the access to financing. Clearly, greater access to information for planners and managers, improved financial management capability at the government and enterprise levels, facilitation of technology transfer, and expanded financing options all are necessary to expand CP project implementation.

Despite these significant barriers, progress is being made on all fronts:

- CP was formally included in the national tenth FYP (2001–5).
- New laws that provide a legal framework for SME and CP development went into effect in 2002 and 2003 respectively. The SME Promotion Law includes a provision for special development funds that could support CP technology investments. The CP Law includes a provision for enterprises not in compliance with relevant discharge standards to conduct CP assessments.
- Theoretically, technology transfer is becoming easier with China's accession to the WTO.
- Information and knowledge transfer is becoming easier with the establishment of CP centers in several cities and rapidly increasing access to the Internet.
- Management acumen is improving as the market economy matures and competitive pressures resulting from WTO membership increase.
- Strengthening the regulatory framework, in particular modifications to the Pollution Levy System, bode well for adopting CP as an environmental compliance tool.
- In the energy sector, large power plants have been converting to low-sulfur coal (an economically attractive alternative to flue-gas desulfurization), and natural gas is being adopted as a primary fuel for power generation and industrial applications. [See Chapter 7 for additional discussion on this topic.]
- Public awareness concerning environmental issues is rising, and consumers are becoming more knowledgeable regarding corporate environmental behavior.
- Reforms in the financial sector continue, albeit slowly.
- Local governments are promoting enterprise development zones (EDZs), which have inherently more efficient power, water, and waste management systems. SMEs and TVEs are actively encouraged to relocate to the EDZs, which potentially expands the scope of CP initiatives to a citywide basis.

Recognizing that the implementation barriers noted earlier still exist, alternative approaches to CP are being designed to achieve greater leverage on initial project investments. For example, the World Bank has funded the start-up of energy management companies (EMCs) modeled on the energy service company (ESCO) business model (Taylor 2002).[13] The EMCs operate with performance contracts, providing turnkey-type survey/assessment and engineering services, and earn profit based on actual client energy savings. The U.S. Department of Commerce is promoting the creation of energy and environmental service companies (EESCOs), also using a performance contract model (Ballard 2003). ADB has evaluated a broader CP service company model, similar to the EESCO concept, but emphasizing financial assistance and corporate restructuring supported by engineering and environmental services (Millison 2002; PA Consulting Co. 2003b). The markets for renewable energy and energy efficiency are growing as the Kyoto Protocol's Clean Development Mechanism (CDM) has been embraced by the national government and restructuring of the power sector proceeds. Positive experience in the energy sector should provide a foundation for broader CP activities.

CP: Great Leap Redux or Green Leap Forward?

Superimposed on a decade of consistent policy statements embracing SD, the past twenty years of China's industrial growth have occurred to a great extent by cloning inefficient, highly polluting process technologies rather than via wholesale technological improvement. Although intellectual property concerns have inhibited or prevented technology transfer, all of the barriers noted above, as well as immense social and political pressure to maintain full employment, have played a role in the development trajectory. "Get rich first, clean up later" was the modus operandi in response to Deng Xiaopeng's statement that "socialism is not poverty." However, as in many countries, economic growth has come at the expense of the environment: estimates of economic losses caused by pollution range from 3 to 5 percent of GDP per year to as high as 13 percent of GDP per year (Smil and Mao 1998). The industrialization of the PRC, from the Great Leap Forward (1958–60) into the 1990s, charitably characterized as a "scorched earth" development approach, is just beginning to show signs of recovery.[14]

China's SME sector, especially TVEs, was the key to growth in the early to mid-1990s, spurred to a great extent by investment from overseas Chinese. TVEs typically used obsolete, highly polluting technology. The resulting environmental problems, combined with other factors, led the State Council to issue a decree in 1996 outlawing various outdated process technologies and requiring enterprises to comply with discharge standards or be closed, merge with larger production units, or modify production processes (see reports in *China Daily* 1996a, 1996b). By the mid-1990s, the SME/TVE sector posed an economic threat to larger state-owned enterprises (SOEs), credit from state-owned commercial banks was tightened, and the SME/TVE sector had to compete for financial support to remain afloat (Becker 2000).

This sector currently is experiencing extensive restructuring, promoted by widespread development of enterprise development zones and "rural urbanization" (PA Consulting Co. 2003b).

With respect to market forces, China's dynamic economic development is still in an early stage. CP adoption appears to be lagging, but is it really or is it just lagging relative to economic growth? Perhaps both phenomena are occurring. CP has been donor driven rather than market driven, although market forces are beginning to pull CP into the mainstream.

With respect to energy efficiency, market forces certainly are influencing policy. Since the mid-1990s, several events have signaled a new national energy policy oriented toward cleaner energy:

- China became a net energy importer, with substantial foreign exchange implications.
- In 1998, a moratorium was imposed on new coal-fired power plant construction in urban areas, which effectively halted new power plant construction for about three years.
- Natural gas development finally was accepted as an economically viable energy alternative, as well as a source for power generation.
- In 2000, the Air Pollution Control Law was revised, with provisions for expanded use of natural gas for power generation; use of low-sulfur coal in large generating plants; and closure of small, obsolete power plants.

Enterprise reforms and financial-sector reforms significantly influence CP adoption, and wider adoption of CP is linked to progress on both fronts. A "green leap" is possible, but it is not yet obvious from recent trends. For example, in 2001 the government announced that by the year 2005, at least 5.5 percent of primary energy production would be from renewable sources. By 2002 the government had signaled that this percentage was just a target that would not be supported by legislation and central government funding. Despite being a signatory to the Kyoto Protocol and having significant potential for CDM project implementation, as of mid-2003 China had no clear renewable energy strategy, at least with respect to projects funded by loans from the ADB and World Bank. As of mid-2004, the National People's Congress was working on draft legislation and had requested technical assistance from the donor community to support further development of a renewable energy law.

Factors for Change and Signs of Hope

"Is your stomach too full?" This was the question posed to one writer when he arrived in China on his worldwide search for environmental consciousness

(Hertsgaard 1998). Not unlike the case in most other countries, China's environmental progress has become serious only after the country has reached a threshold of affluence. There appears to be a paradigm shift occurring, from an earlier belief that environmental investment detracted from economic growth to a greater recognition that environmental investments pay off. Likewise, enterprise managers have a growing appreciation for the difference between pollution control as a management exercise rather than a technology application (Evans and Hamner 2003). Culturally, there is also a broader consensus for restoring balance between human development and environmental protection. In the richer coastal provinces, environmental protection now is perceived as "affordable." In some interior provinces, natural and cultural resource protection is becoming a worthwhile investment in its own right.

China became polluted because it was poor, and it remains statistically poor because it is polluted. Lack of investment in modern industrial technology created huge environmental problems with extensive social costs (for a comprehensive review, see Nehru et al. 1997). Social unrest has also resulted from extensive pollution problems (see, for example, Economy 1997). Yet, few of China's political leaders really believed that environmental problems could hinder economic development until the mid-1990s, when air and water pollution had become so serious that the State Council intervened directly. Beginning at approximately the same time, the foreign exchange outflow for energy imports provided some shock therapy to drive home the idea that inefficient use of resources has real hard-currency implications. The ninth and tenth FYPs reflected this paradigm shift, with much more detailed environmental programs and spending commitments. The tenth FYP (2001–5) includes a goal of investing 1.5 percent of GDP in environmental programs. The plan thus acknowledges the experience of Organization for Economic Cooperation and Development (OECD) countries, in which approximately 2 percent of GDP and twenty to thirty years have been devoted to achieve successful environmental programs (Ecology and Environment 1998). In China, actual investments in environmental protection are estimated to have been 1 percent (or less) of GDP per year during the ninth FYP (1996–2000).

As noted earlier, China's stockpile of solid wastes could soon be well over one billion tons nationwide. Managing these wastes in an environmentally acceptable fashion is a formidable task, but it can be done and, in China's case, must be done, before another billion tons is added to double this stockpile. An appropriate regulatory framework now exists to support the technical aspects of HWM. WTO membership is generating new market forces that support CP as a means of achieving environmental compliance and increasing profits. The specific case of HWM is exemplary of China's environmental challenges in general: uncontrolled disposal can be prevented only if a combination of legal, technical, and financial measures are implemented over a number of years (not months). CP is an example of how such problems can be prevented in the first place and—by simultaneously reducing air, water, and solid wastes—provide direct economic benefits. The amendments to the Air Pollution Control Law that took effect in 2000 signaled a realization that cleaner energy production was possible without sacrificing macroeconomic benefits. The SME Promotion Law and the Cleaner Production Promotion Law, effective in 2002 and 2003 respectively, signaled government support for broader application of CP in the small- and medium-scale industrial sectors. This national legislation has been a necessary complement to China's membership in the WTO and is intended to create additional market pressure to drive sorely needed enterprise reforms.

Environmental management is not glamorous, but, occasionally, it has a very high profile, as in the case of the pending 2008 "Green Olympics" in Beijing. In anticipation of unprecedented media coverage, billions of public dollars are being invested to clean up the city's air and water. However, can this exercise be extended to the country as a whole?

The current generation of political leaders appears to be supporting accelerated industrial and financial reforms, but the government's willingness to tackle environmental and social problems head-on is subject to doubt.[15] The old school of politically based reporting and information control was alive and well in early 2003 as exemplified by the government's failure to control an outbreak of severe acute respiratory syndrome (SARS). The government admitted that a problem existed only after scathing criticism by the World Health Organization (WHO) and foreign governments, and then only because the official truth was challenged by Chinese health care professionals (Becker 2003, Jakes 2003). Some critics compared the SARS episode to the Chernobyl incident, which heralded the break-up of the former Soviet Union (Wei 2003), while others interpreted the PRC government's interventions to control the epidemic as a positive transformational event (Cheow 2003). The SARS crisis may have been instrumental in accelerating the issuance, in 2003, of new regulations and guidelines for hazardous and medical waste management (Van Epp 2003).

China's development progress is often summed up as "two steps forward, one step back." The current environmental situation in large part resulted from central control of industrial development and pollution control, favoring the former at the expense of the latter. Massaged statistics and political slogans did not solve China's problems in the past, nor will they help now. The SARS case is a recent example of that "one step back."

Nevertheless, we can see at least two steps forward. The legal framework for business operations is improving, and widespread enterprise reform is proceeding. Capital markets, perhaps the biggest obstacle to CP adoption, are expanding, albeit slowly. Public awareness is increasing, although civil society remains weak. Social pressures are being channeled into policies that reflect environmental protection as an achievable goal. Generational change is being accompanied by a push for accountable political leadership, modern industrial development, and effective environmental management. This new "long march" is just beginning. Let us hope that it keeps heading in the right direction.

Notes

This chapter is derived in part from work conducted under consulting contracts with the Asian Development Bank (ADB), World Bank, and Government of Indonesia. The author is indebted to Zhuang Ping and Timothy Van Epp for confirming the status of treatment, storage, and disposal facilities (TSDFs) in China. Special thanks are due to Piya Abeygunawardena at the ADB for information about cleaner production programs. The opinions in this chapter are those of the author, and not the official views of the ADB.

1. The U.S. experience is referenced because many HWM and CP programs have adapted the U.S. management approach to local conditions.

2. For analyses of public-information-based programs, see, for example, Afsah, Laplante, and Makarim (1995); Afsah, Laplante, and Wheeler (1996); and Afsah, Blackman, and Ratunanda (2000).

3. See Probst and Beierle (1999) for a more comprehensive comparative discussion of Asian, European, and U.S. HWM program development.

4. This financing calculation was, in essence, an accounting trick, in that interest earned on the prepayment would be subsidizing or reducing the nominal unit cost to the generator.

5. A widely referenced World Bank report (Newfarmer and Johnson 1997) suggests that, in terms of economic impact relative to national gross domestic product (GDP), hazardous waste's impact on development is not as great as that of urban air pollution, acid rain, or water pollution (PA Consulting Co. 2003a).

6. The Government of Indonesia has also coordinated the construction of a large-scale TSDF with the promulgation of its national hazardous waste regulation. At the same time, the PRC has been much more advanced in developing its Pollution Levy System.

7. State Council Decree No. 31 (1996) stated that national industrial enterprises must comply with national discharge and emissions standards by the year 2000, or be closed, modified, or merged with larger production units. This decree also mandated the closure of fifteen sectors of highly polluting small-scale enterprises.

8. Referring again to the U.S. situation, despite extensive treatment technology development, most off-site hazardous waste treatment is by secure land disposal rather than some form of destructive treatment.

9. In China, other more complex intellectual and cultural issues are at play, as

eloquently discussed by Judith Shapiro (2001). See also Backman (1999) for a comparative discussion of business practices in East Asia.

10. For a comprehensive analysis of China's environmental challenges, see McElroy, Nielsen, and Lydon (1998), and other chapters of this volume.

11. An extensive and detailed discussion of the broader application of CP and related concepts can be found in "Natural Capitalism" (Hawken et al. 1999).

12. In March 2003 the SETC was dissolved, with many of its functions transferred to the National Development and Reform Commission.

13. World Bank Project Identification Number CN-PE-3606, US$63 million loan, GEF grant US$22 million.

14. See Shapiro (2001) and Hertsgaard (1998) for a historical and a more modern perspective, respectively. Unfortunately, the gradual environmental recovery noted in the late 1990s has not been sustained: SEPA reported (in 2004) that nationwide sulfur dioxide emissions increased by about 11 percent from 2002 to 2003, vs. a tenth FYP goal of a 10 percent reduction.

15. For example, see Economy 2002 for a critique of environmental implications of the Western Development Strategy; see Chang 2002 for a critique of the "gradualist" economic reform strategy.

Bibliography

Afsah, Shakeb, Benoit Laplante, and Nabiel Makarim. 1995. "Program-Based Pollution Control Management: The Indonesian PROKASIH Program." Working Paper No. 1602. Country Economics Department, Policy Research and External Affairs, (PRDEI) and BAPEDAL, October. www.worldbank.org/NIPR.

Afsah, Shakeb, Benoit Laplante, and David Wheeler. 1996. "Controlling Industrial Pollution: A New Paradigm." World Bank Policy Research Working Paper No. 1672, October. www.worldbank.org/NIPR.

Afsah, Shakeb, Allen Blackman, and Damayanti Ratunanda. 2000. "How Do Public Disclosure Pollution Control Programs Work? Evidence from Indonesia." Resources for the Future Discussion Paper 00–44, Washington, DC, October. www.rff.org. [searchable site]

Alford, William P., and Shen Yuanyuan. 1998. "Limits of the Law in Addressing China's Environmental Dilemma." In Michael McElroy, Chris P. Nielsen, and Peter Lydon, eds., *Energizing China: Reconciling Environmental Protection and Economic Growth.* Cambridge, MA: Harvard University Press.

Backman, Michael. 1999. *Asian Eclipse: Exposing the Dark Side of Business in Asia.* Singapore: John Wiley and Sons (Asia).

Ballard, Stewart. 2003. U.S. Commercial Liaison to Asian Development Bank. "Presentation on EESCOs" to ADB, February.

Becker, Jasper. 2000. In "Getting Rich Is Glorious," *The Chinese, 65–86.* London: John Murray.

———. 2003. "SARS Unmasks Wider Scandal." *International Herald Tribune* (Manila ed.), May 2.

Bersin, Richard, Amanda Horn, Han Xu, Douglas Dopp, and Mohamed Boumerzoug. 2001. "Process and Environmental Benefits with Solvent-Free Stripping." *Solid State Technology* (Apr.). www.solid-state.com.

Bromby, Robin. 1997. "Toxic Waste Threatens Millions in Region," *Australian*

Environment 1 (Dec.). Data attributed to David Nelson at East-West Center in Honolulu, HI, USA.

CERNET [China Education and Research Network]. 2000. "Hazardous Wastes to Be Treated." www.edu.cn/20020221/3020849.shtml.

Chang, Gordon G. 2002. *The Coming Collapse of China.* London: Arrow Random House.

Cheow, Eric Teo Chu. 2003. "SARS and East Asia's Four Transformations," Center for Strategic and International Studies, Pacific Forum PacNet Newsletter Number 28, June 26. Honolulu, Hawaii.

China Daily. 1996a. "State Closes 42,000 Polluting Factories," Oct. 12.

———. 1996b. "Environmental Laws Shut Down 50,000 Factories," Oct. 23.

Clarke, Shelley, Felicity Thomas, Husayn A. Anwar, and Caroline Cook. 1997. *Pollution Control in the People's Republic of China: An Investor's Guide.* London: Environmental Resources Management.

Ecology and Environment, Inc. (E and E). 1998. Final Report for ADB TA No. 2505–PRC: "Strengthening Environmental Standards and Enforcement Policies in the People's Republic of China." Lancaster, NY.

Economy, Elizabeth. 1997. *The Case Study of China, Reforms and Resources: The Implications for State Capacity in the PRC.* Cambridge, MA: Committee on International Security Studies, American Academy of Arts and Sciences.

———. 2002. "China's Go West Campaign: Ecological Construction or Ecological Exploitation?" *China Environment Series* 5.

Evans, J.W., and Burton Hamner. 2003. "Cleaner Production at the Asian Development Bank," *Journal of Cleaner Production* 11: 639–49. www.sciencedirect.com.

Hawken, Paul, Amory Lovins, and L. Hunter Lovins. 1999. *Natural Capitalism: Creating the Next Industrial Revolution.* New York: Little Brown and Co.

Hertsgaard, Mark. 1998. *Earth Odyssey: Around the World in Search of Our Environmental Future.* New York: Broadway Books (Random House).

Hopkins, Andrea. 2002. "Australia Blocks Toxic China Fertilizer Exports," Reuters, May 9.

Jakes, Susan. 2003. "Beijing's SARS Attack," *Time,* Apr. 8.

Lew, D.J. 2001. "Renewable Energy Development in China." Presentation to China Working Group, Environmental Change and Security Project, Woodrow Wilson International Center for Scholars, Washington, DC.

Liu, Gary, Justin Harris, and Chris Adams. 1999. "China Solid Waste Management Technologies," *US Foreign and Commercial Service,* July 1.

Luken, Ralph (Skip), and Ann-Christin Freij. 1994. "Cleaner Industrial Production in Developing Countries: Market Opportunities for Developed Countries and Potential Cost Savings for Developing Countries." Manuscript presented at OECD Workshop on Development Assistance and Technology Cooperation for Cleaner Industrial Production in Developing Countries, Hannover, Germany, Sept. 28–30. (Authors are from the Environment and Energy Branch, Industrial Sectors and Environment Division, United Nations Industrial Development Organization (UNIDO), Vienna.)

McElroy, Michael, Chris P. Nielsen, and Peter Lydon, eds. 1998. *Energizing China: Reconciling Environmental Protection and Economic Growth.* Cambridge, MA: Harvard University Press.

Millison, Dan. 2002. "Great Leap Redux: Toward a Sustainable Cleaner Production Program in China," Report Prepared for ADB TA 3079-PRC, Subproject 6, Williamsburg, VA, and Manila.

Nehru, Vikram, Aart Kraay, and Xiaoqing Yu. 1997. *China 2020: Development Challenges in the New Century.* Washington, DC: World Bank.

Newfarmer, R., and T. Johnson. 1997. "Clear Water Blue Skies, Economic Evaluation of Air and Water Pollution Damage." In Nehru et al., eds., *China 2020: Development Challenges in the New Century.*

"NPC Representatives Call for Legislation on Household Electronics Recycling." 2002. *China Environmental Review* 4 (13) (Apr.). Information attributed to Richard Ferris and Zhang Hongjun.

PA Consulting Co. 2002. Report for Subproject 1. Reports for Asian Development Bank TA-3079-PRC, Washington, DC.

———. 2003a. Report for Subproject 4. Reports for Asian Development Bank TA-3079-PRC, Washington, DC.

———. 2003b. Report for Subproject 6. Reports for Asian Development Bank TA-3079-PRC, Washington, DC.

Pontoniere, Paolo. 2002. "Silicon Valley Group Spurs China to Ban E-waste Imports from US." NCM Online, June 16. http://news.ncmonline.com/news/view_article.html?article_id= 532 .

Probst, Katherine, N., and Thomas C. Beierle. 1999. *The Evolution of Hazardous Waste Programs: Lessons from Eight Countries.* Washington, DC: Center for Risk Management, Resources for the Future. www.rff.org.

Rao, Purba Halady. 2000. *Toward a Green Millennium: Environmental Management Systems in Southeast Asia.* Manila: Asian Institute of Management.

Shapiro, Judith. 2001. *Mao's War Against Nature: Politics and the Environment in Revolutionary China.* Cambridge: Cambridge University Press.

Smil, Vaclav, and Mao Yushi. 1998. *The Economic Costs of China's Environmental Degradation.* American Academy of Arts and Sciences Occasional Paper, Cambridge, MA.

———. 1998. *Project on Environmental Scarcities, State Capacity, and Civil Violence,* Toronto: Committee on International Security Studies.

State Environmental Protection Agency (SEPA). 2003. Notes from U.S. Department of Commerce Environmental Technologies Trade Mission, Washington, DC, Jan.

Taylor, Robert. 2002. "Development of Energy Management Companies in China." Presentation to China Working Group, Environmental Change and Security Project. Woodrow Wilson International Center for Scholars, Washington, DC.

Tianjin government officials. 1998. Personal communication with author.

U.S. Department of Energy. 1998. "China's Energy Demand Now Exceeds Domestic Supply." www.eia.doe.gov/emeu/cabs/china/part2.html#ENERGY.

U.S. Environmental Protection Agency. 2003. "International Trade in Hazardous Waste: An Overview." www.epa.gov/osw/internat/index.htm.

———. 1984, 2003. "Hazardous Waste; Subtitle C of RCRA." www.epa.gov/epaoswer/osw/hazwaste.htm.

Van Epp, Timothy. 2003. Personal communication with author, based on notes from Definitional Mission for U.S. Trade Development Agency, Oct.

Wei Jingsheng. 2003. "SARS Tests Communist Rule in China." *International Herald Tribune* (Manila ed.), Apr. 28.

Wong, Laurence, and Kevin Lai. 2002, 2003. Personal communication with author regarding Onyx Co. operations in Hong Kong and project development in Tianjin, China.

Zhuang Ping. 2002, 2003. Personal communication with author, Wuhan, China.
Zorn, Joe. 1998, 1999. Personal communication with author by employee of Waste Management International (Hong Kong).

Useful Web Sites

Asian Development Bank: www.adb.org
Burton Hamner, independent consultant: www.cleanerproduction.com
Chemical and Pesticides Results Measures (CAPRM): www.pepps.fsu.edu/CAPRM [Via the tab "Draft Indicators" you will find "Design Indicator: Volume of U.S. Imports of Hazardous Waste, by Treatment Method and Country of Origin (7/13/ 01)."]
PRC State Environmental Protection Agency: www.zhb.gov.cn/english/
Sino-Canadian Cleaner Production Cooperation: www.chinacp.org.cn and www. chinacp.com
United Nations Environment Programme (UNEP): www.uneptie.org/pc/cp/
United Nations Industrial Development Organization (UNIDO): www.unido.org
United States Department of Energy (U.S. DOE): www.fe.doe.gov/coal_power/cct/
United States Environmental Protection Agency (U.S. EPA, hazardous waste): www.epa.gov/epaoswer/osw/hazwaste.htm
World Bank: www.worldbank.org

—— Chapter 9 ——

Sandy Desertification in Northern China

Wang Tao and Wu Wei

China suffers from among the most severe land degradation problems in the world. The rapid increase in desertification since the 1970s and its tremendous impact on China's environment, society, and economy have received considerable attention. Sandy desertification is one major type of land desertification in northern China. Based on our nearly thirty years of research and practical experience focusing on land degradation in northern China, we define "sandy desertification" as land degradation, primarily caused by human actions, resulting in wind erosion in the arid, semiarid, and subhumid regions. In China, the sandy desertified lands are located primarily in northern areas, including the provinces of Gansu, Hebei, Heilongjiang, Inner Mongolia, Jilin, Liaoning, Ningxia, Qinghai, Shaanxi, Shanxi, Tibet, and Xinjiang (Map 9.1).

According to our monitoring and assessment studies, in 2000 the total area of sandy desertified land in China was 385,700 square kilometers (km^2) (Table 9.1).[1] This can be broken down as follows: slightly and potentially impacted land, 139,300 km^2; moderately desertified land, 99,770 km^2; and severely and very severely desertified land, 79,090 km^2 and 67,560 km^2, respectively. The sandy desertified lands are located primarily in the interconnecting agropastoral grassland, semiarid rainfed cropland, and oasis-irrigated cropland regions. A comparative analysis of the results of remote-sensing data taken in the late 1950s, 1975, 1987, and 2000 shows that the expansion of sandy desertified land in northern China has been accelerating over the past five decades. The annual rate of expansion was 1,560 km^2/year between the late 1950s and 1975; 2,100 km^2/year between 1975 and 1987; and 3,600 km^2/year from 1987 to 2000.[2] The rapid expansion of desertified land not only seriously endangers the ecosystem but also greatly hinders efforts to improve the standard of living and sustainable development (SD) in desertified regions.

234

Map 9.1

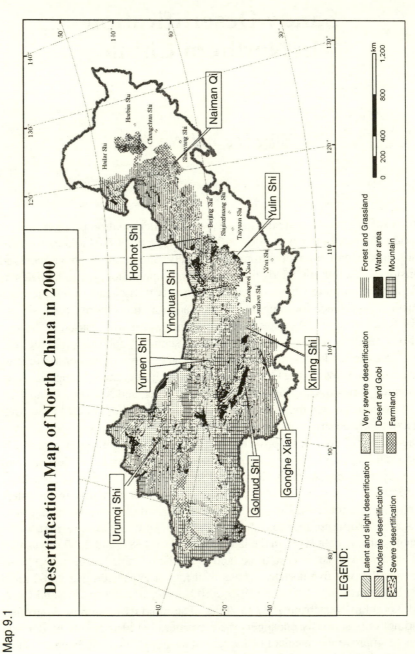

Desertification Map of North China in 2000

LEGEND:

Latent and slight desertification   Very severe desertification

Moderate desertification   Desert and Gobi

Severe desertification   Farmland

Forest and Grassland

Water area

Mountain

Source: Adapted from Wang et al., "Spatial Distribution of Land Desertification."

Table 9.1

Sandy Desertified Lands in China

% Distribution	Regional characteristics	Location
29	Mixed farming-grazing regions; rainfed farming regions	Otindag sandy land, Horqin sandy land, Bashang region of Hebei Province, Houshan region of Inner Mongolia
44	Reactivated fixed dunes and shifting sand spread	In the middle and western parts of the semiarid zone and desert steppe zone (mainly in central Inner Mongolia)
27	Reactivation of fixed dunes	At the margin of oases in the arid zone and the lower reaches of inland rivers (primarily the Alxa region of western Inner Mongolia, northern part of Hexi Corridor region in Gansu, lower reaches of the Tarim River in Xinjiang)

Shortly following the 1977 United Nations Conference on Desertification, China officially launched multidisciplinary and comprehensive research and engineering studies focused on combating this problem. Over the last twenty years, researchers have made encouraging progress. Much work was conducted in regions with fragile ecosystems and intense human activity.[3] Through remote sensing and monitoring of desertification and field investigations in large areas,[4] we have achieved a preliminary understanding of the causes, distribution, and types of sandy desertification in northern China and the damage caused by it.[5] Through multidisciplinary research on the developmental processes associated with sandy desertification (including blown-sand dynamics, biological processes, and anthropogenic processes), a comprehensive, multilevel sandy desertification diagnostic system has been put forward. This chapter provides a brief account of several important aspects of sandy desertification, including the causes, processes, and damage assessment and control measures.

Causes of Sandy Desertification

Sandy desertification is a land degradation process whereby land productivity is diminished, land resources are lost, and a desertlike landscape is created. Only after the causes of sandy desertification are correctly understood can we put forward effective control measures and thoroughly solve the degradation problem. We can divide sandy desertification causes into two categories: natural and anthropogenic.

Natural Causes

The natural occurrence of sandy desertification is a common phenomenon in the arid and semiarid regions of China. For example, wind erosion and moving dunes encroach on oases and river terraces, and cause the destruction of natural vegetation in the wind-affected areas. Sandy desertification due to natural causes can be summed up by the following two points:

1. Global climate change, especially climatic warming and aridification in the midlatitude regions, is a major ecological factor promoting sandy desertification.
2. The presence of adverse factors, such as dry climate, erratic precipitation, sandy soil texture, erosion-prone land surfaces, and strong and frequent winds, provides a dynamic force for erosion.

However, there always exists a degree of self-regulating capacity in nature and the earth's surface ecosystem. Once the system suffers slight natural damage, its internal self-regulating mechanism activates and thereby maintains the overall stability of the ecosystem. So far as we know, sandy desertification due to natural causes is generally small scale, less severe, and more easily reversible than the human-caused variety.

Anthropogenic Causes

Based on many studies, sandy desertification has occurred primarily during the human historical period and has developed rapidly over the last century. Changing natural conditions, mainly the climatic fluctuations over the course of a century, generally are small and therefore insufficient to cause great changes in the natural environment. In contrast, human population pressure and the disturbances due to human economic activities over the course of a century can lead to serious deterioration of the ecosystem and the acceleration of sandy desertification. This chain of events is supported by archaeological data and field investigations. Up to the eighteenth century, while the arid and semiarid regions in northern China were occupied by nomadic people, there was almost no pressure on the ecosystem. However, beginning in the eighteenth century, after the nomadic lifestyle was replaced by agriculture, the ecosystem suffered great damage. It is generally accepted that human causes—including increased population, induced overcultivation, overgrazing, deforestation, overextraction of groundwater, and poor ecological management—destroyed the land cover and ultimately led to wind erosion and sandy desertification (Table 9.2).

Table 9.2

Causes of Sandy Desertification in Northern China

Desertification causes	% Desertified land
Overcultivation	25.4
Overgrazing	28.3
Deforestation (overcutting for firewood)	31.8
Misuse of water resources and vegetation destruction due to industrial construction	9.0
Sand dune encroachment	5.5

According to recent studies, human destruction of ground cover reduces the capacity of soil to hold water, suppresses airflow rise and convergence, enhances surface albedo, intensifies downward airflow, and ultimately leads to climatic aridification. Sandy desertification induced by anthropogenic causes can bring much more rapid and severe direct damage than that resulting from natural causes.

In the sandy-desertification-affected regions of China, the climate is dry, precipitation is sparse and highly variable, strong winds are frequent, the environment is harsh, and the ecosystem is fragile. In addition, the education level of people residing in these areas is generally low. Under such poor economic conditions, the means of production is primitive. Therefore, these areas have a lower population-carrying capacity.

China's massive population and the demand to increase living standards are placing greater pressure on the land. To feed the growing population, people clear vegetation to extend cropland and collect firewood. Under the harsh natural conditions described above, lands denuded of vegetation are nearly impossible to restore to their original landscape. Once overgrazing, cultivation, and industrial construction occur in the grassland regions, grasses gradually degrade and the sandy desertification process takes hold. As sandy desertification expands, the climate becomes drier, and sandy desertification is exacerbated. Anthropogenic sandy desertification creates a vicious cycle. From the preceding data, it is clear that human factors by far have the greatest impact on sandy desertification.

Case Study: Horqin Region of Inner Mongolia

It is useful to focus on how sandy desertification can impact a locality. The Horqin Region of Inner Mongolia provides a good example of the progress and impact of desertification. Comparative study shows that sandy desertified land in this region spread rapidly between 1959 and 1975, increasing by

9,084 km^2, or 21.47 percent. This growth continued through 1987, expanding 18.72 percent, and affecting an additional 9,624 km^2.[6]

A major driving force was the rapidly growing population, primarily consisting of peasants and herdsmen. Between 1949 and 1986, the population in the region increased from 868,000 to 2.6 million. The population pressure and land resource mismanagement resulted in the cultivation of fixed dune land and overgrazing. Since the late 1980s, due to China's one-child policy, population growth has slowed, and strict land resource management measures were adopted.

This coincided with the expansion of scientific research to measure and combat desertification. Horqin benefited from these changes. By the year 2000, sandy desertified land in Horqin had decreased to 50,142 km^2, from a high of 61,008 km^2 in 1987.[7] Most of the reduction occurred in the slight or moderately degraded land, as more severe desertification is harder to combat.

Although climatic factors played a role in the development of desertification in the region, research shows that human activities have had a much greater impact. This primarily has been in the form of changes in land use (from traditional rangeland 100 years ago to mixed agropastoral use) and increased intensity of land use (overcultivation, overgrazing, and firewood collection). In addition, the natural vegetation that was destroyed by human activities accelerated desertification. For example, human activities can result in wind erosion increases of four to ten times the magnitude of natural wind erosion. At least 75 percent of wind erosion can be attributed to human causes. Taken as a whole, it can be concluded that human impact plays a critical role in the process of desertification. This is supported by scientific evidence not only in the Horqin region, but also across the vast desertified area of northern China.[8]

Process of Sandy Desertification

The occurrence and development process of sandy desertification includes blown-sand erosion, transport and deposition of sand due to an imbalanced ecosystem, and the degradation or disappearance of vegetation. The study of the process of sandy desertification primarily involves research on the dynamics of blown sand and the roles of biological and human activities.

Dynamics of Blown Sand

The processes of blown-sand movement encompass mainly (1) sandy surface morphology under wind force, that is, the interaction between wind force and exposed ground surface; (2) reactivation of fixed dunes; and (3) sand dune migration at the margin between sandy desert and oases. Surface roughness reduction caused by human destruction of land cover and intensified blown-sand activity is the basic factor affecting the blown-sand processes of sandy desertification.

Biological Processes

The biological processes of sandy desertification are manifested primarily through the succession of vegetation degradation, that is, the changing landscape pattern. Studies in recent years show that the vegetation succession of sandy grassland is different from that of common grassland and that the difference relates to the degree of sandy desertification. The form and pace of vegetation degradation often have significant variations depending on the cause of sandy desertification.

Grazing-induced grassland sandy desertification generally involves a significant decrease in biodiversity, vegetation cover, grass height, and grass yield. Reduced vegetation cover results in small bare spots on the grassland surface, which continuously expand, connect, and finally turn into desertified land.[9]

Grassland sandy desertification processes caused by wind erosion and water shortage, are similar to those caused by grazing. However, variations in the pace of the process emerge based on shady slope versus sunny slope, wetland versus dry land, and fixed-sand land versus mobile-sand land. Land degradation from wind erosion is significantly faster than that caused by grazing. Both vegetation cover and plant species decrease rapidly, although vegetation height and output do not necessarily decrease.[10] While vegetation degradation in desertified regions results mainly from human activities, the ecosystem has the capacity to restore itself. Once human disturbances are removed, plants in interdune areas can be restored over the course of several years.

Damage Caused by Sandy Desertification

Sandy desertification results in a direct economic loss of about RMB 54 billion, or US$6.532 billion, annually.[11] Although present sandy desertification damage assessments generally are qualitative, it is important to understand the significance of sandy desertification issues and to create a sense of urgency to combat this problem. Sandy desertification has an enormous impact on China's ecosystem and economy, including:

1. Damage to the ecosystem, environmental degradation, lower land productivity, loss of people's livelihoods, aggravated poverty, and ecological refugees
2. Loss of usable land resources and loss of habitable land

3. Negative impact on the safety and normal operation of communities, traffic lines, water conservancy projects, and national defense bases
4. Direct economic losses, as mentioned above, of RMB 54 billion each year
5. Increase in strength and frequency of sand and dust storms.

According to statistical data,[12] strong dust storms occurred five times per year in the 1950s, eight times per year in the 1960s, thirteen times per year in the 1970s, fourteen times per year in the 1980s, and twenty-three times per year in the 1990s. The increase in dust storm frequency coincided with the spread of desertified land in China. A single strong dust storm in 1993 resulted in a direct economic loss of RMB 540 million. During spring 2000, twelve strong sand-raising events and dust storms hit northwest China and to a lesser extent affected large areas of eastern and southern China, including such major cities as Beijing, Tianjin, Nanjing, and Shanghai.

Control of Sandy Desertification

Based on the experience in northern China, there are tremendous ecological, economic, and social benefits to be derived from the rehabilitation of desertified land. To improve the ecosystems of the affected regions, we must adopt an integrated plan and rehabilitation strategy.

With respect to economic development, an approach involving diversified economic activities dominated by forestry should be implemented. In addition, population growth should be effectively controlled.

The rehabilitation projects can be conducted at three levels:

1. Research organizations can undertake sandy desertification control experiments using experimental plots.
2. Research organizations in cooperation with production departments can conduct experiments in the demonstration plots.
3. The government, functional departments, and local people can apply successful techniques for controlling desertification.

In the mixed farming-grazing region in which residential areas, cropland, and grassland are interspersed, certain measures will contribute to local economic development. These include prohibiting grazing; adjusting rainfed, farming-dominated land use; increasing forest and grassland coverage; using intensive management of the land with better water and fertility conditions; and establishing a farmland windbreak forest network and patchy forest or grassland in interdune depressions (Table 9.3).

Table 9.3

Sandy Desertification Control Technologies in Northern China

Techniques/Methods	Sites where applicable	Limitations and benefits	Relative cost of effectiveness	Overall rating[a]
Biological methods				
1 Shelterbelt networks to protect farmland	Within farmland, along the banks of canals	• Only a few tree species suitable • Suffers from long-horned beetle damage • High consumption of water • Good protective results • Creates microclimate for crops • Supplies timber	• Relatively expensive • Simple management • Resulting in yield reduction in the marginal field	4 Effectiveness 4 Durability 4 Maintenance
2 Sand fixation forest for fixing mobile sand dunes	2/3 of leeward side of mobile dunes from bottom	• Hard conditions for shrubs to survive • Labor demanding • Long life (20–40 years) • Fixes sand dunes	• Inexpensive • Relatively easy to maintain	4 Effectiveness 4 Durability 3 Maintenance
3 Windbreak forest	Between farmland and sand dunes	• Labor demanding • High consumption of water • Good ecological and economic benefits	• Relatively inexpensive • More effort to maintain	4 Effectiveness 4 Durability 2 Maintenance
4 Enclosures for grazing land and forest	Desert grassland, forest areas	• Increases biodiversity • Little demand on labor	• Inexpensive • Easy to maintain	4 Effectiveness 4 Maintenance
5 Air seeding for grazing land and afforestation	Loess plateau, desert grazing land	• Requires aircraft • Requires relatively high concentration of rainfall • Efficient for restoration of grazing land and afforestation	• Inexpensive in large areas • Low labor cost	4 Effectiveness 4 Durability 3 Maintenance

(continued)

Table 9.3 (continued)

Techniques/Methods	Sites where applicable	Limitations and benefits	Relative cost of effectiveness	Overall rating[a]
6 Blocking in front and pulling from behind	Dune chains	• Labor demanding • Reduces blown off sand • Stabilizes mobile dunes	• Relatively expensive	4 Effectiveness 4 Durability 3 Maintenance
7 Grass *Kulum*[b] to block wind and sand and to create pasture	Pastureland	• Labor demanding	• More effort to maintain	4 Effectiveness 3 Durability 2 Maintenance
8 Integrated management of small watershed with planting	Loess plateau	• Labor demanding • Can cause blow out • Long life • High social value as it provides cash to local people	• Relatively expensive • More effort to maintain	4 Effectiveness 4 Durability 2 Maintenance
9 Combating soil secondary salinization with vegetation	Mismanaged irrigation areas, lower reaches of rivers	• Labor demanding • Few species • Improves soil	• Costly • More effort to maintain	2 Effectiveness 4 Durability 2 Maintenance
10 Combating industrial mining induced desertification with vegetation	Mining area	• Labor demanding • High consumption of water • Good ecological and economic benefits	• More effort to maintain • Costly	2 Effectiveness 4 Durability 2 Maintenance
Engineering methods 11 Clay sand barriers	2/3 of leeward side of mobile dunes from bottom	• Requires clay • Labor demanding • Prevents rainwater from infiltration (crust on surface) • Long life	• Costly	4 Effectiveness 4 Durability 4 Maintenance

#	Method	Application	Characteristics	Economic features	Rating[a]
12	Straw checkerboard	2/3 of leeward side of mobile dunes from bottom	• Requires local supply of straw • Labor demanding • Short life (2–4 years)	• Inexpensive • Low labor cost because of low opportunity cost for rural labor	4 Effectiveness 2 Durability 3 Maintenance

Engineering measures combined with biological methods

#	Method	Application	Characteristics	Economic features	Rating[a]
13	Straw or clay sand barriers combined with vegetation	2/3 of leeward side of mobile dunes from bottom	• Requires local supply • Labor demanding	• Relatively inexpensive • Easy to maintain	5 Effectiveness 5 Durability 4 Maintenance
14	Building farmland by leveling sand dunes with water	Sand dune	• Requires water • Less labor demanding • Good results	• Inexpensive • Easy to maintain	5 Effectiveness 4 Durability 4 Maintenance
15	Building water conservation project, reclaiming barren land, and improving soil to form new oases	Intermountain basins surrounded by snow-capped peaks	• Requires water • Labor demanding • Long life • High social value as it provides cash to local people	• Relatively expensive • Low labor cost because of low opportunity cost of rural labor	4 Effectiveness 4 Durability 3 Maintenance

Chemical methods

#	Method	Application	Characteristics	Economic features	Rating[a]
16	Covering sand dunes with pitch or making sand barren with asphalt felt	Sand dune	• Requires chemical materials • Labor demanding • Changing soil surface • Long life	• Expensive • Easy to maintain	4 Effectiveness 4 Durability 4 Maintenance
17	Using some chemical materials (such as plastic film, dry water or soil moisture protector) to protect or supply water for afforestation	Arid areas	• Requires chemical materials • Labor demanding • Short life • Good results	• Expensive	4 Effectiveness 1 Durability 2 Maintenance

Notes:
[a] The rating is on an arbitrary scale of 1 (poor) to 5 (excellent).
[b] *Kulum* is a Mongolian word to describe plantings in enclosures of dunes, natural meadows, or plots between dunes where water and soil are suitable.

In addition, efforts should be made to optimally manage the grassland and establish forage bases, rationally arrange drinking-water wells, set grazing-density limits, and build roads. In the arid zone, integrated planning should consider the basin as one ecological unit and undertake the following measures:

- Formulating a rational water allocation plan
- Constructing a farmland forest network inside oases and windbreak tree/shrub belts around oases
- Install mechanical sand fences with sand-anchoring vegetation inside sand fence grids to form a protective system
- Protect transport lines in the dense sand dune regions using mechanical sand fences and sand-anchoring vegetation.

At present, desertification has been only partially controlled in China, and large regions suffer from its spread. Yet, there is room for hope. Some desertified areas in the interlacing agropastoral region and rainfed cropland region have been rehabilitated to the point where they now can be used as farmland and grassland. This rehabilitation results directly from the implementation of better policies and patterns of land use, proving that the process of sandy desertification is reversible. Through a series of experiments using sandy desertification control models in several experimental plots, many successful examples of sandy desertification control and rehabilitation have been established. The monitored results showed that 10 percent of sandy desertified land was controlled, and another 12 percent was improved to the extent of becoming usable land.

Conclusion

China has a long history of desertification that impacts a large swath of the country's land. It is important that we not passively observe the consequences but combat it by aggressively regulating human activity, establishing an interdependent and coordinated man–land relationship, and optimizing the structure and function of man–land systems to attain a new balance and create a benign cycle.[13]

Due to the tremendous impact on economies, the environment, and politics, sandy desertification has drawn worldwide attention. With economic development and increasing societal demands, the pressure on natural resources and the ecosystem is increasing. Given this pressure and the influence of global climate change, sandy desertification poses a serious threat to human existence. The need is urgent to understand the mechanism by which sandy desertification occurs and develop effective means of combating it.

Although scientists have a preliminary understanding of the causes and processes of sandy desertification and have devised control measures, unanswered questions remain. Questions remain because sandy desertification links to natural, social, and economic issues and is a multidisciplinary research field. The challenge is unprecedented, and great effort should be exerted to address interactions between policy and the environment. Sandy desertification is an environmental crisis, but its root causes may lie in the social, economic, and political dimensions.

To combat sandy desertification, an integrated approach is essential. In conclusion, we support the following call to action:

1. Create policy, legal, administrative, and institutional frameworks—complemented by public participation and incentives—that address desertification-related issues
2. Provide socioeconomic alternatives to absorb population groups relocated from overexploited land or displaced by other anti-desertification activities, with safety nets for those particularly disadvantaged
3. Deliver new resource conservation technologies to improve efficiency and output while enhancing economic well-being.

Notes

The authors thank the anonymous reviewers for their critical reviews and comments on the manuscript. This work was supported financially by the China National Key Project for Basic Research on Desertification, No. GT2000048705.

1. Wang et al., "Spatial Distribution of Land Desertification in North China," 73–82.

2. Wang et al., "Time-Space Evolution of Desertification," 230–35. Studies are based on remote sensing and geographic information systems (GIS).

3. Chen, "Influence of Water Resource Development"; Liu, "Internal Dynamic Causes of Desertification"; Wang, "Desertification Processes"; Wang, "Comparative Study of Desertification"; Wang, "Great Attention Should Be Paid to Desertification"; Ze, "Land Use Problems; Zhu, "Land Sandification Problems."

4. Wang, "Comparative Study of Desertification"; Zhu, "Principles and Methods to Compile"; Wang, "Application of Remote Sensing Technique"; Wang and Wang, "Application of Computer Mapping"; Wang, "Thematic Map Compilation with TM"; Zhu and Wang, "Analysis on Trend."

5. Zhu, Liu, and Xiao, "Environmental Features and Restoration"; Zhu and Liu, "Desertification Historic Processes"; Di, Zhang, and Liu, "Land Desertification Features and Control."

6. Wu, "Dynamic Monitor to Evolution of Sandy Desertified Land."

7. Wu, "Remote Sensing Monitoring Methods."

8. Wang and Wu, "Remote Sensing Monitoring and Assessment."

9. Li, Zhao, and Chang, "Several Problems on Vegetation Succession"; Zhao, "Study on Desertification Processes"; Chang and Li, "Dynamical [sic] Change Feature of Plant Diversity."
10. Zhao et al., "Study on Differentiation Law."
11. Zhu, *Study of Desertification/Land Degradation.*
12. Zhu and Wang, "An Analysis on the Trend."
13. Xue and Wang, "Desertification and Sustainable Development."

Bibliography

Chang, Xueli, and Shenggong Li. "Dynamical [sic] Change Feature of Plant Diversity in Fixed Dune Field of Horqin Sandy Land." *Journal of Desert Research* (Suppl. 2) (1998): 33–37.

Chen Hesheng. "Influence of Water Resource Development on Environment in Shule River Basin." *Natural Resources* 2 (1988): 12–23.

Di, Xingmin, Jixian Zhang, and Yangxuan Liu. "Land Desertification Features and Control in Ningxia." *Journal of Desert Research* 2(2) (1982): 1–8.

Li, Shenggong, Aifen Zhao, and Xueli Chang. "Several Problems on Vegetation Succession in Horqin Sandy Land." *Journal of Desert Research* 17 (Suppl.) (1997): 25–33.

Liu, Shu. "Internal Dynamic Causes of Desertification Development in Semiarid Regions." *Journal of Desert Research* 8(1) (1988): 1–8.

State Forestry Bureau. "Northwest China Investigation Group Investigation Report on Great Development of West China and Propagations of Green Homeland Construction." 2000.

Wang, Tao. "Comparative Study of Desertification in Typical Desertified Regions of Northern China." *Journal of Desert Research* 9(1) (1989): 113–37.

———. "Desertification Processes and Prediction in Alagan Region of the Lower Tarim River." *Journal of Desert Research* 6(2) (1986): 16–26.

Wang, Tao, and Wei Wu. "Remote Sensing Monitoring and Assessment of Desertification: Taking Desertified Land in Northern China as an Example." *Quaternary Research* 2 (1998): 108–18.

Wang, Tao, Wei Wu, Guangting Chen, Xian Xue, and Qingwei Sun. "Study of Spatial Distribution of Land Desertification in North China in Recent 10 Years [sic]." *Science in China* (Series D), Vol. 34 Suppl. (2003): 73–82.

Wang, Tao, Wei Wu, Xian Xue, Weimin Zhang, Zhiwen Han, and Qingwei Sun. "Time-Space Evolution of Desertification Land in Northern China." *Journal of Desert Research* 23(3) (2003): 230–35.

Wang, Yimu. "Application of Remote Sensing Technique in the Dynamic Study of Desertification." *MEM Institute of Desert Research,* no. 3 (1986): 82–88.

———. "Thematic Map Compilation with TM Images as Information Source [sic]." In *Study of Renewable Resources.* Beijing: Science Press, 1988, 45–47.

Wang, Yushan. "Great Attention Should Be Paid to Desertification Issues in Ashang Region in Hebei Province." *Journal of Desert Research* 5(3) (1985): 12–14.

Wang, Zhoulong, and Yimu Wang. "Application of Computer Mapping in the Study of Desertification." *Journal of Desert Research* 8(3) (1988): 62–68.

Wu, Wei. "Dynamic Monitor to [sic] Evolution of Sandy Desertified Land in Horqin Region for the Last Five Decades." *China Journal of Desert Research* 23(6) (2003): 646–51.

————. "Remote Sensing Monitoring Methods of Desertification Dynamics and Practice." *Remote Sensing Techniques and Application* 12(4) (1997): 73–89.

Xue, Xian, and Tao Wang. "Desertification and Sustainable Development Problems Viewed from the Angle of System Theory." *Journal of Desert Research* 20(4) (2000): 103–201.

Ze, Ningshu. "Land-Use Problems in Arid and Semiarid Zones of China." *Journal of Desert Research* 6(1) (1986): 1–5.

Zhao, Halin. "Study on Desertification Processes of Grazing Land of Horqin Sandy Land." *Journal of Desert Research* 17 (Suppl.) (1997): 15–24.

Zhao, Halin, Tonghui Zhang, Xueli Chang, and Ruilian Zhu. "Study on Differentiation Law of Plant Diversity and Ecological Niche of Horqin Sandy Grazing Land." *Journal of Desert Research* 19 (Suppl. 1) (1999): 13–20.

Zhu, Zhenda. "Land Sandification Problems in Humid and Subhumid Regions." *Journal of Desert Research* 6(4) (1986): 1–2.

————. "Principles and Methods to Compile Desertification Maps." *Journal of Desert Research* 4(1) (1984): 3–15.

————. *Study of Desertification/Land Degradation of China*. Beijing: China Environment Press, 1994.

Zhu, Zhenda and Guangting Chen. *Land Sandy Desertification in China*. Beijing: Science Press, 1994.

Zhu, Zhenda and Shu Liu. "Desertification Historic Processes and Resource Exploitation Ways Along [sic] Great Wall in Ningxia and Hexi Corridor Region." In *MEM of Institute of Desert Research*, no. 2 (1982): 12–14.

Zhu, Zhenda, and Tao Wang. "An Analysis on the Trend of Land Desertification in Northern China During the Last Decade Based on Examples from Some Typical Areas." *Acta Geographica Sinica* 45(4) (1990): 430–40.

————. "Analysis on Trend of [sic] Land Desertification in Several Typical Regions of China in Recent Ten Years." *Acta Geographica Sinica* 45(2) (1990): 36–49.

Zhu, Zhenda, Shu Liu, and Longshan Xiao. "Environmental Features and Restoration of Desertification in Grassland Regions." *Journal of Desert Research* 1(1) (1981): 2–12.

—— Chapter 10 ——

China's Environment

A Bibliographic Essay

James D. Seymour

During the era of Mao Zedong, little concern was paid to China's environment. However, in the 1980s, as China "opened up," the subject began to enjoy increased attention, not only within China but also in the international community—among foreign governments, nongovernmental organizations (NGOs), academics, and journalists. Now, this once neglected subject has come into its own. There is a huge body of largely science-oriented literature existing in Chinese (largely beyond the scope of this chapter) as well as substantial resources in Western languages on the subject.

These extensive bodies of literature, which often reflect controversies raging within China, have become possible due to the country's modest liberalization and the fact that foreigners are increasingly involved in environmental issues. Whereas, in other social and political matters, the Chinese authorities remain suspicious of foreigners, the authorities have more or less welcomed with open arms those working to improve the environment. As a result, while some of the writings in the field are by academics and journalists, there also is a growing body of literature by practitioners. All three categories of writers have been using the Internet to exchange information and perspectives on progress, remedies, and pitfalls in China's quest for sustainable development (see the "Web-based Resources" listing, p. 263). This chapter provides a general survey of the current English-language literature on China's environment and provides readers with reference information for further exploration of subsets of this important topic.

Chinese Tradition and Attitudes Toward the Environment

Various writers have examined past attitudes toward the environment. In "The Environmental Legacy of Imperial China," Mark Elvin points out how, over the millennia, the Chinese landscape has been vastly transformed, primarily for agricultural purposes.[1] Although the value of the environment was appreciated, he says that "short-term rewards from over-exploitation of resources tended to reduce any inclination to limit exploitation within sustainable limits at a given technological level."[2] Robert B. Marks, in *Tigers, Rice, Silk and Silt: Environment and Economy in Late Imperial South China,* concurs, but asserts that the mid-nineteenth century was a big turning point in ecological development in southern China due to climate change, population shifts, and economic commercialization.[3] The disastrous consequences of these factors are explored by Pierre-Etienne Will in *Bureaucracy and Famine in Eighteenth Century China.*[4]

However, beyond economic considerations, environmental attitudes in China's predominantly agrarian society also must be understood in the contexts of both the Chinese farmers' affection and deep appreciation for the land, and the literati's love of nature on a more aesthetic level. The latter is evident in Richard Edwards's *The World Around the Chinese Artist: Aspects of Realism in Chinese Painting.*[5] The influence of culture on environmental attitudes seems to have been predominately positive and remains so to this day. Bron Taylor, in "Popular Ecological Resistance and Radical Environmentalism," examines the transformation of religions into forces capable of inspiring ecological activism through the articulation and legitimization of environmental ideals and the provision of institutional resources to support environmental protection.[6] An example is explored in "Cultural and Asian Styles of Environmental Movements," by Michael Hsiao. Hsiao describes the case of Taiwan, in which local deities, religious parades, and ghost festivals all are crucial components in the drive to clean up the environment.[7] Similarly, on the mainland, folk religion sometimes plays a constructive role. The fact that the Chinese alligator is associated with the beneficent Chinese dragon may save it from extinction.[8] It must be added, however, that the cultural legacy is not uniformly positive. Daoism teaches accommodation to nature's ways,[9] yet Daoist cosmology *(feng shui)* has been invoked to rationalize pollution in Hong Kong's New Territories.[10]

Nevertheless, contemporary Chinese attitudes have been influenced primarily by economic or political factors rather than cultural considerations. Until the 1990s, China's leaders have dismissed cultural affinities to the environment. During his decades at the helm, Mao Zedong pushed his version of development with reckless disregard for environmental consequences, viewing the environment as an adversary to be conquered. This story is recounted in Judith Shapiro's *Mao's War Against Nature: Politics and the Environment in Revolutionary China.*[11] For Shapiro, "The relationship between humans and nature under Mao is so transparent and extreme that it clearly indicates a link between abuse of people and abuse of the natural environment. . . . Coercive state behavior such as forcible relocations and suppression of intellectual and political freedoms contributed directly to a wide range of environmental problems."[12]

China's Environment During the Reform Era

Other writers find that the environment suffered less under Maoist rule than it would subsequently during China's post-1978 period of unbridled economic growth. S.D. Richardson recounts having seen in 1963 "little of the damage done to the ecosystems and the eager disregard for simple conservation that post-Mao economic change has triggered."[13]

The growth of China-related environmental literature in the West began in 1981 with Henri Isaïa's *La Protection de l'Environnement en Chine*,[14] followed eventually by Baruch Boxer's 1989 article "China's Environmental Prospects."[15] Concurrently, within China, environmental issues were being more openly discussed. Indeed, such controversial projects as the Three Gorges Dam were the targets of scathing criticism.[16] Even after 1989, when most other forms of dissent were repressed, lively discussion on environmental matters continued. One example is the 1990 book by Qu Geping and Li Jinchang discussed below. Except for a political chill in the early 1990s, it has again become more permissible to discuss environmental issues frankly. Sometimes it is even acceptable to recommend imported approaches to these problems without being considered unpatriotic, as Eric Zusman discusses in "Seeking Contradictions in the Field: Environmental Economics, Public Disclosure and Cautious Optimism about China's Environmental Future."[17] These external influences were sometimes reflected in China's high-level policies, as Agnes Gaudu recounted in "Environment in China: From Fast Development to Sustainable Development."[18]

Some Chinese writers focus on population as centrally responsible for China's environmental woes. For example, Qu Geping and Li Jinchang, in *Population and the Environment in China,* argue that overpopulation is the primary constraint to overcoming China's environmental difficulties.[19] Caught up in the wave of market-oriented thinking, they see market-based solutions as a means to develop and distribute such "goods" as water, and especially energy resources, in a rational manner. However, most other writers accept the size of China's population as a "given" rather than central to the problem, and look for solutions to more specific environmental issues.[20] Even population *density* is not seen as a fundamental issue, except (as we shall note below) in ecosystems that are especially fragile.[21]

Energy

While China's reform era has opened up new "frontiers" in environmental discussion and activism, conservative political influences continue to promote environment-blind policies, particularly in such areas as energy generation. A 1985 World Bank study described the extent of the shortfall in meeting China's energy needs.[22] A solution was proposed by the aforementioned Qu and Li: "If energy resources were primarily regarded as national assets, and property relationships more clearly defined, many of the country's energy problems might resolve themselves."[23] On the other hand, in "China's Energy and Resource Uses: Continuity and Change,"[24] Vaclav Smil finds that the experiment in the devolution of state coal mining to collective and private enterprise resulted in enormous waste.[25] (It also resulted in such a high death rate among miners that the industry had to be recentralized.)[26] Because the country is so deficient in oil and natural gas, Smil is not sanguine about China's ability to satisfy its energy needs from fossil fuels under *any* economic order in an environmentally friendly way—with far-reaching geopolitical implications.[27] This view is shared by Frank Wang and Hongfei Li in their discussion of China's energy demands in chapter 7 of the present volume. China does lead the world in nonpolluting energy *potential,* mainly hydropower,[28] but the reality remains that "the dominance of coal in China's fossil fuel consumption is going to change only very slowly."[29] That means large emissions of carbon dioxide (CO_2),[30] a problem for which some, such as Yingzhong Lu, seek a solution in nuclear energy.

Renewable energy has attracted considerable interest.[31] Roger Raufer and Wang Shujuan see wind power as representing an important part of the solution.[32] Although wind-based electricity still is much more expensive than that derived from coal, and has its own drawbacks,[33] the authors believe that government support for wind power is justified by environmental considerations. Raufer and Wang suggest that a phased approach to building a renewable-energy infrastructure—shifting from near-term price supports to a longer-term, market-oriented regime—would be an appropriate means to exploit wind energy in China. For others, the solution lies in solar power.[34] However, the political establishment continues to promote less environmentally benign means of energy production, including the hydropower projects mentioned above.

Rural Environment Issues

China's famine of the early 1960s resulted from multiple errors in development strategies.[35] For example, during the Great Leap Forward (1958), a massive slaughter of sparrows spared crop-eating insects from their natural enemies. Such errors are not confined to distant history. In 2001, authorities in Xinjiang committed a similar mistake, applying pesticides that killed pests' natural enemies, resulting in the devastation of the cotton crop by aphids and red spiders.[36] The pesticide DDT, long banned in the West, continues to be used widely in China—one of the world's largest consumers of pesticides.[37] The serious environmental and health consequences are described by Jessica Hamburger in "Pesticides in China: A Growing Threat to Food Safety, Public Health, and the Environment."[38]

In addition to problematic development strategies, another cause of China's prereform rural environmental problems, as described by Shapiro, was the "disruption of land connections." She recounts that farmers who did not know whether they would have any future rights to their acreage tended to emphasize short-term extraction rather than the long-term fertility of the land.[39] More contemporary-focused studies confirm that this remains a problem.[40] The Land Tenure Law of 1998 was designed to protect the land by giving farmers a stake in the acreage they till. While it has somewhat empowered farmers, the long-term efficacy of this law in protecting land depends on the extent to which people feel assured that the land is theirs for the long term. According to Marilyn Beach, most farmers do not yet have a sufficient degree of this confidence.[41] Thus, the argument is that giving a greater sense of permanence to the family farm would be ecologically beneficial (although a minority holds that small-scale private agriculture is a fundamental part of the problem).[42]

Another rural environmental factor described in the literature is China's loss of arable land. This is documented in "China's Land Resources, Environment and Agricultural Production," by Richard F. Ash and Richard Louis Edmonds,[43] who also speculate on the potential impacts of global warming on Chinese agriculture. The worst-case scenario would see the exacerbation of desertification, which has been occurring as farmers move into pastoral areas with fragile ecosystems. Because grazing areas often are unsuitable for sustained agriculture, they soon desertify. According to Dai Xinyi and Peng Xizhe, "up to 1949 the ecological debts accumulated over time included about 100 million hectares of degraded grassland, 60 thousand square kilometers of human-made desert and one million square kilometers of land affected by erosion."[44] Qu and Li show how true this has been in the northern grasslands[45] and, in chapter 9 of the present volume, Wang Tao and Wu Wei further examine the problem. The effort to combat desertification in western China (Gansu and Xinjiang) is described in James Walls, ed., *Combating Desertification in China.*[46] This subject is explored with respect to the northern steppes by Dee Mack Williams, in *Beyond Great Walls: Environment,*

Identity, and Development on the Chinese Grasslands of Inner Mongolia, in which she examines the unintended consequences of decollectivization and economic development.[47] Hong Jiang, in *The Ordos Plateau of China,* considers the societal impact on grasslands of overreclamation, overgrazing, and excessive gathering of fuelwood and medicinal herbs.[48] .

Another aspect is the loss of farmland as a result of urbanization, an issue that was addressed in the Chinese government's 1994 survey, *Agenda 21: A White Paper on China's Population, Environment and Development in the 21st Century.*[49] The following year, Zhong Fenggan published an article arguing that urbanization in China was not an urgent problem. He noted that China's 30 percent urban population is "not only far below that of developed countries, it also is lower than the average for developing countries."[50] These figures suggest that the urbanization trend will not be reversed. (Efforts to make up the deficit in arable land by draining wetlands have harmful environmental consequences, and fortunately this practice is being resisted and sometimes reversed.)[51]

Given the loss of farmland, will China be able to feed itself? Lester Brown's 1995 book *Who Will Feed China?* argues that it will not.[52] Similar views were presented by a Harvard University–U.S. government follow-up project, which concluded, however, that China could import the grain it requires without overwhelming international grain markets.[53]

China's Political/Economic System

China's post-1978 reforms and evolving economic system have far-reaching implications for the environment. Lester Ross found that more recent pollution control, water management, and market mechanisms applied in the forestry sector yielded more environment-friendly results than had been evident under socialist policies.[54] As we have noted, Qu and Li likewise advocate market-oriented solutions, but, when it comes to land management issues, they foresee the need for considerable state intervention. An increased role of market forces is happening both through the government's de-emphasis on the *rate* of emissions discharge in favor of focusing on overall *amounts* discharged[55] and through more proactive market involvement efforts, as described by Richard D. Morgenstern et al. in chapter 6 of the present volume. Changjin Sun finds that schemes based on a "polluter must pay" policy have been effective, but that far more must be done to bring market forces to bear.[56]

Joshua Muldavin, who has done extensive on-the-ground research, presents a more skeptical view. He argues that changing socioeconomic entitlements have resulted in great disparities of wealth and poverty, driving some impoverished people to commit "desperate ecocide."[57] In "The Limits of

Market Triumphalism in Rural China,"[58] he describes the emergence of a capitalist-socialist hybrid system "that tends to draw on many of the worst aspects of both."[59] He has written elsewhere that environmental degradation is "structurally embedded" in the new order,[60] and that problems will not "simply go away with the completion of the 'transition' to a market economy."[61]

Water

An overview of China's water issues is provided in Vaclav Smil's *The Bad Earth: Environmental Degradation in China.*[62] An earlier work, Robert Carin's study *Irrigation Schemes in Communist China,* describes how irrigation efforts in the 1950s and early 1960s not only fell short of goals, but often resulted in deleterious environmental impacts.[63] Various aspects of water pollution are discussed in a 1990 article by Vanessa Lide.[64] More recently, water issues have received increased scrutiny. A good short overview of the subject is James E. Nickum's "Is China Living on the Water Margin?" in which various uses and misuses of water are described, including irrigation and mining.[65] One aspect of the corruption of China's waters involves the introduction of alien species, a problem focused on by Chen Wei.[66]

Liu Changming, in "Environmental Issues and the South-North Water Transfer Scheme,"[67] comments: "China has good resources of land and water. The problem is that they often are not in the same place."[68] Although many northern provinces are notably dry,[69] there is wide disagreement as to the appropriateness of diverting water from the Yangtze River Basin in the south to the dry northern regions.[70] This huge project, which in size would dwarf the Three Gorges Dam project, worries environmentalists, who often see a better solution in smaller-scale initiatives.[71] These concerns appear to have received little government consideration, and work on the South-North Water Transfer Scheme began in 2002.[72]

Farther south and west, China's water issues take on an international dimension. Indians worry about what Chinese are doing to the Himalayan headwaters.[73] In addition, actions taken among the headwaters of the Mekong River are likely to affect the countries of Southeast Asia. A technical analysis of the latter situation is contained in the collaborative case study *Environmentally Sound Management of Lake Erhai and the Xi'er River Basin.*[74] Focusing on a section of Yunnan's Dali Bai Autonomous Prefecture, this work examines such problems as industrial pollution, sewage, and nonpoint runoff from agriculture and animal husbandry. These environmental assaults, combined with past inappropriate development of water resources and poor forest management, have resulted in serious eutrophication. The writers call for a holistic program of pollution control and resource protection leading to sustainable development, and appear to lack confidence that government policy alone can solve the problems. They add, "A public information element is a critical element in the identification, implementation and supervision of plans and policies. The participation of the public will alter pure governmental behavior to the whole people's consciousness and thus accelerate implementation of the programs and policies."[75] We shall return to the subject of public involvement below.

Economic Development, Quality of Life, and the Environment

Most assessments are optimistic about the potential economic benefits of environmental protection but pessimistic about China's current environmental situation. In 1996, Vaclav Smil, in *Environmental Problems in China: Estimates of Economic Costs*,[76] equated the losses from environmental degradation at 10 to 15 percent of gross domestic product (GDP), which is higher than the World Bank estimate (discussed below), and much higher than Chinese estimates. Still, for Dai and Peng, the problem is not economic growth per se, but the fact that "the Chinese economy has been growing with low efficiency," especially when it comes to industry.[77] For example, in terms of "unit of GDP," China consumes more than double the energy of the United States and almost six times the Japanese rate. Here, these authors find at least a slim reed of hope: if China can reduce the gap in energy *efficiency*, "significant environmental improvements could be made" even before any investment in pollution control.[78] As environmental consultant Pam Baldinger explains, enterprises known as energy service companies are helping to do just that.[79]

Of course, economic progress is likely to entail some environmental costs. Neither environmentalists nor developers can escape the necessity of balancing the two, even though they virtually always seem to take disparate stances. China under Mao, Shapiro asserts, was a clear case in which the environmental costs of "development" came nowhere near being offset by material progress.[80] The reason was that the "reds" refused to listen to the experts. In most cases, development turned out to be illusory, and the environmental costs of the many mistakes were horrendous. For example, rubber was planted in vast areas unsuited to its production, resulting in the loss of richly diverse forests.[81] These massively destructive blunders resulted from the disconnect between political institutions and environmental needs. Unfortunately, this problem has yet to be resolved. Dai and Peng point to the "separation of the economic development decision-making process from the requirements of environmental protection—or the very loose integration of the two."[82]

One aspect of economic development that bears great relevance to the environment is the transportation sector. Michael P. Walsh provides an overview, in an international comparative perspective, in "Transportation and the Environment in China."[83] Emphasis on mass ground transportation would promise many environmental advantages, and D. Tilly Chang offers some hope in "A New Era for Public Transport Development in China."[84] However, as in most other countries, the pressure of the more affluent to place private automobiles at the core of any transportation plan results in mass transit receiving short shrift. Robert E. Paaswell has explored one aspect of the problem in "Transportation Infrastructure and Land Use in China."[85] When it comes to protecting the air from auto emissions, foreign influence can be helpful, as Kelly Sims Gallagher shows in "Foreign Technology in China's Automobile Industry: Implications for Energy, Economic Development, and Environment." China's major automobile manufacturers have joint ventures with foreign companies, such as DaimlerChrysler, Ford, and General Motors. "Although these foreign firms have helped to modernize the automobiles on the road today, emissions control and fuel efficiency technology installed in Chinese cars is considerably behind European, Japanese, and U.S. levels. Foreign firms and the Chinese government share the responsibility to correct this laggardness."[86] Beyond this, however, any solution to the pollution problems posed by transportation will require a holistic, integrated approach, such as is suggested in an article by He Kebin and Cheng Chang.[87]

Ultimately, what one wants to know is how environmental degradation and restoration impact people's quality of life. It is very difficult to get a statistical handle on the impact of pollution on public health, although Judith Banister attempts to do so in "Population, Public Health and the Environment in China."[88] While longevity in China has been increasing, it is obvious that pollution harms public health. Alas, "public health effects are complex and not well documented."[89] More generally, the Stockholm Environment Institute has done an excellent job of pulling together the available relevant information regarding the interaction between society and the environment in the *China Human Development Report 2002: Making Green Development a Choice*,[90] which stresses increased environmental awareness on the part of both the Chinese government and people (a subject further explored by Yok-shiu F. Lee in chapter 2 of the present volume). Especially useful is the Stockholm volume's data annex, containing provincial-level data on economic, social, and demographic indicators.

The World Health Organization reports that China has nine of the world's ten most polluted cities. This report refers primarily to air pollution, a subject on which the literature is relatively thin.[91] The lack is somewhat surprising, given the World Bank's finding that air pollution is an even more serious threat to health than is water pollution.[92]

Politics and Law

In 1979, just as economic reforms were being launched, the government promulgated a "trial" environmental protection law, but for many years the subject received little meaningful official attention.[93] This changed in the mid-1990s, when the government published two "white papers" on the environment: the aforementioned 1994 paper, and another in 1996.[94] It was now clear that the authorities were committed to addressing these problems. However, to what extent was the government *able* to do so? Observers have been skeptical.[95] Abigail R. Jahiel, in "The Organization of Environmental Protection in China," describes China's bureaucracy, and finds it fragmented and wanting.[96] Although the system has some strengths (e.g., an extensive nationwide environmental protection apparatus), it is often not possible for environmental agencies to issue binding mandates, as such units are, at best, of equal rank with economic agencies. Environmental protection bureaus' "dependence on local governments continues to be a fundamental structural impediment to consistent enforcement of environmental policy," she writes.[97] As Marilyn Beach terms it in "Local Environment Management in China,"[98] "decentralization with insufficient attention to rule of law and capacity building has had an adverse effect on the quality of local environmental conditions and agricultural land and threatens to undermine many of the very positive environmental policies and laws created over the past twenty years."[99] Such problems are further explored by Elizabeth Economy in chapter 4 of this volume.

The disconnect between ambitious intentions and local realities is illustrated by the problem of enforcing offshore water quality standards, as Sulan Chen and Juha I. Uitto show in "Governing Marine and Coastal Environment in China: Building Local Government Capacity Through International Cooperation."[100] The central government has devolved such problems onto mid- and lower-level government agencies. Unfortunately, the authors say, the international (i.e., NGOs') attention to this issue has been misdirected toward the central government. "The middle-level agents—local governments, which ultimately implement all environmental policies—have largely been ignored by international organizations. . . . Linking these more empowered local governments with international assistance could fundamentally change the way in which China deals with environmental challenges," write Chen and Uitto.[101]

Kenneth Lieberthal, in "China's Government System and Its Impact on Environmental Policy Implementation," provides a political scientist's perspective on how local government's ineffectiveness impacts the environment, citing documented cases of a local environmental protection bureau's imposing fines on a large local enterprise, but then passing along the amount collected to the local government's general coffers. This transfer of funds was followed by a tax break to the enterprise, roughly in proportion to the amount of the fine. "In this way, the EPA met its responsibilities by imposing the fine and the government met its responsibilities by maintaining the financial health of an important source of local jobs and income. Only the environment lost out in this scenario," writes Lieberthal.[102] Such problems are explored further in an article by Marilyn Beach, who shows how the local officials who are charged with enforcing environmental standards usually have neither the resources nor the will to carry out their mandate.[103] Often, those responsible for curbing pollution are the same people doing the polluting, or at least benefiting financially therefrom.

Michael Palmer, in "Environmental Regulation in the People's Republic of China: The Face of Domestic Law," finds some grounds for hope in China's judiciary, even though there still is insufficient judicial independence.[104] He indicates "the line between environmental regulation and social control may sometimes be difficult to draw in the authoritarian political context of the PRC. . . . The 'Law' . . . still plays an uncertain and ambiguous role."[105] A good overview of China's environmental laws and how they are applied is contained in Xiaoying Ma and Leonard Ortolano's *Environmental Regulations in China: Institutions, Enforcement and Compliance.*[106] One problem, as Kenji Otsuka laments, is the lack of any requirement that environmental legislation be published.[107] An introduction to China's legal framework and related information-access issues is explored by Richard J. Ferris Jr. and Hongjun Zhang in chapter 3 of this volume. Despite the inadequacy of the laws and judicial institutions, however, we are now seeing the beginning of an NGO movement to assist pollution victims to realize their legal rights.[108] One such organization, the Center for Legal Assistance to Pollution Victims, is described by Anna Brettell in "Environmental Disputes and Public Service Law: Past and Present."[109] We discuss NGOs further below.

International Aspects

The literature on China's environment has been heavily affected by foreign involvement. Not only are foreigners in China studying the subject, but foreign governmental and nongovernmental aid directed toward improving the country's environment is flowing to China. Thus, in their essay in chapter 5 of the present volume about external influences on China's environmental policymaking, Eric Zusman and Jennifer L. Turner attribute a great deal of

China's progress to the role played by the international community, which has effectively facilitated communication among China's bureaucracies. The greater the impact of China's environmental degradation on the international community, the greater is the external pressure and assistance for change.

It was in 1997 that world public opinion really began to focus on China's environmental problems and their planetary implications. That year the World Bank published an important report discussed below. On a more popular level, the *Atlantic Monthly* published an article entitled "Our Real China Problem."[110] That year also saw the founding of the China Environment Forum at the Washington-based Woodrow Wilson International Center for Scholars. The forum launched a series of conferences on various aspects of China's environment and began publication of the annual *China Environment Series*. This journal has carried a wide variety of articles pertaining to China's environment reflecting a range of views and contains a comprehensive inventory of environmental and energy projects in China.

Foreign observers are sometimes surprisingly optimistic. For example, China has been given high grades for its support of the 1987 Montreal Protocol concerning the phasing out of ozone-depleting substances.[111] Various writers even claim that China has enjoyed a decline in overall energy use (explained as an unintended consequence of various other policies and developments)[112] and that in recent years, CO_2 emissions have dropped by about one-fifth.[113] Were this true, the United States would be deprived of the "China excuse" for not signing on to the Kyoto Protocol.[114] However, the U.S. Embassy in Beijing refuted claims that energy use and greenhouse emissions were declining,[115] with other international observers generally in agreement. If nothing is done, warns the Japan Environmental Council, Asia in general may contribute over half of the world's CO_2 emissions by the year 2100.[116] While this figure should not be surprising—after all, Asia has about half of the world's population—it nonetheless is worrisome.

The linkages between Chinese and international environmental conditions are explored by Chris Nielsen in "Perspectives on Global and Chinese Environment: Overview of the Harvard University Committee on Environment in China."[117] China's environmental issues particularly affect the country's immediate neighbors. Hong Kong is the most notable example, as Lisa Hopkinson and Rachel Stern demonstrate in *"One Country, Two Systems, One Smog:* Cross-Boundary Air Pollution Policy Challenges for Hong Kong and Guangdong."[118] They link rapid development in the Pearl River Delta to worsening air quality regionwide. Although governments on both sides have taken steps to reduce air pollution, there has been a general failure to include the public in related policymaking. The authors call for the creation of new institutions to provide funding and raise public awareness and pressure.

Another Hong Kong observer, Yok-shiu F. Lee, expects "an uphill and long drawn-out battle . . . to bring forth improvements in this fast-growing and continually deteriorating landscape."[119]

There have been many initiatives by intergovernmental organizations.[120] Both the Asian Development Bank (ADB) and the World Bank have published prolifically about China's environment. The ADB's output tends to laud that institution's own projects.[121] In contrast, the World Bank's publications tend to be more blunt about what China needs to do to improve its environment.[122] The bank's pathbreaking work, *Clear Water, Blue Skies: China's Environment in the New Century*,[123] found that in 1995 air and water pollution damages to health and agriculture alone could be valued at almost 8 percent of China's GDP,[124] virtually eclipsing the nation's annual economic growth. This report, filled with tables and graphs, but written in accessible prose, was a wake-up call that China must no longer practice business as usual. On the other hand, the report also held out promise: "An environmentally sustainable pattern of growth can both increase incomes and improve environmental quality. And with a few crucial adjustments, this future is well within reach of China's current policies and resources. Moreover, the rate of return to these investments is enormous."[125]

Can the private sector play a role? In the case of the automobile industry, we have seen that foreign firms can have a positive impact. A number of writers have noted opportunities for foreign firms that wish to participate in China's pollution-abatement efforts. Bruce Tremayne and Penny de Waal explore these in "Business Opportunities for Foreign Firms Related to China's Environment."[126] In this connection, special reports designed for the international business community have been prepared, including *Environmental Trends and Policies in China: Implications for Foreign Business*,[127] and a November/December 2003 issue of the *China Business Review* entitled "Focus: Green Ambitions."[128]

Private-sector interest notwithstanding, the heavy lifting probably will have to be done by governments and international organizations. As Eduard B. Vermeer shows in "Industrial Pollution in China and Remedial Policies," in return for subscribing to most of the international environmental treaties, China has received considerable foreign aid to help begin the clean-up.[129] Australia, Canada,[130] Europe, Japan,[131] and New Zealand have been providing substantial assistance.[132]

The role of the U.S. government has been mixed. There have been a few sustained efforts, such as that of the U.S. National Oceanic and Atmospheric Administration.[133] There have also been numerous other shorter-term projects, but they have been insufficient to have a major impact.[134] For Kelly Sims, energy issues in particular cry out for bilateral resolution.[135] Notwithstanding some bright spots, U.S.-China bilateral environmental cooperation still is generally characterized as a relationship of unfulfilled promise.[136] In their position paper, Baldinger and Turner[137] argue that there is great potential for more Sino-American cooperation, especially in such areas as energy and global warming.[138] Unfortunately, legal and bureaucràtic obstacles, which they depict in depressing detail, make this unlikely anytime soon, especially given the lack of political commitment by the two governments. The authors point out that the West has a lot to lose from China's mismanagement of environmental concerns, and urge that the United States move these issues to the front burner of the bilateral relationship. They do allow, however, that "the onus for developing rational energy and environmental policies in China rests with the Chinese government and people."[139]

China as a nation has become increasingly active in international environmental efforts. Lester Ross, in "China: Environmental Protection, Domestic Policy Trends, Patterns of Participation in Regimes and Compliance with International Norms,"[140] shows how, "although initially an environmental laggard, China has become a more active participant" in the international environmental regime.[141] The country generally has become more willing to participate in the various international agreements pertaining to the environment; and on certain issues, such as biodiversity, China has become a leader.

What Role for the Public?

Developments in Taiwan illustrate the potential impact of public environmental awareness on environmental policy, as demonstrated by Michael Hsiao in "Environmental Movements in Taiwan." Under martial law, the island saw only four cases of environmental protests. After martial law was lifted in 1987, there were 243 such protests,[142] and eventually such protests would have a profound effect. The same evolution has been true in a number of other Asian countries.[143]

In China, civil society has been slow to develop, despite some assistance and even prodding from the international community.[144] Nevertheless, the victims of environmental assaults are beginning to fight back.[145] There are even some relevant Chinese NGOs, such as Green Voice Environmental Solutions.[146] Elizabeth Knup gives an overview of China's "social organizations" concerned with the environment.[147] Lu Hongyan, in "Bamboo Sprouts After the Rain: The History of University Student Environmental Associations in China," depicts how student groups have become a resource for such involvement.[148] The author analyzes how student environmental associations have expanded their footprint across the country since 1990. His article is based on surveys conducted by Lu and colleagues in 1999 and 2001, covering twenty-seven and ninety-four associations, respectively. However, the usual tendency has been for the domestic scene to be dominated by groups that, paradoxically, are government organized, known (somewhat whimsically) as "GONGOs."[149] Taken in the context of China's tendency to rely on mass campaigns, there still is not a great "space" allowed for genuine civil-society groups to emerge.[150] The need for real public involvement in resource management and pollution abatement has been a recurring theme, including on the part of the World Bank.[151] Foreign NGOs, and similar organizations such as the Wilson Center,[152] have sought to encourage Chinese environmental organizations by including Chinese representatives in various conferences.[153]

To have any influence, environmentalists need to have their views reported in the media. As Ray Cheung has shown,[154] the Chinese press and broadcasters (with the government's blessing and some restrictions) do ventilate environmental issues and often achieve results after other institutions have not succeeded. On the other hand, the media sometimes fail to rise to the occasion, as in not addressing the alarm felt in the western half of the country over the potential impact of China's "Go West" campaign.[155]

We noted earlier the perceived connection between environmentalism and human rights. The link between the two goes beyond the historical issues raised by Judith Shapiro. First, under various international conventions, a decent environment is itself a human right, as asserted in the United Nations' 1994 "Draft Declaration of Principles on Human Rights and the Environment."[156] Nevertheless, people are unlikely to make much progress in achieving their environmental rights unless they can enjoy their *political* rights. The connections between environmentalism and human rights are explored by various writers in a special issue of the journal *China Rights Forum*.[157]

Conclusion

Thus, the literature on this subject documents the fact that China faces enormous challenges in its efforts to implement needed environmental reforms. Doing so is proving especially difficult because, under the current system, despite a new level of openness, the degree of transparency required to resolve the country's most pressing environmental issues is still lacking. Some doubt that the problems can be addressed without a fundamental change in the political order. Others, such as Elizabeth Economy, are less pessimistic, because China's current leaders "appear to be poised to take advantage of their new understanding of the relationship between environmental protection and economic development and reorient their approach."[158] Which view proves closer to reality is a matter of urgent concern to all.

At any rate, in terms of facilitating our understanding of Chinese environmental issues, the body of literature highlighted above is an impressive beginning. Taken together with the burgeoning body of Chinese-language literature, the subject of China's environment and the quest for sustainable development has been well chronicled.[159] This writer looks forward both to more works on the subject as China continues to grapple with its ecological problems, and to more "portability" through Chinese works being translated into English and Western-origin works made accessible to the Chinese public.

Web-based Resources

While much of the literature on China's environment—in numerous languages—exists in the traditional print media, print has been augmented in recent years by Internet resources. Indeed, it is the Internet that makes most analysis and data widely available, and has facilitated the exchange of information and ideas among all parties, Chinese and foreign. The following are the leading Web sites carrying information about the environment.

China Council for International Cooperation on Environment and Development: www.harbour.sfu.ca/dlam/. A collaborative effort of Chinese officials and foreign (mostly Canadian) experts.

ChinaEnvironment: www.chinaenvironment.com. Bilingual site, especially good on water issues and general late-breaking news.

China Internet Information Center: test.china.org.cn/english/environment/33890.htm. China-based, multilingual site, with documents such as government position papers, all searchable.

ChinaSite: www.chinasite.com/Environment.html. Useful links to relevant materials.

Harvard University, Research Guide to China's Environment: http://environment.harvard.edu/activities/sponsored/chinaproject/index.php?&pw=988. A multidisciplinary research program on energy use and the environment in China and related aspects of Sino-American relations.

Index-China: www.index-china.com/index-english/environment-s.html. Commercial site with useful links.

International Fund for China's Environment: www.ifce.org. Washington-based NGO.

Nature Conservancy's Yunnan Great Rivers Project: www.nature.org/aboutus/howwework/about/art7002.html.

Professional Association for China's Environment (PACE): www.chinaenvironment.net. PACE publishes the international online journal *Sinosphere*. (www.chinaenvironment.net/sino/index.html). This important organization has done much to bring together the international community of environmentalists.

Tibet Environmental Watch: www.tew.org/. Rich collection of articles by Tibet supporters based primarily in the United States and India.

Tibetan Plateau Project: www.earthisland.org/tpp/. Project of the San Francisco-based Earth Island Institute.

U.S. Embassy in Beijing: www.usembassy-china.org.cn/sandt/. Site is maintained by the embassy's Environment, Science, Technology and Health Section. Environment-specific materials are listed on the page www. usembassy-china.org.cn/sandt/sandtbak-hp.html#Environment-target.

Woodrow Wilson International Center for Scholars: wwics.si.edu/ index.cfm?fuseaction=topics.home&topic_id=1421. Publishes *China Environment Series* and holds many conferences, reports of which are available on this site.

Notes

1. Mark Elvin, "The Environmental Legacy of Imperial China," in Richard Louis Edmonds, ed., *Managing the Chinese Environment* (Oxford: Oxford University Press, 1998), 9–32. This volume grew out of a conference organized by *China Quarterly* in 1998.

2. Ibid., 31–32.

3. Robert B. Marks, *Tigers, Rice, Silk and Silt: Environment and Economy in Late Imperial South China* (Cambridge: Cambridge University Press, 1998).

4. Pierre-Etienne Will, *Bureaucracy and Famine in Eighteenth Century China* (Palo Alto, CA: Stanford University Press, 1990).

5. Richard Edwards, *The World Around the Chinese Artist: Aspects of Realism in Chinese Painting* (Ann Arbor, MI: University of Michigan Press, 1989).

6. Bron Taylor, "Popular Ecological Resistance and Radical Environmentalism," in Bron Taylor, ed., *Ecological Resistance Movements: The Global Emergence of Radical and Popular Environmentalism* (Albany: State University of New York Press, 1995), 337.

7. Hsin-Huang Michael Hsiao, On-Kwok Lai, Hwa-Jen Liu, Francisco A. Magno, Laura Edles, and Alvin Y. So, "Cultural and Asian Styles of Environmental Movements," in Yok-shiu F. Lee and Alvin Y. So, eds., *Asia's Environmental Movements: Comparative Perspectives* (Armonk, NY: M.E. Sharpe, 1999), 214–17.

8. Carol Kaesuk Yoon, "Rare Alligator Is Threatened, as China Feeds Its People," *New York Times,* Aug. 21, 2001, F4. On the subject of endangered species, see also Martin Williams, "New Hope for Pandas: Drive to Save Dying Species Is Regaining Momentum," *Far Eastern Economic Review* (Dec. 16, 1993): 32–33.

9. Judith Shapiro, *Mao's War Against Nature: Politics and the Environment in Revolutionary China* (New York: Cambridge University Press, 2001), 7.

10. Lee and So, eds., *Asia's Environmental Movements,* 226.

11. Shapiro, *Mao's War.*

12. Ibid., xii, xiv.

13. S.D. Richardson, *Forests and Forestry in China* (Washington, DC: Island Press, 1990). The quotation is from *Far Eastern Economic Review* (June 3, 1993): 38.

14. Henri Isaïa, *La Protection de l'Environnement en Chine* (Paris: Presses universitaires de France, 1981). French observers were among the first to call attention to Chinese environmental problems. An even earlier example is "La lutte contre la pollution," *Nouvelle Chine* (June 1972): 29–30.

15. Baruch Boxer, "China's Environmental Prospects," *Asian Survey* 29 (7) (July 1989): 669–86.

16. Notable were articles by members of the normally quiescent "democratic parties," such as the Democratic League, one of whose members, Qian Weichang, wrote "Revelations from the Gulf War," *Qunyan* 4 (Apr. 7, 1991): 2. Trans. U.S. Foreign Broadcast Information Service (FBIS), June 13, 1991, CAR-91-031: 10–11. Qian argued that, in some future war, the dam could be destroyed with disastrous environmental and social effects.

17. Eric Zusman, "Seeking Contradictions in the Field: Environmental Economics, Public Disclosure and Cautious Optimism about China's Environmental Future," *China Environment Series* 4 (2001): 63–65.

18. Agnes Gaudu, "Environment in China: From Fast Development to Sustainable Development," *China News Analysis* 1618 (Sept. 15, 1998): 1–10.

19. Qu Geping and Li Jinchang, *Population and the Environment in China* (Boulder, CO: Lynne Rienner, 1994).

20. For an interesting and sophisticated critique of Malthusian thinking in the context of Chinese history, see James A. Lee and Wang Feng, *One Quarter of Humanity: Malthusian Mythology and Chinese Realities, 1700–2000* (Cambridge, MA: Harvard University Press, 1999).

21. The relationship between population density and environmental degradation is discussed in "Population, Migration, and the Environment in China," *China Environment Series* 3 (1999–2000): 69–70.

22. World Bank, *China: The Energy Sector* (Washington, DC: World Bank, 1985).

23. Qu and Li, *Population and the Environment,* 139.

24. Vaclav Smil, "China's Energy and Resource Uses: Continuity and Change," in Edmonds, *Managing the Chinese Environment,* 210–27.

25. Ibid., 215.

26. Fubing Su, "The Agency Problem and Institutional Design: Regulating Workplace Safety in China's Coal Industry," presented at the Association for Asian Studies, New York, Mar. 27, 2003.

27. See Michael May, "Energy and Security in East Asia," *China Environment Series* 1 (1997): 16–19; and Philip Andrews-Speed, Xuanli Liao, and Roland Dannreuther, "Searching for Energy Security: The Political Ramifications of China's International Policy," *China Environment Series* 5 (2002): 13–28.

28. See Working Group on Energy Issues, "Hydroelectricity and Nuclear Energy in China: Summary of Working Group Discussion on Energy Issues," *China Environment Series* 1 (1997): 63–66.

29. Edmonds, *Managing the Chinese Environment,* 313. The World Bank likewise notes: "No other major economy is as reliant on coal as is China." The Bank recommends using coal more efficiently and diversifying energy sources. World Bank, *Clear Water, Blue Skies: China's Environment in the New Century* (Washington, DC: World Bank, 1997), 48 and chap. 4, passim.

30. Yingzhong Lu, "The Role of Nuclear Energy in the CO_2 Mitigation Strategy of the People's Republic of China," *China Environment Series* 1 (1997): 20–26.

31. See Qin Xin, "China Environment Forum Meeting Summaries: Renewable Energy in China," *China Environment Series* 5 (2002): 93–95.

32. Roger Raufer and Wang Shujuan, "Navigating the Policy Path for Support of Wind Power in China," *China Environment Series* 6 (2003): 37–54.

33. In the United States there is much disagreement among environmentalists about the desirability of wind power. See Katherine Q. Seelye, "Windmills Sow Dissent for Environmentalists: An Energy Source's Impact Is Debated," *New York Times,* June 5, 2003, A28; and Elinor Burkett, "A Mighty Wind," *New York Times Magazine,* June 15, 2003, 48.

34. W.L. Wallace, Jingming Li, and Shangbin Gao, "The Use of Photovoltaics for Rural Electrification in Northwestern China," presented at the Second World Conference and Exhibition on Photovoltaic Solar Energy Conversion, July 6–10, 1998, Vienna, NREL/CP-520-23920, U.S. DOE National Renewable Energy Laboratory, www.nrel.gov/ncpv/pdfs/photo.pdf.

35. Penny Kane, *Famine in China, 1959–60: Demographic and Social Implications* (London: Macmillan Press, 1988), 48–51.

36. New China News Agency, Sept. 14, 2001; U.S. Foreign Broadcast Information Service, Sept. 14, 2001.

37. Bruce Gilley, "China's Poisoned Chalice," *Far Eastern Economic Review* (Oct. 25, 2001): 50.

38. Jessica Hamburger, "Pesticides in China: A Growing Threat to Food Safety, Public Health, and the Environment," *China Environment Series* 5 (2002): 29–44.

39. Shapiro, *Mao's War,* 18.

40. Peter Ho, "Who Owns China's Land? Policies, Property Rights and Deliberate Institutional Ambiguity," *China Quarterly* 166 (2001): 394–421; and Xiaolin Guo, "Land Expropriation and Rural Conflicts in China," *China Quarterly* 166 (2001): 423–39.

41. Marilyn Beach, "Local Environment Management in China," *China Environment Series* 4 (2001): 30–31. Beach's assessment is based on a survey by the University of Washington's Rural Development Institute.

42. Family farming as usually practiced in China has come in for criticism on environmental grounds. There are both domestic and foreign observers who argue for a more collectivized form of agriculture, as is already practiced in some Chinese localities. Richard Sanders, "Political Economy of Chinese Ecological Agriculture: A Case Study of Seven Chinese Eco-villages," *Journal of Contemporary China* 9 (25) (2000): 349–72.

43. Richard F. Ash and Richard Louis Edmonds, "China's Land Resources, Environment and Agricultural Production," in Edmonds, *Managing the Chinese Environment,* 114–55. An earlier essay on land issues is contained in Vaclav Smil, *The Bad Earth: Environmental Degradation in China* (Armonk, NY: M.E. Sharpe, 1984), 9–77. For Chinese accounts, see Yijun Ma, "How Much Land Does China Still Have? First Report on Land Problem in China," *Zhongguo qingnian bao* (China Youth News), May 13, 1991, trans. in Foreign Broadcast Information Service (FBIS), June 12, 1991, CHI-91-113, 41–42; and Jincai Wu, "An Inch of Land Is an Inch of Gold," New China News Agency (May 31, 1991), trans. FBIS, June 11, 1991, CHI-91-112, 43–44.

44. Dai Xinyi and Peng Xizhe, "Environment and Environment Protection," in

Peng Xizhe and Guo Zhigang, eds., *The Changing Population of China* (Oxford: Blackwell, 2000), 235.

45. Qu and Li, *Population and the Environment,* chap. 7.

46. James Walls, ed., *Combating Desertification in China* (Nairobi: United Nations Environment Programme, 1982).

47. Dee Mack Williams, *Beyond Great Walls: Environment, Identity, and Development on the Chinese Grasslands of Inner Mongolia* (Palo Alto, CA: Stanford University Press, 2002).

48. Hong Jiang, *The Ordos Plateau of China* (Tokyo: United Nations University Press, 1999). This is a case study of the Ih-Ju League in Inner Mongolia, in the area bounded by the Yellow River and the Great Wall.

49. *Agenda 21: A White Paper on China's Population, Environment and Development in the 21st Century* (1994), adopted at the sixteenth executive meeting of the State Council of the People's Republic of China (Beijing), Mar. 25, 1994, www.townsnet.com/tagenda.htm.

50. Zhong Fenggan, "Urbanization," in Peng and Guo, *Changing Population of China*, 172. See also Deborah S. Davis, *Urban Spaces in Contemporary China: The Potential for Autonomy and Community in Post-Mao China* (Cambridge: Cambridge University Press, 1995).

51. David Murphy, "Just Go with the Flow," *Far Eastern Economic Review* (July 18, 2001): 35–36.

52. Lester R. Brown, *Who Will Feed China?* (New York: W.W. Norton, 1995).

53. Summarized in "China's Food Security," *China Environment Series* 3 (1999–2000): 55–57.

54. Lester Ross, *Environmental Policy in China* (Bloomington: Indiana University Press, 1988).

55. Dan Dudek, Zhong Ma, Jianyu Zhang, Guojun Song, and Shuqin Liu, "Total Emission Control of Major Pollutants in China," *China Environment Series* 4 (2001): 43–55.

56. Changjin Sun, "Paying for the Environment in China: The Growing Role of the Market," *China Environment Series* 4 (2001): 32–42.

57. Joshua S.S. Muldavin, "The Paradoxes of Environmental Policy and Resource Management in Reform-Era China," *Economic Geography* 76 (3) (July 2000): 244–71.

58. Joshua S.S. Muldavin, "The Limits of Market Triumphalism in Rural China," *Geoforum* 28 (3–4) (1998): 289–312.

59. Ibid., 307.

60. Joshua S.S. Muldavin, "Environmental Degradation in Heilongjiang: Policy Reform and Agrarian Dynamics in China's New Hybrid Economy," *Annals of the Association of American Geographers* 87 (4) (1997): 579–613.

61. Ibid., 707.

62. Smil, *The Bad Earth,* chap. 3. See also "Conservation and Pollution of Water Resources in China," in *China Environment Series* 3 (1999–2000): 58–60.

63. Robert Carin, *Irrigation Schemes in Communist China* (Hong Kong: Union Research Institute, 1963).

64. Vanessa Lide, "The Perils of Pollution: China Is Awakening to a Wide Range of Environmental Problems," *China Business Review* (July–Aug. 1990): 32–37.

65. James E. Nickum, "Is China Living on the Water Margin?" in Edmonds, *Managing the Chinese Environment,* 156–74.

66. See Xinhua News Agency, "Exotic Species May Threaten Ecology, Expert Warns," July 30, 2002.

67. Liu Changming, "Environmental Issues and the South-North Water Transfer Scheme," in Edmonds, *Managing the Chinese Environment,* 175–86.

68. Ibid., 175.

69. See Jih-Um Kim, "Looking into a Microcosm of China's Water Problems: Dilemmas of Shanxi—A High and Dry Province," *China Environment Series* 5 (2002): 59–63.

70. For an early call to the international community, see Audrey T. Topping, "Ecological Roulette; Damming the Yangtze," *Foreign Affairs* (Sept./Oct. 1995): 132–46.

71. See David Murphy, "New Streams of Thought," *Far Eastern Economic Review* (Jan. 24, 2002): 36–39.

72. Geoffrey York, "China's Water Diversion Raises Eco-activist Alarm: Huge Network of Canals Would Sweep Pollution Across the Country, Critics Warn," *Toronto Globe and Mail,* Feb. 20, 2003, A14.

73. See Piers M. Blaikie and Joshua S.S. Muldavin, "Upstream, Downstream, China, India: The Politics of Environment in the Himalayan Region," *The Annals of the Association of American Geographers* 94(3): 520–48.

74. China International Center for Economic and Technical Exchanges [and] United Nations Environment Programme, Division of Technology, Industry and Economics, International Environmental Technology Centre, *Environmentally Sound Management of Lake Erhai and the Xi'er River Basin* (2000).

75. Ibid., 257. On Yunnan Province, see also Ou Xiaokun, "The Yunnan Great Rivers Project," *China Environment Series* 5 (2002): 74–76.

76. Vaclav Smil, *Environmental Problems in China: Estimates of Economic Costs,* Special Report 5 (Apr.) (Honolulu: East-West Center, 1996).

77. Dai and Peng, "Environment," 240.

78. Ibid.

79. See Pam Baldinger, "Lean and Green: Boosting Energy Efficiency through ESCOs," *China Environment Series* 5 (2002): 90–91. In the same publication, see Timothy Hildebrandt and Jennifer L. Turner, "Powering up the Dragon: World Bank and NGO Energy Efficiency Projects in China," *China Environment Series* 5 (2002): 112–15.

80. Shapiro, *Mao's War,* passim.

81. By the 1990s, China's once vast and fabulously diverse forest was reduced to a mere 14 percent of the country (far worse than Indonesia's 55 percent). Since the Mao years, China's forests have been slightly better managed, and in general there have not been the deliberate assaults on the environment that characterized the Mao years. (The Tibetan plateau is an exception.) For two excellent accounts, see "Forest Issues in China" (summary of a 1998 meeting), *China Environment Series* 3 (1999–2000): 51–54; and Scott Rozelle, Heidi Albers, Guo Li, and Vincent Benziger, "Forest Resources Under Economic Reform in China," *China Information* 7 (1) (summer 1998): 106–25.

82. Dai and Peng, "Environment," 244.

83. Michael P. Walsh, "Transportation and the Environment in China," *China Environment Series* 3 (1999/2000): 28–37.

84. D. Tilly Chang, "A New Era for Public Transport Development in China," *China Environment Series* 3 (1999/2000): 22–27.

85. Robert E. Paaswell, "Transportation Infrastructure and Land Use in China," *China Environment Series* 3 (1999/2000): 12–21.

86. Kelly Sims Gallagher, "Foreign Technology in China's Automobile Industry: Implications for Energy, Economic Development, and Environment," *China Environment Series* 6 (2003): 1.

87. He Kebin and Cheng Chang, "Present and Future Pollution from Urban Transport in China," *China Environment Series* 3 (1999/2000): 38–50.

88. Judith Banister, "Population, Public Health and the Environment in China," in Edmonds, *Managing the Chinese Environment*, 262–91.

89. Ibid., 291.

90. Stockholm Environment Institute, *China Human Development Report 2002: Making Green Development a Choice* (Hong Kong: Oxford University Press, 2002).

91. An early essay on the subject is chapter 4 of Smil's *The Bad Earth.*

92. World Bank, *Clear Water,* 21.

93. For the text of this environmental protection law, see New China News Agency, Sept. 16, 1979; trans. FBIS, Sept. 18, 1979: L1–7.

94. For the text of the 1996 white paper, see trans. FBIS, June 7, 1996, CHI-96-111, 41–55. In prior years, the government had publicized various laws and regulations: "Rules for Implementation of the PRC Law on Prevention and Control of Atmospheric Pollution," New China News Agency, May 27, 1991; "Detailed Rules for Implementation of the PRC Law on Prevention and Control of Atmospheric Pollution," New China News Agency, May 26, 1991, trans. FBIS, CHI-91-108, June 5, 1991: 37–40; and "Law of the People's Republic of China on Preventing and Controlling Environmental Pollution Caused by Solid Waste," trans. FBIS, Nov. 17, 1995, CHI-95-222: 34–42. Regarding the latter problem, see also John Markoff, "Technology's Toxic Trash Is Sent to Poor Nations," *New York Times,* Feb. 25, 2002, A1, C4; and Dan Millison's contribution to the present volume, chapter 8.

95. Lester Ross, Cheng Weixue, Mitchell A. Silk, and Wang Yi, "Cracking Down on Polluters: How Strictly Will New Environmental Measures Be Enforced?" *China Business Review* (July–Aug. 1990): 38–43.

96. Abigail R. Jahiel, "The Organization of Environmental Protection in China," in Edmonds, *Managing the Chinese Environment,* 33–63.

97. Ibid., 59.

98. Marilyn Beach, "Local Environment Management in China," *China Environment Series* 4 (2001): 21–31.

99. Ibid., 30. For a case study of provincial environmental law enforcement, see Benjamin van Rouij, "Organization and Procedure in Environmental Law Enforcement: Sichuan in Comparative Perspective," *China Information* 17 (2) (2003): 36–64.

100. Sulan Chen and Juha I. Uitto, "Governing Marine and Coastal Environment in China: Building Local Government Capacity Through International Cooperation," *China Environment Series* 6 (2003): 67–80. (The quotation is from p. 67.)

101. Ibid., 67.

102. Kenneth Lieberthal, "China's Government System and Its Impact on Environmental Policy Implementation," *China Environment Series* 1 (1997): 3–8. (The quotation is from p. 6.)

103. Beach, "Local Environment Management," passim.

104. Michael Palmer, "Environmental Regulation in the People's Republic of China: The Face of Domestic Law," in Edmonds, *Managing the Chinese Environment,* 64–84.

105. Ibid., 83.

106. Xiaoying Ma and Leonard Ortolano, *Environmental Regulations in China: Insti-*

tutions, Enforcement and Compliance (Lanham, MD: Rowman and Littlefield, 2000).

107. See Kenji Otsuka, "Environmental Law in China," *China Environment Series* 3 (1999–2000): 63–64.

108. Kenji Otsuka, "Networking for Development of Legal Assistance to Pollution Victims in China," *China Environment Series* 5 (2002): 63–65.

109. Anna Brettell, "Environmental Disputes and Public Service Law: Past and Present," *China Environment Series* 4 (2001): 66–68.

110. Mark Hertsgaard, "Our Real China Problem," *Atlantic Monthly* (Nov. 1997): 97–114, www.theatlantic.com/issues/97nov/china.htm.

111. Jimin Zhao and Leonard Ortolano, "The Chinese Government's Role in Implementing Multilateral Environmental Agreements: The Case of the Montreal Protocol," *China Quarterly* 175 (2003): 708–25.

112. Jonathan E. Sinton and David G. Fridley, "Hot Air and Cold Water: The Unexpected Fall in China's Energy Use," *China Environment Series* 5 (2001): 3–20. The same issue contains an article claiming that (in 2000) CO_2 emissions were substantially lower than had been forecast: Jeffrey Logan, "China's Changing Carbon Dioxide Emissions," *China Environment Series* 5 (2001): 60–62.

113. Erik Eckholm, "China Said to Sharply Reduce Emissions of Carbon Dioxide," *New York Times,* June 15, 2001, A1, A8.

114. On China's support for the Kyoto Protocol (which requires little sacrifice on its part), see test.china.org.cn/english/FR/15155.htm.

115. August 2001 report from U.S. Embassy Beijing, www.usembassy-china.org.cn/sandt/estnews-contents.html.

116. Japan Environmental Council, *The State of the Environment in Asia, 1999/2000* (Tokyo: Japan Environmental Council, 2000), iv.

117. Chris Nielsen, "Perspectives on Global and Chinese Environment: Overview of the Harvard University Committee on Environment in China," *China Environment Series* 3 (1999/2000): 3–11.

118. Lisa Hopkinson and Rachel Stern, "One Country, Two Systems, One Smog: Cross-Boundary Air Pollution Policy Challenges for Hong Kong and Guangdong," *China Environment Series* 6 (2003): 19–36.

119. Yok-shiu F. Lee, "Tackling Cross-border Environmental Problems in Hong Kong: Initial Responses and Institutional Constraints," *China Quarterly* 172 (2002): 986–1009 (quotation, p. 1009). On changing public attitudes within Hong Kong itself, see Suh-kyung Yoon, "On a Greener Track," *Far Eastern Economic Review* (Oct. 25, 2001): 56.

120. For a rundown on the activities of multilateral organizations, see Part IV of "Inventory of Environmental Work in China," *China Environment Series* 3 (1999–2000): 169–88.

121. For example, "ADB to Help Bring Clean and Reliable Hydropower Energy to Gansu Province, PRC," News Release no. 177/03, Dec. 8, 2003, www.adb.org/documents/news/2003/nr2003177.asp.

122. For example, World Bank, *China: Air, Land, and Water: Environmental Policies for a New Millennium,* Aug. 2001. Summary: www.worldbank.org.cn/English/content/451e6266206.shtml; text: www.worldbank.org.cn/English/content/china-environment.pdf.

123. World Bank, *Clear Water.*

124. Ibid., 2, 104. As the authors make clear in chapter 2 of the World Bank report, such calculations are an inexact science.

125. Ibid., 40–41.

126. Bruce Tremayne and Penny de Waal, "Business Opportunities for Foreign Firms

Related to China's Environment," in Edmonds, *Managing the Chinese Environment*, 293–317.

127. *Environmental Trends and Policies in China: Implications for Foreign Business* (Washington, DC: *China Business Review*, 2000).

128. "Focus: Green Ambitions," *China Business Review,* special issue (Nov.–Dec. 2003), www.chinabusinessreview.com/public/0311/.

129. Eduard B. Vermeer, "Industrial Pollution in China and Remedial Policies," in Edmonds, *Managing the Chinese Environment,* 230–61.

130. See Geoffrey York, "[Maurice] Strong Aims to Help China Become Leader on Ecology," *Toronto Globe and Mail,* Jan. 22, 2003, 3.

131. But see Joshua S.S. Muldavin, "Aiding Regional Instability?: The Paradox of Japanese Development Assistance to China," *Geopolitics* 5 (3) (winter 2000): 22–47; and "The Geography of Japanese Development Aid to China, 1978–1998," *Environment and Planning A* 32 (2000): 925–46.

132. For a rundown on international aid, see Part II of "Inventory of Environmental Work in China," *China Environment Series* 3 (1999–2000): 105–41.

133. See "Twenty Years of U.S.–China Cooperation in Atmospheric and Oceanic Science," *China Environment Series* 3 (1999–2000): 74–77.

134. For a rundown on short-term projects, see Part I of "Inventory of Environmental Work in China," *China Environment Series* 3 (1999–2000): 78–104; and (for a more comprehensive list) "U.S. Government Environmental Activities," *China Environment Series* 6 (2003): 200–23. See also, listing of projects on the U.S. Embassy's Web site, www.usembassy-china.org.cn/sandt/sandint.htm, reflecting approximately thirty U.S.-China official cooperative efforts in various fields pertaining to energy and environmental protection.

135. Kelly Sims, "Charge to the Bush Administration: U.S. Interests in Energy Cooperation with China," *China Environment Series* 4 (2002): 57–59.

136. On then vice president Al Gore's efforts, see "Briefing on U.S.-PRC Environmental Initiatives," *China Environment Series* 3 (1999–2000): 61–62; and "United States Environmental Priorities in China," ibid., 71–73. See also "Twenty Years of U.S.-China Cooperation," 74–77.

137. Pamela Baldinger and Jennifer L. Turner, *Crouching Suspicions, Hidden Potential: United States Environmental and Energy Cooperation with China* (Washington, DC: Woodrow Wilson International Center for Scholars, 2002).

138. On the latter subject, see the Woodrow Wilson International Center for Scholars's pamphlet *Climate Action in the United States and China* (Washington, DC: 1999); and Keith Bradsher's feature article, "China's Boom Adds to Global Warming Problem," *New York Times,* Oct. 22, 2003, A1, A8.

139. Baldinger and Turner, *Crouching Suspicions,* 7.

140. Lester Ross, "China: Environmental Protection, Domestic Policy Trends, Patterns of Participation in Regimes and Compliance with International Norms," in Edmonds, *Managing the Chinese Environment,* 85–111.

141. Ibid., 91–92.

142. Michael Hsiao, "Environmental Movements in Taiwan," in Lee and So, eds., *Asia's Environmental Movements,* 35.

143. Lee and So, eds., *Asia's Environmental Movements.* See also James David Fahn, *A Land on Fire: The Environmental Consequences of the Southeast Asian Boom* (Boulder, CO: Westview, 2003), chap. 10, which describes the reforms that followed Thailand's 1992 democratic uprising, and discusses the reforms' relevance for the environment.

144. Julia Greenwood Bentley, "The Role of International Support for Civil Society Organizations in China," *Harvard Asia Quarterly* (winter 2003): 11–20.

145. Elisabeth Rosenthal, "Pollution Victims Start to Fight Back in China," *New York Times,* May 16, 2000, A1, A12. See also Caroline Cooper, "Quietly Sowing the Seeds of Activism," *Far Eastern Economic Review* (Apr. 10, 2003): 28–31.

146. See "Green Voice Environmental Solutions," *China Environment Series* 3 (1999–2000): 68.

147. Elizabeth Knup, "Environmental NGOs in China: An Overview," *China Environment Series* 1 (1997): 9–15.

148. Lu Hongyan, "Bamboo Sprouts After the Rain: The History of University Student Environmental Associations in China," *China Environment Series* 6 (2003): 55–66. For a rundown on such organizations, see "Student Environmental Protection Groups," *China Environment Series* 6 (2003): 273–80.

149. See Fengshi Wu, "New Partners or Old Brothers? GONGOs in Transitional Environment Advocacy in China," *China Environment Series* 5 (2002): 45–48. For a rundown of domestic and foreign NGOs and GONGOs, see *China Environment Series* 6 (2003): 224–73.

150. See Jane Sayers, "Environmental Action as Mass Campaign," *China Environment Series* 5 (2002): 77–79.

151. For example, World Bank, *Clear Water,* 70 (with regard to pollution), and 100 (water resources).

152. The Woodrow Wilson International Center for Scholars (the parent of the China Environment Forum) is a U.S.-formed and -funded institution, and so not, strictly speaking, an NGO.

153. The proceedings of one such conference were published as *Green NGO and Environment Journalist* [sic] *Forum: A Meeting of Environmentalists from Mainland China, Taiwan and Hong Kong, April 9–10, 2001* (Washington, DC: Woodrow Wilson International Center for Scholars, and Hong Kong: University of Hong Kong, Centre for Asian Studies, n.d.).

154. Ray Cheung, "Let a Thousand Muckrakers Bloom," *China Environment Series* 4 (2001): 75–76. The media now are allowed to expose violations of official environmental regulations but not to challenge central policies on such matters as the Three Gorges Dam and sovereignty-relevant international issues such as the Kyoto Protocol. The situation was quite different in the late 1980s, when, for example, Dai Qing published her critique of the proposed Three Gorges Dam. See Patricia Adams and John Thibodeau, eds., *Yangtze! Yangtze!* (London: Probe International/Earthscan, 1994). For a balanced account from Germany, see Achim Gutowski, *Der Drei-Schluchten-Staudamm in der VR China–Hintergründe, Kosten-Nutzen-Analyse und Durchführbarkeitsstudie eines grossen Projektes unter Burücksichtigung der Entwicklungszusammenarbeit* (The Three Gorges Dam in China—Background, Cost-benefit Analysis and Feasibility Study of a Large Project with a View to Development Cooperation) (Bremen: Institute for World Economics and International Management, 2000).

155. See Elizabeth Economy, "China's Go West Campaign: Ecological Construction or Ecological Exploitation," *China Environment Series* 5 (2002): 1–12.

156. United Nations, "Draft Declaration of Principles on Human Rights and the Environment," 1994, www1.umn.edu/humanrts/instree/1994-dec.htm.

157. *China Rights Forum* 4 (2002). This journal is published by the New York–based organization, Human Rights in China. Articles in this issue included Judith

Shapiro, "Choking off Debate: How Political Repression Contributes to Environmental Degradation"; Anna Brettell, "Bounded Accountability: The Environmental Complaints System"; Kelly Haggart and Yang Chongqing, "Reservoirs of Repression: State Love Affair with Big Dams Brings Suffering to Chinese People"; Sarah Westerfeld and Jim Pucket, "Toxic Trace: How the West's Obsession with New Technology Is Poisoning China"; Abigail R. Jahiel, "Globalization and the Violation of Environmental Justice"; and an interview with Zheng Yi and a review of his book *China's Ecological Winter* (in Chinese). See also the report of Human Rights Watch/Asia, "The Three Gorges Dam in China: Forced Resettlement, Suppression of Dissent, and Labor Rights Concerns" 7 (2) (Feb. 1995). Summary available at www.hrw.org/summaries/s.china952.html.

158. Economy, "China's Go West Campaign," 9.

159. A guide to the online Chinese-language literature can be found at www.usembassy-china.org.cn/sandt/chenvlnk.htm.

About the Editor and Contributors

Piya Abeygunawardena has worked for the Asian Development Bank since 1994, where he is Principal Project Economist in the Energy Division of the South Asia Department. Previously, he taught in several universities in Europe, Sri Lanka, and the United States. He earned his Ph.D. from Texas A&M University.

Robert Anderson is a consultant in environmental policy with experience in twenty developing countries. Previous positions include Research Director at the American Petroleum Institute, chief of the Benefits Branch at the U.S. Environmental Protection Agency, Research Manager at the Environmental Law Institute, and Assistant Professor at Tufts University. He earned his Ph.D. from Claremont University.

Ruth Greenspan Bell directs the International Institutional Development and Environmental Assistance Program at Resources for the Future, a program that helps developing countries build stronger institutions to implement environmental protection policies and laws. She worked for nearly seventeen years in management positions at the Office of General Counsel at the U.S. Environmental Protection Agency and the Department of State. Bell is a graduate of University of California, Los Angeles, and the School of Law, University of California, Berkeley.

Cynthia W. Cann is an associate professor in the Department of Management/Marketing in the Arthur J. Kania School of Management, University of Scranton. Her research interests include business-to-business (B2B) marketing, international marketing, and environmental business. She recently taught at the Beijing International M.B.A. (BiMBA) program at Peking University in China. She holds a Ph.D. in management/marketing from the State University of New York at Binghamton.

Michael C. Cann is a professor of chemistry and Co-Director of Environmental Science at the University of Scranton. His areas of interest are organic chemistry and environmental chemistry. He is a coauthor of the American Chemical Society publication *Real-World Cases in Green Chemistry*. He has lectured extensively on green chemistry, about which he maintains an extensive Web site. He holds a Ph.D. degree from the State University of New York at Stony Brook in organic chemistry.

Kristen A. Day founded and leads the Calico Group. She is an experienced consultant for U.S.-based multinational corporations in business ethics and corporate social responsibility. Ms. Day is co-chair of Columbia University's University Seminar on China: International Business. She earned her M.B.A. from Columbia University and B.A. in Chinese from Wellesley College.

Elizabeth Economy is C.V. Starr Senior Fellow and Director of Asia Studies at the Council on Foreign Relations. Her book *The River Runs Black: The Environmental Challenge to China's Future* was published by Cornell University Press in 2004. She earned her Ph.D. at the University of Michigan, her A.M. at Stanford University, and her B.A. at Swarthmore College.

Richard J. ("Tad") Ferris Jr. is a Partner at Holland + Knight with the firm's China Practice. His practice focuses on regulatory compliance, investment-risk management and government relations in China and other developing legal regimes. Tad was previously a partner in a leading U.S. environmental law firm and holds leadership positions in a number of China investment-focused organizations. Tad has written extensively on corporate social responsibility practices and environmental, health and safety laws in China. Tad received his legal training at Duke University and Taiwan National University. He frequently lectures at U.S. and Chinese law schools on comparative and international environmental law.

Gao Shangquan is a professor at Peking University and Shanghai Jiao Tong University, and Dean of the School of Management at Zhejiang University. He is former vice minister of the State Commission for Restructuring the Economic System, the agency that played a key role in implementing China's economic reform policy. He is also an appointed member of the United Nations Committee for Development Policy and a senior consultant for the World Bank.

Alan Krupnick is a senior fellow and directs the Quality of the Environment Division at Resources for the Future. Previously, he served as the Senior Economist for Environment and Natural Resources at the Council of Economic Advisers under President Clinton. He holds a Ph.D. in economics from the University of Maryland.

Yok-shiu F. Lee is associate professor in the Department of Geography at the University of Hong Kong. His current research focuses on issues of environmentalism in China and Hong Kong as well as environmental governance problems in the Pearl River Delta region. He holds a Ph.D. from the Massachusetts Institute of Technology in urban planning.

Hongfei Li is a professor and the deputy director of the Liaoning Academy of Social Sciences in China, and a visiting scholar at Harvard University. He has also been a visiting scholar at Columbia University. Dr. Li has completed two major projects under the support of the National Social Sciences Fund of China. He holds a Ph.D. in economics from Liaoning University.

Dan Millison has more than twenty years of professional experience, specializing in hazardous waste management, industrial pollution control, energy efficiency, and clean energy. He has been an active member of the Woodrow Wilson Center's Environmental Change and Security Project China Working Group. He joined the Asian Development Bank in October 2002. He holds an M.S. in civil engineering and a B.A. in geological sciences from Northwestern University.

Richard D. Morgenstern is a Senior Fellow at Resources for the Future. An economist, he previously served in several high-level government policy positions, including as acting Assistant Administrator for Policy and Planning at the U.S. Environmental Protection Agency. His current research focuses on the economic analysis of environmental issues, and on the use of economic incentives in environmental management. He holds a Ph.D. in economics from the University of Michigan.

Jeremy Schreifels is an International Policy Specialist with the U.S. Environmental Protection Agency. He specializes in helping foreign governments develop economic incentive programs, such as emissions trading, to reduce pollution. He has worked in over a dozen countries, including China. He earned a Masters of Environmental Management degree from Duke University.

James D. Seymour is Senior Research Scholar at Columbia University's East Asian Institute. He is the author or coauthor of numerous books, including *New Ghosts, Old Ghosts: Prisons and Labor Reform Camps in China* (1998). He has also been involved in environmental issues in the United States, and is Executive Director of Fire Island Ecology. He earned his bachelor's degree from Yale University and a Ph.D. from Columbia University.

Jennifer L. Turner coordinates the China Environment Forum at the Woodrow Wilson International Center for Scholars in Washington, D.C., where she organizes meetings and study tours on the energy and environmental challenges facing China. She also serves as editor for the center's *China Environment Series*. She holds a Ph.D. in public policy from Indiana University, Bloomington.

Frank Wang has participated in the U.S. National Aeronautics and Space Administration projects in high-energy astrophysics utilizing satellite-borne instruments, and research projects in high-energy physics supported by the U.S. Department of Energy and international collaborators. He is writing a textbook on mathematical physics (Addison-Wesley 2004). He holds a Ph.D. in physics from Columbia University.

Wang Tao is research professor at the Cold and Arid Regions Environmental and Engineering Research Institute, Chinese Academy of Sciences, Lanzhou, China. His research interests include the desert environment, desertification, and land use and sustainable development in arid and semiarid regions. Wang Tao holds a Ph.D. in physical geography from the Chinese Academy of Sciences.

Wu Wei is associate professor in the Department of Environmental Engineering at Peking University. Her research interests include the monitoring and assessment of desertification, land use, and land degradation; and remote sensing and GIS and their applications in information fusion and data mining. She holds a Ph.D. in physical geography from Lanzhou University.

Hongjun Zhang is Senior Counsel with the China Practice at Holland + Knight. Previously, Dr. Zhang served Of Counsel to a leading U.S. environmental law practice and served as Legislative Director in the Environmental Protection and Natural Resources Conservation Committee of China's National People's Congress responsible for drafting and overseeing implementation of environmental and other laws. He was also a Program and Policy Officer at China's State Environmental Protection Administration. Dr. Zhang has published numerous works on Chinese environmental and other legal issues. He received his legal training at Peking University and Harvard Law School.

Eric Zusman is a political science doctoral candidate at the University of California, Los Angeles. He has a dual master's degree from the University of Texas (Austin) in Asian studies and public affairs. He has conducted research in Beijing, Shanghai, and Zhengzhou (Henan Province) on environmental policy in China.

Index

Energy *(continued)*
  nuclear, 188-189, 191, 195
  oil, 9, 181, 184-185, 193-194
  projected consumption of, 191-196
  solar, 21, 189-190, 195, 251
  wind, 21, 189, 195, 217, 219, 251
  See also Coal
Energy Conservation Law, 79
Energy Department (U.S.), 137
Energy and environmental service
    companies (EESCOs), 224
Energy Foundation, 136, 137-138
Energy management companies (EMCs),
    223-224
Enforcement, xxi, 36, 102-120
  bureaucratic impediments to, 107-108,
      110, 117, 123-124
  case initiation, 84-85
  case investigation, 85-86
  compliance challenges and, 88-95
  in courts, 108-110
  in emissions trading program, 170-172
  formal *vs* informal rules, 104
  inspections by central authorities,
      104-106
  legal provisions for, 83-84
  literature on, 257-258
  local responsibility for, 103-104,
      106-112, 115, 117, 123-124,
      257-258
  media influence on, 115-116
  model cities, 110-111, 117
  multinationals and, 111-112
  negligence suits against officials, 110
  nongovernment organizations and,
      111-115
  penalty assessment, 86-87, 110, 171
  public role in, 116-117
  resources for, 87-88
  of waste control regulations, 213
Enterprise development zones (EDZs),
    223
Environmental Defense, 112, 131, 133,
    165
"Environmental Disputes and Public
    Service Law" (Brettell), 258

Environmental Emergency and Incident
    Investigation Center (EEIIC), 87
"Environmental Issues and the
    South-North Water Transfer
    Scheme" (Liu), 254
"Environmentally Sound Management of
    Lake Erhai and the Xi'er River
    Basin," 254-255
"Environmental Movements in Taiwan"
    (Hsiao), 261
Environmental Noise Pollution Control
    Law, 79
Environmental problems
  air pollution. *See* Air pollution
  from dams, 21, 187-188, 195
  economic development and, xix-xx, 5-8,
      35, 68, 102, 224, 226
  population growth and, 4, 10
  public health and, 7, 67, 93, 102, 109,
      151
  public information about, 54
  public perception of. *See* Attitudes,
      environmental
  regional spread of, 67-68, 125-126
  regulatory challenges of, 67-68
  soil erosion, 8
  water pollution. *See* Water pollution
  water shortages, 6-7, 14, 15
*Environmental Problems in China:
    Estimates of Economic Costs* (Smil),
    255
Environmental Protection Agency (EPA,
    U.S.), 164, 175
Environmental protection bureaus (EPBs),
    24, 103, 107-109, 111, 123, 146n3,
    152, 257
Environmental Protection Commission,
    123
Environmental Protection Law (EPL), 76,
    78
Environmental Protection and Natural
    Resources Conservation Committee,
    70
"Environmental Regulation in the
    People's Republic of China"
    (Palmer), 258